Polypores and Similar Fungi of Eastern and Central North America

Polypores and Similar Fungi
of Eastern and Central North America

UNIVERSITY OF TEXAS PRESS

Austin

Alan E. Bessette

Dianna G. Smith

Arleen R. Bessette

Requests for permission to reproduce material from this work should be sent to:
Permissions
University of Texas Press
P.O. Box 7819
Austin, TX 78713-7819
utpress.utexas.edu/rp-form

♾ The paper used in this book meets the minimum requirements of ANSI/NISO Z39.48-1992 (R1997) (Permanence of Paper).

Library of Congress Cataloging-in-Publication Data

Names: Bessette, Alan E., author. | Smith, Dianna G., author. | Bessette, Arleen R., author.
Title: Polypores and similar fungi of eastern and central North America / Alan E. Bessette, Dianna G. Smith, Arleen R. Bessette.
Description: First edition. | Austin : University of Texas Press, 2021. | Includes bibliographical references and index.
Identifiers:
LCCN 2020051260
ISBN 978-1-4773-2272-7 (cloth)
ISBN 978-1-4773-2273-4 (library ebook)
ISBN 978-1-4773-2274-1 (ebook)
Subjects: LCSH: Polyporaceae—North America—Identification. | Polyporaceae—North America—Pictorial works. | LCGFT: Field guides.
Classification: LCC QK629.P7 B48 2021 |
DDC 579.5/97097—dc23
LC record available at https://lccn.loc.gov/2020051260

doi:10.7560/322727

To Harold H. Burdsall, Jr., Robert Lee Gilbertson (1925–2011), and Leif Ryvarden—
Our guides and inspiration.

Contents

Preface

TO DATE, NEARLY 2,000 SPECIES of polypores worldwide have been described, mainly from temperate regions. In North America, approximately 500 species of polypores, belonging to more than 150 genera, have been formally published.

Although mycologists are just beginning to develop an increasingly rich understanding of the complexity of polypores and expect many changes to be forthcoming, a new resource guide that incorporates updated and current prevailing views is needed at this time. Our objective in writing this book was to describe and illustrate the majority of polypores that occur in the eastern and central United States and Canada. Realizing the enormity of this task and knowing that not every polypore species reported to occur in this area can be illustrated, we have partially described, but not illustrated, some species that are extremely rare or uncommonly encountered. With the exception of a few resupinate polypores that are frequently collected or easily identified, this book does not include resupinate species and is not intended to be a resource for their identification. Perhaps this book will inspire some reader to create a new guide devoted exclusively to resupinate fungi.

Previously published reference guides dedicated exclusively to the description of polypore species found in eastern North America contain only black-and-white photographs or lack illustrations altogether. This book illustrates nearly 250 species in color, some of them relatively new to science, as well as common look-alike species.

With the ongoing process of molecular analysis and the construction of phylogenetic trees, the genus names of many polypore species have changed and will continue to change as science's knowledge of their evolutionary relationships increases. Consequently, older, outdated reference works contain many names that are no longer used or considered to be valid. In this book we have attempted to include the most currently accepted genera and species names, knowing it is very likely that many more name changes will have occurred by the time it is published. Some of the polypores listed here as separate species may have been transferred into a single species. We have provided a list of the most relevant taxonomic synonyms with each species description. Additional synonyms can be found on the websites Index Fungorum, MycoBank, Mushroom Observer, or other online sources.

Most readers will be interested in using this resource primarily to learn how to identify particular polypores. The keys, species descriptions, photographs, and bibliography in this guide have been carefully researched and designed to provide readers with an updated resource for identifying this group to genus and species based on macroscopic, microscopic, chemical, and molecular characteristics. However, we want to emphasize from the start that polypores are more than just their fruitbodies. We wish to encourage readers to see and understand them not solely as discrete entities to be identified by their observable morphological characteristics but also as active parts of a greater ecological story.

Acknowledgments

I T IS EASY TO THINK OF BOOKS AS being stationary. Inanimate. Easily picked up and set back down. *Polypores and Similar Fungi of Eastern and Central North America*, for all its weight, is none of those. It is a telling. A journey. The result of our travels, discoveries, learnings, and, most important, friendships that span decades. This book has taken us miles from home, had us crawling on our knees, scaling trees, and moaning for days over chigger bites. We have questioned, debated, searched. We repeatedly returned to the writings of those who blazed the path before us. Along the way, the three of us have had the pleasure of communicating and working with numerous friends and colleagues, old and new, some of whom we have never met face-to-face. We could not have come to this point in our journey without their help.

Heartfelt appreciation goes to Dianna's husband, Howard, who took on the role of personal chef and provided a steady presence in support of her dedication to this book.

Sarah Prentice of the University of Florida Marston Science Library, Gainesville, Florida, once again forayed tirelessly through the literature and provided us access to publications that guaranteed the accuracy of much of this book.

Jason and Jamie Bolin, Chris Matson, Barrie Overton, David Raney, and Phillip Thompson shared collecting sites previously unknown to us where we were able to locate specimens we were searching for. Culinary wizard Tanith Tyrr advised on the edibility of several species and used great restraint by providing us with a rare specimen for study rather than experimenting with it in the kitchen. Keith and Jill LaRoche were trusting enough to allow us, strangers, to come to their home and tromp through their flowerbeds to photograph *Ganoderma lobatum*. Bill and Jennie Sheehan housed and fed us, shared their special woods, and made both laboratory and equipment available during our ongoing quest.

Special thanks to Hal Burdsall, Mike Hopping, Jacob Kalichman, Patrick Leacock, Otto Miettinen, Donna Mitchell, Curtis Peyer, Bill Roody, Leif Ryvarden, Matt Schink, and Matt Smith for sharing their time, mycological knowledge, and expertise through conversation and consultation; their review of images and specimens helped verify species identifications. Michael Kuo and Sarah Prentice were instrumental in our locating and obtaining much-needed color images for this book.

By providing molecular analysis, Linas Kudzma became our eyes when our eyes were not good enough. He was, and continues to be, instrumental in our understanding of specific species.

The number of species illustrated in this book would be significantly lower without the extensive fieldwork of Donna Mitchell and Bill Roody. They were, without question, the indefatigable Polypore Hounds of this project.

We cannot thank Mike Hopping, Donna Mitchell, and Bill Roody enough for their endless patience, persistence, and keen attention to detail in reviewing portions of the manuscript. In addition to reviewing species descriptions, they were the three who read and tested, and read and tested again, and again—more times than can be counted—the identification keys in this book. This is a mind-numbing and exhausting task. The significance of their contributions cannot be overstated.

Our gratitude also to Gary Emberger and Alan Franck, who graciously reviewed the manuscript, offering valuable suggestions and perceptions that resulted in a much improved work.

The beauty and functionality of this book is due in part to Pat Buchanan, who created the original line drawings as well as the map of the North American forest regions. Thanks go also to Erin Greb, of Erin Greb Cartography, for creating the map of the geographic area covered by this book.

One of our greatest wishes was to visually share the diversity and beauty of polypores and similar fungi with you, our readers. The following individuals generously allowed us to use their photographs to help fulfill that wish.

Jason Bolin
Adolf and Oluna Ceska
Neil Dollinger
Gary Emberger
Alan Franck
Django Grootmyers
Drew Henderson
Jason Hollinger
Mike Hopping
Jacob Kalichman
Laurel Kaminsky
Andrew Khitsun
Joan Knapp
David Lewis
Martin Livezey

Justin Mathers
Jared McRae
Daniel Mills
Jonathan Mingori
Daniel Molter
Jamie Newman
Maricel Patino
John Plischke III
David Raney
Bill Roody
Stephen Russell
Christian Schwarz
Bill Sheehan
Luke Smithson
Walt Sturgeon
Huafang Su
David Tate
Garrett Taylor
Phillip Thompson
Tanith Tyrr
Debbie Viess

If we have failed to acknowledge anyone, the fault is entirely ours and we offer our apologies.

The University of Texas Press has supported us in our work for the past twenty-eight years, for which we are deeply appreciative. Very special thanks to our copyeditor, Lorraine Atherton, for her astute observations and gentle suggestions that improved this book in every way.

We are especially grateful to Casey Kittrell, our editor and friend for more than seventeen years. Casey understood the what and the why of this book we were trying to create, and his trust, support, skill, and kindness ensured that there would be a place for our discoveries when this particular mycological journey was done.

Polypores and Similar Fungi of Eastern and Central North America

Introduction

FIGURE 1.

The geographic area covered by this book

Geographic Area Covered by This Book

This book describes and illustrates polypores found in the eastern, central, and southern United States and eastern Canada. As shown in figure 1, this geographic area is divided into three regions: the Northeast Region, North Central Region, and South Region. Each description lists one or more regions where the species is known to occur.

What Is a Polypore?

The word "polypore" can be understood and used in several different senses. The term was originally derived from the Greek words *poly*, meaning "many," and *poros*, meaning "pores."

Taxonomically, the term "polypore" most commonly refers to a group of woody conks that may form relatively long-lasting bracketlike fruitbodies that grow from, and are attached to, living or dead wood. It also has gradually come to incorporate bracket fungi bearing reproductive structures other than pores, such as spines, rigid gills, elaborate mazes, and other unusual forms. Most polypores are saprotrophs, meaning that they break down and feed on some, most, or all of the components of wood. Several are mild pathogens or even parasites. A few long-lasting terrestrial polypores are known to be mycorrhizal associates of trees. They provide water, nitrogen, phosphorus, and other nutrients to these plants in exchange for sugars created in the trees' leaves through photosynthesis.

Most polypores develop tubes that grow on the undersurface of the cap. Within these tubes, reproductive spores are generated. When mature, many billions of spores are released from the tube openings (pores) and dispersed by air currents. Few, if any, will successfully drift onto suitable substrates in a niche adequate for their survival. If the spore does drift to a suitable substrate, it may swell with water and germinate by forming a germ tube. Germ tubes give rise to filamentous monokaryotic hyphae that branch out radially from the swollen spore. If these connect with compatible hyphae, a dikaryotic mycelium of feeding hyphae forms. Hyphae are the tubular filaments of cells that make up the body (mycelium) of the fungus. Polypore hyphal cell walls are composed of glucose polymers (glucans), amino-acid polymers (proteins), and nitrogen-containing polysaccharides (chitin). The apical tips of hyphae are the metabolic centers of feeding, growth, and extension. Hyphae expand in all directions in search of food until a barrier is encountered. In soil, the barrier could be a boulder, a root, or a water pipe, for example. Within a tree, the barrier to further growth and expansion might be a part of the wood that the fungus is unable to break down and digest, or it might even be a competing fungus. As penetrative hyphal tips elongate and break through their preferred food source under hydraulic pressure, their enzymes transform organic material and take in nutrients as smaller molecules while releasing unused molecules into the surrounding medium. Absorbed substances and water are then transported through small openings (septal pores) in hyphal crosswalls (septa) to feed and grow lateral filamentous branches. Although the pores in the crosswalls are minute, they are large enough to permit cytoplasm, ribosomes, and small organelles such as mitochondria to pass between cells. Depending on the species, the mycelium of some polypores can form a miles-long network of hyphae within a relatively small volume of woody substrate in a single tree. The mycelium may

grow internally in this manner sometimes for many years before the associated fruitbody makes an appearance. When conditions are right, the vegetative mycelium produces a primordium, which gradually develops into a fruitbody that will eventually release mature spores. Some polypores produce a simple, often shelflike or fan-shaped fruitbody, while others form more elaborate overlapping fruitbodies, especially when growing on vertical surfaces (fig. 2). Once nutrients from carbon, nitrogen, and certain inorganic ions required by the mycelium of a species of polypore are exhausted, growth slows, and death occurs from the oldest areas of the mycelium outward.

Over the course of the past few hundred years, the term "polypore" reflected the diverse ways in which scientists understood and organized knowledge of certain fungi based on both their observable morphological characteristics and the reaction of their tissues and spores to chemicals. Subsequently, technological innovations in optical, electronic, laser, and scanning microscopy enabled mycologists to better understand polypore structures. The study of polypore environmental and ecological requirements and functions, as well as the recent use of DNA sequencing, has also advanced the understanding of this broadly defined group of fungi.

Recent use of phylogenetic analysis has revealed that although many previous assumptions regarding polypore lineages have been spot-on, there are notable cases that are not. Poroid morphologies, it turns out, evolved a number of times in several different and distantly related fungal orders as an adaptive response to similar environmental circumstances and challenges. In other words, some fungi that have traditionally been treated in field guides as polypores do not share a common ancestor. They are considered to be polyphyletic. Morphological features that represent convergent evolution in the Kingdom Fungi include fruitbodies that are conks, are stipitate, have tough gills or mazelike or ribbonlike fertile surfaces, or have typ-

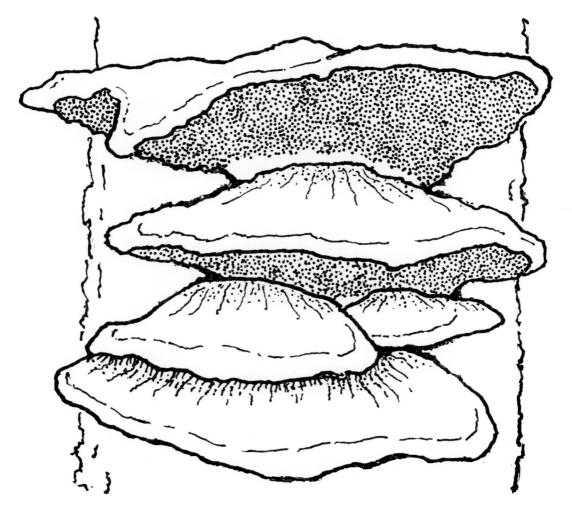

FIGURE 2. Overlapping fruitbodies

ical mushroom caps and stalks. Currently, these unrelated poroid fungi are being assigned to different orders and families in the Basidiomycota that more accurately reflect their genetic relationships rather than their morphological similarities with other pored fungi.

This book contains fungi that have been determined by DNA analysis to be true members of the monophyletic order Polyporales. As stated earlier, we have included only a few resupinate polypores. Additionally, we have included species from 12 other fungal orders that morphologically resemble polypores.

Macrocharacteristics of Polypores

When describing the macroscopic features of polypores, we have used nontechnical terms whenever possible. Most known polypores are bracket or shelf fungi that grow from living or dead wood. They produce shelflike, hoof-shaped, semicircular or shell-shaped fruitbodies that are firmly, and of-

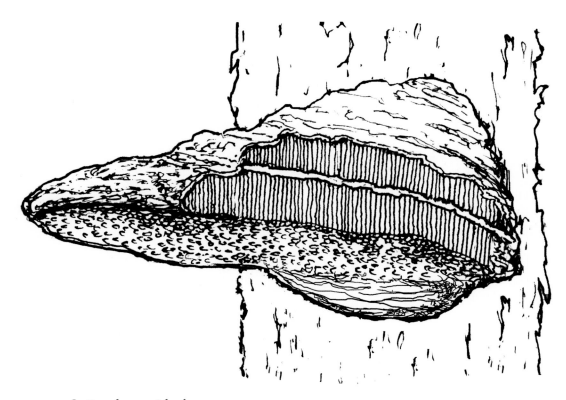

FIGURE 3. Sectioned perennial polypore

ten broadly, attached to the substrate. Occasionally polypores have a somewhat triangular shape. Some species have caps that overlap each other like tiles on a roof, whereas others grow singly or in loose groups. All polypores and some crust fungi that grow on the top of fallen logs tend to develop into rosettes: roundish, almost circular caps that resemble a stemless flower bouquet. For example, a fruiting of Turkey-tail fungi (*Trametes versicolor*) growing from the top of a stump or log will usually form a rosette. Three terms used to describe different forms of attachment are stalked, substipitate, and sessile. When a stalk is present, it may be attached at the center (central), attached away from the center but not marginal (eccentric), or attached at the base or margin of the fruitbody (lateral). Substipitate species are attached to the substrate by a rudimentary extension of the fruitbody. Ses-

sile species are often broadly attached at the margin or base.

Several polypores have bands of different colors (zonation). These zones are typically sulcate or depressed. Between these zones, raised ridges of growth can be observed. There are, of course, exceptions. In *Trametes versicolor*, these zones have dense short hairs that disappear as the cap matures. Some polypores, such as *Fulvifomes robiniae*, develop angular cracks and radial lines.

Perennial polypores actively grow for more than one year (fig. 3). New layers of cells are added to the cap, and new tubes and a new fertile surface are created annually.

The margin, the most distal portion from the point of attachment, is actively expanding outward and downward and is often differently colored from the rest of the cap surface. During this growth phase, if the substrate of an existing polypore has rotated or changed from its original position and has caused the tube layer's direction to be altered, the tubes will close off. New tubes will form and reorient geotropically, ensuring that they are once again vertically aligned.

In most cases, a polypore's tubes are laterally attached to each other and are usually the same color as the pore surface. The Beefsteak Polypore, *Fistulina hepatica*, is one exception. Its tubes are not laterally fused and are easily separated one from another. It and other polypores exhibiting this feature are referred to as cephaloid.

Microcharacteristics of Polypores: Hyphal Systems

Polypores are composed of one, two, or three types of hyphae: generative, skeletal, and binding.

Generative hyphae consist of connected and inflated filaments of thin-walled tubules that are usually branched and have simple septa or clamp connections. They make the reproductive structures that will bear the spores of the next generation. All fungi consist at least of generative hyphae. If generative hyphae are difficult to locate, try examining microscopic preparations made from the margin or the edges of dissepiments.

Skeletal hyphae are structures that strengthen and support polypores. They provide rigidity for the fruitbody. Skeletal hyphae are thick-walled, long, and usually unbranched. They have few septa and no clamp connections. In tough polypores, there are numerous skeletal hyphae.

Binding hyphae are usually very narrow, thick-walled, and highly branched. They bind and lock generative and skeletal hyphae together and are the structures responsible for the tough, woody consistency of the more complex fruitbodies.

Most gilled mushrooms and some polypores consist solely of generative hyphae and are termed monomitic. Examples of some monomitic polypore genera include *Abortiporus, Albatrellus, Bjerkandera, Coltricia, Coltriciella, Fistulina, Fomitopsis, Gloeoporus, Hapalopilus, Inonotus, Ischnoderma, Meripilus, Oxyporus, Phaeolus, Postia, Pseudofistulina, Pycnoporellus, Spongipellis*, and *Tyromyces*. All of the above-mentioned genera represent annual polypores, with the exception of *Oxyporus*. The texture of many monomitic polypores is soft, fibrous, rubbery, or corky. The rest are relatively stiff.

A fungus that is made up of two kinds of hyphae, either generative and skeletal or generative and binding, is called dimitic. Some examples of dimitic genera are *Bondarzewia, Cerioporus, Ganoderma, Grifola, Laetiporus, Phellinus, Polyporus, Rhodofomes*, and *Xylodon*. Dimitic fungi almost always consist of generative and skeletal hyphae. An exception includes dimitic species of the *Laetiporus sulphureus* complex, which consist of generative and binding hyphae.

Trimitic fungi are composed of all three types of hyphae. Examples of trimitic genera include *Cerrena, Daedalea, Daedaleopsis, Globifomes, Hexagonia, Niveoporofomes*, and *Trametes*.

Macromorphology offers no obvious clues as to the types of hyphae found in any particular polypore. Microscopic examination of the flesh is needed to determine its composition. We have included the hyphal system of each fully described polypore species in this book under "Microscopic Features" within each description.

Polypore Nomenclature and Taxonomy: A Brief History

Taxonomy involves the description, identification, naming, and classification of organisms into intelligible groupings. Using a hierarchical structure based on given sets of shared characteristics, taxonomy often reflects cultural and philosophical beliefs combined with experiential knowledge.

The study of polypores and other fungi had a

head start in Europe, where eighteenth-century naturalists, inspired by Francis Bacon (1561–1626), René Descartes (1596–1650), Isaac Newton (1642–1727), and the ideals of enlightened philosophers promoted during the Age of Reason, sought to discover, describe, and define where fungi fit within developing taxonomic systems. Incorporating the binomial system adopted from the Sami natives in northern Sweden, Carl Linnaeus (1707–1778), like his pre-Darwinian contemporaries, had a vision of nature that reflected an organism's place based on its perceived worthiness and its proximity to or distance from the Prime Mover, Almighty God. Just as Newton uncovered the clockwork regularity of the planets' motions around the sun, Linnaeus wanted to uncover the natural order the Creator intended in crafting the Garden of Eden for Man's benefit by grouping all of nature into the three categories, or kingdoms (Animals, Plants, and Minerals), first proposed by Aristotle in the fourth century BC. The polymath's primary interest, like that of many educated contemporaries, was in plants as a potential source of medicines that might provide cures for diseases. Lacking visible sexual organs of stamens and pistils, fungi were difficult to understand (microscopes were not in common use yet). These strange "plants," along with algae, mosses, ferns, and lichens, were assigned to the class Cryptogamia.

Basing his fungal taxonomy on morphological characters, Linnaeus was determined to name all pored fungi *Boletus*. Christiaan Hendrik Persoon (1761–1836) likewise assigned all fungi with tubular structures ending in pores to the genus *Boletus*, whether the pored fungi were fleshy or stiff, grew from the ground or wood, and had stalks or were sessile.

In his *Systema Mycologicum* of 1821, Elias Magnus Fries (1794–1878) considered the soft, ephemeral, spongy-pored mushrooms with their removable tubes sufficiently different from the comparatively more durable and long-lived poly-pores to be deemed independent groups of fungi. The latter were designated members of the Polypore Tribe. As Fries and his successors discovered pored specimens having a more limited set of defined shared characteristics, they were assigned to new genera within the Polyporaceae family; however, through the nineteenth century most species in this family retained the generic name *Polyporus*. Understandably, lamellate (gilled) polypores were problematic for early mycologists. Like Linnaeus, Fries considered them agarics (members of the family Agaricaceae).

Several American mycologists, including Thomas U. Walter (1740–1789), Lewis David de Schweinitz (1780–1834), Moses Ashley Curtis (1808–1872), Henry William Ravenel (1814–1887), William Alphonso Murrill (1869–1957), Lee Oras Overholts (1890–1946), Rolf Singer (1906–1994), and Josiah Lincoln Lowe (1905–1997) made major contributions to the study of North American polypores.

The most recent major addition to our understanding of polypores of the Western Hemisphere was incorporated into the monumental collaborative work of two mycologists, Robert Lee Gilbertson (1925–2011) of the University of Arizona and Leif Ryvarden (b. 1935) of the University of Oslo, in their two-volume publication *North American Polypores* (1986). Drawing on advances in worldwide mycological studies, Gilbertson and Ryvarden incorporated updated information on various forms of rot, preferred substrates, spore sizes, shapes and colors, sexuality, chemical reactions, and details on the hyphal systems of the various fungi treated. The authors also added new genera but intentionally left out of their approach references to phylogeny and evolution. At the time of publication, they concluded that not enough was known yet to attempt sorting out how the described polypores might be related to one another.

Even after Darwin's theory of evolution was accepted by leaders in various scientific disciplines, many taxonomists continued to assume that organisms with similar observable characteristics were related and unchanging over time. Through the use of phylogenetic analysis of genetic information contained in the cells of fruitbodies, we have since learned that some fungal look-alikes, such as polypores (understood in the morphological sense), are genetically different from each other. Poroid morphologies, it turns out, evolved a number of times in several different and distantly related fungal orders as an adaptive response to similar environmental circumstances and challenges. Also, several fungal species previously considered more closely related to cap and stalk agarics, coral-like fungi, or club fungi are now known to be more closely related to polypores in the order Polyporales rather than to their morphological counterparts in other fungal orders.

Recently developed complementary systems of classifying the relationships between organisms are altering the way we currently describe and understand fungi. These include cladistics, systematics, and biosystematics, which are similar in that they have overlapping definitions for both existing and extinct organisms. Increasingly, however, they are being influenced by the use of molecular sequencing data to infer the evolutionary relationships between individual or groups of organisms. The current trend is to base taxonomy on the molecular analysis of nucleotide or protein sequences as well as on shared morphological characteristics derived from a common ancestor. The information obtained from this process is used to construct phylogenetic trees, which represent evolutionary relationships among organisms.

All creatures in a particular clade have a distinct set of derived traits not found in clades representing other organisms. Consequently, there are some fruitbodies that have been treated in field guides as polypores because they look like polypores, but they do not share a recent common ancestor. As such, they are considered polyphyletic. All descendants can be visualized as part of a branching diagram that illustrates their evolutionary relationships and which represents a monophyletic group. Two organisms sharing the highest proportion of derived characteristics are presumed to have diverged more recently from a common ancestor than two organisms sharing fewer derived traits.

Advances in microscopy, chemistry, mineralogy, archeology, paleogeography, plate tectonics, physics, mathematics, and computer sciences are further helping to augment information derived from various competing taxonomic schemes. Numerous monographs have been published worldwide in the past 50 years, including several studies by Ryvarden, Miettinen, Ginns, and others, that delimited polypores previously unrecognized as separate species. They also reorganized the placement of genera from one order to another, or in uncertain taxonomic positions.

As our understanding of fungal relationships based on molecular sequencing increased, the need to change the names of some fungi became apparent. For example, at the time of this writing, 175 species described in Gilbertson and Ryvarden's two-volume monograph required name changes and nearly 100 additional new species have been recorded. Amateur mycologists are often frustrated by the recent storm of name changes, preferring to use common names or former scientific names found in existing field guides. Mycology is both a relatively young science and a dynamic discipline. It will evolve in response to technological improvements available to us and will enable us to expand and refine our current observational skills. Ongoing scientific discoveries will continue to enhance our understanding of the complexity of polypores and their interactions with trees, animals, insects, and other life-forms. Without question, this will result in continued taxonomic reorganization with corresponding ongoing revisions in nomenclature.

Historical and Contemporary Uses of Polypores

Certain polypores have traditionally been employed by our ancestors as well as modern survivalists to create a mobile source of fire, heat, and light that can easily be carried from one encampment site to a more distant one. Wood debris that might be used to construct a fire pit is often too wet to ignite without great effort. Most wilderness guides include instructions for campers, hikers, and backwoodsmen on the identification and use of polypores for starting fires. The friction caused by twisting a spindlelike stick deep into the dried flesh of the Birch Polypore (*Fomitopsis betulina*), the Tinder Conk (*Fomes excavatus*), the Willow Bracket or False Tinder Polypore (*Phellinus igniarius*), the Hemlock Varnish Shelf (*Ganoderma tsugae*), the sterile Birch Conk commonly known as Chaga (*Inonotus obliquus*), the Artist's Conk (*Ganoderma applanatum*), and others will smoke, ignite, and transform the fungus into long-burning embers of charcoal. The dried-out tubular pore layer of these polypores provides a conduit for moisture evaporation. The release of aromatic smoke from the Birch Polypore has also been employed by apiarists for anesthetizing bees. Smoldering embers of *Fomes excavatus* have been used ritually to drive away illness, malevolent spirits, and odors. They have also been used as an insect repellent. The dense perennial polypore *Fomes excavatus* was found with the 5,300-year-old mummified body of the Tyrolean Iceman (known as Ötzi) in 1991 on the Austrian-Italian border situated in the Ötztal Alps. Ötzi presumably carried it for the purpose of transporting fire from one campsite to another. The other fungus discovered on Ötzi was *Fomitopsis betulina*, also known for its usefulness in starting fires as well as for its alleged curative properties in folk medicines. This annual polypore of birch trees has also been utilized as recently as the nineteenth century as a razor strop or blade sharpener by barbers (and possibly by barber-surgeons in previous centuries). Building on traditional uses, contemporary Eastern Europeans are known to grind up the singed remains and combine them with water to fashion a rough facial cleanser.

OTHER USES

For thousands of years Native North American peoples made iqmik by mixing ash from *Phellinus igniarius* (punk ash), and possibly other related polypore species of the Hymenochaetaceae family, wrapped in the leaves of indigenous plants containing alkaloids. This form of smokeless chewing tobacco combines alkaline ash and plant alkaloids and serves to heighten the nicotine kick. Iqmik, also known as blackbull, was both common and widespread. It is still used by many populations, especially in the southwestern regions of Alaska. While viewed by some users as a healthy alternative to commercially available tobacco products, iqmik is responsible for severe nicotine poisoning and is currently considered to be a serious health concern.

Amadou is a spongy material derived from *Fomes excavatus* and other polypores. Skilled crafters from the Corund region in Hungary fashion it into a suedelike fabric used in hats, purses, assorted knick-knacks, and other items. The tradition has been handed down in particular families who collect suitable specimens in forests for extensive processing and manufacturing by hand.

Trimitic polypores have been utilized in modern times to fabricate special nontoxic colored gift-wrap paper, note cards, and wall decor. Manufacturers of fashionable but stiff new blue jeans use the enzymes from Turkey-tail fungi, *Trametes versicolor*, to quickly bleach, soften, and age the denim. Another popular use, especially among weavers and knitters, is in colorful dyes: polypores and other fungi are combined with specific mordants and pH modifiers to dye wool, silk, and other fabrics. Among the most popular species for making dyes are the Dyer's Polypore, *Phaeolus schweinitzii*, a beautiful, velvety parasite growing from the roots of conifers, which produces both pale and vivid yellows, golds, browns, and greens, as well as the comparatively innocuous-appearing Tender Nesting Polypore, *Hapalopilus rutilans*, especially valued by collectors because it yields coveted and rare natural purple pigments. Several polypores have also been used in many different cultures as styptics, to stop bleeding, and as bandages. To learn more about the use of fungi as medicine, please consult our review in Appendix D.

POLYPORES AS FOOD

Much has been written about the presumed use of mind-altering fungi by our prehistoric ancestors based on our interpretations of rock paintings and sculptures dating back to 9000 BC. Less speculative is our documented knowledge of their use among indigenous cultures in Central America from at least 1500 AD, and undoubtedly before. We know that elite inhabitants of the Roman empire relished some polypores, boletes, truffles, and some cap and stalk mushrooms. Select fungi were also popular edibles in parts of Africa, the Middle East, Eastern Europe, and Russia. The story is quite different for much of Western Europe, where scholarly writings and attitudes regarding the visible world were largely based on the encyclopedic natural philosophy of the Greek polymath Aristotle (384–322 BC).

In the Aristotelian tradition, Christian natural philosophers posited that some living organisms, such as worms, frogs, rats, beetles, and mushrooms, sprouted spontaneously out of muddy soil, sewage, or rotten food. Fungi were considered strange and dangerous plants that suddenly erupted and, just as abruptly, putrefied into noxious oblivion. Mushrooms and other fungi were generally associated with decay, death, evil,

witches, and the devil. By the mid-nineteenth century, a Frenchman had begun cultivating the now ubiquitous *Agaricus bisporus*, but until fairly recently the populations of Great Britain and the United States were generally fungiphobic. On the other hand, edible boletes and other cap and stalk mushrooms, polypores, and truffles were relished in the Mediterranean region, parts of Africa and the Middle East, Eastern Europe, and Russia.

In regions of Asia that comprise modern China, Japan, Korea, and southeast Asia, numerous species of fungi were subjects addressed in many thousands of family recipe books, medical literature, pharmaceutical works, personal journals, and poems for well over 2,000 years. China's recent experiments in cultivating polypores and other mushrooms for use as food, as energizing and healing nutriments, and as medicine have piqued our interest in learning more about the fungi we find in our woodlands, fields, parks, and lawns. Although the softer polypores, such as the Chicken Mushroom and Hen of the Woods, have been popular for decades, fascination with the nutritional and potential curative properties of other edible polypores and cultivable fungi has bolstered the popularity of incorporating fungi and commercially available fungal supplements into our diets throughout the world. Scores of us are initially drawn to learning about fungi because we want to know which ones are edible. After all, what could be better than strolling through the woods to forage for wild foods we can harvest and bring home to our kitchens to prepare for a delicious meal? Foraging, like fishing, hunting, and growing our own food, is a pleasurable experience that replicates experiences of our hunter-gatherer ancestors and facilitates and enriches our connections to our environment.

Regarding the edibility of polypores, it is appropriate to provide a few words of caution, especially to novice mushroom collectors. First, there are no shortcuts to knowing which are safe to eat and which are poisonous. The myth that all polypores are edible is, like other myths about fungi, patently wrong. Whether one is interested in trying fungi as food or as medicine, the novice needs to learn about each one individually and thoroughly. We now know, for example, that *Hapalopilus rutilans*, a valued polypore sought after for dyeing, is highly toxic. Consuming it causes severe damage to the kidneys and central nervous system. There are even recent questions about the safety of consuming teas made from *Inonotus obliquus* (Chaga), the sterile conk found on birch trees, which many believe is capable of preventing and curing a plethora of diseases.

Our current knowledge regarding the edibility of fungi is still for the most part based on centuries of trial and error. Relatively few fungi have been subject to testing for contaminants. Every so often we discover that a fungus previously described as edible turns out to be potentially mutagenic, such as species of *Gyromitra*. Other edible species including *Coprinus comatus*, *Laccaria laccata*, and *Lycoperdon perlatum* accumulate heavy metals, which can build up over time in the body and presumably cause health issues for immune-compromised individuals. Even choice edibles do not agree with everyone's constitution. The reasons are many and varied: some specimens may be too old, riddled with insects, or insufficiently cooked; a number are known to cause negative reactions when consumed with alcohol, others may trigger allergic reactions, and some are just generally poorly tolerated. Occasionally, individuals become ill simply from overindulgence. We don't all have cast-iron bellies like Charles "Old Iron Guts" McIlvaine (1840–1909), author of *One Thousand American Fungi*. He prided himself on having eaten hundreds of different fungal species, many of which we now consider extremely bitter, acrid, and at least moderately toxic.

The edibility of a choice polypore can also be a matter of personal taste. Ask any experienced mushroom foragers which polypores they relish most, and they will exclude some that others love. We don't always enjoy the texture, taste, or aroma of polypores others judge as choice. Our opinions may be based on the way the fungi are prepared. Different cooking techniques such as grilling, frying, boiling, or broiling, as well as the selection of spices, herbs, vegetables, oils, butter, or dairy accompaniments, can make a huge difference in one's perception of a cooked edible polypore.

Most known nontoxic polypores are too tough, woody, mealy, small, or tasteless to be considered suitable for eating. Several, however, are regarded as excellent edibles and are generally plentiful in the midwestern, eastern, and southeastern forests of North America. They include some of the terrestrial polypores as well as some wood-decaying polypores, such as the Black-staining Polypore, Chicken Mushroom, and Hen of the Woods. All of these are relatively soft in texture when young but can become too tough if picked when mature and beginning to dry out. When collecting edible polypores one should take care to avoid any that show signs of advanced age, mold, discoloration, or infestation by insects and other arthropods.

Evolution of Polypores and Their Host Trees

Many fungi can be identified by morphological characteristics alone, but the identification of others has come to depend on the results of genetic sequencing and the analysis of ancestral lineages. Therefore, it seems appropriate to address the issues involved in our current understanding of developing relationships between fungi and their hosts from an ecological and evolutionary perspective. Piecing this puzzle together is especially difficult because the fossil record contains so little evidence of fungal fruitbodies or other soft-bodied organisms. Preserved remnants of extinct organisms are largely limited to permineralized organisms with skeletons or shells that were quickly bur-

TABLE 1. Intervals of Geologic Time

Eon	Era	Period	Number of Years Ago
Phanerozoic (541 Mya–present)	Cenozoic (65.5 Mya–Present)	Quaternary	2.6 Mya–present
		Tertiary	65.5–2.6 Mya
	Mesozoic (252–65.5 Mya)	Cretaceous	145–65.5 Mya
		Jurassic	200–145 Mya
		Triassic	252–200 Mya
	Paleozoic (541–252 Mya)	Permian	299–252 Mya
		Carboniferous	359–299 Mya
		Devonian	419–359 Mya
		Silurian	444–419 Mya
		Ordovician	488–444 Mya
		Cambrian	541–488 Mya
Proterozoic (2.5 Bya–541 Mya)	Neoproterozoic (1 Bya–541 Mya)	Ediacaran	635–541 Mya
		Cryogenian	750–635 Mya
		Tonian	1 Bya–750 Mya
			2.5–1 Bya
Archean			4–2.5 Bya
Hadean			4.5–4 Bya

ied in anaerobic sediments at the bottom of seas, lakes, or rivers. With few notable exceptions, fossils of recognizable fungi prior to 115 million years ago (Mya) are difficult to come by. Proof of cap and stalk fungi currently exists in collections discovered in amber derived from gymnosperms. The apparent absence of recognizable fungal fossils from earlier periods, however, should not be interpreted as evidence of their nonexistence.

Over the past twenty to thirty years, scientists with broad interests in paleogeography, paleoceanography, earth science, geology, mineralogy, plate tectonics, volcanology, meteorology, chemistry, physics, botany, mycology, and other specializations have been collaborating to determine when, and in what form, fungi, plants, and animals colonized shallow wetlands, deltas, ponds, and the damp edges of post-Cambrian continental land. Some preliminary findings are described here. For a list of the geological intervals mentioned in this section, see table 1, which shows their order and ages.

In a 2017 paper associated with the Swedish Royal Museum of Natural History (Bengston et al. 2017), researchers claim to have discovered fossilized structures resembling mycelium and spores within volcanic material dating to 2.4 billion years ago (Bya). Another paper, published in the May 2019 issue of *Nature*, reports the discovery of a microscopic branching multicellular chitinous fungus found encased in shale of a once shallow estuary in Canada's Northwest Territories (Loron et al. 2019). It has been determined to be between one billion and 900 million years of age. Although these revelations are still controversial, many mycologists believe that single-celled fungi existed about a billion years ago. Fungal filaments found in shale from the Democratic Republic of Congo date to between 810 and 715 Mya. The authors suggest the fungi lived in a biofilm coating sediment along a lake and fed on bacteria, cyanobacteria, and decaying algae (Bonneville et al. 2020).

Cambrian Period fossils have been discovered in ancient rock deposits dating to more than half a billion years ago in Australia, Canada, Russia, Morocco, India, China, and the British Isles. Researchers examine and use these fossilized materials to interpret the evolutionary history of life in changing marine and terrestrial environments. The ancestor of modern plants, animals, and fungi is presumed to have survived in pockets of glacial ice and in oceans as single-celled organisms, which later diverged from each other, diversified, and eventually made landfall between 600 and 500 Mya. The first fungi, like their closely related counterparts in the animal kingdom, were mobile organisms that moved through coastal waters by means of a whiplike appendage called a flagellum. Early terrestrial fungi descended from chytridlike parasitic and saprotrophic unicellular fungi that lost their flagella, more than once, and moved onto the supercontinent of Gondwanaland along with photosynthetic organisms like cyanobacteria and algae. Their habitats were along the edges of freshwater pools or protected marine environments on otherwise barren rock landscapes. It is presumed that early ascomycetes and basidiomycetes may have diverged between 500 Mya and 400 Mya, if not before, assuming their evolution did not greatly precede early terrestrial plant fossils. The oldest documented fungal fossils associated with plants date to about 450 Mya. At least some of these early fungi adopted a dynamic branching cylindrical hyphal growth habit and septa to allow the passage of cytoplasmic material within a network of attached cells. It is doubtful, however, that the earliest representatives produced visible fruitbodies that we would recognize today. Fossil specimens of fungi from the Devonian are limited to spores and mycelial structures of the ancient Glomeromycota lineage. They have been discovered embedded in the fossilized tissues of liverworts embedded in Scotland's Rhynie chert dating to the early Devonian around 410 Mya. These fossils provide evidence for early symbioses that were essential for the evolution of fungi and land plants.

Lichens—organisms that consist of a mutualistic relationship between algae (Kingdom Protista) and cyanobacteria (Kingdom Monera), or fungi (Kingdom Fungi)—are adapted to survive in extreme conditions. It is conceivable, but not yet confirmed, that they appeared before bryophytes (liverworts, hornworts, and mosses). These nonvascular plants consisted of flat naked stems without roots, branches, or leaves. Growing horizontally in flooded low-lying swampy continental edges and coastal areas, they were dependent on watery surroundings for their proliferation via spores, and their colonization by early diverging arbuscular mycorrhizal fungal lineages from the subphylum Glomeromycotina, to keep them from drying out. Ground-hugging club mosses followed, along with tiny plants with needlelike leaves, vertically oriented spore-bearing branch tips, and rhizomatous roots. Seedless mosses, ferns, and horsetails arrived on the scene about 410 Mya. Fossil fungal finds from around 400 Mya include chytrid zoospores, sporangia of zygomycetes, and fruitbodies of ascomycetes. Waste from dead vegetation was consumed by fungi, bacteria, and early invertebrates. The tallest land-dwelling organism in existence between roughly 430 to 360 Mya may have been the terrestrial megafungus *Prototaxites*, at 26 feet tall and 3 feet wide. Scientists have debated for decades whether it was a conifer, a red or brown alga, a liverwort, a lichenized fungus, or a basidiomycete. A recent analysis based on examination of hyphae using scanning electron microscopy finally assigned it to the subdivision Taphrinomycotina of the Ascomycota in the Kingdom Fungi.

Pioneering ecosystems of the Devonian incorporated taller versions of the first plants. Growing between 30 and 40 feet tall, fossilized trunks of cladoxylopsids were topped with an array of photosynthetic branches covered in projecting twigs. Each tree was a conglomerate of numerous mini-trees that increased the hollow trunk's length and diameter at the expense of tearing the tissues holding them together. Its base eventually collapsed in on itself, creating a wider support. Cladoxylopsids were superseded by *Archaeopteris* and other fern-like sporulating tree forms that flourished along with mosses, cycads, and giant ferns during the Age of Amphibians and the start of the Carboniferous Period, or Coal Era. At 60 to 98 feet tall, with trunks up to 5 feet in diameter, *Archaeopteris* was the longest lived of several tree species. It eventually made up 90 percent of the earth's forests, but those forests were limited to tropical and subtropical watery regions around wetlands, river basins, and coastal plains. Throughout the late Devonian Period, and during much of the Carboniferous Period, they had a profound impact on the carbon dioxide and oxygen content of the atmosphere and the concomitant ecosystems and soil chemistry. Oxygen levels resulting from the escalating growth of vegetation were sufficiently high to enable insects and other animals to grow to gigantic proportions.

While early terrestrial plants, animals, and fungi were taking up residence along shorelines in the years between the mid-Cambrian through the Devonian, there were two great landmasses on the planet, each composed of fractured continental segments drifting on several tectonic plates. Laurasia was in the tropics, and Gondwana extended southward to the Antarctic. During the 60 million years of the Carboniferous these landmasses rifted, twisted, bumped, and advanced northward at varying rates from their previous tropical and Antarctic positions on the globe and collided. Their impacts closed oceans and created a single landmass, known as Pangea, that covered about a quarter of the planet's surface (fig. 4). Mountains, deep continental shelves, shallow seas, floodplains, and deltas were created, including the northern Appalachians, the highest mountain formation in Earth's entire geologic history. They extended almost horizontally in the equatorial belt from the eastern coast of America to the Nordic mountains. Weath-

ering and erosion created streams and lakes and contributed to the buildup of sediments in the surrounding lowlands and many new niches for evolving organisms.

For the first 40 million years of the Carboniferous Period (359–320 Mya) temperatures throughout the planet were uniformly high. Precipitation was largely confined to tropical and subtropical land encompassing eastern North America, northern Europe, and northern Asia. Swampy, warm, humid conditions favored rapid plant diversification and expansion. Ancient club mosses, ferns, quillworts, scale trees, spike mosses, and zosterophylls, rather than the woodier gymnosperms or angiosperms, formed the main source of carbon for the development of coal beds measuring up to 39 feet deep. Neither wood-degrading macrofungi in the basidiomycetes nor lignin appear to have been major components of these boggy forests. Fossil evidence of basidiomycetes is limited to the discovery of hyphae with clamp connections associated with the fern *Botryopteris antiqua* and dat-

FIGURE 4. Pangea

ing to roughly 330 Mya during the Carboniferous. Along with ascomycetes and bacteria, early representatives of jelly fungi may also have been at work breaking down the components of wood. Giant lycophytes, mosses, and ferns were preserved in a low-oxygen, low-pH environment. This seedless vascular carbon source accumulated in layers of sedimentation and was subjected to extreme pressure, heat, and the effects of subduction and tectonic movements for tens of millions of years. With little significant fungal or microbial activity present, the compounded vegetation turned to peat and then coal.

Toward the end of the Carboniferous Period, the continental plates making up the southern hemisphere of Pangea became colder and drier as they drifted back toward the South Pole. The high oxygen levels of the previous 40 million years, fed by the equatorial swamp forests, initiated planetary cooling and resulted in a series of widespread glaciations, lower sea levels, increasingly arid conditions in continental interiors, and a precipitous drop in carbon dioxide levels. By the start of the Permian Period (299 Mya), the arborescent lycopod forests were dying out and being replaced by fern forests, cycads, and ancestors of modern conifers that took advantage of new terrestrial habitats resulting from continental uplift. The earliest conifers were better suited to adapt to the desert conditions and temperature extremes of Pangea's drier and rockier interior, but most trees and other plants still required water for reproduction to occur. Animal life during these 47 million years included ancestors of dinosaurs and modern mammals, turtles, snakes, and lizards, creatures better adapted to drier conditions. During these many millions of years fungi expanded their repertoire of enzymes to make the most of novel opportunities to flourish as saprotrophs, parasites, and symbiotic partners with nearly all evolving life-forms.

The Permian ended around 252 Mya with the worst of five extinctions in Earth's history, the Permian-Triassic extinction event, or the Great Dying. Within a span of less than 60,000 years, upwards of 96 percent of all marine life was eradicated, as well as nearly all insects and 70 percent of terrestrial vertebrates. Causes included ocean stagnation and the buildup of carbon dioxide resulting from inadequate circulation due to the existence of the megacontinent Pangea. It took at least another 10 million years for surviving marine, insect, and most terrestrial life-forms to recover and diversify. Remarkably, organisms in the highly adaptable Kingdom Fungi may have avoided comparable levels of extermination. Organic matter in sedimentary rocks of the time confirms the presence of fungal remains in every climate and environment.

Extinction events and continental movements provided opportunities for resilient life-forms to diversify and adapt to novel ecological challenges. An increase in diversification of all life-forms from 180 Mya through the Cretaceous Period (145 to 66 Mya) was accompanied by Pangea's gradual breakup again into the two large fractured supercontinents of Gondwanaland in the Southern Hemisphere and Laurasia to the north (fig. 5).

Gymnosperms dominated Earth's forests from the Jurassic Period (199.6 to 145.5 Mya) to about 50 Mya and were an important source of nutrients for newly evolving white rot and, eventually, for

FIGURE 5. Gondwanaland and Laurasia

brown rot macrofungi. Primitive flowering plants appeared in the late Triassic Period from an extinct branch of gymnosperms, providing another source of food. Fungi meanwhile expanded the tools in their chemical arsenals to digest newly evolved substances in the plant and animal world. They evolved a huge number of morphologies, from resupinate fruitbodies on the underside of logs to amorphous jellies to corals, followed by evolving macrofungi in the Agaricomytina related to the Cantharellales, Sebacinales, and Auriculariales. They subsequently included early decomposers in the Hymenochaetales, Gloeophyllales, Corticiales, Russulales, Thelephorales, and Polyporales. Cap and stem agaric mushrooms were among the last to evolve, beginning with saprotrophs in the Boletales and Agaricales from late in the Jurassic and the Cretaceous. Around 100 Mya the appearance of similarly shaped mycorrhizal fungi coincided with the emergence of the genus *Pinus*. These were polyphyletic, having convergently evolved from a variety of forms and from completely different lineages. The species of macrofungi we are familiar with evolved and diversified during the most recent 66 million years of the Cenozoic Era. All benefited immensely from having their spore surfaces raised above their preferred substrates.

The Cenozoic began with the Cretaceous-Tertiary extinction, an event that extinguished much of the flora and fauna of the Cretaceous and ended the long successful reign of the dinosaurs. It was triggered by the seven-mile-wide asteroid strike in the Yucatán, 66 Mya. Recovery from the effects of the bombardment was slow, but fungi, once again, made the most of this devastating event. After a slow start, and a succession of alternating glaciations and warm and dry conditions, this immense geological period of 66 million years witnessed the evolution of a prodigious diversity of species of fungi, plants, and animals. By 50 Mya angiosperms finally overshadowed gymnosperms. The Cenozoic witnessed rapid diversification of

mycorrhizal, saprotrophic, and parasitic macrofungi resulting in the further proliferation of species resembling currently existing macrofungi, including the polypores. Fungal-farming leaf-cutting ants were the principal herbivores in tropical rain forests, while their counterparts among the termite genera practiced fungiculture in semiarid ecosystems. Larger even-toed ungulates replaced small mammals as the prevailing fauna. Eventually megafauna came to dominate expanding grasslands.

These ecological changes were stimulated by the continued breakup and separation of the landmasses forming the continents of Laurasia and Gondwanaland, under way by the beginning of the Jurassic. All the continents inched toward their current positions. The world's continental and oceanic species were increasingly isolated and evolved to adapt to new climatic challenges, oceanic currents, and ecological niches. Developments associated with continued continental drift, perturbations in global temperatures, sea levels, and evolutionary pressures on organisms to adapt to new habitats will continue the evolutionary process by providing new opportunities and challenges for polypores and other fungi.

Forest Regions

The last of six or seven major glaciations known to have occurred in the past 3 billion years covered large parts of the Northern Hemisphere. A series of glaciations interrupted by extended warming began 34 million years ago during the Oligocene and ended approximately 11,700 years ago in the Pleistocene. The retreat of these glaciers altered the geographical terrain of North America, leaving behind the Great Lakes, Niagara Falls, the Wisconsin Kettle Moraine, and the terminal moraines that formed the eastern islands off Massachusetts and New York. Boreal biomes of trees dominated the colder north, with mixed coniferous-deciduous forests in the central areas and primarily broadleaf trees in the south. As temperatures warmed, broadleaf trees in our most biologically diverse southern mixed forests gradually advanced northward.

Prior to the settlement of North America by Europeans, roughly one-half of the North American continent was forested. Today's forests are a shadow of their former existence. Deforestation to clear land for agriculture, settlements, and other uses has reduced forests to less than one-third of pre-colonial times. Timber production leveled more than two-thirds of America's forests at least once, surpassing agriculture by 1880 as the main cause of deforestation. Since then some farmlands in the east have reverted to forests, but many are gradually disappearing for business developments or homesites. Less than 1 percent of old-growth forest remains. Overall, our forests are getting younger and are exhibiting more homogeneity than in the past. Eastern forests extending from the Mississippi River to the Atlantic Ocean differ from western forests in being dominated by broadleaf trees, rather than conifers. The latter are better adapted to shallower soils and drier climate conditions. The same tree species that inhabited pre-colonial America still exist, although there has been a shift away from late successional taxa such as hemlock and beech in favor of early and mid-successional species, such as poplar and red maple.

Six major forest regions exist within the eastern and central United States and Canada (fig. 6). From north to south, they are the Northern Coniferous Forest, Northern Broadleaf Forest, Central Broadleaf Forest, Southern Oak-Pine Forest, Bottomland Broadleaf Forest, and Tropical Forest.

Forest regions provide a huge number of ecosystem services for humans and other organisms. They give us clean water, clean air, climate control, food, and habitats for wildlife. Rainfall, temperature extremes, soil structure, and slope elevation in eastern forests are factors that influence the kinds of trees that grow in any particular region.

The Northern Coniferous Forest is dominated by a mix of spruce, fir, tamarack, pine, and juniper. Broadleaf trees including birch, poplar, aspen, alders, and willows also make up a significant part of this region. The Northern Broadleaf Forest is composed of numerous tree species including fir, cedar, spruce, hemlock, and pine but is dominated by species such as beech, birch, ash, cherry, elm, and oak. The Central Broadleaf Forest is also made up of some conifer species along with a very large number of broadleaf species. Hickory, maple, beech, ash, locust, and cherry are commonly encountered, but the region is dominated by oaks. The Southern Oak-Pine Forest includes at least ten species of oaks and eight species of pines. The large number of broadleaf species found here also include maples, hickory, holly, magnolia, tupelo, and sweet gum. The Bottomland Broadleaf Forest, the second smallest of the forest regions, consists of wet areas that are often flooded for part or all of the year. Numerous broadleaf trees, especially oaks, river birch,

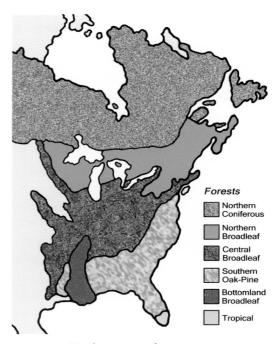

Forests

- Northern Coniferous
- Northern Broadleaf
- Central Broadleaf
- Southern Oak-Pine
- Bottomland Broadleaf
- Tropical

FIGURE 6. North American forest regions

tupelo, hickory, and maples, are common here. Cedar, pine, and cypress are the dominant conifers in this region. The Tropical Forest occurs only in the southernmost portion of Florida. Twelve native species of palms are found in this region, including Florida silver palm, Florida royal palm, and the Everglades palm. Examples of the numerous tropical species of trees and shrubs found here include pigeon plum, ficus, live oak, black olive, mahogany, wild tamarind, and gumbo limbo. Our southern forests are the most biologically diverse forests in North America. They were critical habitats, acting as species reservoirs for the regeneration of forests in terrain once covered by deep layers of glacial ice in the Arctic and the north temperate zones.

A natural forest ecosystem consists of a diversity of native plants, animals, fungi, bacteria, and other organisms. A successful balance is achieved when environmental conditions are suitable for all of its inhabitants, ensuring that future generations are able to survive the periodic challenges of ecological changes in weather patterns and invasive diseases and competing plants.

Polypore diversity is most pronounced in the world's old-growth forests. Polypores are also abundant on fallen dead wood. A woodland with plenty of standing and fallen dead wood is able to support more species of fungi, birds, insects, and soil organisms than a tidied-up parkland. A mixed forest of North America consisting of older coniferous and broadleaf trees will have a greater variety of fungal associates than nontropical forests consisting predominantly of conifers or of broadleaf trees, especially if the forest takes up a large expanse of territory uninterrupted by logging, grazing, or farm cultivation. Those of us living east of the Mississippi and the Great Lakes regions to the southern Gulf and eastern coasts of North America have access to an incredibly rich area of forest and fungal diversity, although increasingly little of it resembles the forests of pre-colonial times.

Most of today's conservation lands, parks, and woodlands are second- or third-growth forests situated on abandoned farmlands with altered soil composition and plants. Alien fungi, plants, and insect pests are competing with native organisms, upsetting the ecological balance and threatening diversity. Although today's fledgling forests continue to support a surprising number of fungi and other living entities, they exhibit more homogeneity than those found in past natural forests.

Forests consisting of a single type of tree species are cultivated monocultures. The trees in these forests are most susceptible to damage caused by parasitic or saprotrophic fungi and insects that may specialize in attacking the planted species. Single tree species are cultivated by lumber companies and farmers to meet our demands for wood and food. Industrial logging removes stored carbon, often results in erosion from heavy rains, and decreases biodiversity. Replacing forests with pine plantations reliant on insecticides to control insect pests in order to provide short-term benefits for logging companies, rather than allowing them to regenerate naturally, serves to degrade the environment and promote further global warming. These trees are typically harvested when the trunks are long and tall. They are not allowed to reach maturity, because mature trees tend to be habitats for numerous organisms that result in imperfect wood. Such forests will not be as productive for fungal growth as a natural forest.

Types of Fungal Decay

Given sufficient space, water, nutrients, and light, a tree seed can take root, grow strong, and defy decay for hundreds of years. A healthy tree will be able to live a long life resisting and surviving breaches caused by animal, insect, and fungal invaders by using various toxic chemical deterrents, as well as barriers such as bark and lignin, to prevent infestation and decay of heartwood. Cells in sapwood can detect fungal and insect penetration and limit their progression. By releasing volatile compounds and communicating via connections with mycorrhizal fungi, infected trees alert neighbors to discourage invasion by emitting similar repellents. Conifer resins respond to attempted breaches by sealing off intrusions, often trapping invaders in hardened amber. Fungi that manage to penetrate the outer bark and enter the inner bark can also be temporarily walled off by the formation of cankers.

But trees are not immortal. Trees become susceptible to invasion because they suffer wind damage, heavy snow, ice storms, lightning, fires, frost cracks, too much or too little rain, and sun scalding. Entry by fungi, insects, and other invasive species occurs at potential weak spots, including lenticels, furrows, and cracks at junctions with branches. Debarking scrapes made by bears, moose, porcupines, and deer; wounds from trimming or lumbering equipment; roots severed by lawn mowers, bulldozers, or backhoes, all provide fungi and insect fungal farmers access to debarked and damaged wood. Covering tree roots with too much topsoil, wood chips, asphalt, or concrete for streets and sidewalks also limits the tree's access to sufficient oxygen, water, and nutrients. Excretions of animals that frequent trees, such as squirrels, chipmunks, field mice, moles, rabbits, sapsuckers, woodpeckers, and other birds, typically contain fungal spores, fungal filaments, and yeasts. Should they be deposited on exposed damp wood, they can serve as vectors for inoculation. Once penetration of hyphae takes place, it can be expected that a succession of fungi will enter the tree to feed on remains amenable to their respective enzymatic activities, provided the wood is wet but not waterlogged or dry. Wood with a moisture content above 26 to 32 percent is suitable for the initiation of fungal infiltration, expansion, and colonization.

Wood rot, as the term is used in this book, is defined as the deterioration of wood caused by the enzymatic activities of fungi and certain bacteria. Wood-decomposing polypores traditionally have been assigned to one of two major categories, white rot fungi or brown rot fungi, depending on whether they are capable of degrading all of the components of wood or only specific portions. Recent analysis suggests that although this dichotomous categorization is useful, there are known instances of fungi that are capable of obtaining their nutritional requirements by using enzymatic mechanisms not found in either group. Soft rot is an additional and important type of rot caused by ascomycetes, rather than polypores, and will not be discussed further in this book.

WHITE ROT FUNGI

Broadly speaking, white rot fungi produce digestive enzymes capable of breaking down all three of the components of wood (cellulose, hemicellulose, and lignin) to meet their nutritional requirements. The several types of white rot include white pocket rot, spongy white rot, stringy white rot, and heart rot. The residual material found during the late stages of white rot decay consists of the cellulose fibers that remain (fig. 7). These fibers are typically stringy, hydrophilic, and whitish due to bleaching from oxidation and the loss of lignin. Soft and wispy, these cellulose strands are capable of absorbing water and contributing moisture to the surrounding soil. They are unstable, however, and will eventually disappear because of the decomposition activity of soil bacteria.

There is considerable interest in using white rot fungi that are capable of selectively decomposing lignin before breaking down cellulose and hemicellulose for purposes of biopulping. The resulting components are enriched with nutrients that can also serve as a supplementary food for ungulates, whose fungal gut microorganisms can break these down.

Today white rot fungi are the dominant type of decay fungi of dead tree wood. In fact, they are significantly more plentiful and varied than their brown rot fungal counterparts. Although they are

FIGURE 7. White rot

angiosperm specialists, white rot fungi are major decomposers of dead broadleaf tree wood and
conifers. In the distant geologic past, they were
the principal recyclers of the earliest conifers,
the dominant group of trees until about 50 million years ago. Between 180 and 140 Mya, angiosperm lineages began to take root and diversify,
giving white rot fungi a novel meganiche to ex-
ploit. White rot fungi existed prior to the evolution
of brown rot fungi, possibly since the close of the
Carboniferous Period.

BROWN ROT FUNGI

Brown rot fungi produce oxalic acid and hydrogen
peroxide, chemicals that break cellulose and hemicellulose fibers into smaller sections, which are
further broken down into sugars that are gradually

absorbed by the fungus. As is the case with white
rot, there are several different kinds of brown rot:
brown heart rot, cubical brown rot, root and butt
rot, and brown pocket rot. Brown rot fungi leave
the substrate so crumbly that the lignin remaining after the cellulose is digested is powdery dry. It
usually appears to form cubical blocks that eventually disintegrate into a fine dust while contributing to soil formation (fig. 8). This residual material
is extremely stable and can persist in soil for hundreds of years, unless degraded by soil fungi.

Fewer than 6 percent of wood decay polypores
are brown rot fungi. Today they are most prevalent
in conifer woods throughout the Northern Hemisphere in cooler zones of the planet where there are
fewer species of broadleaf trees. Examples include
Fomitopsis palustris and *Gloeophyllum sepiarium*.
Notable brown rot polypores that are generalists

FIGURE 8. Brown rot

and fruit on broadleaf wood are *Fomitopsis betu-lina, Daedalea quercina, Laetiporus cincinnatus,* and *Laetiporus sulphureus.*

As noted previously, various saprotrophic and parasitic white rot and brown rot polypores should not be viewed as two completely distinct kinds of wood decay fungi. Some fall within a continuum of rot types in which cell layers are partially or to-tally removed and replaced by the mycelia of spe-cific fungi. Finally, it is important to note that a single tree can be host to both brown rot and white rot fungi.

Guidelines for Collecting and Preserving Polypores

Mushrooming is a relatively inexpensive hobby, but if you are someone who is serious about ex-panding your knowledge and perhaps even help-ing advance the science of mycology, you may want to have on hand some or all of the following items that we have found to be essential or useful:

1. Collecting basket or backpack
2. Small notebook, pen or pencil
3. 10× hand lens
4. Sheathed knife
5. Sheathed small hatchet
6. Smart phone or camera and tripod
7. Labeling tags
8. Insect repellent
9. Waxed paper, waxed paper sandwich bags, brown paper bags, or aluminum foil—but not plastic bags!

When collecting a polypore for identification, record the tree species it is growing on or under. If you are unable to identify the tree, note whether it is a broadleaf or conifer. Photographing the habitat and taking one or more documentary photos of the polypore itself often provides valuable information for later use. Note whether the polypore is connected to a root, growing from the soil, or growing on wood. If your unknown polypore is growing on wood, record whether the polypore is growing from a part of the tree that is dead or alive, and whether there is bark on the substrate. Gently bruise the fertile surface and note any immediate or delayed color change. The information you gather will contribute to the identification process and help to determine whether your unknown polypore is pathogenic, saprotrophic, or mycorrhizal.

The taste and odor of a polypore's flesh are important features used for identifying specimens. Note the odor, if any, of an intact specimen. Cut off a small section from your specimen and note any odor you detect. If you choose to taste a specimen, *be advised that some are acrid and may irritate, burn, or numb your mouth if they are chewed for an extended period. However, you cannot be poisoned, and there is no significant risk, if you do not swallow the tissue.* To safely taste a polypore (even poisonous ones), place a small piece onto the tip of your tongue, chew it with your front teeth for a few seconds, and then spit it out. If the taste is mild (not bitter or acrid), wait a minute and then chew a second small piece for 15 to 30 seconds and again spit it out. Some polypores develop bitter or acrid tastes slowly, or the taste may be subtle.

To preserve a polypore, place it or a portion of it in a dehydrator with the temperature set at 95 to 100 degrees Fahrenheit for a minimum of 24 hours. Higher temperature settings of 105 to 115 degrees Fahrenheit may be used in humid conditions. Drying temperatures above 115 degrees may destroy DNA if the dried collection is needed for molecular analysis. Although drying polypores in an oven set at a low temperature sometimes works, it is not recommended because drying temperatures are difficult to regulate and are often too high. Drying is absolutely necessary for two reasons: (1) a collection that holds moisture will quickly become contaminated with other fungal organisms, especially molds; (2) polypores, whether soft- or hard-textured, are highly susceptible to insect infestation. Some polypores you collect may already contain insects; if left untreated, they will eventually destroy your specimens. Proper dehydration prevents contamination by molds and destruction by insects. After drying, polypore specimens should be placed in resealable plastic bags and placed in a freezer for a minimum of two weeks to kill any remaining insects or insect eggs. Specimens removed from the freezer may be kept in paper cartons, plastic containers, waxed paper, resealable bags, etc., preferably stored at room temperature or colder. Remember not to open the container after removing it from the freezer until it has reached room temperature. Opening a cold container directly from the freezer may allow moisture and molds to enter and eventually destroy the collection.

The Identification Process: How to Identify Polypores

Once you get home, and before using the identification keys or reading the species descriptions, carefully observe the features of your unknown polypore. (See "Guidelines for Collecting and Preserving Polypores" above.) Start by making a spore deposit using one or more specimens, as described in appendix C, "How to Make a Spore Deposit."

Then measure the width of the specimens and note their overall shape. Examine the upper surface color(s) and note the presence or absence of any staining reactions. Record whether the surface features are smooth or wrinkled, concentrically zoned, sulcate, soft or hard, encrusted or not, and whether they exhibit any other noticeable characteristics. Using a hand lens or a dissecting microscope, determine whether the surface is glabrous, tomentose, hirsute, or tufted. Check the thickness, shape, and color of the margin.

Now examine the fertile surface, noting its

color(s), staining reactions, and its margin to see if it is sterile or not. Note the shape(s) of the pores. Measure the number of pores per millimeter. Repeat this measurement several times to obtain an accurate range.

Using a single-edge razor blade or sharp knife, cut off a portion of the fruitbody from the point of attachment through to the margin. A sharp saw may be needed for large, thick specimens. Measure the thickness of the flesh and note its color(s) and consistency. Observe whether the flesh layer is uniform or duplex (consisting of two distinct zones of different textures). Also, check for the presence or absence of a thin black line above the tubes or near the upper surface. Measure the depth of the tube layer and note its color. Check whether your unknown specimen has a single tube layer or more than one arranged in layers. Using a cotton-tipped swab, apply a small amount of KOH (potassium hydroxide) to both the upper and fertile surfaces, and to the flesh, and record any color reactions.

Many polypores can be identified by their macrocharacteristics alone, but some will require microscopic examination. See appendix A, "Microscopic Examination of Polypores," for instructions.

We find that performing the above steps on some known species is great practice and helps make the identification process easier.

Using This Book

This book is intended to serve as a guide for the identification of polypores and similar fungi of the eastern United States and Canada. With few exceptions, we have intentionally excluded descriptions and illustrations of fully resupinate species. The keys following this introduction ("Keys to Polypores and Similar Fungi") are based on macroscopic features. Following the keys, the species descriptions and their illustrations make up the bulk of the book; they include both macroscopic and microscopic information. The species descriptions are arranged alphabetically by genus.

Each description begins with the currently accepted scientific name for the species, followed by the author(s), synonyms, and one or more known common names. Macroscopic and microscopic features, as well as information on habit, habitat, geographic distribution, and season, are included, and at least one color illustration is provided for each fully described species. Features are measured in metric units, usually centimeters (cm) or millimeters (mm). Spore size is given as length by width in micrometers, usually as a range; for example, 4.5–6 × 3.5–4.5 μm. If spores (or other features) outside a given size range are encountered, the outlier measurement is noted in parentheses, as in 8–11(14) × 2.5–4(5) μm. The edibility status is provided for each species. Additionally, information about ecological impact, derivation of the species name, and a brief discussion of similar species is included in the "Remarks" section at the end of the description. We have used nontechnical terms except where unavoidable. All technical terms are defined in the glossary.

When attempting to identify an unknown polypore, it is possible (and tempting) to thumb through the illustrations looking for a match. We strongly recommend resisting this urge and encourage you first to use the series of identification keys. It may seem more difficult and time consuming, but using the keys requires you to think about and observe your specimen more closely than you might normally have done. The keys may also direct your attention to features not visible, or easily seen, in the color images. This combination of verbal reasoning and visual attention increases your ability to recognize and "know" your unknown polypore much more clearly than you would simply by matching it with images.

Explanation and Use of the Keys

The next section, "Keys to the Polypores and Similar Fungi," was constructed to assist the reader with the process of identifying unknown species of polypores. Although the keys are intended to be a useful tool, they are not meant to be used alone. They, and the species descriptions, are based on macroscopic features of the fruitbody, including its growth habit, habitat, and geographical distribution. Fresh, mature specimens in good condition are more likely to be correctly identified than specimens that are immature or very old. The keys contain leads to more than 250 species; however, some polypores that are very rare or unlikely to be collected may not be included in the keys.

In this book we typically refer to two measurements when describing the physical dimensions of a fruitbody: width and thickness. Width represents the greatest diameter across the upper surface of the fruitbody when viewed from above. Thickness, as used here, is a measurement of the distance from the upper surface to the bottom of the fertile surface. Although some references include a length measurement (the distance from the point of attachment to the margin), in most instances it is of little value in determining species identification. When necessary or helpful, we have used the word "projecting," followed by the measurement, to describe the distance from the point of attachment to the margin.

The keys are constructed of paired numerical couplets, each of which provides two options. Start by carefully reading the information provided in both choices of the first couplet. Select the choice (either 1a or 1b) that most accurately describes your specimen, then proceed to the subkey or numerical couplet indicated by your choice (e.g., "Key A" or "2"). Continue reading the information in each couplet to which you are directed until you have reached a tentative identification. At this point, refer to the full description and color illustration of the suggested species. Examine your specimen and compare its features to the descriptions and color images before deciding on a final identification. Be sure to read the information provided in the "Remarks" section of each description, since it is possible that your polypore may be included there as a similar species. In some instances, when several polypores share multiple features, a couplet will terminate at a small cluster of species. When this occurs, examine the photographs provided, carefully read the descriptions, and compare the features for each species. If at some point neither choice in a couplet matches your unknown polypore, you may have made an error, or your specimen may not be included in this book.

Keys to Polypores
and Similar Fungi

1a. Fertile surface lacking pores, spines, jagged teethlike projections, or lamellae . . . . **Key A** (p. 26)

1b. Fertile surface with conspicuous pores, spines, jagged teethlike projections, or lamellae 2

2a. Fruitbody growing, or appearing to grow, on the ground but may be attached to decaying buried wood, roots, or a sclerotium . . . . **Key B** (p. 28)

2b. Fruitbody growing on wood 3

3a. Fruitbody growing on broadleaf wood, fan-shaped; upper surface gelatinous, reddish orange to pinkish red or dark red; stalk lateral or eccentric; flesh tastes sour: *Fistulina hepatica*, p. 117

3b. Fruitbody not as above 4

4a. Fruitbody growing on conifer wood, nearly round to hoof-shaped, sessile, whitish to tan or pale yellow-brown; fertile surface covered by a whitish to yellowish membranous veil: *Cryptoporus volvatus*, p. 107

4b. Fruitbody not as above 5

5a. Fertile surface poroid, lacking spines and not teethlike in age, not lamellate or labyrinthine, pinkish buff to rosy pink, becoming brownish pink or pinkish brown when mature, or bright yellow, yellow-orange, pale orange, orange to orange-red, brownish orange, or dark red . . . . **Key C** (p. 31)

5b. Fertile surface not as above 6

6a. Fruitbody upper surface typically shiny and appearing varnished, covered with a thin crust, sometimes sulcate, usually not cracked or deeply fissured when mature . . . . **Key D** (p. 32)

6b. Fruitbody upper surface not as above 7

7a. Fruitbody typically robust and conklike, often hoof-shaped; upper surface usually dull and not appearing varnished, sometimes covered with a thin, dull, hard crust in age, often sulcate, sometimes cracked or deeply

fissured when mature; flesh richly colored, yellow-brown, reddish brown, dark brown, or purplish black . . . . **Key E** (p. 33)

7b. Fruitbody stature or upper surface or flesh not as above 8

8a. Fertile surface with conspicuous spines or teethlike projections, or poroid to lamellate at first and becoming finely to distinctly teethlike in age . . . . **Key F** (p. 35)

8b. Fertile surface not as above 9

9a. Fertile surface lamellate and not becoming teethlike in age . . . . **Key G** (p. 38)

9b. Fertile surface not as above 10

10a. Fertile surface poroid, notably elongated to sinuous or labyrinthine . . . . **Key H** (p. 39)

10b. Fertile surface not as above 11

11a. Fruitbody with a distinct stalk that is central, eccentric, or lateral; fertile surface poroid; pores circular, angular, or irregular . . . . **Key I** (p. 41)

11b. Fruitbody sessile or with a rudimentary stalk or contracted stalklike base, or entirely resupinate; fertile surface poroid; pores circular, angular, slightly elongated, or irregular 12

12a. Fruitbody growing on conifers . . . . **Key J** (p. 43)

12b. Fruitbody growing on broadleaf trees 13

13a. Fruitbody upper surface ground color white to creamy white, buff, pale orange, tan, pale gray, greenish gray, or straw-colored, occasionally zonate with darker brown bands or developing yellowish to ochraceous tones as it matures, sometimes staining blue to grayish blue, brownish, or reddish when bruised or as it ages . . . . **Key K** (p. 46)

13b. Fruitbody upper surface ground color darker than the previous choices, or fruitbody entirely resupinate 14

14a. Fertile surface white, whitish, creamy white, buff to pale tan or grayish, sometimes becoming pale brown in age or staining brown when bruised . . . . **Key L** (p. 50)

14b. Fertile surface more richly colored, sometimes staining brown when bruised . . . .
. . . . **Key M** (p. 52)

Key A

Fruitbody fertile surface lacking pores, spines, jagged teethlike projections, or lamellae; sometimes
smooth, but often rough, uneven, warted, wrinkled, pitted, or with ridges.

1a. Fruitbody growing, or appearing to grow,
on the ground but may be attached to buried
roots or wood 2
1b. Fruitbody growing on wood 6
2a. Fruitbody up to 35 cm wide, a rounded,
lettucelike cluster of flattened branches attached to a common, partially buried stalklike base; upper and lower surfaces smooth,
whitish, creamy white to pale yellow or tan:
  Sparassis americana, p. 314
  Sparassis spathulata, p. 315
2b. Fruitbody not as above 3
3a. Fruitbody up to 25 cm wide, consisting of
a rosette cluster of tightly packed branches
arising from a common base; upper and
lower surfaces rough and uneven, whitish to
creamy white, sometimes grayish, pinkish,
or brownish in age:
  Hydnopolyporus palmatus, p. 179
  Podoscypha aculeata, p. 276
3b. Fruitbody not as above 4
4a. Fruitbody up 15 cm wide, a semi-erect ro-
sette of caps arising from a central stalk; cap
funnel- to vase-shaped, often laterally fused;
upper surface purple or brownish with a
white to yellowish margin; fertile surface
wrinkled and colored like the upper surface:
  Thelephora vialis, p. 333
4b. Fruitbody not as above 5
5a. Fruitbody 1–3 cm wide, shelflike, irregularly
fan-shaped to semicircular, broadly attached

to the substrate; upper surface dark brown to
blackish with a white margin; fertile surface
smooth, dark brown to blackish with purplish tints:
  Thelephora cuticularis, p. 330
5b. Fruitbody 1.3–7 cm wide, partially erect and
spreading, sometimes enveloping the stems
and branches of host plants, composed of circular to fan-shaped stalkless caps in overlapping clusters; upper surface rusty brown to
grayish brown, becoming blackish brown in
age; fertile surface somewhat wrinkled and
finely warted, grayish to pinkish brown or
darker brown:
  Thelephora terrestris, p. 331
  Thelephora terrestris f. *concrescens*, p. 332
6a. Fruitbody 2–10 cm wide, vase- to bowl-
shaped with a short stalk; inner surface conspicuously longitudinally ribbed:
  Cymatoderma caperatum, p. 108
6b. Fruitbody not as above, sessile or resupinate
to effused-reflexed 7
7a. Fruitbody growing on living birch trunks,
rarely on elm, beech, or ironwood, an irregular growth resembling charred wood, deeply
cracked and brittle with a golden brown
interior:
  Inonotus obliquus, p. 196
7b. Fruitbody not as above 8
8a. Fruitbody semicircular to fan-shaped; up-
per surface finely pubescent, coral pink when
young and fresh, becoming salmon-buff in
age; fertile surface consisting of a network of
radiating branched ridges, pinkish ochre to
salmon-buff:
  Byssomerulius incarnatus, p. 82
8b. Fruitbody not as above 9
9a. Fruitbody a spreading, often coalescing
crust with projecting caps; upper surface
finely velvety, bright white, becoming pale
yellow and appearing translucent and gelatinous in age; lower surface consisting of re-

ticulate ridges and shallow pits, orange or yellow or pinkish orange, becoming dark orange when old:

Phlebia tremellosa, p. 264

9b. Fruitbody not as above 10

10a. Fruitbody 1–6 cm wide, up to 1.5 mm thick, effused-reflexed and forming a semicircular to fan-shaped cap that is often laterally fused; upper surface typically undulating, zonate, tomentose, grayish orange to dark cinnamon brown; fertile surface smooth or slightly velvety, often deeply cracked in age, whitish to pale orange or pinkish buff:

Xylobolus subpileatus, p. 380

10b. Fruitbody not as above 11

11a. Fruitbody 1–3 cm wide, shelflike, irregularly fan-shaped to semicircular, broadly attached to the substrate; upper surface dark brown to blackish with a white margin; fertile surface smooth, dark brown to blackish with purplish tints:

Thelephora cuticularis, p. 330

11b. Fruitbody not as above 12

12a. Fruitbody up to 4.5 cm wide, often laterally fused up to 15 cm in diameter, semicircular; upper surface matted tomentose to densely hairy, dark reddish brown to grayish brown, sometimes with blackish zones, becoming uneven, pitted, zonate, and sulcate as it ages; fertile surface soon developing radially elongated, crowded wrinkles and warts, weakly to distinctly zonate, reddish brown to grayish brown:

Punctularia strigosozonata, p. 292

12b. Fruitbody not as above 13

13a. Fruitbody a spreading crust of effused-reflexed caps, often laterally fused; cap up to 2 cm wide and 0.4 mm thick, fan-shaped, narrowly attached to the substrate; upper surface concentrically zonate, variously colored from yellow-orange to grayish orange or brownish, shiny when dry; fertile surface smooth or conspicuously cracked, bright yellow-orange to pale orange when fresh, becoming pale orange-brown when dry:

Stereum complicatum complex, p. 322

13b. Fruitbody not as above 14

14a. Fruitbody a dense cluster of sessile caps narrowly attached to the substrate; cap up to 3 cm wide and 1.5 mm thick, fan- to shell-shaped, often laterally fused; upper surface concentrically zonate with reddish brown, yellow-orange, and grayish bands, sometimes with dark brown bands, dull when dry; fertile surface smooth or warty, yellowish to reddish brown or grayish brown:

Stereum hirsutum complex, p. 324

14b. Fruitbody not as above 15

15a. Fruitbody a spreading crust of caps, often laterally fused; cap up to 1.5 cm wide, fan- to shell-shaped; upper surface shiny, pale gray to silvery or buff, with radiating silky fibers or tiny furrows; fertile surface smooth, buff to yellowish or brownish, not staining when cut or bruised:

Stereum striatum, p. 328

15b. Fruitbody not as above 16

16a. Fertile surface uneven, warted, pinkish buff to pale grayish brown, staining dark red when cut or bruised; fruitbody consisting of caps up to 6 cm wide, often laterally fused; growing on oaks:

Stereum gausapatum complex, p. 323

16b. Fruitbody not as above 17

17a. Fertile surface uneven, wrinkled and warted or sometimes nearly smooth, grayish, yellow-brown, or ochre, sometimes with a pale violet tint; marginal portion paler, quickly staining blood red when cut or bruised; growing on conifers:

Stereum sanguinolentum, p. 326

17b. Fruitbody not as above 18

18a. Fruitbody consisting of fan-shaped to oyster shell-shaped caps, up to 8 cm wide, overlapping or sometimes laterally fused; upper surface concentrically zoned with reddish brown, gray, yellow, and orange bands, sometimes greenish when coated with algae, often whitish at the margin; fertile surface smooth, reddish brown to reddish buff or buff, sometimes staining yellow when cut or bruised:

> *Stereum ostrea* complex, p. 325
>
> *Stereum subtomentosum* complex, p. 329

18b. Fruitbody not as above 19

19a. Fruitbody a thin spreading crust, becoming confluent and spreading to form patches 20 cm or more in diameter; upper surface narrowly shelflike and projecting 3–10 mm, brownish black, with irregular concentric ridges and radial folds; fertile surface uneven, roughened, finely cracked, whitish to grayish, pale yellow, or pale tan:

> *Cystostereum murrayi*, p. 109

19b. Fruitbody not as above 20

20a. Fruitbody a thin spreading crust with small, shelflike, semicircular to fan-shaped, sessile caps, 1–2 cm wide, often laterally fused and extending 20–30 cm or more, projecting 6–10 mm from the substrate; upper surface densely matted and woolly, becoming nearly glabrous in age, yellowish brown to dark brown, zonate; margin orange-yellow to bright golden yellow:

> *Hydnoporia tabacina*, p. 182

20b. Fruitbody not as above 21

21a. Fruitbody effused-reflexed, often fused laterally and overlapping, 1–4 cm wide, up to 1 mm thick and projecting 1–4 cm from the substrate; upper surface uneven, with rounded concentric ridges, finely tomentose or nearly glabrous, ochre-brown to dark reddish brown or blackish brown:

> *Hymenochaete rubiginosa*, p. 184

21b. Fruitbody not as above 22

22a. Fruitbody a thin spreading crust, resupinate; fertile surface rough and uneven, conspicu-

ously cracked and reddish brown to grayish brown, or smooth and velvety, not cracked and rusty red to cinnamon-ochre:

> *Hydnoporia corrugata*, p. 180
>
> *Hymenochaete cinnamomea*, p. 180
>
> *Hymenochaete fuliginosa*, p. 180

22b. Fruitbody not as above 23

23a. Fruitbody resupinate at first, becoming effused-reflexed and forming patches several centimeters or more in diameter, with caps projecting up to 4 cm from the substrate; upper surface finely tomentose to hirsute, grayish to brown, indistinctly zoned; margin undulating, whitish; fertile surface bright pink-violet to dark violet, becoming brown-violet as it ages:

> *Chondrostereum purpureum*, p. 95

23b. Fruitbody not as above 24

24a. Fruitbody typically resupinate, circular, often radially furrowed from the point of attachment and fused laterally to form extensive rows; fertile surface uneven, warty, color highly variable, orange-red to coral-red, pinkish gray, or tan with an orangish margin:

> *Phlebia radiata*, p. 262

24b. Fruitbody a resupinate to effused-reflexed spreading crust; upper surface velvety to matted and woolly, sometimes warted and uneven or cracking in age, brownish with purplish tints or bright purple to nearly dark violet:

> *Phlebiopsis crassa*, p. 265

Key B

Fruitbody fertile surface with conspicuous pores, spines, jagged teethlike projections, or lamellae; growing, or appearing to grow, on the ground but may be attached to decaying buried wood, roots, or a sclerotium.

1a. Fruitbody a dense overlapping cluster or compound cluster of caps attached to branches arising from a thick common base; sometimes laterally fused and forming a rosette 2

1b. Fruitbody not as above 8

2a. Fruitbody up to 20 cm wide, consisting of numerous fan-shaped to spatula-like caps with rudimentary stalks, usually forming in a rosette cluster; cap white to pale tan; margin thin, wavy, entire or fimbriate to irregularly split:

    Hydnopolyporus palmatus, p. 179

2b. Fruitbody not as above 3

3a. Fruitbody 20–75 cm wide, a compound rosette of overlapping fan-shaped caps attached to a central stalk; cap upper surface whitish to grayish, pale yellow, or tan; margin sometimes wavy and blunt; widely distributed in the Northeast, North Central, and South regions:

    Bondarzewia berkeleyi, p. 73

3b. Fruitbody not as above 4

4a. Fruitbody up to 50 cm wide, a cluster or rosette of overlapping caps, 10–30 cm wide and 1–2.5 cm thick; upper surface rusty red to rusty brown, wrinkled and warted, often zonate and radially lined; fertile surface cinnamon to chestnut brown with angular pores, 2–3 per mm; growing at the base of oaks, sweet gum, or tupelo trees in the South region:

    Inocutis ludoviciana, p. 186

4b. Fruitbody not as above 5

5a. Fruitbody up to 55 cm wide, a large rosette of laterally fused caps; upper surface bright orange to pinkish orange; margin and fertile surface white to pale cream or pinkish cream:

    Laetiporus cincinnatus, p. 297

5b. Fruitbody not as above 6

6a. Fruitbody up to 50 cm wide, a compound cluster of pale grayish brown to light yellow-brown or dull white caps arising from a strongly branched stalk; caps circular, each with a separate stalk branch; fertile surface white:

    Polyporus umbellatus, p. 280

6b. Fruitbody not as above 7

7a. Fruitbody up to 50 cm wide, a cluster of overlapping caps, grayish tan to pale dull orange with black stains when young, becoming yellowish brown or grayish to blackish brown when mature; margin and fertile surface staining black when bruised:

    Meripilus sumstinei, p. 225

7b. Fruitbody up to 60 cm wide, a cluster of overlapping gray to brownish gray or dark brown caps attached to branches arising from a short and thick common stalk; fertile surface white; margin and fertile surface not staining black when bruised:

    Grifola frondosa, p. 171

8a. Fruitbody upper surface appearing varnished and shiny, covered with a thin crust, or dull and covered with a thin crust 9

8b. Fruitbody not as above 12

9a. Fruitbody growing in association with conifers, especially pines. .10

9b. Fruitbody growing in association with broadleaf trees, especially oaks 11

10a. Fruitbody with a prominent central or lateral stalk:

    Ganoderma curtisii f.sp. *meredithiae*, p. 148

    Ganoderma tsugae, p. 160

10b. Fruitbody sessile:

    Heterobasidion irregulare, p. 175

11a. Fruitbody sessile or sometimes with a rudimentary stalk:

    Ganoderma lobatoideum, p. 149

    Ganoderma lobatum, p. 150

    Ganoderma sessile, p. 158

11b. Fruitbody with a prominent lateral, eccentric, or central stalk:

    Foraminispora rugosa, p. 134

    Ganoderma curtisii, p. 146

    Ganoderma ravenelii, p. 146

12a. Fruitbody consisting of a cap and conspicuous central, eccentric, or lateral stalk; flesh
cinnamon to dark rusty brown 13
12b. Fruitbody not as above 14
13a. Fertile surface decurrent:
    Coltricia montagnei, p. 101
    Coltricia perennis, p. 103
13b. Fertile surface not decurrent:
    Coltriciella oblectabilis, p. 104
    Coltricia cinnamomea, p. 103
    Coltricia focicola, p. 103
14a. Fruitbody consisting of a cap and conspicuous central, eccentric, or lateral stalk; flesh
white to buff, pale yellow ochraceous,
or tan 15
14b. Fruitbody sessile or with an inconspicuous
or rudimentary stalk 22
15a. Fertile surface distinctly lamellate; fruitbody attached to a sclerotium and buried
wood; growing with conifers or broadleaf
trees along the Gulf Coast states:
    Panus tephroleucus, p. 249
15b. Fertile surface distinctly poroid 16
16a. Fruitbody growing with conifers 17
16b. Fruitbody growing with broadleaf trees . . .21
17a. Cap upper surface grayish blue to dull gray;
fertile surface blue to grayish blue:
    Neoalbatrellus caeruleoporus, p. 231
17b. Cap upper surface and fertile surface not as
above 18
18a. Cap upper surface white to creamy white,
pale buff to pinkish buff, pale grayish, pale
brown, or tan:
    Albatrellus confluens, p. 60
    Albatrellus ovinus, p. 63
    Albatrellus subrubescens, p. 64
    Sistotrema confluens, p. 311
18b. Cap upper surface not as above 19
19a. Cap upper surface often forming coarse
scales, greenish yellow to dull yellow-orange,
yellowish green, or olivaceous, sometimes
brownish:

Albatrellus ellisii, p. 62
Laeticutis cristata, p. 206
19b. Cap upper surface not as above 20
20a. Cap upper surface color variable, often mottled with a mixture of dingy white, grayish,
brown, and black, smooth or finely scaly;
fruitbody up to 15 cm wide and 4 cm thick;
stalk gray to pale sordid olivaceous brown:
    Boletopsis grisea, p. 72
20b. Cap upper surface grayish brown, reddish
brown to pale purplish brown, dark yellow
brown, or blackish brown:
    Jahnoporus hirtus, p. 204
    Picipes melanopus, p. 270
    Scutiger pes-caprae, p. 310
21a. Fruitbody upper surface azonate; stalk central or lateral, radicating:
    Polyporus radicatus, p. 279
    Pseudofistulina radicata, p. 290
21b. Fruitbody upper surface azonate or zonate;
stalk not radicating:
    Abortiporus biennis, p. 59
    Laeticutis cristata, p. 206
    Microporellus dealbatus, p. 228
    Polyporoletus sublividus, p. 278
    Xanthoporus peckianus, p. 61
22a. Fruitbody usually a cluster of overlapping, semicircular to fan-shaped caps, up to
15 cm or more wide; upper and fertile surfaces whitish to buff at first, sometimes with
ochraceous tints or darker spots in age; flesh
white when fresh, becoming buff to ochraceous with an unpleasant odor in age; usually in grassy areas; reported from Texas:
    Amylosporus campbellii, p. 370
22b. Fruitbody not as above 23
23a. Fruitbody growing with broadleaf trees, especially oaks:
    Pseudoinonotus dryadeus, p. 291
    Trametes lactinea, p. 341
23b. Fruitbody growing with conifers, especially
pines:

Heterobasidion irregulare, p. 175
Onnia circinata, p. 240
Onnia tomentosa, p. 241
Phaeolus schweinitzii, p. 254
Trametes lactinea, p. 341

Key C

Fruitbody growing on wood; fertile surface poroid, lacking spines and not teethlike in age, not lamellate or labyrinthine, pinkish buff to rosy pink, becoming brownish pink to pinkish brown when mature, or bright yellow, yellow-orange, pale orange, orange to orange-red, or dark red.

1a. Fertile surface pinkish buff to pink at first, becoming brownish pink to pinkish brown when mature.............................2

1b. Fertile surface bright yellow, pale to dark orange, brownish orange, orange-red, or dark red 4

2a. Upper surface rose pink or pinkish brown to reddish brown, darkening to grayish brown or brownish black in age:
   Rhodofomes cajanderi, p. 301
   Rhodofomes roseus, p. 302
   Rhodofomitopsis feei, p. 301

2b. Upper surface not as above 3

3a. Fertile surface and tubes stretchable and separable from the flesh; fruitbody annual, up to 10 cm wide and 5 mm thick at the base; upper surface white to creamy white, becoming ochraceous to grayish ochre in age; widely distributed in the Northeast, North Central, and South regions:
   Gloeoporus dichrous, p. 170

3b. Fertile surface and tubes not stretchable and separable from the flesh; pores 5–6 per mm, fruitbody perennial, up to 30 cm wide and 6 cm thick, effused-reflexed or shelflike to hoof-shaped, typically enlarged to substipitate at the point of attachment; upper surface

pinkish buff to light buff or green; widely distributed in the South region:
   Rigidoporus ulmarius, p. 304

4a. Fruitbody growing on the trunks of conifers; fertile surface lemon yellow, becoming bright creamy yellow in age; upper surface bright to dull orange, fading to orange-yellow then whitish in age:
   Laetiporus huroniensis, p. 209

4b. Fruitbody not as above 5

5a. Fruitbody growing on broadleaf trees; fertile surface bright sulfur yellow; upper surface bright to dull orange, fading to orange-yellow then whitish in age:
   Laetiporus sulphureus, p. 212

5b. Fruitbody not as above 6

6a. Fruitbody upper surface pale orange at first, becoming pale to dark orange-brown or rusty brown in age; fertile surface sometimes whitish at first then pale to dark orange.....7

6b. Fruitbody not as above 8

7a. Pores 1.5–2.5 per mm; growing on conifers or sometimes broadleaf trees; fruitbody 4–12 cm wide, widely distributed in the Northeast, North Central, and upper South regions:
   Pycnoporellus fulgens, p. 296

7b. Pores 6–9 per mm; growing on broadleaf trees, especially magnolia and oaks; fruitbody up to 22 cm wide and 2 cm thick, widely distributed along the Gulf Coast states:
   Rigidoporus lineatus, p. 303
   Rigidoporus microporus, p. 303

8a. Fruitbody a cluster of overlapping shelf-like orange to pale orange caps growing on oak trees; cap up to 20 cm wide, fan-shaped, growing on standing trunks or logs of oaks:
   Laetiporus gilbertsonii var. *pallidus*, p. 208
   Piptoporellus species, South region, p. 272

8b. Fruitbody solitary or in groups on logs and branches; upper surface orange to orange-red; fertile surface orange to orange-red or dark red:

> *Trametes cinnabarina*, p. 337
> *Trametes sanguinea*, p. 346

Key D

Fruitbody growing on wood; upper surface typically shiny and appearing varnished, covered with a thin crust, sometimes sulcate, usually not cracked or deeply fissured when mature.

1a. Fruitbody growing in association with conifers. 2

1b. Fruitbody growing in association with broadleaf trees 5

2a. Fruitbody with a prominent central or lateral stalk. 3

2b. Fruitbody sessile or with a rudimentary stalk. 4

3a. Fruitbody growing on living pine trees or on decaying pines or stumps; widely distributed in the South region:

> *Ganoderma curtisii* f.sp. *meredithiae*, p. 148

3b. Fruitbody growing on living or decaying hemlock or fir; widely distributed in the Northeast and North Central regions:

> *Ganoderma tsugae*, p. 160

4a. Fruitbody growing in the Northeast and North Central regions, uncommon or absent in the South region:

> *Fomitopsis mounceae*, p. 130
> *Fomitopsis schrenkii*, p. 131

4b. Fruitbody growing in the Gulf Coast states:

> *Ganoderma colossus*, p. 144
> *Ganoderma tuberculosum*, p. 162

5a. Fruitbody solitary, in groups or overlapping clusters on the trunks of palm trees; widely distributed in the South region, especially the Gulf Coast states:

> *Ganoderma zonatum*, p. 163

5b. Fruitbody not as above 6

6a. Fruitbody with a prominent central or lateral stalk:

> *Ganoderma curtisii*, p. 146
> *Ganoderma martinicense*, p. 152
> *Ganoderma ravenelii*, p. 146

6b. Fruitbody sessile 7

7a. Fruitbody shelflike, semicircular to fan-shaped, broadly attached; upper surface ochraceous, forming a hard reddish brown cuticular layer that spreads from the base outward and often becomes blackish as it ages, weathering to whitish on older specimens; pores circular, 5–7 per mm; fertile surface white to creamy white, tan, purplish brown to dull brown, grayish or smoky:

> *Fomitella supina*, p. 121
> *Trametes cubensis*, p. 341

7b. Fruitbody not as above .8

8a. Fruitbody shelflike, semicircular to fan-shaped, broadly attached; upper surface white to creamy white at first, forming a hard reddish to bay cuticular layer that spreads from the base outward and becomes dark reddish brown to purplish brown as it ages; pores angular near the margin, sinuous to conspicuously labyrinthine on more mature portions, 2–3 per mm; fertile surface white to cork-colored:

> *Earliella scabrosa*, p. 114

8b. Fruitbody not as above; pores circular or angular, but not sinuous to conspicuously labyrinthine 9

9a. Fertile surface whitish to pale orange or light ochraceous, sometimes staining yellow when bruised; widely distributed in the Northeast, North Central, and upper South regions:

> *Fomitopsis mounceae*, p. 130

9b. Fertile surface, staining reaction, or geographic distribution not as above. 10

10a. Fruitbody widely distributed in the Northeast, North Central, and South regions; upper surface dark red to reddish brown, becoming ochraceous outward; fertile surface

white at first, becoming yellowish then dull brown in age, staining brown when bruised:
　　Ganoderma sessile, p. 158

10b. Fruitbody distributed along the Gulf Coast states; upper surface yellow to pale brown, chestnut-colored to reddish brown or violet-brown; fertile surface whitish to yellowish or brownish, sometimes staining brown when bruised:
　　Ganoderma colossus, p. 144
　　Ganoderma parvulum, p. 156
　　Ganoderma tuberculosum, p. 162

Key E

Fruitbody typically robust and conklike, often hoof-shaped; upper surface usually dull and not appearing varnished, sometimes covered with a thin, dull, hard crust in age, often sulcate, sometimes cracked or deeply fissured when mature; flesh richly colored, yellow-brown, reddish brown, dark brown, or purplish black.

1a. Fruitbody growing on living sabal palms; known only from Florida:
　　Fomitiporia apiahyna, p. 123

1b. Fruitbody not as above 2

2a. Fruitbody growing on living acacia, desert willow, or mesquite; known only from Texas:
　　Fulvifomes badius, p. 136
　　Inocutis texana, p. 188

2b. Fruitbody not as above 3

3a. Fruitbody growing on cherry, peach, plum, or hawthorn trees; widely distributed:
　　Phellinopsis conchata, p. 256
　　Phellinus pomaceus, p. 256

3b. Fruitbody not as above 4

4a. Fruitbody growing on standing black locust or rarely on a few other broadleaf trees; widely distributed:
　　Fulvifomes robiniae, p. 138

4b. Fruitbody not as above 5

5a. Fruitbody growing on branch scars or

wounds of standing aspen; distributed in the Northeast and North Central regions:
　　Phellinus tremulae, p. 260

5b. Fruitbody not as above 6

6a. Fruitbody growing on conifers. 7

6b. Fruitbody growing on broadleaf trees 8

7a. Fruitbody up to 20 cm wide and 10 cm or more thick, shelflike to irregular at first, becoming hoof-shaped as it matures; margin rounded, reddish brown when actively growing, then blackish; fertile surface brownish yellowish to yellow-brown or ochre-orange; pores circular to angular or labyrinthine, 1–3 per mm; flesh typically lustrous:
　　Porodaedalea pini, p. 282

7b. Fruitbody up to 10 cm wide and 5 cm thick, shelflike to hoof-shaped; upper surface roughened, shallowly sulcate, reddish brown at first, becoming blackened and deeply cracked in age; pores circular, 7–10 per mm; flesh yellowish brown, lustrous:
　　Fulvifomes merrillii, p. 138

8a. Fruitbody growing on standing broadleaf trees, especially birch and alder, but not oak; distributed in the Northeast and North Central regions, occasionally in the upper South region 9

8b. Fruitbody growing on other broadleaf trees, especially oak, sweet gum, magnolia, and walnut. 12

9a. Fruitbody resupinate at first, becoming effused-reflexed on vertical surfaces, often fused laterally, typically up to 18 cm wide and spreading vertically or horizontally, but sometimes much larger; upper surface dark brown to blackish, sometimes cracked; fertile surface pale brown when fresh, staining darker brown when bruised, becoming darker reddish brown in age; pores with very thick dissepiments; flesh up to 4 cm thick, dull yellow to yellow-brown at first, becoming dark reddish brown in age:
　　Phellinus lundellii, p. 259

9b. Fruitbody not as above 10

10a. Fruitbody 6–20 cm wide; upper surface pale to dark gray or brown; margin extending beyond the fertile surface and curved downward; fertile surface often stains dark brown when bruised; pores 3–4 per mm; widely distributed in the Northeast and North Central regions:

  Fomes excavatus, p. 118

10b. Fruitbody not as above 11

11a. Flesh reddish brown with white flecks of tissue intermixed:

  Phellinus igniarius, p. 258

11b. Flesh yellowish brown or reddish brown, lacking white flecks of tissue intermixed:

  Fomitiporia bakeri, p. 124
  Fulvifomes everhartii, p. 137
  Phellinopsis conchata, p. 256

12a. Fertile surface white; widely distributed:

  Ganoderma applanatum, p. 143
  Ganoderma lobatum, p. 150
  Ganoderma megaloma, p. 154

12b. Fertile surface more richly colored 13

13a. Flesh shiny yellowish brown or reddish brown with white flecks of tissue intermixed or white radial streaks in the tubes and near the point of attachment:

  Fomitiporia calkinsii, p. 125
  Fomitiporia texana, p. 126
  Phellinus igniarius, p. 258
  Phellinus lundellii, p. 259

13b. Flesh variously colored, lacking white flecks of tissue or white radial streaks. 14

14a. Fruitbody 7–18 cm wide; upper surface grayish with concentric zones of reddish brown and grayish brown, often darker brown to blackish brown in age; margin even; fertile surface soon staining brown to dark brown when bruised; pores 4–5 per mm; widely distributed in the South region:

  Fomes fasciatus, p. 120

14b. Fruitbody not as above 15

15a. Fruitbody 6–20 cm wide; upper surface pale to dark gray or brown; margin extending beyond the fertile surface and curved downward; fertile surface not staining when bruised; pores 3–4 per mm; widely distributed in the Northeast and North Central regions:

  Fomes excavatus, p. 118

15b. Fruitbody not as above 16

16a. Fruitbody up to 20 cm wide, shelflike and semicircular, sometimes lobed, usually concentrically zoned or sulcate, yellowish brown to reddish brown or dark brown; flesh reddish brown:

  Ganoderma lobatoideum, p. 149
  Ganoderma lobatum, p. 150

16b. Fruitbody not as above 17

17a. Fruitbody shelflike and semicircular, up to 20 cm wide and 5 cm thick; upper surface sulcate, warted and slightly cracked, dark brown to purplish black; fertile surface dark brown to purplish black; pores 6–9 per mm; flesh dark chestnut to purplish black; known only from the Gulf Coast states:

  Nigrofomes melanoporus, p. 238

17b. Fruitbody not as above 18

18a. Fruitbody hoof-shaped to somewhat triangular, up to 20 cm wide and 8 cm thick; upper surface yellowish brown to gray-brown, blackish gray, or black; flesh reddish brown:

  Fulvifomes everhartii, p. 137

18b. Fruitbody not as above 19

19a. Fruitbody shell-shaped to semicircular or irregular, up to 15 cm wide and 4 cm thick; upper surface glabrous, azonate, rough and uneven, color variable, yellowish to grayish or rusty brown, sometimes blackish, especially as it ages, often a mixture of these colors, usually coated with moss or algae; widely distributed in the Northeast, North Central, and South regions:

  Phellinopsis conchata, p. 256

19b. Fruitbody not as above 20

20a. Fruitbody growing at the base of oak, sweet gum, or tupelo trees, up to 50 cm wide, sessile or substipitate, consisting of a cluster or rosette of fan-shaped, overlapping caps, 10–30 cm wide and 1–2.5 cm thick; upper surface wrinkled, warted, and radially lined, rusty red to rusty brown; fertile surface buff to brown, quickly staining dark brown when bruised; pores angular, thin-walled, and becoming lacerated, 2–3 per mm, sometimes up to 1 mm wide; widely distributed in the South region:

  Inocutis ludoviciana, p. 186

20b. Fruitbody growing on standing oak trees, 10–30 cm wide; upper surface tomentose or covered with stiff hairs, golden yellow to bright reddish orange, becoming rusty brown to blackish in age:

  Inonotus hispidus, p. 195
  Inonotus quercustris, p. 197

Key F

Fruitbody growing on wood; fertile surface with conspicuous spines or teethlike projections, or poroid to lamellate at first and becoming finely to distinctly teethlike in age.

1a. Fertile surface with conspicuous spines or teethlike projections, not poroid or lamellate at first and becoming teethlike only in age; specimens may be poroid only near the margin 2

1b. Fertile surface distinctly poroid or lamellate at first and becoming teethlike only in age 12

2a. Fertile surface orange to salmon; upper surface zonate, grooved, with erect velvety hairs, dull white or ochraceous to pale grayish orange, greenish with algae:

  Steccherinum ochraceum, p. 318

2b. Fertile surface not as above 3

3a. Fertile surface yellow-brown or grayish brown, staining darker brown when bruised; fruitbody with an odor of cinnamon, especially when drying or placed on a dehydrator:

  Steccherinum subrawakense, p. 321

3b. Fertile surface not as above 4

4a. Fruitbody a resupinate, spreading, sulfur yellow crust with pale to bright yellow, waxy spines, growing on the underside of decaying branches of apple or other fruit trees:

  Sarcodontia setosa, p. 305

4b. Fruitbody not as above .5

5a. Fertile surface dull yellow-brown to reddish brown, with jagged teethlike projections up to 2 mm long:

  Hydnoporia olivacea, p. 181

5b. Fertile surface not as above 6

6a. Fertile surface white at first, becoming smoky gray to pinkish brown at maturity; spines up to 3 mm long, typically fused and appearing forked at their tips:

  Mycorraphium adustum, p. 230

6b. Fertile surface not as above 7

7a. Fruitbody resupinate to very slightly effused-reflexed; fertile surface white to yellowish at first, becoming buff to brownish in age; spines densely crowded, up to 1.4 cm long:

  Radulodon americanus, p. 300
  Radulomyces copelandii, p. 300

7b. Fruitbody not as above .8

8a. Fruitbody an effused-reflexed, spreading crust of overlapping fused caps, up to 5 cm or more wide; upper surface azonate, white to creamy white; fertile surface white to creamy white, poroid near the margin; tubes soon splitting and becoming jagged or teethlike; teeth up to 7 mm long:

  Irpex lacteus, p. 199
  Steccherinum oreophilum, p. 320

8b. Fruitbody not as above 9

9a. Fruitbody a leathery to tough spreading crust of effused-reflexed overlapping caps; cap 2–5 cm wide, fan-shaped; upper surface azonate, white to creamy white; fertile surface white to creamy white, with conspicuous flattened teeth; teeth up to 1.5 cm long:
Spongipellis pachyodon, p. 316

9b. Fruitbody not as above 10

10a. Fruitbody effused-reflexed, consisting of sessile, shelflike caps up to 8 cm wide, often laterally fused and spreading up to 18 cm or more; upper surface whitish to orangish yellow, darkening in age; fertile surface consisting of flattened or conical spines, 5–10 mm long, easily removed from the flesh, olive-green to yellow, becoming reddish brown from maturing spores:
Gyrodontium sacchari, p. 172

10b. Fruitbody not as above 11

11a. Fruitbody fan-shaped to semicircular sometimes in fused or overlapping clusters, sessile, 3–10 cm wide; flesh white, exuding a creamy white, sticky sap when squeezed; upper surface densely woolly or with matted hairs, whitish at first, becoming ochraceous orange to pinkish buff or pale tan; fertile surface covered with crowded short spines, 2.5–5 mm long:
Climacodon pulcherrimus, p. 98

11b. Fruitbody in dense overlapping fan-shaped clusters, sessile, 10–30 cm wide, 2.5–5 cm thick, and up to 80 cm high; flesh white but not exuding a sticky sap when squeezed; upper surface hairy to roughened and uneven, whitish to creamy yellow when young, becoming yellow-brown in age; fertile surface composed of crowded, spines, 6–20 mm long:
Climacodon septentrionalis, p. 99

12a. Fruitbody upper and fertile surfaces white to creamy white, buff, straw- to cork-colored or pale gray 13

12b. Fruitbody more richly colored 19

13a. Fruitbody consisting of numerous fan-shaped to spatula-like caps with rudimentary stalks, usually forming a rosette cluster; margin thin, wavy, entire or fimbriate to irregularly split:
Hydnopolyporus palmatus, p. 179

13b. Fruitbody not as above 14

14a. Fruitbody 4–15 cm wide, consisting of overlapping or sometimes solitary sessile caps with a tomentose to glabrous upper surface, growing on conifers; fertile surface white to creamy white, buff or cork-colored, not smoky brown to blackish in age:
Antrodia heteromorpha, p. 68
Climacocystis borealis, p. 96

14b. Fruitbody not as above 15

15a. Fruitbody up to 8 cm wide and 1–2 mm thick, semicircular to fan-shaped, often fused laterally, flexible; upper surface covered with coarse, elongated, upright or somewhat flattened hairs, becoming tomentose in age, distinctly zonate, white to grayish or brown; fertile surface white to cream, becoming smoky brown to blackish as it matures; pores angular, 1–3 per mm, frequently breaking up and becoming finely incised and teethlike in age:
Trametes villosa, p. 350

15b. Fruitbody not as above; growing on broadleaf trees. 16

16a. Fruitbody up to 12 cm wide and 3 cm thick, semicircular, broadly attached, watery and sappy when fresh, or corky and tough; jagged teeth up to 3 cm long:
Antrodia heteromorpha, p. 68
Tyromyces galactinus, p. 370

16b. Fruitbody not as above 17

17a. Fruitbody up to 8 cm wide and 1–2 mm thick, semicircular to fan-shaped, often fused laterally, flexible; upper surface covered with coarse, elongated, upright or somewhat flattened hairs, distinctly zonate, white to grayish or brown; fertile surface white to cream, becoming smoky brown to blackish in age; pores angular, 1–3 per mm, frequently breaking up and becoming finely incised and teethlike in age:

Trametes villosa, p. 350

17b. Fruitbody not as above 18

18a. Fruitbody resupinate; fertile surface white to creamy white or grayish, with jagged teeth up to 3 mm long:

Xylodon paradoxus, p. 381

18b. Fruitbody shelflike or hoof-shaped, up to 18 cm wide, up to 4 cm thick; fertile surface white, becoming pale buff to ochraceous, with jagged teeth up to 1 cm long:

Spongipellis delectans, p. 317
Spongipellis unicolor, p. 317

19a. Fertile surface bright orange to yellow-orange, becoming dull yellow then eventually white in age; upper surface bright orange:

Pycnoporellus alboluteus, p. 294

19b. Fruitbody not as above 20

20a. Fertile surface lamellate at first, becoming teethlike in age, brown; upper surface zonate; widely distributed in the South region:

Gloeophyllum striatum, p. 167

20b. Fruitbody not as above 21

21a. Fruitbody encircling living twigs of pawpaw (*Asimina* species); fertile surface concave, honey yellow to reddish brown:

Inonotus amplectens, p. 190

21b. Fruitbody not as above 22

22a. Fertile surface whitish to pale buff at first, becoming gray to smoky gray or grayish brown at maturity; pores labyrinthine, often teethlike in age; upper surface often covered with green algae:

Cerrena unicolor, p. 93

22b. Fruitbody not as above 23

23a. Fruitbody shell- to kidney-shaped, pale brown; fertile surface depressed from the margin, white at first, becoming brown in age; growing on birch trees:

Fomitopsis betulina, p. 127

23b. Fruitbody not as above 24

24a. Fruitbody upper surface appressed-velvety, white at first, becoming zonate with various shades of pale to dark brown, with conspicuous radial striae (use a hand lens); pores 5–6 per mm:

Cerrena drummondii, p. 92

24b. Fruitbody not as above 25

25a. Fertile surface cinnamon-buff to tan at first, then cinnamon or darker brown in age; pores 1–3 per mm, angular to irregular when young, conspicuously labyrinthine as they mature, then breaking up and becoming coarsely teethlike in age:

Trametopsis cervina, p. 352

25b. Fertile surface not as above 26

26a. Fertile surface white to cream at first, becoming buff to cork-colored in age; upper surface white to creamy white at first, becoming pale sordid brown with a distinctive white margin as it ages:

Antrodia heteromorpha, p. 68

26b. Fertile surface white to cream at first, becoming smoky brown to blackish in age, or some other color at first or in age; margin not white and distinctive 27

27a. Fertile surface white to cream, becoming smoky brown to blackish in age; upper surface covered with coarse, elongated, upright or somewhat flattened hairs, becoming tomentose in age, distinctly zonate, white to grayish or brown:

Trametes villosa, p. 350

27b. Fertile surface ochraceous to ochraceous orange, violet to dark purple-brown, dark cinnamon to rusty brown or gray to nearly black, sometimes fading to pale buff in age. 28

28a. Fruitbody 2–6 cm wide, 1–3 mm thick, semicircular to fan-shaped; upper surface finely velvety in numerous narrow concentric zones, light to dark rusty brown; fertile surface dark cinnamon to rusty brown; pores

3–5 per mm, typically elongating and forming sinuous, concentrically arranged ridges
on mature specimens:
   Hymenochaete iodina, p. 183

28b. Fruitbody not as above 29

29a. Fertile surface gray or dark purplish brown
to nearly black; upper surface white to ochraceous buff; margin conspicuously fimbriate;
widely distributed in the South region:
   Trichaptum sector, p. 361

29b. Fertile surface not as above 30

30a. Fertile surface ochraceous to ochraceous orange; pores circular to angular then weakly
labyrinthine, sometimes arranged in more
or less concentric rows, 1–2 per mm, growing
on broadleaf trees, especially oaks:
   Spongipellis unicolor, p. 317

30b. Fertile surface violet to purple-brown, fading to buff or brown in age 31

31a. Fruitbody growing on conifers:
   Trichaptum abietinum, p. 353
   Trichaptum fuscoviolaceum, p. 356

31b. Fruitbody growing on broadleaf trees 32

32a. Fruitbody growing on aspen, cottonwood,
and poplar species; widely distributed in
the northern portions of the Northeast and
North Central regions; upper surface covered with coarse hairs, faintly zonate, pale
buff to pale gray, often developing yellowish
tints as it dries:
   Trichaptum subchartaceum, p. 362

32b. Fruitbody not as above 33

33a. Fruitbody upper surface covered with a
dense layer of coarse, stiff, forked, brown or
grayish hairs that are darkest near the point
of attachment, weakly zonate or sometimes
azonate; fertile surface violet at first, drying
brown; pores angular or circular, splitting,
coalescing and becoming sinuous to labyrinthine and teethlike in age; reported from
southern Georgia and Florida:
   Trichaptum perrottetii, p. 360

33b. Fruitbody upper surface appressed-fibrillose
to finely velvety at first, becoming nearly glabrous in age, distinctly zonate; fertile surface
violet to purple-brown fading to buff; widely
distributed in the Northeast, North Central,
and South regions:
   Trichaptum biforme, p. 354

Key G

Fruitbody growing on wood; fertile surface lamellate and not becoming teethlike in age.

1a. Fruitbody with a distinct stalk 2

1b. Fruitbody with a rudimentary stalk or
sessile 6

2a. Fruitbody upper surface violet to purplish
when young, becoming pinkish tan to red-
dish brown in age 3

2b. Fruitbody upper surface white to buff, or yellowish to ochraceous, with or without small
scales 4

3a. Upper surface glabrous and smooth:
   Panus conchatus, p. 247

3b. Upper surface distinctly hairy:
   Panus lecomtei, p. 248

4a. Fruitbody 1–5 cm wide; upper surface yellowish to ochraceous, lacking tiny scales:
   Neofavolus suavissimus, p. 236

4b. Fruitbody not as above 5

5a. Fruitbody upper surface covered by small
brown to grayish brown scales over a whitish
to yellowish ground color; stalk white with
conspicuous brown scales:
   Lentinus tigrinus, p. 218
   Neolentinus lepideus, p. 237

5b. Fruitbody 2.5–7.5 cm wide, convex with a depressed center, often funnel-shaped; upper surface covered with dense, long, pale yellowish
brown to dark reddish brown radiating hairs:
   Lentinus berteroi, p. 216
   Lentinus crinitus, p. 216

6a. Fertile surface ochraceous to yellow-brown, reddish brown, or dark brown:
>*Gloeophyllum striatum*, p. 167
>*Gloeophyllum trabeum*, p. 168
>*Osmoporus mexicanus*, p. 242

6b. Fertile surface white to creamy white, tan, grayish to pinkish gray, or purplish to purple-brown 7

7a. Fertile surface purplish to purple-brown; upper surface covered with coarse hairs, faintly zonate, gray to purplish gray or tan:
>*Trichaptum laricinum*, p. 358

7b. Fertile surface white to creamy white, tan, or grayish to pinkish gray 8

8a. Fertile surface consisting of subdistant, white, pinkish gray, gray, or pinkish brown gills that are split lengthwise along the free edge:
>*Schizophyllum commune*, p. 306
>*Schizophyllum fasciatum*, p. 308

8b. Fertile surface distinctly lamellate and not split along the free edge. 9

9a. Fruitbody 3–10 cm wide; upper surface velvety to hairy, with numerous, distinct, multicolored concentric zones of variable color; margin acute:
>*Lenzites betulinus*, p. 222

9b. Fruitbody not as above 10

10a. Fruitbody 1–2.5 cm wide; upper surface finely tomentose, faintly concentrically zonate, yellow-orange to reddish brown or yellow-brown; margin incurved to inrolled, undulating, sometimes scalloped or lobed, whitish to pale yellow:
>*Plicaturopsis crispa*, p. 274

10b. Fruitbody upper surface glabrous, rough and uneven at first, becoming nearly smooth in age, with conspicuous concentric zones, radially striate, variously colored; fertile surface whitish to grayish at first, becoming pale brown, bruising pinkish brown:
>*Daedaleopsis septentrionalis*, p. 112

Key H

Fruitbody growing on wood; fertile surface poroid, notably elongated to sinuous or labyrinthine.

1a. Fruitbody growing on conifers. 2

1b. Fruitbody growing on broadleaf trees 6

2a. Fruitbody 2.5–10 cm wide; upper surface bright yellowish red to reddish brown, becoming grayish or blackish in age; fertile surface golden brown to rusty brown; pores fairly thick:
>*Gloeophyllum sepiarium*, p. 166

2b. Fruitbody not as above 3

3a. Fruitbody perennial or sometimes annual, up to 15 cm wide, shelflike, semicircular to elongated, arising from a resupinate or effused-reflexed, glancing, bright yellowish brown base; upper surface tomentose to hispid, sulcate, zonate, dull reddish brown; pores slightly labyrinthine to angular, 1–3 per mm:
>*Porodaedalea chrysoloma*, p. 281

3b. Fruitbody not as above 4

4a. Fruitbody perennial, up to 15 cm wide and 8 cm thick, resupinate at first, becoming shelflike to hoof-shaped; upper surface light reddish brown at first, becoming dark brown to blackish as it matures, sometimes cracked in age; fertile surface brownish yellowish to yellow-brown or ochre-orange; pores circular to angular or labyrinthine, 1–4 per mm:
>*Porodaedalea pini*, p. 282

4b. Fruitbody not as above 5

5a. Fruitbody upper surface cinnamon-brown, consisting of several small caps, each up to 4 cm wide; fertile surface white or whitish, becoming pale brown in age:
>*Neoantrodia variiformis*, p. 234

5b. Fruitbody upper surface white to cream, pale buff or pale sordid brown; fruitbody sometimes forming extensive patches or clusters of fused caps arising from a resupinate sur-

face; fertile surface white to creamy white, cork-colored or pale ochraceous:
    Antrodia albida, p. 67
    Antrodia heteromorpha, p. 68
    Brunneoporus juniperinus, p. 77

6a. Fruitbody upper surface predominantly white to creamy white, buff or grayish, sometimes with ochraceous to orange or brownish tints 7

6b. Fruitbody upper surface more richly colored 10

7a. Fertile surface white to grayish brown; pore walls thick and tough:
    Daedalea quercina, p. 110

7b. Fertile surface not as above 8

8a. Fertile surface decurrent, white at first, becoming creamy white to pale ochraceous; pores hexagonal or radially elongated:
    Favolus tenuiculus, p. 116
    Neofavolus alveolaris, p. 235

8b. Fertile surface not as above 9

9a. Fruitbody effused-reflexed or forming numerous narrow, overlapping, sessile caps on a decurrent fertile surface; pores variable, angular to sinuous and elongated to nearly lamellate or labyrinthine:
    Antrodia albida, p. 67
    Antrodia heteromorpha, p. 68

9b. Fruitbody shelflike, semicircular to fan- or kidney-shaped; pores variable, often circular, radially elongated and labyrinthine or nearly lamellate, especially near the margin:
    Trametes aesculi, p. 336
    Trametes gibbosa, p. 339

10a. Fruitbody 4–10 cm wide, up to 1.3 cm thick; upper surface separated from the flesh by a thin, dark zone, covered with a dense layer of coarse, elongated hairs, whitish, grayish, or pale brown, frequently covered by green algae; fertile surface whitish to pale buff at first, becoming gray to smoky gray or grayish brown at maturity:
    Cerrena unicolor, p. 93

10b. Fruitbody not as above 11

11a. Fruitbody 2–6 cm wide, 1–3 mm thick, semicircular to fan-shaped; upper surface finely velvety in numerous narrow concentric zones, light to dark rusty brown; fertile surface dark cinnamon to rusty brown; pores 3–5 per mm, typically elongating and forming sinuous, concentrically arranged ridges on mature specimens:
    Hymenochaete iodina, p. 183

11b. Fruitbody not as above 12

12a. Fruitbody shelflike, semicircular to fan-shaped, broadly attached; upper surface white to creamy white at first, forming a hard reddish to bay cuticular layer that spreads from the base outward and becomes dark reddish brown to purplish brown as it ages; pores angular near the margin, sinuous to conspicuously labyrinthine on more mature portions, 2–3 per mm; fertile surface white to cork-colored:
    Earliella scabrosa, p. 114

12b. Fruitbody not as above 13

13a. Fruitbody upper surface wrinkled, rough and scaly, zonate, yellow-brown to reddish brown or grayish brown; fertile surface whitish to pale brown, bruising pinkish brown:
    Daedaleopsis confragosa, p. 111

13b. Fruitbody not as above 14

14a. Fruitbody fertile surface cinnamon-buff to tan at first, then cinnamon or darker brown in age; pores 1–3 per mm, angular to irregular when young, conspicuously labyrinthine as they mature, then breaking up and becoming coarsely teethlike in age; upper surface covered with short, coarse hairs, zonate or sometimes faintly zonate, variously colored, pinkish buff, brownish orange, pinkish cinnamon, or darker cinnamon:
    Trametopsis cervina, p. 352

14b. Fruitbody not as above 15

15a. Fruitbody upper surface weakly zonate or sometimes azonate covered with a dense

layer of coarse, stiff, forked, brown or grayish hairs that are darkest near the point of
attachment; fertile surface violet at first,
drying brown; pores angular or circular,
splitting, coalescing and becoming sinuous to labyrinthine and teethlike in age; reported from southern Georgia and Florida:
  Trichaptum perrottetii, p. 360

15b. Fruitbody upper surface distinctly zonate
with light to dark brown or purplish brown
zones, sometimes slightly grayish green
when coated with algae, often radially wrinkled when mature; pores hexagonal to angular, becoming elongated to sinuous in age,
1–2 per mm:
  Hexagonia papyracea, p. 178

Key I

Fruitbody growing on wood, with a distinct stalk
that is central, eccentric, or lateral; fertile surface
poroid; pores circular, angular or irregular.

1a. Fruitbody very small, typically less than 1 cm
wide; stalk or stalklike base pendant 2

1b. Fruitbody not as above 3

2a. Fruitbody with a cap and distinct stalk;
cap 3–10 mm wide, circular, rusty brown or
black; fertile surface rusty brown:
  Coltriciella dependens, p. 104

2b. Fruitbody 1–5 mm wide, circular with a
stalklike base; upper surface and fertile surface whitish to pale brown:
  Porodisculus pendulus, p. 284

3a. Fruitbody white to creamy white, pinkish
buff to dull buff, or pale straw-colored 4

3b. Fruitbody more richly colored 9

4a. Fruitbody a small cap with an eccentric to
lateral stalk; cap 3–16 mm wide, white to
pinkish buff:
  Panellus pusillus, p. 246

4b. Fruitbody not as above 5

5a. Fruitbody consisting of large, lobed caps
that often form rosettes up to 36 cm wide; individual caps up to 17 cm wide:
  Picipes admirabilis, p. 266

5b. Fruitbody not as above 6

6a. Fruitbody a cluster of overlapping caps with
short stalks; pores hexagonal or radially
elongated, decurrent:
  Favolus tenuiculus, p. 116
  Neofavolus alveolaris, p. 235

6b. Fruitbody not as above 7

7a. Fruitbody cap centrally depressed to funnel-
shaped; pores angular, 3–4 per mm, strongly
decurrent; stalk base dark yellow-brown to
blackish brown; growing on decaying broadleaf branches, logs, and stumps:
  Bresadolia uda complex, p. 76

7b. Fruitbody not as above 8

8a. Pores minute, 6–8 per mm; upper surface white when young, becoming creamy
white to ochraceous, sometimes zonate with
darker grayish or brownish zones:
  Microporellus obovatus, p. 229

8b. Pores 3–5 per mm; upper surface white
to buff becoming straw-colored or
ochraceous:
  Loweomyces fractipes, p. 224
  Osteina obducta, p. 243

9a. Fruitbody cap depressed to funnel-shaped. . .
. 10

9b. Fruitbody cap not as above 14

10a. Fruitbody upper surface orange-yellow to
reddish orange, azonate, fading to pale yellow or tan in age; pores angular to hexagonal
and radially arranged, 1–2 per mm:
  Neofavolus alveolaris, p. 235

10b. Fruitbody upper surface and pores not as
above. 11

11a. Cap margin finely fringed with short hairs:
  Lentinus arcularius, p. 214
  Lentinus brumalis, p. 215
  Lentinus tricholoma, p. 220

11b. Cap margin not as above. 12

12a. Cap upper surface glabrous or nearly so, pale gray to pale grayish brown or reddish brown with a darker center; stalk reddish brown near the apex and black below or reddish brown and darkening to blackish in age:
>   *Picipes badius*, p. 267
>   *Picipes lowei*, p. 268
>   *Picipes tubaeformis*, p. 271

12b. Cap upper surface not as above 13

13a. Stalk base dark yellow-brown to blackish brown or black; cap concave and depressed at first, soon funnel-shaped:
>   *Bresadolia craterella*, p. 74
>   *Picipes virgatus*, p. 74

13b. Stalk base paler, yellowish white to ochraceous or pale brown, not dark yellow-brown to blackish brown or black on any portion:
>   *Bresadolia craterella*, p. 74

14a. Flesh yellowish or reddish brown to rusty brown; stalk 2–7 cm long or sometimes rudimentary, up to 5 cm thick, enlarged upward, pale to dark brown:
>   *Phaeolus schweinitzii*, p. 254

14b. Flesh white, whitish, creamy white, buff, or tan. 15

15a. Fruitbody occurring as two morphologically distinct forms, one a distorted mass of whitish and brownish tissue covered with pores, or with a cap and stalk; upper surface staining reddish brown when bruised:
>   *Abortiporus biennis*, p. 59

15b. Fruitbody not as above 16

16a. Stalk tan to yellowish brown or chestnut brown on the upper portion, black on the lower portion; cap 3–6 cm wide, tan to yellowish brown or chestnut brown:
>   *Cerioporus leptocephalus*, p. 85

16b. Stalk and cap not as above 17

17a. Stalk reddish brown near the apex, black below; cap 4–20 cm wide, reddish brown with a blackish brown center:
>   *Picipes badius*, p. 267

17b. Stalk and cap not as above 18

18a. Stalk central 19

18b. Stalk eccentric or lateral 22

19a. Cap large, 10–26 cm wide, circular to fan-shaped, pinkish brown to darker brown; attached to the roots of oak or pine trees; widely distributed in the South region:
>   *Laetiporus persicinus*, p. 210

19b. Cap not as above 20

20a. Cap large, 3–25 cm wide, fan- to petal-shaped, bright orange to pinkish orange; fruitbody a large rosette of convex to nearly flat, laterally fused caps attached to a central branching stalk; fertile surface white to pale cream:
>   *Laetiporus cincinnatus*, p. 207

20b. Cap not as above 21

21a. Cap margin finely fringed with short hairs:
>   *Lentinus arcularius*, p. 214
>   *Lentinus brumalis*, p. 215
>   *Lentinus tricholoma*, p. 220

21b. Cap margin not as above; cap distinctly zonate, variously colored with a mixture of buff to brown, pale grayish brown, or pale smoky gray colors:
>   *Microporellus dealbatus*, p. 228

22a. Cap large, 5–30 cm wide, kidney- to fan-shaped, or semicircular, with large, flattened, reddish brown scales on a creamy white to dingy yellowish or pale yellow-brown ground color:
>   *Cerioporus squamosus*, p. 88

22b. Cap not as above 23

23a. Fruitbody growing on dead broadleaf branches and logs; fertile surface white, becoming pale straw-colored; pores minute, 6–8 per mm:
>   *Microporellus obovatus*, p. 229

23b. Fruitbody not as above 24

24a. Fruitbody growing on the bark of dead, fallen wood or well-decayed broadleaf stumps or roots; upper surface zonate; fer-

tile surface white to creamy white, becoming ochraceous in age; pores 6–9 per mm:
> *Microporellus dealbatus*, p. 228
> *Trullella polyporoides*, p. 364

24b. Fruitbody growing on decaying conifer wood, rarely broadleaf wood; upper surface azonate; fertile surface white to yellowish; pores 3–5 per mm:
> *Osteina obducta*, p. 243

Key J

Fruitbody sessile or with a rudimentary stalk or contracted stalklike base, or entirely resupinate, growing on conifers; fertile surface poroid; pores circular, angular, slightly elongated, or irregular.

1a. Fruitbody upper surface white to creamy white, straw-colored, or grayish well into maturity, sometimes darkening or staining in age, or when bruised or drying 2

1b. Fruitbody upper surface more richly colored 11

2a. Fertile surface orange-brown to pinkish brown or purplish brown, with a whitish margin when actively growing, gelatinous and stretchable when fresh, drying hard and resinous:
> *Gloeoporus dichrous*, p. 170

2b. Fertile surface not as above 3

3a. Fruitbody upper surface and fertile surface typically with bluish tints, sometimes bruising intensely blue:
> *Postia livens*, p. 286
> *Postia simulans*, p. 286

3b. Fruitbody upper surface and fertile surface not as above. 4

4a. Fruitbody upper surface and fertile surface staining reddish brown when bruised or on drying:
> *Fuscopostia fragilis*, p. 142
> *Postia leucomallella*, p. 142

4b. Fruitbody upper surface and fertile surface not as above. 5

5a. Fruitbody upper surface with a cuticle that peels easily, sometimes with small, circular depressions that often exude watery drops when fresh, white to creamy white or pale gray, drying buff to pale brown, sometimes staining reddish or brownish when bruised:
> *Calcipostia guttulata*, p. 83
> *Postia stiptica*, p. 84
> *Postia tephroleuca*, p. 288

5b. Fruitbody upper surface not as above. 6

6a. Fruitbody up to 10 cm or longer, effused-reflexed and forming numerous variable, overlapping, sessile caps on a decurrent fertile surface:
> *Antrodia albida*, p. 67
> *Antrodia heteromorpha*, p. 68
> *Antrodiella semisupina*, p. 69
> *Postia undosa*, p. 96

6b. Fruitbody not as above 7

7a. Fruitbody usually a cluster of overlapping, semicircular to fan-shaped caps, up to 15 cm or more wide; upper and fertile surfaces whitish to buff at first, sometimes with ochraceous tints or darker spots in age; flesh white when fresh, becoming buff to ochraceous with an unpleasant odor in age; usually growing on juniper; reported from Texas:
> *Amylosporus campbellii*, p. 370

7b. Fruitbody not as above 8

8a. Fruitbody consisting of overlapping sessile caps up to 15 cm wide; upper and fertile surfaces white to creamy white or straw-colored; flesh white to cream, odor and taste not distinctive; growing on a variety of conifers, but not juniper; found in the Northeast, North Central, and upper South regions:
> *Climacocystis borealis*, p. 96

8b. Fruitbody not as above 9

9a. Fruitbody consisting of semicircular, shelf-like caps, 3–10 cm wide, typically in large, overlapping clusters; upper and fertile surfaces white to cream; flesh creamy white, odor unpleasant; widely distributed in the South region:

   Fomitopsis palustris, p. 133

9b. Fruitbody not as above 10

10a. Fruitbody solitary or an overlapping cluster of caps up to 5 cm wide; upper and fertile surfaces whitish to cream or buff, becoming pale brown in age; flesh white to buff, odor pleasant; found in the Northeast, North Central, and mountainous areas of the upper South region:

   Postia balsamea, p. 96

10b. Fruitbody up to 8 cm wide and 1–2 mm thick, semicircular to fan-shaped, often fused laterally, flexible; upper surface covered with coarse, elongated, upright or somewhat flattened hairs, distinctly zonate, white to grayish; fertile surface white to cream, becoming smoky brown to blackish in age; pores angular, 1–3 per mm, frequently breaking up and becoming finely incised and teethlike in age:

   Trametes villosa, p. 359

11a. Fruitbody 5–15 cm wide; upper surface and fertile surface white at first, staining dark reddish brown when bruised or in age; flesh odor strong of iodine; usually on spruce; distributed in the Northeast and North Central regions:

   Amylocystis lapponica, p. 66

11b. Fruitbody not as above 12

12a. Fruitbody 4–20 cm wide; upper surface dark red-brown to blackish brown, paler toward the margin; fertile surface white to ochraceous, staining brown when bruised; flesh odor not distinctive:

   Ischnoderma benzoinum, p. 200

12b. Fruitbody not as above 13

13a. Fruitbody up to 12 cm wide, upper surface white to pale pink or pale reddish purple at first, becoming purplish brown in age; fertile surface white to pink or pale reddish purple at first, becoming dark purplish brown in age:

   Leptoporus mollis, p. 223

13b. Fruitbody not as above 14

14a. Fruitbody 2–12 cm wide; upper surface violet to vinaceous brown at first, becoming purplish brown to dark violet at maturity; fertile surface purplish brown to dark violet:

   Nigroporus vinosus, p. 238

14b. Fruitbody not as above 15

15a. Fruitbody 2–7.5 cm wide; fertile surface pale gray at first, becoming dark smoky gray to blackish at maturity:

   Bjerkandera adusta, p. 70

15b. Fruitbody not as above 16

16a. Fertile surface white, whitish, ivory, buff, or grayish, sometimes becoming pale brown in age. 17

16b. Fertile surface ochre-orange, bright yellowish brown, yellowish brown to ochraceous brown, pinkish brown, grayish brown, rusty brown, or dark brown to blackish (may be white when very young) 23

17a. Fruitbody perennial, 2.5–25 cm wide, velvety or glabrous, becoming encrusted, brown at first, becoming blackish in age; on roots, stumps, or trunks of pines or hemlock:

   Heterobasidion irregulare, p. 175

17b. Fruitbody not as above 18

18a. Fruitbody 2–10 cm wide; pores circular to angular, 3–5 per mm; upper surface silky to velvety, conspicuously zonate with various colors:

   Trametes ochracea, p. 343
   Trametes versicolor, p. 348

18b. Fruitbody not as above 19

19a. Fruitbody 5–25 cm wide; pores circular to angular, 2–3 per mm; upper surface concen-

trically zoned and often shallowly furrowed, with pale to dark brown or grayish bands on a whitish to grayish ground color:
> *Trametes lactinea*, p. 341

19b. Fruitbody not as above 20

20a. Fruitbody effused-reflexed, forming extensive patches of individual caps arising from a resupinate surface, often laterally and vertically fused; pores angular to sinuous, 1–3 mm wide, often split and labyrinthine on older specimens; growing on standing trunks of juniper:
> *Brunneoporus juniperinus*, p. 77

20b. Fruitbody not as above 21

21a. Fruitbody resupinate at first, becoming effused-reflexed and forming groups or dense clusters of overlapping caps; cap 2–10 mm wide, knobby or rounded, sloped forward; upper surface finely tomentose then glabrous in age, ochraceous to pale cinnamon brown, faintly zonate; fertile surface white to cork-colored or buff, becoming more sordid brown as it ages; pores rounded, 2–3 per mm:
> *Neoantrodia serialis*, p. 233

21b. Fruitbody not as above 22

22a. Fruitbody narrowly effused-reflexed, rarely resupinate, typically with several sessile caps on the upper portion; pores round to angular, sometimes irregular to labyrinthine, 1–2 per mm; upper surface finely tomentose, cinnamon brown, slightly zonate:
> *Neoantrodia variiformis*, p. 234

22b. Fruitbody up to 30 cm wide and 8(13) cm thick, shelflike to hoof-shaped, smooth, glabrous, sulcate; pores circular, (3)4–5(6) per mm:
> *Fomitopsis ochracea*, p. 132

23a. Fruitbody growing on the roots or standing trunks of juniper species, soft and flexible or hard and woody 24

23b. Fruitbody growing on other types of conifers 26

24a. Fruitbody up to 12 cm wide, perennial, hoof-shaped, hard and woody; upper surface with conspicuous annular layers:
> *Pyrofomes juniperinus*, p. 298

24b. Fruitbody not as above 25

25a. Fruitbody 3–7 cm wide, annual, semicircular to fan-shaped, soft and flexible:
> *Inonotus juniperinus*, p. 299

25b. Fruitbody up to 20 cm wide; upper surface brown to blackish, becoming encrusted and cracked in age; flesh shiny, yellowish brown, with white radial streaks near the tubes and point of attachment; usually growing on oaks:
> *Fomitiporia calkinsii*, p. 125
> *Fomitiporia texana*, p. 126

26a. Fruitbody up to 3 mm thick, petal- to fan-shaped; fertile surface white at first but soon becoming tan to grayish brown; growing on standing trunks or downed logs of decaying bald cypress; widely distributed in the Gulf states:
> *Cerrena drummondii*, p. 92

26b. Fruitbody not as above 27

27a. Fruitbody growing on the ground, on roots, or on the butt of standing trees, circular or irregular, with a short stalk; upper surface velvety or tomentose, or sometimes nearly glabrous in age; flesh up to 1 cm thick:
> *Onnia circinata*, p. 240
> *Onnia tomentosa*, p. 241

27b. Fruitbody not as above 28

28a. Fruitbody perennial or sometimes annual, up to 15 cm wide, shelflike, semicircular to elongated, arising from a base that is resupinate or effused-reflexed, glancing, bright yellowish brown; upper surface tomentose to hispid, sulcate, zonate, dull reddish brown; pores slightly labyrinthine to angular, 1–3 per mm:
> *Porodaedalea chrysoloma*, p. 281

28b. Fruitbody not as above 29

29a. Fruitbody perennial, up to 6 cm wide, effused-reflexed, sessile and shelflike or fully resupinate; fertile surface reddish brown; pores circular to angular, 4–7 per mm, with thick, entire dissepiments; upper surface uneven and sulcate, reddish brown or sometimes blackish in age with a paler brown margin; flesh reddish brown:

    Fuscoporia viticola, p. 141

29b. Fruitbody not as above 30

30a. Fruitbody up to 8 cm wide and 1–2 mm thick, semicircular to fan-shaped, often fused laterally, flexible; upper surface covered with coarse, elongated, upright or somewhat flattened hairs, distinctly zonate, white to grayish or brown; fertile surface white to cream, becoming smoky brown to blackish in age; pores angular, 1–3 per mm, frequently breaking up and becoming finely incised and teethlike in age:

    Trametes villosa, p. 350

30b. Fruitbody perennial, up to 15 cm wide and 8 cm thick, resupinate at first, becoming shelflike to hoof-shaped; upper surface light reddish brown at first, becoming dark brown to blackish as it matures, sometimes cracked in age; fertile surface brownish yellowish to yellow-brown or ochre-orange; pores circular to angular or labyrinthine, 1–4 per mm:

    Porodaedalea pini, p. 282

Key K

Fruitbody growing on broadleaf trees, sessile or with a rudimentary stalk or contracted stalklike base; upper surface ground color white to creamy white, buff, pale orange, tan, pale gray, greenish gray, or straw-colored, occasionally zonate with darker brown bands or developing yellowish to ochraceous tones as it matures, sometimes staining blue to grayish blue, brownish, or reddish when bruised or as it ages.

1a. Fruitbody soft and spongy; upper surface typically with bluish tints, sometimes bruising intensely blue; fertile surface whitish to pale gray, usually staining blue:

    Postia caesiosimulans, p. 286
    Postia livens, p. 287
    Postia populi, p. 286
    Postia simulans, p. 286

1b. Fruitbody not as above 2

2a. Fruitbody firm and tough; upper surface developing greenish blue to grayish blue stains, especially along the margin, as it ages:

    Niveoporofomes spraguei, p. 239

2b. Fruitbody not as above 3

3a. Fertile surface orange-brown to pinkish brown or purplish brown, with a whitish margin when actively growing, gelatinous and stretchable when fresh, drying hard and resinous:

    Gloeoporus dichrous, p. 170

3b. Fertile surface not as above 4

4a. Fruitbody up to 14 cm wide and 4 cm thick; upper surface with a cuticle that peels easily, sometimes with small, circular depressions that often exude watery drops when fresh, white to creamy white or pale gray, drying buff to pale brown, sometimes staining reddish or brownish when bruised:

    Calcipostia guttulata, p. 83
    Postia stiptica, p. 84
    Postia tephroleuca p. 288

4b. Fruitbody upper surface not as above. 5

5a. Fruitbody up to 20 cm wide, 2–12 cm thick, shelflike and broadly attached or semicircular with a contracted base, soft and fleshy or sappy when fresh; upper surface azonate, sometimes longitudinally uneven and roughened or tufted with agglutinated hairs and small pits in age; flesh up to 8 cm thick:

    Pappia fissilis, p. 250
    Spongipellis spumeus, p. 317

Spongipellis unicolor, p. 317

Vanderbylia robiniophila, p. 375

5b. Fruitbody not as above 6

6a. Fruitbody annual, at first a small cup- to fan-shaped sterile structure which develops one or more circular caps; cap upper surface concentrically zoned, with zones of contrasting colors, white to grayish white, yellowish, or pale brown:

Poronidulus conchifer, p. 285

6b. Fruitbody not as above 7

7a. Fruitbody soft and spongy or soft and waxy when fresh 8

7b. Fruitbody firm, rigid or woody. 15

8a. Fruitbody up to 6 cm wide; upper and fertile surfaces staining reddish brown when bruised or on drying:

Fuscopostia fragilis, p. 142

8b. Fruitbody not as above 9

9a. Fruitbody up to 5 cm wide; upper and fertile surfaces not staining when bruised, but may darken on drying; flesh up to 3 mm thick:

Antrodiella semisupina, p. 69

Postia balsamea, p. 96

Postia undosa, p. 96

9b. Fruitbody not as above 10

10a. Fruitbody 2–6 cm wide; fertile surface dull white to ochraceous buff, with a pale olive tint when mature, not staining brown when bruised; flesh up to 2 cm thick, easily crumbled, with a fragrant odor:

Tyromyces fumidiceps, p. 369

10b. Fruitbody not as above 11

11a. Fruitbody 2–10 cm wide; fertile surface white to creamy white, lacking a pale olive tint when mature, not staining brown when bruised, drying yellowish to ochraceous; flesh up to 2 cm thick, with a non-anise fragrant odor when fresh:

Tyromyces chioneus, p. 368

11b. Fruitbody not as above 12

12a. Fruitbody 2–10 cm wide; fertile surface white, staining beige to pale brown when bruised; flesh up to 2 cm thick, white to pale gray or brown, with a strong odor of anise:

Tyromyces humeanus, p. 368

12b. Fruitbody not as above 13

13a. Fruitbody 2–12 cm wide; fertile surface white, not staining when bruised; flesh up to 2 cm thick, white to creamy white, with a slightly fragrant odor:

Tyromyces galactinus, p. 370

13b. Fruitbody not as above 14

14a. Fruitbody up to 12 cm wide and 2.5 cm thick, finely velvety at first, soon becoming uneven and slightly warted or roughened with small, projecting, pointed fascicles of white to bright orange hairs over a pale orange to whitish ground color; widely distributed along the Gulf Coast states:

Tyromyces kmetii, p. 372

14b. Fruitbody usually a cluster of overlapping, semicircular to fan-shaped caps, up to 15 cm or more wide; upper and fertile surfaces whitish to buff at first, sometimes with ochraceous tints or darker spots in age; flesh white when fresh, becoming buff to ochraceous with an unpleasant odor in age; growing on citrus or chinaberry; reported from Texas:

Amylosporus campbellii, p. 370

15a. Fruitbody 3–20 cm wide, fan- to kidney-shaped, often overlapping and laterally fused; upper surface often covered with mosses at the base on mature specimens; usually growing on standing maple trees:

Oxyporus populinus, p. 244

15b. Fruitbody not as above 16

16a. Fruitbody up to 6 cm wide and 8 mm thick, shelflike, semicircular to fan-shaped, sappy when fresh; upper surface hairy and velvety when young, becoming appressed-velvety to finely roughened as it ages, azonate; fertile

surface white to pale straw-colored; pores
3–5 per mm:

    Loweomyces subgiganteus, p. 250

16b. Fruitbody not as above 17

17a. Fruitbody up to 10 cm or longer, effused-
reflexed and forming numerous variable,
overlapping, sessile caps on a decurrent fertile surface; caps up to 10 cm wide, shelflike, semicircular to fan-shaped; upper surface finely velvety and azonate at first, white
to creamy white, becoming glabrous, sometimes sulcate, and zonate in age; fertile surface highly variable:

    Antrodia albida, p. 67

    Antrodia heteromorpha, p. 68

    Antrodiella semisupina, p. 69

17b. Fruitbody not as above 18

18a. Fertile surface pale gray to dark smoky gray,
purplish brown, or nearly black; upper surface tomentose to velvety, sometimes nearly
glabrous in age 19

18b. Fertile surface not as above 22

19a. Fruitbody shelflike, semicircular to fan-
shaped, broadly attached; upper surface
ochraceous, forming a hard, reddish brown
cuticular layer that spreads from the base
outward and often becomes blackish as it
ages, weathering to whitish on older specimens; pores circular, 5–7 per mm; fertile surface purplish brown to dull brown, grayish
or smoky:

    Fomitella supina, p. 121

19b. Fruitbody not as above 20

20a. Fruitbody up to 10 cm wide and 1–4 mm
thick; upper surface zonate, white to
ochraceous buff; margin conspicuously
fimbriate; widely distributed in the South
region:

    Trichaptum sector, p. 361

20b. Fruitbody not as above 21

21a. Fruitbody up to 7.5 cm wide and 8 mm thick;
upper surface azonate to faintly zonate,
whitish to tan or pale smoky gray; margin

not fimbriate (use a hand lens); flesh lacking
a dark layer near the tubes:

    Bjerkandera adusta, p. 70

21b. Fruitbody up to 15 cm wide and 2 cm thick;
upper surface zonate or azonate, buff to tan;
margin not fimbriate (use a hand lens); flesh
with a dark layer near the tubes:

    Bjerkandera fumosa, p. 71

22a. Fertile surface purple to violaceous, fading
to buff; upper surface covered with coarse
hairs, pale buff to pale gray; margin rounded,
typically purple to violaceous; on aspen, cottonwood, and poplar in the Northeast and
North Central regions:

    Trichaptum subchartaceum, p. 362

22b. Fertile surface not as above 23

23a. Fruitbody up to 14 cm wide and 1.4 cm thick;
upper surface finely tomentose to nearly glabrous, azonate; flesh up to 3.5 mm thick, zonate, soft-corky, white to creamy white; odor
pleasant, aniselike; widely distributed:

    Trametes suaveolens, p. 347

23b. Fruitbody not as above 24

24a. Fruitbody large, 5–35 cm wide, up to 8 cm
thick; upper surface typically sulcate, sometimes uneven and warted 25

24b. Fruitbody smaller and thinner 28

25a. Fruitbody upper surface glabrous, smooth or
concentrically sulcate, often slightly uneven
and warted, azonate or faintly zonate, sometimes with ochraceous to orange tints, often partially covered from the base outward
with green algae:

    Trametes aesculi, p. 336

25b. Fruitbody not as above 26

26a. Fruitbody upper surface distinctly velvety or
fuzzy, especially when observed with a hand
lens, warted and uneven, typically concentrically zonate or sulcate, sometimes with very
pale ochraceous or gray tints as it ages, often
covered from the base outward with green
algae:

    Trametes gibbosa, p. 339

26b. Fruitbody not as above 27

27a. Fruitbody 5–25 cm wide; pores circular to angular, 2–3 per mm; upper surface concentrically zoned and often shallowly furrowed, with pale to dark brown or grayish bands on a whitish to grayish ground color:

Trametes lactinea, p. 341

27b. Fruitbody up to 30 cm wide and 8(13) cm thick; pores circular, (3)4–5(6) per mm; upper surface azonate, sulcate, whitish to grayish, cork-colored to ochraceous, or brown to blackish, often a mix of these colors:

Fomitopsis ochracea, p. 132

28a. Fruitbody upper surface distinctly zonate 29

28b. Fruitbody upper surface azonate or faintly zonate 32

29a. Pores 1–3 per mm, angular, thin-walled, often breaking up and becoming incised and finely teethlike in age, not conspicuously labyrinthine, then coarsely teethlike; upper surface covered with coarse, elongated, upright or somewhat flattened hairs, white to grayish or brown:

Trametes villosa, p. 350

29b. Pores not as above. 30

30a. Pores 3–4 per mm, circular to angular; upper surface covered with coarse, elongated hairs, often concentrically sulcate, frequently pale gray nearly overall, sometimes with tan, yellowish, or brown zones, greenish gray when coated with algae; flesh duplex, gray upper layer separated from the lower white layer, at least at the base, by a thin black line, often with an anise odor when fresh:

Trametes hirsuta, p. 340

30b. Pores, upper surface, and flesh not as above 31

31a. Pores 3–5 per mm, angular; upper surface tomentose to finely velvety, becoming nearly glabrous, creamy white to buff; flesh uniform, white to creamy white, lacking a thin black line; widely distributed in the Northeast, North Central, and South regions:

Trametes pubescens, p. 345

31b. Pores 5–6 per mm, circular to angular, sometimes slightly elongated radially; upper surface tomentose or glabrous, zonate, white to ochraceous, becoming buff to pale dull brown; flesh white, lacking a thin black line; widely distributed in the South region:

Trametes membranacea, p. 344
Trametes pavonia, p. 344

32a. Pores 3–5 per mm, angular; upper surface tomentose to finely velvety, becoming nearly glabrous, creamy white to buff; flesh uniform, white to creamy white, lacking a thin black line; widely distributed in the Northeast, North Central, and South regions:

Trametes pubescens, p. 345

32b. Fruitbody not as above 33

33a. Fruitbody up to 16 cm wide and 6 cm thick; pores 6–8 per mm, circular to angular; upper surface glabrous, white at first, becoming pale brown and eventually developing a dark, resinous, cuticular layer that spreads from the base outward in older specimens; widely distributed along the Gulf Coast states:

Trametes nivosa, p. 342

33b. Fruitbody not as above 34

34a. Fruitbody up to 15 cm wide and 6 cm thick, semicircular to somewhat triangular or irregular, fibrous-tough and corky when fresh, drying very hard and rigid; upper surface smooth to slightly rough, azonate, creamy white to pale buff or grayish when young, buff to pale brown as it dries; pores 2–5 per mm, but some may be up to 1 mm wide:

Fomitopsis durescens, p. 128
Fomitopsis palustris, p. 133

34b. Fruitbody not as above 35

35a. Fruitbody up to 2.5 cm wide and 1.5 cm thick; pores 4–7 per mm, circular to angular then partly sinuous; distributed along the Gulf Coast states or in Wisconsin:

Truncospora floridana, p. 366

Truncospora mexicana, p. 366

Truncospora tropicalis, p. 366

Truncospora wisconsinensis, p. 367

35b. Fruitbody not as above 36

36a. Fruitbody up to 8 cm wide and 2.5 cm thick; upper surface creamy white to pale yellowish brown when young, becoming darker brown to blackish in age; pores 5–7 per mm; growing on various broadleaf trees, especially oak:

Truncospora ohiensis, p. 367

36b. Fruitbody not as above 37

37a. Fruitbody up to 20 cm wide, consisting of numerous fan-shaped to spatula-like caps with rudimentary stalks, usually forming a rosette cluster; cap white to pale tan; margin thin, wavy, entire or fimbriate to irregularly split:

Hydnopolyporus palmatus, p. 179

37b. Fruitbody up to 25 cm wide, consisting of semicircular to fan-shaped, pale gray caps; fertile surface white to buff or pale yellow; stalk lateral, pale brown to nearly black toward the base; flesh white, odor of anise with hints of sweet almond:

Picipes lowei, p. 268

Key L

Fruitbody sessile or with a rudimentary stalk or contracted stalklike base, or fruitbody entirely resupinate; upper surface when present richly colored, not white to creamy white, pale gray, or straw-colored; fertile surface poroid, white, whitish, creamy white, or buff to pale tan, sometimes becoming pale brown in age or staining brown when bruised; pores circular, angular, slightly elongated, or irregular.

1a. Flesh more than 1 cm thick 2

1b. Flesh less than 1 cm thick 9

2a. Fruitbody shell- to kidney-shaped, pale brown; fertile surface depressed from the margin, white at first, becoming brown in age; growing on birch trees:

Fomitopsis betulina, p. 127

2b. Fruitbody not as above 3

3a. Fruitbody semicircular to fan-shaped or rounded, whitish when very young, soon yellow then brownish, darkening from the base outward as it ages; fertile surface staining brownish when bruised; usually solitary but sometimes in groups, growing on oak:

Buglossoporus quercinus, p. 80

3b. Fruitbody not as above 4

4a. Fertile surface rapidly staining dark brown when bruised; fruitbody shelflike, dull brownish orange to dark brown; often growing in overlapping clusters:

Ischnoderma resinosum, p. 202

4b. Fertile surface not as above 5

5a. Fruitbody upper surface concentrically zoned; fruitbody 5–25 cm wide; pores 2–3 per mm:

Trametes lactinea, p. 341

5b. Fruitbody not as above 6

6a. Fruitbody up to 12 cm wide and 2.5 cm thick, finely velvety at first, soon becoming uneven and slightly warted or roughened with small, projecting, pointed fascicles of white to bright orange hairs over a pale orange to whitish ground color; widely distributed along the Gulf Coast states:

Tyromyces kmetii, p. 372

6b. Fruitbody not as above 7

7a. Fruitbody upper surface distinctly sulcate, azonate; fruitbody up to 30 cm wide; pores (3)4–5(6) per mm:

Fomitopsis ochracea, p. 132

7b. Fruitbody not as above 8

8a. Fruitbody upper surface not sulcate, slightly zonate; fruitbody up to 16 cm wide; pores 4–6 per mm:

Vanderbylia fraxinea, p. 374

8b. Fruitbody upper surface not sulcate; fruitbody up to 55 cm wide, a large rosette of convex to nearly flat, laterally fused, bright orange to pinkish orange caps:

    Laetiporus cincinnatus, p. 207

9a. Fruitbody upper surface distinctly zonate or sulcate 10

9b. Fruitbody upper surface azonate or faintly zonate and not sulcate .18

10a. Fruitbody sessile or effused-reflexed, sometimes overlapping and laterally fused; pores typically 1–2 per mm, but some may be more than 1 mm wide:

    Cerioporus mollis, p. 86
    Neoantrodia variiformis, p. 234

10b. Fruitbody not as above 11

11a. Fruitbody effused-reflexed, consisting of overlapping caps up to 6 cm wide; pores variable, angular to rounded hexagonal or slightly elongated, typically 3–5 per mm when growing on horizontal surfaces, up to 1 mm wide on vertical surfaces; upper surface distinctly hairy or tomentose, sometimes nearly glabrous in age, pale ochraceous to brown, sometimes grayish to blackish in age:

    Brunneoporus malicola, p. 79
    Cerioporus stereoides, p. 89

11b. Fruitbody not as above 12

12a. Fruitbody 5–25 cm wide; pores circular to angular, 2–3 per mm; upper surface with pale to dark brown or grayish bands on a whitish to grayish ground color:

    Trametes lactinea, p. 341

12b. Fruitbody not as above 13

13a. Fruitbody 2–10 cm wide, silky to velvety, multizonate with various colors; margin thin and sharp 14

13b. Fruitbody not as above 15

14a. Fruitbody upper surface variously colored, often with shades of orange, green, blue, brown, or gray; pores 3–5 per mm; widely distributed in the Northeast, North Central, and South regions:

Trametes ochracea, p. 343
Trametes versicolor, p. 348

14b. Fruitbody upper surface tan to dingy pale yellowish brown at first, developing reddish brown bands from the base outward, color variable from zone to zone; pores 4–6 per mm; widely distributed in the South region:

    Trametes ectypa, p. 338

15a. Fruitbody upper surface covered with coarse, elongated, upright or somewhat flattened hairs; pores 1–4 per mm, thin-walled, sometimes breaking up and becoming finely incised and teethlike:

    Trametes hirsuta, p. 340
    Trametes villosa, p. 350

15b. Fruitbody upper surface glabrous or nearly so 16

16a. Fruitbody up to 9 cm wide and 7 cm thick; upper surface reddish brown to brown when young, becoming grayish brown to blackish as it matures, often covered with algae or moss, becoming cracked in age; usually growing on ash trees:

    Perenniporia fraxinophila, p. 252

16b. Fruitbody not as above 17

17a. Fruitbody up to 8 cm wide and 2.5 cm thick; upper surface creamy white to pale yellowish brown when young, becoming darker brown to blackish in age; pores 5–7 per mm; growing on various broadleaf trees, especially oak:

    Truncospora ohiensis, p. 367

17b. Fruitbody up to 3 cm wide and 3–10 mm thick, semicircular to nearly pendant; upper surface whitish at first soon becoming dark brown to black, with a paler margin; pores 4–5 per mm; growing on various broadleaf trees:

    Datroniella scutellata, p. 111

18a. Fruitbody sessile, effused-reflexed or resupinate and often elongated on the substrate; upper surface tomentose or distinctly hairy:

Cerioporus stereoides, p. 89

Trametella trogii, p. 334

18b. Fruitbody not as above 19

19a. Fruitbody effused-reflexed, consisting of overlapping caps up to 4 cm wide; pores variable, angular to rounded or slightly elongated, typically 3–4 per mm when growing on horizontal surfaces, up to 1 mm wide on vertical surfaces; upper surface not distinctly hairy, pale ochraceous to pale brown, becoming grayish to blackish in age:

Brunneoporus malicola, p. 79

19b. Fruitbody not as above 20

20a. Fruitbody shelflike, semicircular to fan-shaped, broadly attached; upper surface ochraceous, forming a hard, reddish brown cuticular layer that spreads from the base outward and often becomes blackish as it ages, weathering to whitish on older specimens; pores circular, 5–7 per mm; fertile surface white to creamy white, tan, purplish brown to dull brown, grayish or smoky:

Fomitella supina, p. 121

Trametes cubensis, p. 122

20b. Fruitbody not as above, not forming a hard, reddish brown cuticular layer 21

21a. Fruitbody effused-reflexed; upper surface uniformly dark brown; pores 3–4 per mm:

Neoantrodia serialiformis, p. 232

21b. Fruitbody resupinate or effused-reflexed; upper surface ochraceous to pale cinnamon brown; pores 2–3 per mm:

Neoantrodia serialis, p. 233

Key M

Fruitbody sessile or with a rudimentary stalk or contracted stalklike base, or fruitbody entirely resupinate; upper surface richly colored, not white to creamy white, pale gray, or straw-colored; fertile surface poroid, richly colored, not white, whitish, creamy white, or buff to pale tan, sometimes staining brown when bruised; pores circular, angular, slightly elongated, sinuous, or irregular.

1a. Fruitbody solitary or in groups encircling or attached to living twigs of pawpaw, oleander, or orange trees, dark yellowish orange to dark brown:

Inonotus amplectens, p. 190

Phylloporia fruticum, p. 190

1b. Fruitbody not as above 2

2a. Fruitbody solitary, in groups or clusters on living sabal palms, sometimes on other woody substrates; reported only from Florida:

Fomitiporia apiahyna, p. 123

2b. Fruitbody not as above 3

3a. Fruitbody composed of small, overlapping caps in a rounded to hoof-shaped or columnar mass; caps 2–5 cm wide, petal-like, laterally fused, with a long, overhanging margin:

Globifomes graveolens, p. 164

3b. Fruitbody not as above 4

4a. Fruitbody shelflike, semicircular to fan- or kidney-shaped, tough or leathery; upper surface zonate, violet to purplish brown; fertile surface grayish brown to dark brown or purplish brown to dark violet; pores minute, 7–8 per mm:

Nigroporus vinosus, p. 238

4b. Fruitbody not as above 5

5a. Fruitbody upper surface distinctly zonate or sulcate. 6

5b. Fruitbody upper surface azonate or faintly zonate and not distinctly sulcate, or fruitbody entirely resupinate 24

6a. Fruitbody hard and woody, concentrically sulcate, often hoof-shaped, typically cracked in age. 7

6b. Fruitbody not as above 11

7a. Fruitbody 6–20 cm wide; upper surface pale to dark gray or brown; margin extending beyond the fertile surface and curved downward; fertile surface not staining when bruised; pores 3–4 per mm; widely distributed in the Northeast and North Central regions:

    Fomes excavatus, p. 118

7b. Fruitbody not as above 8

8a. Fruitbody 7–18 cm wide; upper surface grayish with concentric zones of reddish brown and grayish brown, often darker brown to blackish brown in age; margin even; fertile surface staining brown to dark brown when bruised; pores 4–5 per mm; widely distributed in the South region:

    Fomes fasciatus, p. 120

8b. Fruitbody not as above 9

9a. Fruitbody up to 20 cm wide; upper surface brown to blackish, becoming encrusted and cracked in age; flesh yellowish brown, with white radial streaks near the tubes and point of attachment; usually growing on oaks:

    Fomitiporia calkinsii, p. 125
    Fomitiporia texana, p. 126

9b. Fruitbody not as above 10

10a. Fruitbody up to 20 cm wide; upper surface dark gray to brownish black, becoming encrusted; pores 3–5 per mm; flesh somewhat shiny, yellowish brown, lacking white radial streaks; growing on birch trunks:

    Fomitiporia bakeri, p. 124

10b. Fruitbody 1–6 cm wide; upper surface strigose or glabrous, brown to dark brown, grayish or blackish, not encrusted; pores 1–2 per mm; flesh up to 2 mm thick; growing on dead broadleaf trees:

    Cerioporus mollis, p. 86

11a. Fruitbody effused-reflexed, consisting of overlapping caps up to 4 cm wide; pores variable, angular to rounded or slightly elongated, typically 3–4 per mm when growing on horizontal surfaces, up to 1 mm wide on vertical surfaces; upper surface not dis-

tinctly hairy, pale ochraceous to pale brown, becoming grayish to blackish in age:

    Brunneoporus malicola, p. 79

11b. Fruitbody not as above 12

12a. Fruitbody effused-reflexed, up to 8 cm wide, semicircular or elongated; upper surface tomentose to velvety, soft to touch, with narrow yellowish brown to pale cinnamon brown or darker brown zones, radially striate or sulcate; fertile surface sometimes soft and smooth to touch, yellow-brown to cinnamon brown; pores circular, 2–4 per mm or 4–6 per mm; distributed in the South region, most commonly in southeast Georgia and Florida, west along the Gulf Coast states:

    Coriolopsis byrsina, p. 106
    Funalia floccosa, p. 106

12b. Fruitbody not as above 13

13a. Fruitbody broadly sessile, 3–12(20) cm wide, semicircular or elongated; upper surface densely hairy, brownish to dirty grayish; fertile surface brown to grayish; pores very large, 1–3 mm wide; flesh brown to rusty brown; widely distributed from Florida to Texas northward through the North Central and uppermost Northeast regions:

    Trametella gallica, p. 335

13b. Fruitbody not as above 14

14a. Fruitbody sessile, not effused-reflexed, 3–15 cm wide, 1–3 mm thick, semicircular to fan-shaped or kidney-shaped; upper surface soft and velvety at first, becoming nearly glabrous, with light to dark brown or purplish brown zones; fertile surface brown with purplish brown near the margin; pores hexagonal to angular, becoming elongated to sinuous in age, 1–2 per mm; widely distributed along the Gulf Coast states:

    Hexagonia papyracea, p. 178

14b. Fruitbody not as above 15

15a. Fruitbody 3–15 cm wide growing on living broadleaf shrubs, especially currants, rose bushes, and honeysuckles; with perennial, semicircular, solitary, or overlapping caps that often enclose the stems on which they are growing; upper surface with a soft and spongy tomentum separated from the flesh by a distinct black line that is absent near the margin; widespread in the Northeast and North Central regions:

Phylloporia ribis, p. 335

15b. Fruitbody not as above 16

16a. Fruitbody 2–7 cm wide, growing on living broadleaf bushes, with annual, semicircular, solitary, or overlapping caps; upper surface with a soft and spongy tomentum that is separated from the flesh by a thin black line that is absent near the margin; known only from Florida and the tropics:

Phylloporia chrysites, p. 335

16b. Fruitbody not as above 17

17a. Fruitbody up to 22 cm wide and 12 cm thick, hoof-shaped; upper surface tomentose or glabrous, often zonate, becoming cracked, buff to reddish brown; fertile surface buff at first, becoming dark reddish brown; pores 1–3 per mm; flesh with intermixed brown and whitish hyphae:

Inocutis dryophila, p. 185

17b. Fruitbody not as above 18

18a. Fruitbody 5–20 cm wide, shelflike, semicircular to somewhat elongated; upper surface reddish brown to umber; margin concolorous, fertile surface grayish brown to brown; pores circular, minute, 5–9 per mm; flesh reddish brown; widely distributed in the South region:

Phellinus wahlbergii, p. 261

18b. Fruitbody not as above 19

19a. Fruitbody 4–16 cm wide; pores angular, 3–5 per mm; upper surface conspicuously woolly-tomentose or radially fibrillose, uneven and knobby or warted, weakly to distinctly zonate, sometimes sulcate, develop-

ing rusty brown and yellowish brown zones as it matures, spongy, often with moisture drops along the margin or on the fertile surface when fresh, becoming blackened and cracked in age:

Inonotus cuticularis, p. 192

19b. Fruitbody not as above 20

20a. Fruitbody up to 5 cm wide and 5–15 mm thick, fan-shaped to circular with a narrowed base; upper surface zonate, finely tomentose, bright yellowish brown; fertile surface dull purplish brown; pores circular to angular, 5–6 per mm; known only from the Gulf Coast states:

Inocutis porrecta, p. 189

20b. Fruitbody not as above 21

21a. Fruitbody perennial, up to 6 cm wide, effused-reflexed, sessile and shelflike or fully resupinate; fertile surface reddish brown; pores circular to angular, 4–7 per mm, with thick, entire dissepiments; upper surface uneven and sulcate, reddish brown or sometimes blackish in age with a paler brown margin; flesh reddish brown:

Fuscoporia viticola, p. 141

21b. Fruitbody not as above 22

22a. Fruitbody growing at the base of oak, sweet gum, or tupelo trees, up to 50 cm wide, sessile or substipitate, consisting of a cluster or rosette of fan-shaped, overlapping caps, 10–30 cm wide and 1–2.5 cm thick; upper surface wrinkled, warted, and radially lined, rusty red to rusty brown; fertile surface buff to brown, quickly staining dark brown when bruised; pores angular, thin-walled, and becoming lacerated, 2–3 per mm, sometimes up to 1 mm wide:

Inocutis ludoviciana, p. 186

22b. Fruitbody not as above 23

23a. Fruitbody annual, up to 5 cm wide and 1 cm thick, consisting of sessile caps usually overlapping, sometimes effused-reflexed, with a sweet odor resembling the scent of vanilla or cinnamon; fertile surface pale to dark brown with a shiny grayish tint; upper surface finely velvety, zonate or somewhat sulcate, grayish or pale brown to cinnamon with an orange tint; pores round, 6–7 per mm:

> *Metuloidea fragrans*, p. 226

23b. Fruitbody annual, 1–5 cm wide, effused-reflexed or sessile; fertile surface yellowish brown, becoming dark brown; pores angular, 2–5 per mm, with thin dissepiments that become lacerated and develop tiny hairs that are best observed at an oblique angle using a lens; upper surface bright ochraceous orange at first, soon becoming golden brown to yellowish brown or reddish brown, blackening in age; flesh lustrous, faintly zonate, yellowish brown and reddish brown:

> *Xanthoporia radiata*, p. 378

24a. Fruitbody 4–16 cm wide; pores angular, 3–5 per mm; upper surface conspicuously woolly-tomentose or radially fibrillose, uneven and knobby or warted, weakly to distinctly zonate, sometimes sulcate, developing rusty brown and yellowish brown zones as it matures, spongy, often with moisture drops along the margin or on the fertile surface when fresh, becoming blackened and cracked in age:

> *Inonotus cuticularis*, p. 192

24b. Fruitbody not as above 25

25a. Fruitbody upper surface golden yellow or bright orange to bright reddish orange, often darkening in age, sometimes fading to yellowish orange when dry or in age 26

25b. Fruitbody upper surface not as above, or fruitbody entirely resupinate. 27

26a. Fruitbody 5–20 cm wide; upper surface velvety, soft and watery when fresh, bright orange, becoming brownish orange and smooth or rough with tufts of agglutinated hyphae as it ages; fertile surface bright red-

dish orange; flesh bright orange, becoming dark orange to brownish in age; addition of KOH to the upper surface produces a red to carmine reaction:

> *Hapalopilus croceus*, p. 173

26b. Fruitbody 10–30 cm wide; upper surface tomentose or covered with stiff hairs, golden yellow to bright reddish orange, becoming rusty brown to blackish in age:

> *Inonotus hispidus*, p. 195
> *Inonotus quercustris*, p. 197

27a. Fruitbody up to 15 cm wide and 2 cm thick; upper surface tomentose to glabrous, zonate or azonate, buff to tan; margin not fimbriate (use a hand lens); fertile surface buff at first, soon becoming pale smoky gray, staining darker when bruised; flesh with a dark layer near the tubes:

> *Bjerkandera fumosa*, p. 71

27b. Fruitbody not as above 28

28a. Fruitbody 3–20 cm wide, fan-shaped to semicircular, sometimes laterally fused; upper surface covered with conspicuous erect, stiff hairs that fall off in age, dark brown to blackish; widely distributed in the South region:

> *Hexagonia hydnoides*, p. 177

28b. Fruitbody not as above 29

29a. Fruitbody up to 20 cm wide; a brown cushionlike mass of soft and fleshy, moist, and velvety tissue that exudes clear droplets from the entire surface and becomes crumbly and dusty with elongated, aggregated, stringy masses of hyphae:

> *Inonotus rickii*, p. 198

29b. Fruitbody not as above 30

30a. Fruitbody upper surface covered by a dense layer of dark brown, coarse, stiff, forked hairs; fertile surface violet at first, drying brown; pores angular to circular, 2–3 per mm, splitting to form teeth in age; reported from southern Georgia and Florida:

> *Trichaptum perrottetii*, p. 360

30b. Fruitbody upper surface not as above, or fruitbody entirely resupinate 31

31a. Fruitbody effused-reflexed, consisting of overlapping caps up to 4 cm wide; pores variable, angular to rounded or slightly elongated, typically 3–4 per mm when growing on horizontal surfaces, up to 1 mm wide on vertical surfaces; upper surface not distinctly hairy, pale ochraceous to pale brown, becoming grayish to blackish in age:

    Brunneoporus malicola, p. 79

31b. Fruitbody not as above 32

32a. Fruitbody effused-reflexed, usually forming several overlapping caps that arise from the effused portion; caps 3–11 cm wide 33

32b. Fruitbody not as above 35

33a. Fruitbody upper surface finely tomentose to glabrous, yellow-brown, often covered with a bright yellow mass of spores, sometimes forming a sterile black, cracked and crusty conk; fertile surface grayish brown, glancing; pores angular, becoming lacerated in age, 3–5 per mm; flesh up to 1 cm thick, golden brown to dark yellowish brown, shiny on cut surfaces:

    Inonotus glomeratus, p. 194

33b. Fruitbody upper surface not as above 34

34a. Fruitbody upper surface coated with a dense layer of fibrils that become matted in age, pale yellow-brown at first, darkening in age, often becoming rusty brown from deposited spores; fertile surface pale yellowish brown when young, becoming dark reddish brown in age; pores angular, often lacerated, 1–3 per mm; flesh up to 2 cm thick, shiny, bright yellow at first, becoming dark rusty brown:

    Inocutis rheades, p. 187

34b. Fruitbody upper surface densely hairy especially at the base, brownish, but soon dirty grayish; fertile surface brown to grayish; pores angular, large, 1–3 mm wide; flesh rusty brown to dark brown:

    Trametella gallica, p. 335

35a. Fruitbody solitary or in groups, fan-shaped to semicircular, thickened at the point of attachment; upper surface pinkish brown to reddish brown or pale brown; margin sharp, curved, concolorous; fertile surface ochraceous to cinnamon-brown; pores angular, 2–4 per mm; flesh pale cinnamon; all parts stain bright violet to purplish with KOH:

    Hapalopilus rutilans p. 174

35b. Fruitbody not as above 36

36a. Fruitbody up to 12 cm wide, fan- to shell-shaped or semicircular, up to 3 cm thick at the point of attachment; upper surface brownish yellow to bright rusty yellow when young, soon becoming dark yellowish brown to rusty brown; margin sharp, yellow at first, becoming brown in age; fertile surface reddish brown at first, becoming dark purplish brown as it ages; pores variable, 5–8 per mm; flesh mustard yellow to bright yellowish brown:

    Fuscoporia gilva, p. 140

36b. Fruitbody not as above 37

37a. Fruitbody 2–8 cm wide, convex, fan- to kidney-shaped, ochraceous to ochre, darkening in age, attached to wood by a small whitish disk; pores hexagonal to angular, 1–3 per mm:

    Hexagonia cucullata, p. 176

37b. Fruitbody not as above 38

38a. Fruitbody up to 8 cm wide and 1–2 mm thick, semicircular to fan-shaped, often fused laterally, flexible; upper surface covered with coarse, elongated, upright or somewhat flattened hairs, becoming tomentose in age, white to grayish or brown; fertile surface white to cream, becoming smoky brown to blackish as it matures; pores angular, 1–3 per mm, breaking up and becoming finely incised and teethlike in age:

    Trametes villosa, p. 350

38b. Fruitbody not as above 39

39a. Fruitbody 13–36 cm wide, up to 15 cm thick, shelflike or top-shaped to somewhat rounded, sometimes laterally fused; upper surface buff to brown, typically exuding amber droplets when fresh; flesh bright yellowish brown to reddish brown, distinctly mottled with whitish streaks when cut:
Pseudoinonotus dryadeus, p. 291
39b. Fruitbody not as above 40
40a. Fruitbody usually growing on oak, up to 22 cm wide and 12 cm thick, hoof-shaped, becoming cracked in age; flesh consisting mainly of a hard granular core of intermixed brown and whitish hyphae; widely distributed in the Northeast, North Central, and South regions:
Inocutis dryophila, p. 185
40b. Fruitbody not as above 41
41a. Fruitbody growing at the base of oak, sweet gum, or tupelo trees, up to 50 cm wide, sessile or substipitate, consisting of a cluster or rosette of fan-shaped, overlapping caps, 10–30 cm wide and 1–2.5 cm thick; upper surface wrinkled, warted, and radially lined, rusty red to rusty brown; fertile surface buff to brown, quickly staining dark brown when bruised; pores angular, thin-walled, and becoming lacerated, 2–3 per mm, sometimes up to 1 mm wide:
Inocutis ludoviciana, p. 186

41b. Fruitbody not as above 42
42a. Fruitbody growing on living mesquite or acacia, up to 8 cm wide and 5 cm thick, shelflike to hoof-shaped, becoming radially and concentrically cracked into angular scales; flesh consisting mainly of a hard granular core of intermixed brown and whitish hyphae; reported only from Texas and Arizona:
Inocutis texana, p. 188
42b. Fruitbody not as above 43
43a. Fruitbody resupinate; fertile surface bright yellow to yellow-brown, typically rough and uneven; pores round to angular, of highly variable size, 1–6 per mm; growing under the bark or outer layers of sapwood of broadleaf trees, usually oak or hickory, eventually rupturing the bark:
Xanthoporia andersonii, p. 376
43b. Fruitbody resupinate; fertile surface pinkish, salmon, or lilac with a grayish tint or purple to purple-violet 44
44a. Fertile surface whitish when very young, soon pink or salmon, becoming purple to purple-violet as it ages or when bruised, purple-brown to wine-red when dry; pores rounded to oblong or elongated, 3–5 per mm:
Cerioporia purpurea, p. 91
44b. Fertile surface lilac with a grayish tint; pores rounded to angular, 5–6 per mm:
Skeletocutis lilacina, p. 312

Species Descriptions and Illustrations

Abortiporus biennis (Bull.) Singer

= *Heteroporus biennis* (Bull.) Lázaro Ibiza
= *Polyporus biennis* (Bull.) Fr.

COMMON NAMES: Aborted Polypore, Blushing Rosette

MACROSCOPIC FEATURES: FRUITBODY annual, occurring as two morphologically distinct forms, one a distorted mass of whitish and brownish tissue covered with pores, and the other a nondistorted form as follows: CAP 8–16 cm wide, convex to nearly flat, almost circular to rosettelike at first, becoming irregularly undulating and lobed in age. UPPER SURFACE smooth to slightly pitted, finely tomentose, whitish to pale yellow when very young, soon becoming ochre to yellow-brown at maturity; margin thin, lobed to crenate, paler than the center, staining reddish brown when bruised. FERTILE SURFACE whitish, staining reddish brown when bruised. PORES elongate and sinuous, somewhat decurrent, 1–3 per mm; tubes up to 6 mm deep. STALK 4–7 cm long, 2–3 cm thick, central or lateral, buff or concolorous with the upper surface, typically with adhering debris. FLESH duplex, white to creamy white or tan, soft on the outer portion, firm and corky on the inner portion, staining reddish when cut; odor unpleasant, taste not distinctive.

MICROSCOPIC FEATURES: Spores 4.5–6 × 3.5–4.5 μm, elliptical, smooth, hyaline, with oil drops; hyphal system monomitic, clamp connections present.

OCCURRENCE: Solitary, in groups, or in overlapping clusters on various broadleaf trees, rarely on conifers, often on the ground attached to buried roots; widely distributed in the Northeast, North Central, and South regions; year-round.

EDIBILITY: Inedible.

REMARKS: Pathogenic, causing a white trunk rot of living or dead broadleaf trees. The epithet *biennis* means "lasting for two years."

Abortiporus biennis

Albatrellus confluens (Alb. & Schwein.) Kotl. & Pouzar

= *Polyporus confluens* (Alb. & Schwein.) Fr.

MACROSCOPIC FEATURES: FRUITBODY annual, consisting of a cap and stalk, growing on the ground with conifers. CAP 5–14 cm wide, convex, circular to fan-shaped or lobed and irregular. UPPER SURFACE smooth when young, sometimes cracked in age, azonate, pinkish buff; margin incurved and entire at first, becoming uplifted, wavy, and partially eroded at maturity. FERTILE SURFACE white to pale yellow, becoming salmon-pink when dry. PORES circular to angular, 3–5 per mm; tubes up to 5 mm deep. STALK 2.5–8 cm long, 1–2.5 cm thick, tapered downward or nearly equal, central or lateral, smooth, glabrous, creamy white to pinkish buff. FLESH 6–20 mm thick, soft when fresh, creamy white, drying pinkish buff; odor aromatic or not distinctive, taste like cabbage or bitter.

MICROSCOPIC FEATURES: Spores 4–5 × 2.5–3.5 μm, ovoid to elliptic, smooth, hyaline, weakly amyloid; hyphal system monomitic, clamp connections present.

Albatrellus confluens

OCCURRENCE: In fused clusters or sometimes solitary on the ground with conifers; widely distributed in the Northeast, North Central, and South regions; summer–early winter.

EDIBILITY: Edible, but sometimes bitter.

REMARKS: Mycorrhizal, not a wood-rotting fungus. The epithet *confluens* means "blended into one," a reference to its growth habit. *Albatrellus ovinus* has a white to grayish or tan cap. Peck's Polypore, *Xanthoporus peckianus* = *Albatrellus peckianus* (not illustrated), has a circular to kidney-shaped cap, usually depressed at the center and concave to funnel-shaped at maturity. The upper surface is glabrous to minutely fibrillose, azonate to faintly zoned, smooth, yellow or cinnamon-buff to pale brown, often with a sharp, incurved margin. The fertile surface is decurrent, white, pale yellow or bright yellow when fresh. It has 4–6 circular to angular pores per mm and tubes up to 2 mm deep. The stalk is central to lateral, up to 4 cm long and 1 cm thick, and is yellow to light buff. The flesh is up to 3 mm thick, pale yellow to light buff, and the odor and taste are not distinctive. The spores are ovoid to ellipsoid, hyaline, smooth, inamyloid, $3.5–4.5 \times 2.5–3$ μm, and clamp connections are lacking. It may be solitary or in groups of several caps that arise from a branched base, growing on the ground in broadleaf woods with basswood or beech, or attached to buried roots. It is widely distributed in the Northeast and North Central regions during summer–early winter.

Albatrellus ellisii (Berk.) Pouzar

= *Polyporus ellisii* Berk.
= *Scutiger ellisii* (Berk.) Murrill

MACROSCOPIC FEATURES: FRUITBODY annual, consisting of a cap and stalk, growing on the ground with conifers. CAP 5–20 cm wide, circular, semicircular, fan-shaped, or irregularly lobed. UPPER SURFACE dry, azonate, covered with coarse scales composed of matted fibers, greenish yellow to dull yellow-orange; margin incurved at first. FERTILE SURFACE attached to slightly decurrent, creamy yellow, becoming more yellowish in age, slowly staining greenish when bruised. PORES circular to angular, 1–2 per mm, sometimes lacerated on mature specimens; tubes up to 3 mm deep. STALK 5–12 cm long, 2–6 cm thick, nearly equal or tapered downward to a narrow base, solid, coated with matted fibers, greenish yellow to dull yellow-orange. FLESH up to 1 cm thick, firm, azonate, cream-colored to pale tan; odor and taste not distinctive.

MICROSCOPIC FEATURES: Spores 8–14 × 5–8 µm, ellipsoid to lacrimoid with a prominent apiculus, smooth, hyaline, inamyloid; hyphal system monomitic, clamp connections present.

OCCURRENCE: Solitary, in groups, or in clusters on the ground in conifer or mixed woods, especially with pines; widely distributed in the Northeast, North Central, and South regions, but not commonly collected; summer–early winter.

EDIBILITY: Unknown.

REMARKS: Mycorrhizal, not a wood-rotting fungus. The epithet *ellisii* refers to New York mycologist Job Bicknell Ellis (1829–1905), who had more than 100 species named in his honor. *Laeticutis cristata* is similar but usually grows with broadleaf trees and has smaller spores that measure 5–7 × 4–5 µm. *Scutiger pes-caprae* has a woolly to scaly, reddish brown to dark brown cap with yellow flesh showing between the scales.

Albatrellus ellisii

Albatrellus ovinus (Schaeff.) Kotl. & Pouzar

= *Polyporus ovinus* (Schaeff.) Fr.
= *Scutiger ovinus* (Schaeff.) Murrill

COMMON NAME: Sheep Polypore
MACROSCOPIC FEATURES: FRUITBODY annual, consisting of cap and stalk, growing on the ground with conifers. CAP 5–16 cm wide, convex, circular to kidney-shaped, sometimes fused. UPPER SURFACE dry, glabrous, smooth at first, becoming cracked with white to pale yellow flesh showing in the cracks at maturity, white, becoming pale grayish or tan; margin incurved at first. FERTILE SURFACE decurrent, white to pale yellow, sometimes with olivaceous or grayish tints, not staining when bruised. PORES angular near the stalk, round near the margin; 2–4 per mm; tubes up to 4 mm deep. STALK 2.5–9 cm long, 1–3.5 cm thick, central or eccentric, enlarged downward or nearly equal, often with a swollen base, dry, glabrous, white to pale yellowish brown. FLESH up to 2 cm thick near the stalk, firm, white to creamy white, drying yellowish; odor and taste not distinctive.

MICROSCOPIC FEATURES: Spores 3.5–5 × 2.5–3.5 μm, ovoid to subglobose, smooth, hyaline; hyphal system monomitic, clamp connections absent.

OCCURRENCE: Scattered or in groups on the ground with conifers; widely distributed in the Northeast, North Central, and South regions, summer–early winter.

EDIBILITY: Edible.

REMARKS: Mycorrhizal, not a wood-rotting fungus. The epithet *ovinus* means "pertaining to sheep." It has a white spore deposit. *Albatrellus confluens* has a pinkish buff to pale orange cap that is often fused with others, 3–5 pores per mm, and grows on the ground with conifers. Also compare with *Boletopsis grisea*, which has a pale brown spore deposit.

Albatrellus ovinus

Albatrellus subrubescens (Murrill) Pouzar

= *Albatrellus ovinus* var. *subrubescens* (Murrill)
  L. G. Krieglst.
= *Polyporus subrubescens* (Murrill) Murrill
= *Scutiger subrubescens* Murrill

MACROSCOPIC FEATURES: FRUITBODY annual, consisting of a cap and stalk, growing on the ground, usually with conifers. CAP 6–15 cm wide, convex and circular to kidney-shaped, sometimes fused and irregular, often slightly depressed to somewhat funnel-shaped. UPPER SURFACE dry, glabrous to minutely tomentose, smooth but becoming wrinkled or cracked and scaly in age, whitish to pale buff; margin incurved at first, becoming uplifted, wavy or lobed, and partially eroded in age. FERTILE SURFACE strongly decurrent, whitish at first, becoming light yellow to pale greenish yellow at maturity, often developing reddish orange tints, sometimes slowly staining brown when bruised. PORES angular near the stalk, rounded near the margin; 2–4 per mm; tubes up to 2 mm deep. STALK 2–7.5 cm long, 6–30 mm thick, central or eccentric, nearly equal or tapered in either direction, usually with an enlarged base, whitish to buff, often with reddish orange or brownish orange tints. FLESH thick, firm, brittle to fibrous-tough, white to creamy yellow, drying yellowish; odor and taste not distinctive.

MICROSCOPIC FEATURES: Spores 3.5–5 × 2.5–3.5 μm, ovoid to subglobose, smooth, hyaline, amyloid; hyphal system monomitic, clamp connections absent.

OCCURRENCE: Solitary, scattered, or in groups on the ground under pines or with mixed pine and broadleaf trees; distributed along the Gulf Coast states; summer–winter.

EDIBILITY: Unknown.

REMARKS: Mycorrhizal, not a wood-rotting fungus. The epithet *subrubescens* means "somewhat reddish," a reference to the reddish orange tints that often develop on the stalk or fertile surface. The addition of FeSO$_4$ to the flesh produces a gray to gray-blue reaction. *Albatrellus ovinus* is a very similar species with a more northern distribution. It grows on the ground with conifers, especially spruce or balsam fir, and has inamyloid spores. *Albatrellus confluens* has a pinkish buff to pale orange cap that is often fused with others, a central or eccentric white stalk, 3–5 pores per mm, and grows on the ground under conifers during summer through early winter.

Albatrellus subrubescens

Amylocystis lapponica (Romell) Bondartsev & Singer

= *Leptoporus lapponicus* (Romell) Pilát
= *Polyporus lapponicus* Romell

MACROSCOPIC FEATURES: FRUITBODY annual, sessile, 5–15 cm wide, rounded to fan- or shell-shaped. UPPER SURFACE tomentose to hispid, azonate, pale buff at first, soon becoming dark reddish brown when bruised or in age; margin rounded or acute. FERTILE SURFACE white at first, becoming dark reddish brown when bruised or mature. PORES angular, 3–4 per mm; tubes up to 4 mm deep. FLESH 0.5–2 cm thick, corky to fibrous-tough, azonate, pale buff or slightly darker; odor typically strong of iodine when fresh, taste unpleasant to slightly bitter or not distinctive.

MICROSCOPIC FEATURES: Spores 8–11 × 2.5–3.5 μm, cylindrical, smooth, hyaline, inamyloid; cystidia 30–45 × 5–9 μm, mostly thick-walled, fusiform, strongly amyloid; hyphal system monomitic, clamp connections present.

OCCURRENCE: Solitary or in overlapping, often fused clusters on decaying conifer wood, especially spruce; Northeast and North Central regions; early spring–fall.

EDIBILITY: Inedible.

REMARKS: Saprotrophic, causing a brown cubical rot of dead conifer wood. *Amylocystis* means "with amyloid cystidia." The epithet *lapponica* means "of Lappland," a reference to its circumboreal distribution. It sometimes fruits near melting snow in early spring.

Amylocystis lapponica

Antrodia albida (Fr.) Donk

= *Trametes albida* Lév.

MACROSCOPIC FEATURES: FRUITBODY annual, up to 10 cm or longer, effused-reflexed and forming numerous narrow, overlapping, sessile caps on a decurrent fertile surface. CAP up to 3 cm wide, shelflike, semicircular to fan-shaped, tough to somewhat woody. UPPER SURFACE finely velvety and azonate at first, white to creamy white, becoming glabrous, sometimes sulcate, and distinctly zonate in age; margin sharp. FERTILE SURFACE white to creamy white. PORES variable, angular to sinuous and elongated to nearly lamellate, 2–3 per mm; tubes up to 1.5 cm deep. FLESH up to 3 mm thick, tough, white; odor and taste not distinctive.

MICROSCOPIC FEATURES: Spores 10–14 × 3.5–5 μm, nearly cylindrical, smooth, hyaline; hyphal system dimitic, clamp connections present.

OCCURRENCE: Typically forming overlapping caps on various species of broadleaf trees, more rarely on conifers, especially dead branches of junipers; widely distributed in the Northeast, North Central, and South regions; year-round.

EDIBILITY: Inedible.

REMARKS: Pathogenic, causing a brown rot. The epithet *albida* means "white." *Brunneoporus juniperinus* grows only on the trunks of living juniper species. It has a pale buff to cork-colored upper surface that becomes encrusted and gray to black in age, a white margin, a white to pale ochraceous fertile surface, much larger labyrinthine pores that are 1–3 mm wide, and smaller spores that measure 6.5–9 × 2.5–3.5 μm. *Neoantrodia serialis* is resupinate to effused-reflexed and grows in clusters and overlapping fused groups, often several feet long, on decaying conifers or sometimes broadleaf trees. It has smaller spores that measure 6.3–8(10) × 2.2–4 μm.

Antrodia
albida

Antrodia heteromorpha (Fr.) Donk

= *Daedalea heteromorpha* Fr.

MACROSCOPIC FEATURES: FRUITBODY annual, sometimes resupinate, but usually effused-reflexed and consisting of numerous, overlapping, sessile caps on a decurrent fertile surface. CAP up to 10 cm wide, often wider when laterally extended, corky and tough. UPPER SURFACE finely tomentose, white to creamy white at first, becoming nearly glabrous and pale sordid brown, weakly zonate, smooth or sulcate; margin sharp, white, often narrow. FERTILE SURFACE white to creamy white, buff or cork-colored. PORES angular to sinuous or labyrinthine, 1–2 per mm, sometimes larger, splitting and becoming teethlike in age; tubes up to 3 cm deep. FLESH thin, white; odor and taste not distinctive.

MICROSCOPIC FEATURES: Spores 10–13 × 5–7 μm, cylindrical to oblong-ellipsoid, hyaline, inamyloid; hyphal system dimitic, clamp connections present.

OCCURRENCE: In overlapping clusters, often laterally extended, on stumps, standing trunks, or logs of conifers or broadleaf trees; widely distributed in the Northeast, North Central, and South regions; year-round.

EDIBILITY: Inedible.

REMARKS: Pathogenic, causing a brown rot. The epithet *heteromorpha* means "having different shapes." *Brunneoporus malicola* has a pale ochraceous to pale brown upper surface and smaller spores.

Antrodia heteromorpha

Antrodiella semisupina (Berk. & M. A. Curtis) Ryvarden

= *Antrodia semisupina* (Berk. & M. A. Curtis)
  Ryvarden
= *Polyporus semisupinus* Berk. & M. A. Curtis

MACROSCOPIC FEATURES: FRUITBODY annual, sessile to effused-reflexed, rarely resupinate, often fused laterally and overlapping, sometimes forming a rosette. CAP mostly fan-shaped, up to 3 cm wide and 5 mm thick, wider when fused, often broadly attached. UPPER SURFACE soft and waxy when fresh, tough when dry, sometimes appearing semitranslucent, velvety to appressed velvety, azonate, and white to creamy white at first, becoming nearly glabrous, somewhat zonate, and ochraceous to pale straw-colored as it ages. FERTILE SURFACE typically decurrent or effused, creamy white to pale straw-colored, darkening

in age. PORES round to angular with thin dissepiments, 5–7 per mm; tubes up to 3 mm deep. FLESH up to 2 mm thick, tough and cartilaginous, white; odor and taste not distinctive.

MICROSCOPIC FEATURES: Spores 2–3.5 × 2–3 μm, ellipsoid, smooth, hyaline, inamyloid; hyphal system trimitic, clamp connections present.

OCCURRENCE: On decaying broadleaf wood, rarely on conifers; widely distributed in the Northeast, North Central, and upper South regions; summer–early winter.

EDIBILITY: Inedible.

REMARKS: Saprotrophic on dead wood, causing a white rot. The epithet *semisupina* means "somewhat prostrate on the substrate with the surface turned upward."

Antrodiella semisupina

Bjerkandera adusta (Willd.) P. Karst.

= *Gloeoporus adustus* (Willd.) Pilát
= *Polyporus adustus* (Willd.) Fr.

COMMON NAMES: Scorched Bracket, Smoky Polypore

MACROSCOPIC FEATURES: FRUITBODY annual, sessile, broadly attached to wood, 2–7.5 cm wide, up to 8 mm thick, convex to nearly flat, shelf-like, often overlapping or sometimes forming rosettes, tough to somewhat woody. UPPER SURFACE tomentose at first, becoming nearly glabrous in age, azonate to faintly zonate, whitish to tan or pale smoky gray; margin acute, whitish when young, darkening when bruised. FERTILE SURFACE pale gray at first, becoming dark smoky gray to blackish at maturity. PORES angular to irregularly rounded, 4–7 per mm; tubes up to 1 mm deep. FLESH up to 6 mm thick, tough, pale buff, lacking a dark layer near the tubes; odor not distinctive, taste somewhat sour or not distinctive.

MICROSCOPIC FEATURES: Spores 5–6 × 2.5–3.5 μm, short cylindrical, smooth, hyaline; hyphal system monomitic, clamp connections present.

OCCURRENCE: Overlapping caps or rosettes on broadleaf trees or sometimes conifers, sometimes resupinate on the undersurface of decaying logs; widely distributed in the Northeast, North Central, and South regions; summer–early winter.

EDIBILITY: Inedible.

REMARKS: Saprotrophic on broadleaf logs and slash, sometimes on conifers. The epithet *adusta* means "scorched," a reference to the smoky gray colors. *Bjerkandera fumosa* has a larger fruitbody, up to 15 cm wide, with a darker upper surface and a paler fertile surface. It has thicker flesh, up to 1.5 cm, and sometimes has an anise odor.

Bjerkandera adusta

Bjerkandera fumosa (Pers.) P. Karst.

= *Gloeoporus fumosus* (Pers.) Pilát
= *Polyporus fumosus* (Pers.) Fr.

COMMON NAMES: Big Smoky Bracket, Smoked Bracket

MACROSCOPIC FEATURES: FRUITBODY annual, sessile, up to 15 cm wide and 2 cm thick, semicircular, often laterally fused. UPPER SURFACE tomentose to glabrous, zonate or azonate, smooth or roughened with tufts of hyphae, buff to tan; margin thin, wavy, whitish when actively growing, becoming dingy yellow to brown in age. FERTILE SURFACE buff at first, soon becoming pale smoky gray, staining darker when bruised. PORES circular to angular, 2–5 per mm; tubes up to 4 mm deep. FLESH up to 1.5 cm thick, azonate, fibrous-tough, whitish to buff or ochre-brown, separated from the tubes by a thin dark layer; odor of anise, disagreeable, or not distinctive; taste not distinctive.

MICROSCOPIC FEATURES: Spores 5–6 × 2–3.5 μm, cylindrical, smooth, hyaline, inamyloid; hyphal system monomitic, clamp connections present.

OCCURRENCE: Solitary or in overlapping clusters on decaying broadleaf wood; widely distributed in the Northeast, North Central, and South regions; year-round.

EDIBILITY: Inedible.

REMARKS: Saprotrophic on decaying broadleaf wood. The epithet *fumosa* means "smoky." *Bjerkandera adusta* has a smaller and thinner fruitbody, up to 7.5 cm wide, with a darker fertile surface. It has thinner flesh, up to 6 mm, and it lacks an anise or disagreeable odor.

Bjerkandera fumosa (A)

Bjerkandera fumosa (B)

Boletopsis grisea (Peck) Bondartsev & Singer

= *Boletopsis subsquamosa* (Fr.) Kotl. & Pouzar
= *Polyporus griseus* Peck
= *Scutiger griseus* (Peck) Murrill

COMMON NAME: Kurotake

MACROSCOPIC FEATURES: FRUITBODY annual, with a stalk and cap, growing on the ground, usually with conifers. CAP 5–14 cm wide, circular, convex to broadly convex, usually somewhat depressed. UPPER SURFACE dry, smooth, becoming slightly fibrillose-scaly over the center in age, azonate, color variable, often mottled, dingy white, grayish, brownish and black, darkening when bruised or in age; margin slightly inrolled when young, becoming elevated, wavy, and sometimes sulcate or split in age. FERTILE SURFACE subdecurrent, white at first, becoming grayish or brownish when dry. PORES circular, 1–3 per mm; tubes up to 8 mm deep. STALK 3–8 cm long, 2–3 cm thick, central or slightly eccentric, nearly equal, solid, fibrillose-scaly, grayish to olive-brown.

FLESH thick, firm, white to pale grayish; odor not distinctive when fresh, fragrant or spicy when dry; taste somewhat bitter.

MICROSCOPIC FEATURES: Spores 5–7 × 4–5 μm, angular and irregular, appearing warty, hyaline to pale brown; hyphal system monomitic, clamp connections present.

OCCURRENCE: Solitary, scattered, or in groups on the ground with conifers, sometimes with oaks; widely distributed in the Northeast, North Central, and South regions, but not commonly collected; late summer–fall.

EDIBILITY: Edible, but sometimes bitter.

REMARKS: Mycorrhizal with conifers, especially pines, possibly with oak. The epithet *grisea* means "gray," a reference to the overall colors of this fungus. It resembles a bolete, but the tube layer does not cleanly separate from the cap, the flesh is too tough, and the spores are not typical of boletes. It has a pale brown spore deposit.

Boletopsis grisea

Bondarzewia berkeleyi (Fr.) Bondartsev & Singer

= *Grifola berkeleyi* (Fr.) Murrill
= *Polyporus berkeleyi* Fr.

COMMON NAME: Berkeley's Polypore
MACROSCOPIC FEATURES: FRUITBODY annual, 20–75 cm wide, a compound rosette of overlapping caps attached to a central stalk. CAP 6–25 cm wide, fan-shaped, convex to flattened, sometimes depressed, laterally fused. UPPER SURFACE dry, radially wrinkled and shallowly pitted, obscurely to conspicuously zoned, whitish to grayish, pale yellow or tan; margin wavy and blunt. FERTILE SURFACE white to creamy white. PORES angular to irregular, 0.5–2 per mm; tubes up to 2 cm deep. STALK 4–12 cm long, 3–5 cm thick, central, solid, roughened, dingy yellow to brownish, arising from an underground sclerotium. FLESH up to 3 cm thick, corky to tough, white; odor not distinctive, taste mild when young, bitter in age.
MICROSCOPIC FEATURES: Spores 7–9 × 6–8 μm, globose, ornamented with prominent ridges and spines, hyaline, amyloid; hyphal system dimitic, clamp connections absent.
OCCURRENCE: Solitary or scattered on the ground at the base of broadleaf trees and stumps, especially oak; widely distributed in the Northeast, North Central, and South regions; summer–fall.
EDIBILITY: Edible when young and tender, becoming tough and bitter in age.
REMARKS: Pathogenic, causing a white stringy rot of heartwood in the butt and roots of living broadleaf trees. The epithet *berkeleyi* honors British mycologist Miles Joseph Berkeley (1803–1889). Although the typical fruitbody diameter is 20–75 cm, mature specimens may be more than 100 cm wide. The globose, amyloid spores with spines and ridges are most unusual for polypores. Molecular analysis has confirmed that *Bondarzewia berkeleyi* is related to *Lactarius* and *Russula* and is classified in the Russulales.

Bondarzewia berkeleyi

Bresadolia craterella (Berk. & M. A. Curtis) Audet

= *Polyporus craterellus* Berk. & M. A. Curtis
= *Polyporus fagicola* Murrill

COMMON NAME: Beech Polypore

MACROSCOPIC FEATURES: FRUITBODY annual, with a cap and stalk, attached to dead broadleaf wood. CAP up to 14 cm wide, 2–8 mm thick, circular, flat with a depressed center, or sometimes funnel-shaped, fibrous-tough, flexible when fresh. UPPER SURFACE finely tomentose to nearly glabrous, typically azonate or sometimes with one or more zones, distinctly radially wrinkled, with small reddish brown scales over an ochraceous to tan ground color; margin thin, very finely lacerated. FERTILE SURFACE white to pale yellow. PORES decurrent, angular, 1–2 per mm; tubes up to 5 mm deep. STALK up to 6 cm long, 3–8 mm wide, central to eccentric, somewhat roughened to hispid, yellowish white to ochraceous or pale brown; base variable, not black on any portion, or sometimes blackish brown to black. FLESH 1–4 mm thick, white; odor and taste not distinctive.

MICROSCOPIC FEATURES: Spores 10–14 × 4–6 µm, cylindrical to oblong-ellipsoid, smooth, hyaline, inamyloid; hyphal system dimitic, clamp connections present.

OCCURRENCE: Solitary, scattered, or in groups on dead broadleaf branches, logs, or stumps; widely distributed in the Northeast, North Central, and South regions; mostly late spring–fall, but may be year-round in the South region.

EDIBILITY: Edible.

REMARKS: Saprotrophic on decaying broadleaf wood. The genus name *Bresadolia* honors Italian mycologist Giacomo Bresadola (1847–1929); the epithet *craterella* means "like a little crater or cup," a reference to the depressed shape of the cap. *Cerioporus squamosus* is similar but much larger, and its stalk is brown to blackish at the base. *Picipes virgatus* (not illustrated) has a depressed to funnel-shaped, reddish brown, circular cap, up to 10 cm wide. The upper surface has radially elongated fibrillose lines that partly expose the yellowish to ochraceous flesh, and the stalk is central, dark brown, up to 3 cm long and 1 cm wide. The fertile surface is strongly decurrent, with circular to angular pores that measure 3–4 per mm. It grows on dead broadleaf wood in the South region.

Bresadolia craterella

Bresadolia uda complex (Jungh.) Audet

MACROSCOPIC FEATURES: FRUITBODY annual, with a cap and stalk, attached to dead broadleaf wood. CAP 3–9 cm wide, up to 1.5 cm thick toward the center, circular, flat with a depressed center, or sometimes funnel-shaped, fibrous-tough, flexible when fresh. UPPER SURFACE glabrous, smooth, azonate, whitish to buff, developing ochraceous tones as it dries; margin thin, sterile, concolorous. FERTILE SURFACE white to creamy white, slowly staining ochraceous when bruised or drying. PORES angular, 3–4 per mm; tubes up to 2 mm deep, creamy white and darker than the flesh. STALK 2.5–4.5 cm long, 7–15 mm thick, tapered downward, with an expanded apex, distinctly velvety or fuzzy and roughened on the upper portion, glabrous and smooth below, whitish on the upper portion, yellow-brown to blackish brown toward the base. FLESH up to 1 cm thick, fibrous-tough, white; odor and taste not distinctive.

MICROSCOPIC FEATURES: Spores 8–10 × 3–4.5 μm, ellipsoid, smooth, hyaline, inamyloid; hyphal system dimitic, clamp connections present.

OCCURRENCE: Solitary or in groups on decaying broadleaf branches, logs, and stumps; known only from Florida; year-round.

EDIBILITY: Unknown.

REMARKS: The species described and depicted here is most likely an undescribed species related to *Bresadolia uda*. Additional molecular analysis is required to resolve this issue. Compare with *Bresadolia craterella*, which has small, reddish brown scales over an ochraceous to tan ground color and larger spores.

Bresadolia uda complex

Brunneoporus juniperinus (Murrill) Zmitr.

= *Antrodia juniperina* (Murrill) Niemelä &
  Ryvarden
= *Subantrodia juniperina* (Murrill) Audet

MACROSCOPIC FEATURES: FRUITBODY perennial, sessile or effused-reflexed, forming extensive patches or clusters of individual caps arising from a resupinate surface, often laterally and vertically fused, growing on wood. CAP up to 5 cm or more wide, irregularly rounded to fan-shaped or semicircular, hard and woody. UPPER SURFACE tomentose and buff to cork-colored at first, becoming glabrous and pale brown, sometimes encrusted, dull and gray to blackish in age; margin whitish when

Brunneoporus juniperinus (A)

actively growing. FERTILE SURFACE whitish to pale ochraceous, becoming pale brown then darker brown in age. PORES angular to sinuous, 1–3 mm wide, often split and labyrinthine on older specimens; tubes up to 4 cm deep. FLESH up to 2 cm thick, corky, creamy white; odor and taste not distinctive.

MICROSCOPIC FEATURES: Spores 6.5–9 × 2.5–3.5 μm, cylindrical to narrowly ellipsoid, smooth, hyaline, inamyloid; hyphal system dimitic, clamp connections present.

OCCURRENCE: In groups or large clusters, usually on standing trunks of junipers; widely distributed in the Northeast, North Central, and South regions; year-round.

EDIBILITY: Inedible.

REMARKS: Pathogenic, causing a brown cubical heartrot of living junipers. The epithet *juniperinus* means "inhabiting junipers."

Brunneoporus juniperinus (B)

Brunneoporus malicola (Berk. & M. A. Curtis) Audet

= *Antrodia malicola* (Berk. & M. A. Curtis) Donk
= *Coriolellus malicola* (Berk. & M. A. Curtis) Murrill

MACROSCOPIC FEATURES: FRUITBODY annual, effused-reflexed, consisting of narrow, overlapping, sessile caps on a decurrent fertile surface, sometimes resupinate. CAP up to 4 cm wide, corky and tough. UPPER SURFACE finely tomentose at first, soon agglutinated and glabrous, sometimes uneven and slightly roughened, azonate to distinctly zonate, pale ochraceous to pale brown, becoming grayish to blackish in age; margin acute to slightly rounded, sometimes well demarcated, whitish to pale brown. FERTILE SURFACE evenly pale cinnamon to woody brown, staining darker brown when fresh material is bruised, often sterile near the margin. PORES round and regular, 3–4 per mm when growing on horizontal substrates, more irregular and angular to sinuous, up to 1 mm wide on vertical substrates; tubes up to 5 mm deep. FLESH 1–3 mm thick, pale brown; odor and taste not distinctive.

MICROSCOPIC FEATURES: Spores 6–10 × 2.7–4 μm, cylindrical to narrowly ellipsoid, often arcuate close to the apiculus, smooth, hyaline, inamyloid; hyphal system dimitic, clamp connections present.

OCCURRENCE: In overlapping groups or clusters on decaying broadleaf wood; widely distributed in the Northeast, North Central, and South regions; year-round.

EDIBILITY: Inedible.

REMARKS: Saprotrophic, causing a brown rot of various broadleaf trees. The epithet *malicola* means "inhabiting apple trees." *Antrodia heteromorpha* has a white to creamy white upper surface that becomes pale sordid brown in age, and larger spores.

Brunneoporus malicola

Buglossoporus quercinus (Schrad.) Kotl. & Pouzar

= *Buglossoporus pulvinus* (Pers.) Donk
= *Piptoporus quercinus* (Schrad.) P. Karst.
= *Polyporus quercinus* (Schrad.) Fr.

MACROSCOPIC FEATURES: FRUITBODY annual, flexible and fleshy when fresh, hard when dry, consisting of a cap and contracted stalklike base, growing on oak. CAP up to 15 cm wide, 1–5 cm thick, shelflike to slightly convex, semicircular to fan-shaped or rounded. UPPER SURFACE finely appressed-velvety when young, soon becoming glabrous and smooth, whitish when very young, soon yellow then brownish, darkening from the base outward as it ages, sometimes slightly pitted or warty; margin rounded. FERTILE SURFACE smooth and white when ac-

Buglossoporus quercinus (A)

tively growing, staining brownish when bruised, becoming darker brown and sometimes cracked when old. PORES circular, 2–4 per mm; tubes up to 4 mm deep. STALK a short, broad, lateral extension of the cap, sometimes rudimentary, colored like the cap. FLESH up to 4 cm thick, tough when fresh, hard when dry, white; odor and taste not distinctive.

MICROSCOPIC FEATURES: Spores 6–8 × 2.5–3.5 µm, cylindrical to fusiform, usually bent close to the apex, smooth, hyaline, inamyloid; hyphal system dimitic in the flesh, monomitic in the trama, clamp connections present.

OCCURRENCE: Solitary or in groups on decaying oak trunks, stumps, and logs; widely distributed in the Northeast region; spring–summer.

EDIBILITY: Inedible.

REMARKS: Saprotrophic on decaying heartwood of oaks. The epithet *quercinus* means "growing on oak." Compare with *Fomitopsis betulina*, which grows on birch wood.

Buglossoporus quercinus (B)

Byssomerulius incarnatus (Schwein.) Gilb.

= *Merulius incarnatus* Schwein.

= *Phlebia incarnata* (Schwein.) Nakasone & Burds.

COMMON NAME: Coral-pink Merulius

MACROSCOPIC FEATURES: FRUITBODY annual, consisting of sessile caps, 3–8 cm long, 2–4 cm wide, semicircular to fan-shaped, somewhat leathery to cartilaginous. UPPER SURFACE moist or dry, subglabrous to finely pubescent, coral-pink when young and fresh, becoming salmon-buff in age. FERTILE SURFACE a network of radiating branched ridges, pinkish ochre to salmon-buff. FLESH 2–4 mm thick, spongy to leathery, whitish to buff.

MICROSCOPIC FEATURES: Spores 4–5 × 2–3 μm, elliptic, smooth, hyaline, inamyloid; clamp connections present.

OCCURRENCE: In overlapping clusters on logs and stumps of broadleaf trees, often intertwined with fruitbodies of the *Stereum ostrea* complex or other *Stereum* species; widely distributed in the Northeast, North Central, and South regions; summer–winter.

EDIBILITY: Inedible.

REMARKS: Recent reports suggest that it may be parasitic on *Stereum* species. The epithet *incarnatus* means "flesh-colored," a reference to the upper surface of the fruitbody.

Byssomerulius incarnatus

Calcipostia guttulata (Sacc.) B. K. Cui, L. L. Shen & Y. C. Dai

= *Oligoporus guttulatus* (Sacc.) Gilb. & Ryvarden
= *Postia guttulata* (Sacc.) Jülich
= *Tyromyces guttulatus* (Sacc.) Murrill

MACROSCOPIC FEATURES: FRUITBODY annual, sessile, soft and spongy, up to 12 cm wide and 2 cm thick, shelflike, semicircular to fan-shaped, broadly convex to somewhat flattened, attached to wood. UPPER SURFACE azonate to faintly zoned, glabrous, smooth, with a cuticle that peels easily, with numerous small circular depressions, white and often exuding watery drops when fresh, drying buff to pale brown, sometimes staining reddish or brownish when bruised; margin sharp, wavy. FER-TILE SURFACE white to creamy white. PORES circular to angular, 4–6 per mm; tubes up to 5 mm deep. FLESH up to 1.5 cm thick, fibrous, azonate, white to creamy white; odor not distinctive, taste bitter.

MICROSCOPIC FEATURES: Spores 4–5 × 2–2.5 µm, cylindrical to oblong, smooth, hyaline, inamyloid; hyphal system monomitic, clamp connections present.

OCCURRENCE: Solitary or in overlapping clusters on conifers or broadleaf trees, sometimes on duff attached to buried wood; widely distributed in the Northeast, North Central, and upper South regions; summer–early winter.

Calcipostia guttulata (A)

EDIBILITY: Inedible.

REMARKS: Saprotrophic on decaying conifers or broadleaf trees. The epithet *guttulata* means "sprinkled with dots of resin or oil," a reference to the watery drops. The Bitter Bracket Fungus, *Postia stiptica* = *Oligoporus stipticus* (not illustrated), widely distributed in the Northeast, North Central, and upper South regions, is very similar, but its upper surface is rough and often has small black spots. The flesh also tastes very bitter, and it grows on dead conifers or broadleaf trees. Also compare with *Postia tephroleuca*.

Calcipostia guttulata (B)

Cerioporus leptocephalus (Jacq.) Zmitr.

= *Cerioporus varius* (Pers.) Zmitr. & Kovalenko
= *Polyporus elegans* (Bull.) P. Karst.
= *Polyporus leptocephalus* (Jacq.) Fr.
= *Polyporus varius* (Pers.) Fr.

COMMON NAME: Elegant Black-footed Polypore
MACROSCOPIC FEATURES: FRUITBODY annual, consisting of a cap and stalk attached to wood. CAP 3–6 cm wide, up to 1 cm thick, circular to kidney-shaped or fan-shaped. UPPER SURFACE glabrous, azonate, tan to yellowish brown or chestnut brown; margin thin, acute. FERTILE SURFACE attached to somewhat decurrent, pale buff, staining brown when bruised. PORES circular to angular, minute, 5–7 per mm; tubes up to 2 mm deep. STALK up to 7 cm long and 1 cm thick, central to lateral, glabrous, colored like the cap on the upper portion, black on the lower portion. FLESH up to 7 mm thick, corky, azonate, pale buff.

MICROSCOPIC FEATURES: Spores 7.5–10 × 2.5–3 μm, cylindrical to slightly allantoid, smooth, hyaline; hyphal system dimitic, clamp connections present.
OCCURRENCE: Usually solitary or sometimes in groups on decaying broadleaf wood, occasionally on conifers; widely distributed in the Northeast, North Central, and South regions; late spring–early winter.
EDIBILITY: Inedible.
REMARKS: Saprotrophic, on decaying broadleaf wood. The epithet *leptocephalus* means "thin head," a reference to the cap of this polypore. Currently, there is widespread confusion as to whether *Cerioporus leptocephalus* and *Cerioporus varius* are the same or different species. *Picipes badius* has a larger cap, up to 20 cm wide, that is chestnut brown to dark blackish brown with a darker center, white to buff decurrent pores, and a black stalk.

Cerioporus leptocephalus

Cerioporus mollis (Sommerf.) Zmitr. & Kovalenko

= *Daedalea mollis* Sommerf.
= *Datronia mollis* (Sommerf.) Donk.

COMMON NAME: **Common Mazegill**
MACROSCOPIC FEATURES: FRUITBODY annual, effused-reflexed or occasionally resupinate or sessile, 1–6 cm wide and up to 1 cm thick, fan- to shell-shaped, often fusing laterally, broadly attached to wood. UPPER SURFACE concentrically zonate and sulcate, hairy or glabrous, brown to dark brown, grayish or blackish; margin thin. FERTILE SURFACE whitish to buff when young, becoming brown in age. PORES angular to labyrinthine, 1–2 per mm, sometimes greater than 1 mm wide on older specimens; tubes up to 3 mm deep. FLESH thin, up to 1 mm thick, pale buff, separated from the darker upper surface by a thin black layer; odor and taste not distinctive.

MICROSCOPIC FEATURES: Spores 10–12 × 3–4.5 μm, cylindrical, smooth, hyaline; hyphal system dimitic, clamp connections present.

OCCURRENCE: Overlapping and often confluent on numerous species of broadleaf trees; widely distributed in the Northeast, North Central, and upper South regions; summer–fall, sometimes overwintering.

EDIBILITY: Inedible.

REMARKS: Saprotrophic, causing a white rot of dead broadleaf wood. The epithet *mollis* means "smooth or soft."

Cerioporus mollis (A)

Cerioporus mollis (B)

Cerioporus squamosus (Huds.) Quél.

= *Polyporus squamosus* (Huds.) Fr.

COMMON NAMES: Dryad's Saddle, Pheasant's-back Polypore, Scaly Polypore

MACROSCOPIC FEATURES: FRUITBODY annual, consisting of a cap and stalk attached to wood. CAP 5–30 cm wide, up to 5 cm thick, kidney- to fan-shaped or semicircular, fleshy-fibrous when young, becoming fibrous-tough in age. UPPER SURFACE ground color creamy white to dingy yellowish or pale yellow-brown, with large, flattened, reddish brown scales that are often concentrically arranged; margin thin, entire, or sometimes conspicuously lobed. FERTILE SURFACE decurrent, white to yellowish. PORES elongate-angular, 1–2 per mm; tubes up to 1 cm deep. STALK 1–6 cm long, up to 4 cm thick, lateral or eccentric, sometimes rudimentary, white on the upper portion, brown to blackish at the base. FLESH up to 4 cm thick, soft-corky to fibrous-tough, white; odor and taste farinaceous.

MICROSCOPIC FEATURES: Spores, 10–18 × 4–7 μm, cylindrical, smooth, hyaline; hyphal system dimitic, clamp connections present.

OCCURRENCE: Solitary, in groups, or in overlapping clusters on decaying broadleaf wood; widely distributed in the Northeast and North Central regions and in the northern portion of the South region; spring–early winter.

EDIBILITY: Edible when young and tender.

REMARKS: Pathogenic, causing a white heartrot of broadleaf trees. The epithet *squamosus* means "scaly," referring to the cap surface. *Bresadolia craterella* is smaller, up to 14 cm wide, has fewer and smaller scales, and a yellowish white to ochraceous stalk.

Cerioporus squamosus

Cerioporus stereoides (Fr.) Zmitr. & Kovalenko

= *Antrodia stereoides* (Fr.) Bondartsev & Singer
= *Datronia stereoides* (Fr.) Ryvarden

MACROSCOPIC FEATURES: FRUITBODY annual, effused-reflexed or sometimes resupinate, attached to wood. CAP up to 6 cm wide, 2–5 mm thick, elongate or semicircular, sessile. UPPER SURFACE tomentose to radially strigose, often azonate but sometimes zonate, brown; margin thin, sharp. FERTILE SURFACE pale pinkish buff. PORES round to hexagonal, 4–5 per mm, with thick dissepiments that appear granular when viewed with a lens; tubes up to 6 mm deep. FLESH up to 2 mm thick, duplex, lower portion pale brown, separated from the darker brown upper portion by a thin black layer.

MICROSCOPIC FEATURES: Spores 10–13 × 4.5–6 μm, cylindrical, hyaline, smooth, inamyloid; hyphal system dimitic, clamp connections present.

OCCURRENCE: Solitary or in groups, sometimes laterally fused on decaying broadleaf wood, especially aspen and paper birch; Northeast and North Central regions; year-round.

EDIBILITY: Inedible.

REMARKS: Saprotrophic on decaying broadleaf wood. The epithet *stereoides* means "resembling *Stereum* species." *Cerioporus mollis* has larger angular to labyrinthine pores, thin flesh up to 1 mm thick, and smaller cylindrical spores.

Cerioporus stereoides (A)

Cerioporus stereoides (B)

Ceriporia purpurea (Fr.) Donk

= *Gloeoporus purpureus* (Fr.) Zmitr. & Spirin
= *Merulioporia purpurea* (Fr.) Bondartsev & Singer

MACROSCOPIC FEATURES: FRUITBODY annual, resupinate, tightly attached to the substrate, forming porose patches several centimeters or more long, soft and waxy when young, hard and brittle when dry; margin distinctly demarcated, sterile and white when immature. FERTILE SURFACE whitish when very young, soon pink or salmon, becoming purple to purple-violet as it ages or when bruised, purple-brown to wine-red when dry; PORES rounded to oblong or elongated, 3–5 per mm; tubes 2–4 mm long.

MICROSCOPIC FEATURES: Spores 6–7 × 2–2.5 μm, allantoid, smooth, hyaline, inamyloid, often with several small oil drops.

OCCURRENCE: On branches, logs, or trunks of fallen broadleaf trees; widely distributed in the Northeast, North Central, and South regions; year-round.

EDIBILITY: Inedible.

REMARKS: The epithet *purpurea* means "purple." Compare with *Skeletocutis lilacina*, which is similarly colored but has 5–6 pores per mm, and smaller spores. Also compare with *Phlebiopsis crassa*, which is similarly colored but lacks pores.

Ceriporia purpurea

Cerrena drummondii (Klotzsch) Zmitr.

= *Polyporus drummondii* Klotzsch
= *Trametes drummondii* (Klotzsch) Ryvarden

MACROSCOPIC FEATURES: FRUITBODY annual, up to 6 cm wide and 3 mm thick, petal- to fan-shaped and tapered to a narrowed, lateral, somewhat thickened stalklike base, flexible when fresh, rigid when dry. UPPER SURFACE appressed-velvety, white at first, soon becoming multizonate with various shades of pale to dark brown, with conspicuous radial striae (use a lens) when dry; margin very thin, wavy, uneven, often torn. FERTILE SURFACE white at first, becoming tan to dark grayish brown in age. PORES angular, 5–6 per mm, becoming finely lacerated and teeth-like in age; tubes up to 1 mm deep. FLESH up to 1 mm thick, white, becoming buff toward the upper surface; odor and taste not distinctive.
MICROSCOPIC FEATURES: Spores 3.5–4.5 ×

2–2.5 μm, cylindrical to ellipsoid, smooth, hyaline, inamyloid, often very difficult to find; hyphal system trimitic, clamp connections present.
OCCURRENCE: Solitary, in groups, or in overlapping clusters, often laterally fused, on standing trunks or downed logs of decaying bald cypress; widely distributed in the Gulf Coast states; year-round.
EDIBILITY: Inedible.
REMARKS: Saprotrophic on decaying wood of bald cypress. *Trametes membranacea* (not illustrated), widely distributed in the South region, is similar, but it grows on broadleaf trees. It is up to 8 cm wide, semicircular to fan-shaped with a contracted base, and the upper surface is zonate, velvety when young and soon turning glabrous. Both the upper and fertile surfaces are dull white at first but then become creamy white to pale tan. The angular pores, 5–6 per mm, often become lacerated; spores measure 4.5–6 × 2–2.5 μm.

*Cerrena
drummondii*

Cerrena unicolor (Bull.) Murrill

= *Daedalea unicolor* (Bull.) Fr.

COMMON NAME: Mossy Maze Polypore
MACROSCOPIC FEATURES: FRUITBODY annual, 4–10 cm wide, sessile, fan-shaped to semicircular or irregular in outline, sometimes laterally fused and often forming extensive rows. UPPER SURFACE covered with coarse, elongated hairs, distinctly zonate, whitish to grayish, olivaceous, ochraceous, or pale brown, sometimes green when covered with algae; margin sharp, often lobed and wavy. FERTILE SURFACE whitish to pale buff at first, becoming gray to smoky gray or grayish brown at maturity. PORES 1–4 per mm, labyrinthine, splitting and becoming teethlike in age; tubes up to 1 cm deep. FLESH up to 3 mm thick, corky to fibrous-tough, whitish to pale brown, with a thin dark zone separating the upper surface from the flesh; odor and taste not distinctive.
MICROSCOPIC FEATURES: Spores 5–7 × 2.5–4 µm, cylindrical-ellipsoid, smooth, hyaline; hyphal system trimitic, clamp connections present.
OCCURRENCE: Typically in overlapping clusters, sometimes solitary or scattered, on broadleaf trees or rarely on conifers; widely distributed in the Northeast, North Central, and South regions; year-round.
EDIBILITY: Inedible.

Cerrena unicolor

REMARKS: Saprotrophic on decaying broadleaf wood. The epithet *unicolor* means "one color." The hairy cap surface, grayish fertile surface, and labyrinthine pores are good field identification features. *Trametopsis cervina* is similar but has a zonate or sometimes faintly zonate upper surface and does not have a thin dark zone separating the upper surface from the flesh. *Hymenochaete iodina* is distributed along the Gulf Coast states on decaying oaks. It has a small and thin, sessile, semicircular to fan-shaped fruitbody, 1–6 cm wide and 1–3 mm thick. The upper surface is finely velvety in numerous narrow concentric zones that are light to dark rusty brown. The fertile surface is dark cinnamon to rusty brown, with angular pores, 3–5 per mm, that sometimes become teethlike or fused concentrically and sinuous in age. The upper surface is separated from the rusty brown flesh by a black zone. It has oblong-ellipsoid, hyaline spores that measure $3.5–4.5 \times 2–2.5$ µm, lacks clamp connections, and has dark brown, acute, hymenial setae with a bent base.

Chondrostereum purpureum (Pers.) Pouzar

= *Stereum purpureum* Pers.

COMMON NAME: Silver Leaf Fungus

MACROSCOPIC FEATURES: FRUITBODY resupinate at first, becoming effused-reflexed and forming patches several centimeters or more in diameter, with caps projecting up to 4 cm from the substrate. UPPER SURFACE dry, finely tomentose to hirsute, grayish to brown, indistinctly zoned; margin undulating, whitish when actively growing, even or slightly fringed. FERTILE SURFACE uneven, wrinkled and finely warty or nearly smooth, bright pink-violet to dark violet, becoming brown-violet as it ages. FLESH 1–2.5 mm thick, tough, with a black line that separates the upper surface from the flesh when observed in cross section; odor and taste not distinctive.

MICROSCOPIC FEATURES: Spores 6.5–8 × 2.5–3.5 μm, elliptical to cylindrical, smooth, hyaline, inamyloid; clamp connections present.

OCCURRENCE: On broadleaf wood, rarely on conifers; widely distributed in the Northeast, North Central, and upper South regions; year-round.

EDIBILITY: Inedible.

REMARKS: The epithet *purpureum* means "purple." Silver Leaf Fungus is a pathogen of fruit trees in the rose family, especially cherry and plum. It causes a progressive and often fatal disease of stone fruit trees called silver leaf or silver blight.

Chondrostereum purpureum

Climacocystis borealis (Fr.) Kotl. & Pouzar

= *Polyporus borealis* Fr.

COMMON NAME: Boreal Polypore

MACROSCOPIC FEATURES: FRUITBODY annual, consisting of overlapping sessile caps attached to wood or roots. CAP 4–15 cm wide, up to 4 cm thick, fan-shaped to semicircular, broadly attached, soft and watery when fresh, becoming brittle when dry. UPPER SURFACE slightly convex to nearly flat, tomentose to hirsute when fresh, becoming partly glabrous when the hairs agglutinate on drying, and forming small tufts of short, stiff hairs, white to cream or straw-colored. FERTILE SURFACE often obliquely oriented, white to cream or pale straw-colored. PORES angular, sometimes irregular and split, 1–2 per mm; tubes up to 5 mm deep. FLESH up to 2 cm thick, duplex with a dense lower layer, white to cream; odor and taste not distinctive.

MICROSCOPIC FEATURES: Spores 4.5–6.5 × 3–4.5 µm, broadly ellipsoid, smooth, hyaline, inamyloid; cystidia abundant, up to 50 µm long, 5–12 µm wide, ventricose and tapered, acute or rounded, thin-walled on the proximal portion, distinctly thickened toward the distal portion; hyphal system monomitic, clamp connections present.

OCCURRENCE: Sometimes solitary, but more often in overlapping clusters at the base or on roots of living conifers, also on logs and stumps; widespread in the Northeast and North Central regions, also in the mountainous areas of the South region; year-round.

EDIBILITY: Inedible.

REMARKS: Pathogenic, causing a white mottled rot in the butt and roots of conifers. *Climacocystis* means "growing in an overlapping fashion like a staircase and having cystidia." The epithet *borealis* means "northern," a reference to its distribution. *Postia balsamea* = *Oligoporus balsameus* (not illustrated) has an annual, sessile, soft and spongy fruitbody consisting of solitary or overlapping caps, up to 5 cm wide, that are shelflike, semicircular or laterally fused and elongated. The upper surface is faintly zonate, radially fibrillose, smooth or shallowly sulcate, whitish when fresh, becoming pale brown as it ages. It has a sharp and wavy margin. The fertile surface is whitish to creamy white or buff with 5–6 angular pores per mm and tubes up to 5 mm deep. The flesh is up to 3 mm thick, azonate, corky, white to buff, with no distinctive odor or taste. It has oblong to cylindrical, smooth, hyaline, inamyloid spores, 3.5–4.5 × 2.5–3 µm, and clamp connections. It may be solitary or in overlapping clusters on conifers, rarely on broadleaf trees, and it is widely distributed in the Northeast, North Central, and mountainous areas of the upper South regions during summer–early winter. *Postia undosa* = *Oligoporus undosus* (not illustrated), widely distributed in the Northeast and upper South regions, has an effused-reflexed fruitbody with the upper surface tomentose to glabrous, azonate, smooth to shallowly sulcate, and white to pale buff. The fertile surface is creamy white with angular to irregular pores, 1–3 per mm. It has soft, whitish flesh and allantoid, hyaline, smooth, inamyloid spores that measure 4.5–6 × 1–1.5 µm. It grows mostly on conifers but occasionally on broadleaf trees.

Climacocystis borealis

Climacodon pulcherrimus (Berk. & M. A. Curtis) Nikol.

= *Donkia pulcherrima* (Berk. & M. A. Curtis) Pilát
= *Steccherinum pulcherrimum* (Berk. & M. A. Curtis) Banker

COMMON NAME: Charming Tooth

MACROSCOPIC FEATURES: FRUITBODY annual, sessile, 3–10 cm wide, fan-shaped to semicircular, arising from a confluent spreading base. UPPER SURFACE densely woolly or with matted hairs, whitish at first, becoming ochraceous-orange to pinkish buff or pale tan; margin often undulating or lobed. FERTILE SURFACE covered with crowded short spines, 2.5–5 mm long, whitish at first, becoming orangish to pinkish buff in age. FLESH flexible, fibrous, white, exuding a creamy white, sticky sap when squeezed; odor variously described as woody or resembling preserved figs, taste not distinctive.

MICROSCOPIC FEATURES: Spores 4–6 × 1.5–3 μm, elliptic, smooth, hyaline.

OCCURRENCE: In overlapping or fused clusters on decaying broadleaf wood; widely distributed in the Northeast, North Central, and South regions; year-round.

EDIBILITY: Inedible.

REMARKS: Saprotrophic on broadleaf trees. The epithet *pulcherrimus* means "beautiful." The upper surface and flesh stain pinkish to red with KOH. Compare with *Steccherinum ochraceum*.

Climacodon pulcherrimus

Climacodon septentrionalis (Fr.) P. Karst.

= *Hydnum septentrionale* Fr.
= *Steccherinum septentrionale* (Fr.) Banker

COMMON NAME: Northern Tooth

MACROSCOPIC FEATURES: FRUITBODY annual, sessile, 10–30 cm wide, 2.5–5 cm thick, and up to 80 cm high, fan-shaped. UPPER SURFACE hairy to roughened and uneven, whitish to creamy yellow when young, becoming yellow-brown in age. FERTILE SURFACE composed of crowded, flexible spines, 6–20 mm long, whitish with lacerated tips. FLESH tough, flexible, zonate, whitish; odor and taste not distinctive when young, becoming like spoiled ham and bitter in age.

MICROSCOPIC FEATURES: Spores 4–5.5 × 2.5–3 µm, elliptic, thick-walled, smooth, hyaline.

OCCURRENCE: In dense, overlapping clusters growing from a common base on wounds of standing broadleaf trunks, especially maple and beech; widely distributed in the Northeast, North Central, and upper South regions; summer–fall.

EDIBILITY: Inedible.

REMARKS: Pathogenic, causing a heartrot of broadleaf trees. *Climacodon* means "ladder tooth," a reference to the overlapping layers of spines. The epithet *septentrionalis* means "northern."

Climacodon septentrionalis

Coltricia cinnamomea (Jacq.) Murrill

= *Polyporus cinnamomeus* (Jacq.) Pers.

COMMON NAMES: Fairy Stool, Shiny Cinnamon
Polypore

MACROSCOPIC FEATURES: FRUITBODY annual,
a small to medium polypore with a circular, thin
cap and stalk, grows on the ground. CAP 1.2–5 cm
wide, circular to irregular, flat to depressed, sometimes laterally fused with other caps, fibrous-
tough. UPPER SURFACE concentrically zoned,
silky, shiny, bright reddish cinnamon to amber-
brown and dark rusty brown; margin faintly striate, often torn, thin, sharp. FERTILE SURFACE
not decurrent, yellowish brown to reddish brown.
PORES angular, 2–4 per mm; tubes up to 2 mm
deep. STALK 1–4 cm long, 1.5–6 mm thick, central,
nearly equal or tapered downward, velvety, dark
reddish brown. FLESH up to 1 mm thick, fibrous-
tough, rusty brown, black in KOH.

MICROSCOPIC FEATURES: Spores 6–10 × 4.5–7 μm,
oblong to broadly ellipsoid, smooth, golden yellow
to nearly hyaline, weakly dextrinoid; hyphal system monomitic, clamp connections absent.

OCCURRENCE: Solitary, in groups, or fused together on the ground, usually along roadsides
and on paths in woods; widely distributed in the
Northeast, North Central, and South regions; late
spring–early winter.

EDIBILITY: Inedible.

REMARKS: Mycorrhizal, evolved from saprotrophic ancestors. The epithet *cinnamomea* refers to
the color of the upper surface. *Coltriciella oblectabilis* = *Coltricia pseudocinnamomea* (not illustrated)
is similar but typically smaller and has finely verrucose spores that measure 7–10 × 4–5 μm. It grows
on the ground or on well-decayed stumps in broadleaf or mixed oak and pine forests throughout the
South region.

Coltricia cinnamomea

Coltricia montagnei (Fr.) Murrill

= *Cyclomyces greenei* Berk.
= *Polyporus greenei* Lloyd
= *Polyporus montagnei* Fr.

COMMON NAMES: Green's Polypore, Montagne's Polypore

MACROSCOPIC FEATURES: FRUITBODY annual, with a cap and stalk, growing on the ground. CAP 3.5–14 cm wide, circular to fan-shaped, convex to flat, sometimes depressed. UPPER SURFACE azonate or inconspicuously zoned, velvety to hairy or fibrous-scaly, uneven or wrinkled, ochre, or cinnamon to dark rusty brown; margin wavy, sometimes torn. FERTILE SURFACE decurrent, completely poroid or concentrically lamellate, or a mixture of both types, yellow-brown to rusty brown or grayish brown, darkening in age. PORES angular and radially elongated near the stalk; tubes up to 4 mm deep; lamellae thick, firm, concentrically arranged. STALK 3–7 cm long, tapered downward, central to eccentric, velvety, reddish brown to dark brown. FLESH up to 2 cm thick, soft and spongy, becoming fibrous in age, cinnamon to rusty brown; odor and taste not distinctive.

Coltricia montagnei (A)

MICROSCOPIC FEATURES: Spores 9–15 × 5–7.5 μm, ellipsoid, smooth, pale golden yellow to pale brown, slightly dextrinoid; hyphal system monomitic, clamp connections absent.

OCCURRENCE: Scattered or in groups on the ground, usually under broadleaf trees; widely distributed in the Northeast, North Central, and South regions; summer–early winter.

EDIBILITY: Inedible.

REMARKS: Saprotrophic or possibly mycorrhizal, not a wood-rotting fungus. All parts stain black with KOH. The epithet *montagnei* honors French mycologist Jean Pierre Montagne (1784–1866).

Coltricia montagnei (B)

Coltricia perennis (L.) Murrill

= *Polyporus perennis* (L.) Fr.

COMMON NAME: Tiger's Eye

MACROSCOPIC FEATURES: FRUITBODY annual, consisting of a cap and stalk, growing on the ground, sometimes confluent with adjacent specimens when growing in groups. CAP 2–11 cm wide, circular to irregular, flat to depressed or funnel-shaped, often fused with adjacent specimens, fibrous-tough. UPPER SURFACE concentrically zoned, dull, velvety to felted, brownish orange to pale cinnamon-brown, becoming dark brown or grayish in age; margin thin, sharp, wavy. FERTILE SURFACE decurrent, grayish, becoming yellow-brown to dark brown in age, staining brown when bruised. PORES angular, 2–4 per mm; tubes up to 3 mm deep. STALK 1.5–7 cm long, 3–10 mm thick, central, nearly equal, velvety, brown. FLESH 1–2 mm thick, fibrous-tough, rusty brown, black in KOH.

MICROSCOPIC FEATURES: Spores 6–10 × 3.5–5.5 µm, elliptic, smooth, pale yellowish brown, slightly dextrinoid; hyphal system monomitic, clamp connections absent.

OCCURRENCE: Solitary, in groups, or sometimes fused together, on the ground, usually with conifers; widely distributed in the Northeast, North Central, and South regions; late spring–early winter.

EDIBILITY: Inedible.

REMARKS: Mycorrhizal. The epithet *perennis* means "continually recurring." The cap margin of *Coltricia focicola* (not illustrated) is often incised or lobed. It has large, nondecurrent pores, 1–2 per mm, often irregular; it grows on burned-over soil or fireplaces; and its spores measure 7–11 × 4–5 µm. *Coltricia cinnamomea* is smaller, has a shiny cap bright reddish cinnamon to dark rusty brown, and a nondecurrent fertile surface.

Coltricia perennis

Coltriciella dependens (Berk. & M. A. Curtis) Murrill

= *Polyporus dependens* Berk. & M. A. Curtis

COMMON NAME: Wasp's Nest Polypore
MACROSCOPIC FEATURES: FRUITBODY annual, consisting of a cap with a distinct stalk that is pendant, often inside rotten logs. CAP typically circular, 3–10 mm wide, 2–8 mm thick, soft and brittle or fragile when dry, with a vertical margin. UPPER SURFACE finely velvety, variably rusty brown, becoming nearly glabrous with some faint radial lines or furrows in age. FERTILE SURFACE initially rusty brown, then black and resembling a wasp nest. PORES angular, 2–3 per mm; tubes up to 6 mm deep. STALK up to 1 cm long, 1–3 mm thick, pendant, often inconspicuous, FLESH 2–5 mm thick, soft, rusty brown.
MICROSCOPIC FEATURES: Spores 7.5–10 × 4.5–5.5 μm, oblong-ellipsoid, with a prominent apiculus, finely verrucose, pale golden brown; hyphal system monomitic, clamp connections absent.
OCCURRENCE: Solitary or in groups on well-decayed conifer or broadleaf logs, usually inside or on the underside; widely distributed in the Northeast, North Central, and South regions; year-round.
EDIBILITY: Inedible.
REMARKS: Pathogenic, causing a white rot. The epithet *dependens* means "hanging down." *Coltriciella oblectabilis* = *Coltricia pseudocinnamomea* (not illustrated) is not pendant and has rusty brown flesh. It has a central stalk and resembles a small *Coltricia cinnamomea*, but it has finely verrucose spores that measure 7–10 × 4–5 μm. It grows on the ground or on well-decayed stumps in broadleaf or mixed oak and pine forests throughout the South region.

Coltriciella
dependens (A)

Coltriciella dependens (B)

Coriolopsis byrsina (Mont.) Ryvarden

= *Polyporus byrsinus* Mont.
= *Trametes byrsina* (Mont.) Pat.

MACROSCOPIC FEATURES: FRUITBODY annual, effused-reflexed, solitary and up to 8 cm wide, or with numerous smaller caps, semicircular or sometimes laterally fused and elongated, thin, flexible, broadly attached. UPPER SURFACE tomentose to velvety, soft to touch, with narrow yellowish brown to pale cinnamon brown or darker brown zones, sulcate; margin thin, wavy, sterile below. FERTILE SURFACE soft and smooth to touch, yellow-brown to golden brown. PORES circular, 4–6 per mm, with thick dissepiments; tubes typically less than 1 mm deep, up to 2 mm near the base. FLESH up to 2 mm thick but usually thinner, ochraceous to tan; odor and taste not distinctive.

MICROSCOPIC FEATURES: Spores 9–14 × 4.5–6 μm, oblong-ellipsoid to cylindrical, smooth, hyaline, inamyloid; hyphal system trimitic, clamp connections present.

OCCURRENCE: Solitary, in groups, or in clusters on decaying broadleaf wood, especially oaks; distributed in the South region, most commonly in southeast Georgia and Florida, west along the Gulf Coast states; year-round.

EDIBILITY: Inedible.

REMARKS: Saprotrophic, causing a white rot. The epithet *byrsina* means "pertaining to a hide." This polypore may be difficult to determine when the fruitbody is sterile. *Funalia floccosa* = *Coriolopsis rigida* (photo below), widely distributed in the South region, is very similar. It has a hirsute, ochraceous to brown upper surface, a cinnamon brown fertile surface, often with a slighty bluish ashy gray tint, and 2–4 pores per mm. The flesh stains black in KOH and the spores measure 8–11(14) × 2.5–4(5) μm.

Coriolopsis byrsina

Funalia floccosa

Cryptoporus volvatus (Peck) Shear

= *Polyporus volvatus* Peck

COMMON NAMES: Cryptic Globe Fungus, Pouch Fungus, Veiled Polypore

MACROSCOPIC FEATURES: FRUITBODY annual, rounded, sessile, attached to tree trunks and stumps, 1.5–8.5 cm wide, nearly round to hoof-shaped. UPPER SURFACE azonate, glabrous, whitish to tan or pale yellow-brown, often coated with a clear, varnishlike layer, smooth or wrinkled. FERTILE SURFACE whitish at first, becoming pale to dark brown, covered by a thick whitish to yellowish membranous veil that tears open at maturity. PORES circular, 3–5 per mm; tubes up to 6 mm deep. FLESH up to 2 cm thick, soft-corky, white; odor not distinctive, taste slightly bitter.

MICROSCOPIC FEATURES: Spores 9–16 × 3–5 μm, cylindrical, smooth, hyaline, inamyloid; hyphal system trimitic, clamp connections present.

OCCURRENCE: Solitary or in groups on conifers, especially pines; widely distributed in the Northeast and North Central regions, rarely reported in the South region; late spring–early winter.

EDIBILITY: Inedible.

REMARKS: Saprotrophic, causing a soft, grayish white rot of sapwood in conifers recently killed by fire or bark beetles. *Cryptoporus* means "hidden pores." The veil may function to retain moisture and high relative humidity for sporulation during dry weather periods. The breakdown of the veil is often assisted by various insects and other tiny arthropods, which bore holes through the membrane.

Cryptoporus volvatus

Cymatoderma caperatum (Berk. & Mont.) D. A. Reid

= *Stereum caperatum* (Berk. & Mont.) Berk.
= *Thelephora caperata* Berk. & Mont.

COMMON NAME: Goblet Fungus

MACROSCOPIC FEATURES: FRUITBODY annual, 2–10 cm wide, wrinkled to folded in the shape of a vase or bowl, attached to wood by a short stalk. INNER SURFACE concave, undulating, typically uneven or deeply folded, moist when fresh, often with a dense coating of whitish hairs that become more visible as it dries or in age; color variable, whitish, yellow, pinkish to lavender or purple, and darkest toward the margin, often yellowish or brownish downward. OUTER SURFACE conspicuously longitudinally ribbed, glabrous and shiny when moist and fresh, color highly variable, a mixture of whitish to pinkish, lavender or purple and darkest toward the margin when fresh, often brownish downward, becoming yellowish to whitish in age; margin divided into slightly concave, somewhat zonate, rounded or pointed teeth-like lobes with finely torn edges. STALK 1–3.5 cm long, 3–12 mm thick, nearly equal down to an enlarged base, solid, whitish with yellow or brownish tints, sometimes with yellowish hairs at the base. FLESH thin, papery to somewhat cartilaginous, whitish.

MICROSCOPIC FEATURES: Spores 8–11 × 3–4 μm, subcylindrical, smooth, hyaline, inamyloid; clamp connections present.

OCCURRENCE: Solitary, scattered, or in groups on decaying broadleaf logs and branches; widely distributed in the South region; summer–early winter.

EDIBILITY: Inedible.

REMARKS: Saprotrophic on broadleaf trees. *Cymatoderma* means "wavy skin." The epithet *caperatum* means "wrinkled or folded."

Cymatoderma caperatum

Cystostereum murrayi (Berk. & M. A. Curtis) Pouzar

= *Stereum murrayi* (Berk. & M. A. Curtis) Burt
= *Stereum tuberculosum* Fr.
= *Thelephora murrayi* Berk. & M. A. Curtis

MACROSCOPIC FEATURES: FRUITBODY perennial, 2–10 cm wide, effused-reflexed or sometimes resupinate, thin and crustlike, becoming confluent and spreading to form patches 20 cm or more wide. UPPER SURFACE narrowly shelflike and projecting 3–10 mm, brownish black, with irregular concentric ridges and radial folds, sometimes covered with moss. FERTILE SURFACE dull, uneven, roughened, finely cracked, whitish to grayish, pale yellow or pale tan. FLESH thin, whitish to yellowish; odor pleasant or not distinctive, sometimes described as similar to shredded coconut; taste not distinctive.

MICROSCOPIC FEATURES: Spores 4–5 × 2–2.5 μm, elliptical, sometimes flattened on one side, smooth, hyaline, inamyloid; hyphal system dimitic, clamp connections present.

OCCURRENCE: On decaying broadleaf logs, especially beech; widely distributed in the Northeast and North Central regions; year-round.

EDIBILITY: Inedible.

REMARKS: The upper surface of the cap is often bent backward, forming a distinctive whitish margin.

Cystostereum murrayi

Daedalea quercina (L.) Pers.

= *Lenzites quercina* (L.) P. Karst.
= *Trametes quercina* (L.) Pilát

COMMON NAME: Thick-maze Oak Polypore
MACROSCOPIC FEATURES: FRUITBODY annual, sessile, 5–20 cm wide, semicircular to kidney-shaped, convex to nearly flat, leathery to corky or woody. UPPER SURFACE velvety, becoming smooth then sulcate or cracked in age; predominantly white, becoming concentrically zoned with one or more shades of brownish yellow, tan, brown, or black; margin blunt and whitish. FERTILE SURFACE whitish to grayish brown. PORES labyrinthine with tough, thick walls, sometimes elongated near the margin. FLESH up to 1 cm thick, tough, dull white to pale brown; odor and taste not distinctive.

MICROSCOPIC FEATURES: Spores 5–6 × 2–3.5 µm, cylindrical, smooth, hyaline; hyphal system trimitic, clamp connections present.

OCCURRENCE: Solitary or in overlapping groups on decaying broadleaf wood, especially oak; widely distributed in the Northeast, North Central, and South regions; year-round.

EDIBILITY: Inedible.

REMARKS: Pathogenic, causing a brown heart-rot. The epithet *quercina* refers to oaks. *Daedaleopsis confragosa* is similar but has thin-walled pores. *Lenzites betulinus* is also similar, but it has conspicuously lamellate pores that sometimes fork.

Daedalea quercina

Daedaleopsis confragosa (Bolton) J. Schröt.

= *Daedalia confragosa* (Bolton) Pers.

COMMON NAME: Thin-maze Flat Polypore

MACROSCOPIC FEATURES: FRUITBODY annual, sessile, 3–16 cm wide, up to 3 cm thick, slightly convex to nearly flat, semicircular to kidney-shaped. UPPER SURFACE coarsely wrinkled, rough and scaly at first, becoming finely velvety to nearly smooth in age, with concentric zones, yellow-brown to reddish brown or grayish brown; margin thin and wavy, white when actively growing. FERTILE SURFACE tough, whitish to pale brown, bruising pinkish brown. PORES variable, circular or radially elongated, sometimes labyrinthine, up to 1 mm wide; tubes up to 1 cm deep. FLESH up to 2 cm thick, tough, whitish to pale brown; odor and taste not distinctive.

MICROSCOPIC FEATURES: Spores 7–11 × 2–3 μm, cylindrical, slightly curved, smooth, hyaline, inamyloid; hyphal system trimitic, clamp connections present.

OCCURRENCE: Solitary, scattered, or in groups on decaying wood, especially broadleaf trees; widely distributed in the Northeast, North Central, and South regions; year-round.

EDIBILITY: Inedible.

REMARKS: Saprotrophic on decaying broadleaf wood and conifers. The epithet *confragosa* means "rough and scaly." *Daedaleopsis septentrionalis* is nearly identical, but it has grayish, distinctly lamellate pores. *Daedalea quercina* has a larger and thicker fruitbody, a conspicuously labyrinthine fertile surface with tough, thick walls, and much smaller spores that measure 5–6 × 2–3.5 μm.

Daedaleopsis confragosa

Daedaleopsis septentrionalis (P. Karst.) Niemelä

= *Gloeophyllum septentrionalis* (P. Karst.) P. Karst.
= *Lenzites septentrionalis* P. Karst.

MACROSCOPIC FEATURES: FRUITBODY annual, sessile, 3–10 cm wide, 1–3 cm thick at the base, slightly convex to nearly flat, semicircular to kidney-shaped. UPPER SURFACE glabrous, rough and uneven at first, becoming nearly smooth in age, with conspicuous concentric zones, radially striate, variously colored, creamy white, yellow, tan, grayish, or pale brown; margin thin and wavy. FERTILE SURFACE tough, whitish to grayish at first, becoming pale brown, bruising pinkish brown. PORES distinctly lamellate, thin, wavy, dichotomously forked. FLESH up to 1.2 cm thick, tough, whitish to very pale brown; odor and taste not distinctive.

MICROSCOPIC FEATURES: Spores 7–12 × 2–3.5 μm, cylindrical, slightly curved, smooth, hyaline, inamyloid; hyphal system trimitic, clamp connections present.

OCCURRENCE: Solitary or in overlapping groups on decaying branches and logs of birch; widely distributed in the Northeast and North Central regions; year-round.

EDIBILITY: Inedible.

REMARKS: Saprotrophic, causing a white rot of decaying birch. *Daedaleopsis* means "resembling the genus *Daedalea*." The epithet *septentrionalis* means "northern." *Daedaleopsis confragosa* is nearly identical, but its fertile surface is labyrinthine or sometimes elongated.

Daedaleopsis septentrionalis

Datroniella scutellata (Schwein.) B. K. Cui, Hai J. Li & Y. C. Dai

= *Cerioporus scutellatus* (Schwein.) Zmitr.
= *Datronia scutellata* (Schwein.) Gilb. & Ryvarden
= *Polyporus scutellatus* Schwein.

MACROSCOPIC FEATURES: FRUITBODY annual, sessile, up to 3 cm wide and 1 cm thick, semicircular to nearly pendant, sometimes effused-reflexed, hard and woody, usually broadly attached. UPPER SURFACE velvety and whitish when very young, soon becoming glabrous and dark brown to black, often sulcate in zones; margin typically paler than the basal portion. FERTILE SURFACE white to buff, becoming pale brown in age. PORES circular to slighty angular, 4–5 per mm; tubes up to 7 mm deep. FLESH 1–3 mm thick, yellowish buff to pale brown with a conspicuous black crust on top; odor and taste not distinctive.

MICROSCOPIC FEATURES: Spores 8–12 × 3–3.5 μm, cylindrical, smooth, hyaline, inamyloid; hyphal system trimitic, clamp connections present.

OCCURRENCE: Solitary, scattered, or in groups on broadleaf trees; widely distributed in the Northeast, North Central, and South regions; year-round.

EDIBILITY: Inedible.

REMARKS: Saprotrophic, causing a white rot in decaying broadleaf trees. The epithet *scutellata* means "covered with small scales or plates."

Datroniella scutellata

Earliella scabrosa (Pers.) Gilb. & Ryvarden

= *Earliella corrugata* (Pers.) Murrill
= *Earliella cubensis* Murrill
= *Polyporus scabrosus* Pers.

MACROSCOPIC FEATURES: FRUITBODY annual to perennial, resupinate, effused-reflexed, or pileate, sessile, broadly attached to wood. CAP 3–12 cm wide and up to 1 cm thick at the base, semicircular to fan-shaped, tough and leathery. UPPER SURFACE glabrous and smooth when young, zonate, white to creamy white at first, soon covered by a hard reddish to bay cuticle from the base outward, becoming dark reddish brown to purplish brown, radially wrinkled, rough and uneven; margin wavy or lobed, curved downward, narrowly sterile on lower portion, whitish. FERTILE SURFACE white to cork-colored. PORES angular near the margin, becoming sinuous to conspicuously labyrinthine on more mature portions, 2–3 per mm when angular, up to 6 mm long when mature and sinuous; tubes up to 5 mm deep. FLESH up to 5 mm thick, tough, white, with a dis-

Earliella scabrosa (A)

Earliella scabrosa (B)

tinct dark line near the cuticle; odor and taste not distinctive.

MICROSCOPIC FEATURES: Spores 7–11 × 3–4 μm, cylindrical to oblong-ellipsoid, hyaline, inamyloid; hyphal system trimitic, clamp connections present.

OCCURRENCE: Solitary, in groups, or in overlapping clusters on decaying branches, logs, and stumps of numerous broadleaf trees, also on structural timbers; widely distributed along the Gulf Coast states; fall–early winter.

EDIBILITY: Inedible.

REMARKS: Pathogenic and saprotrophic, causing a white rot. The epithet *scabrosa* means "rough or gritty." Compare with *Fomitella supina*, which has a purplish brown to dull brown, grayish or smoky fertile surface that stains darker brown when bruised, and circular pores that measure 5–7 per mm.

Favolus tenuiculus P. Beauv.

= *Favolus brasiliensis* (Fr.) Fr.
= *Polyporus tenuiculus* (P. Beauv.) Fr.

MACROSCOPIC FEATURES: FRUITBODY annual, a cluster of overlapping caps with short stalks attached to wood. CAP 2–10 cm wide, fan-shaped to semicircular, soft and flexible when fresh, becoming brittle when dry. UPPER SURFACE glabrous to slightly roughened, azonate, white, becoming creamy white to pale ochraceous; margin thin, acute. FERTILE SURFACE decurrent, white at first, becoming cream to pale ochraceous. PORES hexagonal or radially elongated, sometimes finely incised, typically 1–3 per mm but sometimes up to 2 mm wide; tubes up to 3 mm deep. STALK short and lateral or sometimes rudimentary. FLESH up to 3 mm thick, white to pale ochraceous; odor and taste not distinctive.

MICROSCOPIC FEATURES: Spores 9–12 × 2–3.5 μm, cylindrical to somewhat boat-shaped with tapered ends, smooth and hyaline; hyphal system dimitic, clamp connections present.

OCCURRENCE: Usually in overlapping clusters, but sometimes solitary or in groups on decaying broadleaf logs and stumps; widely distributed in the South region; summer–early winter.

EDIBILITY: Unknown.

REMARKS: Saprotrophic, causing a white rot of decaying broadleaf trees. It is a common species of the tropics that extends northward to the Gulf states and Georgia. The epithet *tenuiculus* means "very thin," a reference to the cap.

Favolus tenuiculus

Fistulina hepatica (Schaeff.) With.

= *Ceriomyces hepaticus* Sacc.
= *Fistulina hepatica* var. *monstrosa* Peck

COMMON NAME: Beefsteak Polypore
MACROSCOPIC FEATURES: FRUITBODY annual, fan-shaped, gelatinous, 7–26 cm wide, fan- to spoon-shaped. UPPER SURFACE smooth to velvety, gelatinous, often viscid to slimy, reddish orange to pinkish red or dark red, becoming brownish in age, typically exuding red juice when squeezed; margin rounded or sharp, wavy or sometimes lobed. FERTILE SURFACE whitish to pinkish yellow, becoming reddish brown in age or when bruised. PORES circular, 1–3 per mm; tubes up to 1.5 cm deep, crowded but distinctly independent and easily separable when viewed with a hand lens. STALK up to 8 cm long, 1.5–3 cm thick, lateral to eccentric or sometimes rudimentary, colored like the cap. FLESH 2–5 cm thick, tender and juicy, becoming fibrous in age, dingy white to pinkish or reddish, with darker and paler zones, slowly darkening when exposed; odor not distinctive, taste acidic.

MICROSCOPIC FEATURES: Spores 4–6 × 2.5–4 μm, oval to tear-shaped, smooth, hyaline, inamyloid; hyphal system monomitic, clamp connections present.

OCCURRENCE: Solitary or in groups on oak trunks and stumps; widely distributed in the Northeast, North Central, and South regions; summer–early winter.

EDIBILITY: Edible.

REMARKS: Pathogenic, causing a brown rot. *Fistulina* means "having small, hollow tubes." The epithet *hepatica* means "resembling liver." *Pseudofistulina radicata* has a smaller, pale yellowish brown cap, a whitish fertile surface, and a rooting stalk attached to buried wood.

Fistulina hepatica

Fomes excavatus (Berk.) Cooke

= *Fomes fomentarius* (L.) Fr.
= *Polyporus fomentarius* (L.) Fr.
= *Pyropolyporus fomentarius* (L.) Teng

COMMON NAMES: Ice Man Fungus, Tinder Conk, Tinder Polypore

MACROSCOPIC FEATURES: FRUITBODY perennial, sessile, 6–20 cm wide, hoof-shaped or convex, hard and woody. UPPER SURFACE shallowly sulcate and zonate, hard, thick, crusty, thickened at the central point of attachment, finely cracked and roughened or smooth, pale to dark gray or brown; margin blunt, extending beyond the fertile surface and curved downward, sometimes wavy and uneven, typically brown. FERTILE SURFACE depressed from the margin, pale brown, often staining dark brown when bruised. PORES circular, 3–4 per mm, with thick walls. Tube layer light brown, becoming stuffed with whitish mycelium. FLESH up to 3 cm thick, with a thicker granular core above it, fibrous-tough to woody, yellowish brown; odor and taste not distinctive. The granular core is mottled with a mixture of pale and darker areas.

MICROSCOPIC FEATURES: Spores 12–20 × 4–7 μm, cylindrical, smooth, hyaline, inamyloid; sclerids present in the flesh, thick-walled, irregular, sometimes lobed or branched, reddish brown in KOH; hyphal system trimitic, clamp connections present.

OCCURRENCE: Solitary, in groups, or in clusters on decaying broadleaf wood, especially birch and beech; widely distributed in the Northeast, North Central and upper portions of the South regions; year-round.

EDIBILITY: Inedible.

REMARKS: Pathogenic, causing a white rot of heartwood of living or dead broadleaf trees. *Fomes* means "tinder," a reference to its use for lighting a fire. The epithet *excavatus* means "having a hollowed out hymenium." *Fomes fasciatus* has a more southern distribution and much smaller spores. Also compare with *Fomitiporia calkinsii*, which has smaller pores, 6–8 per mm, and white radial streaks near the tubes and point of attachment.

Fomes excavatus

Fomes fasciatus (Sw.) Cooke

= *Polyporus fasciatus* (Sw.) Fr.

COMMON NAME: Southern Clam Shell
MACROSCOPIC FEATURES: FRUITBODY perennial, sessile, 7–18 cm wide, convex, hoof- to fan-shaped or semicircular. UPPER SURFACE finely tomentose and slightly roughened when young, becoming hard and nearly smooth at maturity, concentrically sulcate, grayish with concentric zones of reddish brown, grayish brown, or blackish brown, often darker brown to blackish brown in age; margin curved and somewhat blunt, even. FERTILE SURFACE pale brown to dark grayish brown, darkening in age, staining brown to dark brown when bruised. PORES circular, 4–5 per mm. FLESH up to 4 cm thick at the base, hard and crusty near the upper surface, fibrous to granular and corky below, lustrous golden brown; odor and taste not distinctive.

MICROSCOPIC FEATURES: Spores 10–14 × 4–5 μm, cylindrical, smooth, hyaline, inamyloid; sclerids present in the flesh, thick-walled, irregular, sometimes lobed or branched, reddish brown in KOH; hyphal system trimitic, clamp connections present.
OCCURRENCE: Solitary, scattered, or in groups, on living and dead broadleaf trees, especially oaks; widely distributed in the South region; year-round.
EDIBILITY: Inedible.
REMARKS: Pathogenic, causing a white rot of broadleaf trees. The epithet *fasciatus* means "bundled or banded," a reference to the concentric zones of this polypore. Compare with *Fomes excavatus*, which has a more northern distribution and has much larger spores.

Fomes fasciatus

Fomitella supina (Sw) Murrill

= *Polyporus supinus* (Sw) Fr.

MACROSCOPIC FEATURES: FRUITBODY annual or perennial, sessile, up to 15 cm wide and 4 cm thick, shelflike, semicircular to fan-shaped, broadly attached, occasionally circular when growing on top of downed wood. UPPER SURFACE highly variable, minutely tomentose or nearly glabrous, azonate and smooth at first, ochraceous when young, developing a thin reddish brown cuticular layer that spreads from the base outward and often becoming blackish as it ages, sometimes with green tints when coated with algae, usually becoming whitish nearly overall on older weathered specimens; margin slightly rounded, sometimes with two or more lobes. FERTILE SURFACE purplish brown to dull brown, grayish or smoky, staining darker brown when bruised. PORES circular, 5–7 per mm, with thick, entire dissepiments; tubes up to 5 mm deep, indistinctly stratified in perennial specimens. FLESH up to 2 cm thick, duplex with an upper pale zone above and darker below, firm and fibrous, rigid, ochraceous to brown; odor and taste not distinctive.

MICROSCOPIC FEATURES: Spores 6–9 × 3–3.5 μm, cylindrical, smooth, hyaline, inamyloid; hyphal system trimitic, clamp connections present.

Fomitella supina (A)

OCCURRENCE: Solitary or in overlapping groups on dead broadleaf trees and downed logs; widely distributed in the South region; summer–early winter.

EDIBILITY: Inedible.

REMARKS: Saprotrophic, causing a white rot of dead broadleaf trees. The epithet *supina* means "lying flat." *Trametes cubensis* (not illustrated) is nearly identical macroscopically and microscopically. It differs by having a white to cream fertile surface that becomes tan in age, white to creamy white flesh, and branched hymenial binding hyphae with sharply pointed ends. Specimens of *Trametes lactinea* are often misidentified as *Trametes cubensis*. In our opinion, *Trametes cubensis* is either extremely rare or does not occur in North America. Also compare with *Trametes nivosa*, which has white to creamy white flesh.

Fomitella supina (B)

Fomitiporia apiahyna (Speg.) Robledo, Decock & Rajchenb.

= *Fomes apiahynus* Speg.
= *Phellinus apiahynus* (Speg.) Rajchenb &
   J. E. Wright
= *Phellinus elegans* (Speg.) J. E. Wright & Blumenf.

Fomitiporia apiahyna

MACROSCOPIC FEATURES: FRUITBODY perennial, sessile, 2–5 cm wide, hoof-shaped to semicircular and shelflike. UPPER SURFACE glabrous, concentrically zonate and sulcate, dark brown to nearly black, sometimes covered with moss or algae; margin acute. FERTILE SURFACE grayish brown, sometimes yellowish toward the margin. PORES circular, very small, 7–9 per mm; tubes up to 2 mm thick. FLESH up to 2 mm deep, woody, vivid golden brown.

MICROSCOPIC FEATURES: Spores 5–6 × 4.5–5 μm, subglobose to globose, thick-walled, smooth, hyaline, dextrinoid; setae absent; hyphal system dimitic, clamp connections absent.

OCCURRENCE: Solitary, in groups, or in clusters on living sabal palms, sometimes on other woody substrates; reported only from Florida; year-round.

EDIBILITY: Inedible.

REMARKS: Pathogenic, causing a white rot. The key identifying features are its very small size, dark concentrically zoned and sulcate cap, very small pores, subglobose to globose dextrinoid spores, and lack of setae. *Fomitiporia calkinsii* is similar but grows on broadleaf trees, especially oaks, and has larger dextrinoid spores.

Fomitiporia bakeri (Murrill) Vlasák & Kout

= *Fomes bakeri* (Murrill) Sacc. & Trotter
= *Phellinus bakeri* (Murrill) A. Ames
= *Pyropolyporus bakeri* Murrill

MACROSCOPIC FEATURES: FRUITBODY perennial, 8–20 cm wide, 3–5 cm thick, semicircular and shelflike to hoof-shaped, sessile, slightly decurrent. UPPER SURFACE concentrically sulcate, rough and uneven, becoming encrusted and finely cracked in age, dark gray to brownish black, sometimes colonized by algae, mosses, or lichens; margin very broad and rounded, smooth, pale rusty brown when young, becoming pale grayish brown at maturity. FERTILE SURFACE yellowish brown to grayish brown. PORES circular, 3–5 per mm; tubes 5–7 mm deep per season. FLESH 1.5–2 cm thick, woody, somewhat shiny, yellowish brown.

MICROSCOPIC FEATURES: Spores 5–7 μm, globose, smooth, hyaline; hyphal system dimitic, clamp connections absent.

OCCURRENCE: Solitary or in groups on birch trunks; widely distributed in the upper Northeast and North Central regions; year-round.

EDIBILITY: Inedible.

REMARKS: Pathogenic, causing white rot. The epithet *bakeri* honors agronomist, entomologist, and mycologist Charles Fuller Baker (1872–1927). Illustrations of *Fomitiporia bakeri* appearing in some publications have been misidentified and mislabeled as *Phellinus cinereus*. Recent molecular analysis has demonstrated that collections of *Phellinus cinereus* are either *Phellinus alni* or *Phellinus nigricans*, neither of which occurs in the central or eastern United States or in Canada.

Fomitiporia bakeri

Fomitiporia calkinsii (Murrill) Vlasák & Kout

= *Fomes calkinsii* (Murrill) Sacc. & D. Sacc.
= *Pyropolyporus calkinsii* Murrill

MACROSCOPIC FEATURES: FRUITBODY perennial, sessile, up to 18 cm wide and 7 cm thick, hoof-shaped to shelf-like, hard and woody. UPPER SURFACE tomentose and rusty brown at first, becoming nearly glabrous, blackish, incrusted, concentrically sulcate and cracked in age; margin thick, entire, rounded, yellowish brown to rusty brown, sometimes blackish in age. FERTILE SURFACE dark reddish- or grayish brown, non-staining. PORES circular, very regular, 6–8 per mm, with thick, entire dissepiments; tubes up to 5 mm deep, pale brown, whitish within. FLESH up to 3 cm thick, shiny, weakly zonate, hard and woody, yellowish brown to reddish brown, with white radial streaks especially near the point of attachment.
MICROSCOPIC FEATURES: Spores 5–7 × 5–6 μm, subglobose, hyaline, smooth, thick-walled, dextrinoid; setae lacking; hyphal system dimitic, clamp connections absent.

OCCURRENCE: Solitary or in groups on broadleaf trees, especially oak and hickory; widely distributed in the South region and also reported from the lower Northeast and lower North Central regions; year-round.
EDIBILITY: Inedible.
REMARKS: Pathogenic, causing a white rot of broadleaf trees. The epithet *calkinsii* honors amateur mycologist and naturalist William Wirt Calkins (1842–1914). It is macroscopically and microscopically very similar to *Fomitiporia robusta* (not illustrated), a European species which is molecularly distinct. Whether or not *Fomitiporia robusta* occurs in eastern North America remains to be determined. *Phellinus igniarius* has a similar hoof-shaped to shelf-like fruitbody with a pale cinnamon brown to dark purplish brown fertile surface and white flecks in its flesh. The pores are slightly larger and measure 5–6 per mm. It has abundant to rare setae and grows on a wide variety of broadleaf trees.

Fomitiporia calkinsii

Fomitiporia texana (Murrill) Nuss

= *Phellinus texanus* (Murrill) A. Ames

MACROSCOPIC FEATURES: FRUITBODY perennial, sessile, up to 18 cm wide, hoof-shaped. UPPER SURFACE matted tomentose and pale brown at first, becoming nearly glabrous, blackish, encrusted, concentrically sulcate and cracked in age, sometimes with green tints when coated with algae; margin thick, entire, rounded, yellowish brown to rusty brown, sometimes blackish in age. FERTILE SURFACE pale brown to rusty brown. PORES circular, 4–6 per mm; tubes up to 3 mm deep, pale brown, whitish within. FLESH up to 3 cm thick, hard and woody, yellowish brown, mottled with streaks of paler tissue.

MICROSCOPIC FEATURES: Spores 7–9 × 6.5–9 μm, subglobose, hyaline, smooth, thick-walled, strongly dextrinoid; setae lacking or occasional, 20–60 × 5–10 μm, subulate to ventricose, thin- or thick-walled; hyphal system dimitic, clamp connections absent.

OCCURRENCE: Solitary or in groups on broadleaf trees, especially oaks, also on conifers, especially juniper; known only from Texas; year-round.

EDIBILITY: Inedible.

REMARKS: Pathogenic, causing a white rot of broadleaf trees and junipers. The epithet *texana* means "of Texas." Compare with *Fomitiporia calkinsii*, which has slightly smaller spores, grows only on broadleaf trees, and is more widely distributed.

Fomitiporia texana

Fomitopsis betulina (Bull.) B. K. Cui, M. L. Han & Y. C. Dai

= *Fomes betulinus* (Bull.) Fr.
= *Piptoporus betulinus* (Bull.) P. Karst.

COMMON NAME: Birch Polypore

MACROSCOPIC FEATURES: FRUITBODY annual, 5–26 cm wide, shell- to kidney-shaped, fibrous-tough to corky when fresh. UPPER SURFACE smooth when young, often tearing or breaking into scales or patches in age, pale brown with darker brown streaks; margin inrolled, most obviously so at maturity. FERTILE SURFACE depressed from the margin, white and smooth when young, becoming pale brown to yellowish brown in age. PORES circular to angular, becoming teethlike or jagged on older specimens, 3–5 per mm; tubes up to 1 cm deep. STALK up to 6 cm long and thick, sometimes rudimentary, white to reddish brown or brown. FLESH 1–5 cm thick, fibrous-tough, azonate, white; odor and taste not distinctive.

MICROSCOPIC FEATURES: Spores 5–6 × 1.5–2 μm, cylindrical to allantoid, smooth, hyaline, inamyloid; hyphal system dimitic, clamp connections present.

OCCURRENCE: Solitary or in groups on decaying birch trees; widely distributed in the Northeast, North Central, and upper South regions; year-round.

EDIBILITY: Edible, but fibrous-tough and somewhat bitter.

REMARKS: Saprotrophic, causing a brown cubical rot of decaying birch trees. *Fomitopsis* means "having the appearance of a *Fomes*." The epithet *betulina* means "occurring on birch trees."

Fomitopsis betulina

Fomitopsis durescens (Overh. ex J. Lowe) Gilb. & Ryvarden

= *Pilatoporus durescens* (Overh. ex J. Lowe) Zmitr.

= *Polyporus durescens* Overh. ex J. Lowe

MACROSCOPIC FEATURES: FRUITBODY annual, sessile, up to 15 cm wide and 6 cm thick, semicircular to somewhat triangular or irregular, fibrous-tough and corky when fresh, drying very hard and rigid. UPPER SURFACE glabrous or nearly so, smooth to slightly rough, azonate, creamy white to pale buff or grayish when young, becoming yellowish to pale brown as it dries; margin moderately thick, rounded, finely tomentose, creamy white to grayish or brownish. FERTILE SURFACE white to creamy white or grayish, ochraceous when dry. PORES circular to angular, 4–5 per mm; tubes up to 1 cm deep, darker than the flesh. FLESH up to 5 cm thick, tough and fibrous-corky when fresh, very hard and rigid when dry, azonate, white; odor and taste not distinctive.

MICROSCOPIC FEATURES: Spores 6–8 × 1.5–2.5 μm, narrowly cylindric to slightly curved, smooth, hyaline, inamyloid; hyphal system trimitic, clamp connections present.

OCCURRENCE: Solitary or in overlapping groups or clusters on decaying broadleaf trunks and stumps; widely distributed in the Northeast, North Central, and South regions; summer–early winter.

EDIBILITY: Inedible.

REMARKS: Saprotrophic, causing a brown cubical rot of dead broadleaf wood. The epithet *durescens* means "hard or woody." *Fomitopsis palustris* is very similar and grows on conifers or broadleaf trees, but differs by having larger pores, 2–4 per mm, with some up to 1 mm wide, and thicker spores that measure 6.5–8 × 2.5–3 μm. *Trametes nivosa* is also similar, but the formation of a dark, resinous, cuticular layer in older specimens is a key identification feature.

Fomitopsis durescens (A)

Fomitopsis durescens (B)

Fomitopsis mounceae J.-E. Haight & Nakasone

COMMON NAME: Red-belted Polypore

MACROSCOPIC FEATURES: FRUITBODY perennial, sessile, up to 30 cm wide and 8(13) cm thick, usually shelflike, rarely triangular or hoof-shaped, hard and woody. UPPER SURFACE glabrous, smooth to uneven, sulcate, azonate or weakly zonate, often with a sticky resinous coating, color variable, brownish orange, reddish brown or blackish, especially toward the point of attachment, usually with a distinct, shiny, reddish brown band near the margin; margin moderately thick, rounded, smooth, yellowish white to orange-white, pale orange or grayish orange. FERTILE SURFACE not receding, whitish to pale orange or light ochraceous, sometimes staining yellow when bruised. PORES circular, 3–5(6) per mm. FLESH up to 4 cm thick, woody, dense, azonate, creamy white to buff, becoming brown when dried; odor and taste not distinctive.

MICROSCOPIC FEATURES: Spores 5.8–7.1 × 3–4 μm, ellipsoid to cylindrical, smooth, hyaline, inamyloid; hyphal system dimitic, clamp connections present.

Fomitopsis mounceae (A)

OCCURRENCE: Solitary or in groups on standing conifer and broadleaf trees and downed logs; widely distributed in the Northeast, North Central, and upper South regions; year-round.

EDIBILITY: Inedible.

REMARKS: The epithet *mounceae* honors Canadian mycologist Irene Mounce (1894–1987) for her contributions to mycology, especially polypores. *Fomitopsis ochracea* is similar, but the upper surface lacks a conspicuous reddish brown band near the margin and the sticky resinous coating. It sometimes has a receding fertile surface, and the spores are 4–7 × 3–5 μm. *Fomitopsis schrenkii* (not illustrated) is also similar but occurs only in the western and southwestern regions of North America, with the exception of a few collections, including the type from western South Dakota. It grows mainly on conifers, rarely on broadleaf trees, sometimes has a reddish brown band near the margin, and rarely has a receding fertile surface. The spores measure 5.7–6.7 × 3.7–4.3 μm. *Fomitopsis pinicola* sensu stricto is described and illustrated in many American field guides, but molecular analysis has demonstrated that it is restricted to Eurasia and does not occur in North America.

Fomitopsis mounceae (B)

Fomitopsis ochracea Ryvarden & Stokland

MACROSCOPIC FEATURES: FRUITBODY perennial, sessile, up to 30 cm wide and 8(13) cm thick, shelflike to hoof-shaped, hard and woody. UPPER SURFACE dull, smooth, glabrous, sulcate, azonate, color variable, whitish to grayish, cork-colored to ochraceous, or brown to blackish, often a mix of these colors, lacking a conspicuous reddish brown band near the margin; margin thick, round, lacking a resinous layer. FERTILE SURFACE sometimes receding, creamy white to cork-colored, not staining when bruised. PORES circular, (3)4–5(6) per mm. FLESH up to 4 cm thick, woody, dense, creamy white to pale brown, darkening as it dries; odor and taste not distinctive.

MICROSCOPIC FEATURES: Spores 4–7 × 3–5 µm, broadly ellipsoid, smooth, hyaline, inamyloid; hyphal system dimitic, clamp connections present.

OCCURRENCE: Solitary or in groups on standing conifer and broadleaf trees and logs; widely distributed in the Northeast, North Central, and upper South regions; year-round.

EDIBILITY: Inedible.

REMARKS: Pathogenic, causing a brown cubical rot of living and dead conifer and broadleaf trees. The epithet *ochracea* means "ochre-colored, yellowish buff." *Fomitopsis mounceae* is similar, but the upper surface usually has a conspicuous reddish brown band near the margin, it never has a receding fertile surface, and the spores are 5.8–7.1 × 3–4 µm. *Fomitopsis schrenkii* (not illustrated) is also similar but occurs only in the western and southwestern regions of North America, with the exception of a few collections, including the type from western South Dakota. It grows mainly on conifers, rarely on broadleaf trees, sometimes has a reddish brown band near the margin, and rarely has a receding fertile surface. The spores measure 5.7–6.7 × 3.7–4.3 µm. *Fomitopsis pinicola* sensu stricto is described and illustrated in many American field guides, but molecular analysis has demonstrated that it is restricted to Eurasia and does not occur in North America.

Fomitopsis ochracea

Fomitopsis palustris (Berk. & M. A. Curtis) Gilb. & Ryvarden

= *Polyporus palustris* Berk. & M. A. Curtis
= *Trametes palustris* (Berk. & M. A. Curtis) Ryvarden
= *Tyromyces palustris* (Berk. & M. A. Curtis) Murrill

MACROSCOPIC FEATURES: FRUITBODY annual, sessile, caps 3–10 cm wide, semicircular, shelf-like, typically in large, overlapping clusters. UPPER SURFACE white to creamy white, becoming pale buff in age, smooth to faintly zonate and shallowly sulcate, tomentose to nearly glabrous; margin moderately thick, rounded, concolorous. FERTILE SURFACE white to creamy white, becoming pale buff in age. PORES circular to angular, mostly 2–4 per mm, but some up to 1 mm wide; tubes up to 1.5 cm deep. FLESH up to 4 cm thick, creamy white, azonate, fibrous to corky; odor unpleasant.

MICROSCOPIC FEATURES: Spores 6.5–8 × 2.5–3 μm, cylindrical to slightly allantoid, smooth, hyaline, inamyloid; hyphal system dimitic, clamp connections present.

OCCURRENCE: Solitary or in overlapping clusters on conifers, especially pines, sometimes on broadleaf trees; widely distributed in the South region; year-round.

EDIBILITY: Inedible.

REMARKS: Saprotrophic, causing a brown cubical rot of decaying trees. The epithet *palustris* means "in marshy places." As the illustration shows, it is sometimes a food source for beetles. *Fomitopsis meliae* (not illustrated) is nearly identical, if not the same species. It also has spores that measure 6.5–8 × 2.5–3 μm, but the pores number 5–7 per mm and the tube depth is up to 5 mm. *Fomitopsis durescens* is very similar but differs by having smaller pores, 4–5 per mm, and narrower spores that measure 6–8 × 1.5–2.5 μm.

Fomitopsis palustris

Foraminispora rugosa (Berk.) Costa-Rezende, Drechsler-Santos & Robledo

= *Amauroderma avellaneum* Murrill
= *Amauroderma dubiopansum* (Lloyd) Ryvarden
= *Amauroderma sprucei* (Pat.) Torrend

MACROSCOPIC FEATURES: FRUITBODY annual, 3–13.5 cm wide, consisting of a cap and stalk. CAP shape highly variable, semicircular to fan-shaped, spatula- to spoon-shaped or irregular. UPPER SURFACE slightly to distinctly concentrically sulcate and radially wrinkled, frequently zonate, covered by a thin crust, dull, glabrous, brown to dark brown; margin acute, often strongly incurved, wavy and lobed, grayish orange or pale to dark brown. FERTILE SURFACE color highly variable, from very pale orange to reddish yellow or bright orange to brick red. PORES circular, 7–8 per mm, with thick dissepiments; tubes 2–10 mm deep, colored like the flesh or darker, whitish within. STALK 5–15 cm long, 5–25 mm thick, central, ec-centric, or lateral, more or less rounded, nearly equal or sometimes with a slightly bulbous base, occasionally with one or more aborted branches, glabrous, smooth, covered with a hard, horny crust, brown to dark brown. FLESH 3–15 mm thick, fibrous, white to creamy white; odor and taste not distinctive.

MICROSCOPIC FEATURES: Spores 7.5–10.5 × 7–9.5 µm, subglobose to globose, double-walled, yellowish, slightly dextrinoid; hyphal system trimitic with hyaline, dextrinoid skeletal hyphae, clamp connections present.

OCCURRENCE: Solitary or in groups on the ground, growing in association with broadleaf trees, especially oak, attached to buried wood; reported from Florida; year-round.

EDIBILITY: Inedible.

REMARKS: Opportunistic pathogen, causing a white rot.

Foraminispora rugosa

Fulvifomes badius (Cooke) G. Cunn.

= *Fomes badius* Cooke
= *Phellinus badius* (Cooke) G. Cunn.
= *Polyporus badius* Berk.

MACROSCOPIC FEATURES: FRUITBODY perennial, sessile, up to 16 cm wide and 9 cm thick, hoof-shaped. UPPER SURFACE tomentose and pale brown at first, soon becoming cracked, dull, and blackened; margin up to 1.5 cm wide, rounded, yellowish brown. FERTILE SURFACE yellowish brown. PORES circular to angular, 4–6 per mm; tubes up to 2 cm deep per layer. FLESH up to 2 cm thick, easily splitting, bright yellowish brown, with a granular core consisting of intermixed yellowish brown and white tissue with scattered dark reddish brown, hard, glossy granules.

MICROSCOPIC FEATURES: Spores 5–7 × 4–6 µm, ovoid, smooth, thick-walled, dark reddish brown, inamyloid; hyphal system dimitic, clamp connections absent.

OCCURRENCE: Solitary or in groups on acacia, desert willow, or mesquite; reported from Texas, Arizona, New Mexico, and Mexico; summer–early winter.

EDIBILITY: Inedible.

REMARKS: Pathogenic, causing a white rot of heartwood. The epithet *badius* means "chestnut colored." Compare with *Inocutis texana*, which has larger pores that measure 1–3 per mm.

Fulvifomes badius

Fulvifomes everhartii (Ellis & Galloway) Murrill

= *Fomes everhartii* (Ellis & Galloway) H. Schrenk
   & Spauld.

= *Mucronoporus everhartii* Ellis & Galloway

= *Phellinus everhartii* (Ellis & Galloway) A. Ames

COMMON NAME: Everhart's Polypore

MACROSCOPIC FEATURES: FRUITBODY perennial, sessile, hoof-shaped, up to 13 cm wide and 8 cm thick, hard and woody. UPPER SURFACE very finely tomentose at first, becoming glabrous and encrusted in age, typically sulcate and cracked, yellowish brown to black; margin thick, rounded, concolorous. FERTILE SURFACE glancing with a golden luster, dark yellowish to reddish brown. PORES circular to angular, 5–6 per mm; tubes up to 7 mm deep. FLESH up to 5 cm thick, faintly zonate, hard and woody, reddish brown.

MICROSCOPIC FEATURES: Spores 4–5 × 3–4 μm, ovoid to subglobose, with a slightly thickened wall, smooth, pale yellow; setae 16–36 × 5–9 μm, subulate to ventricose, thick-walled, dark brown, frequent to abundant; hyphal system dimitic, clamp connections absent.

OCCURRENCE: Solitary or in groups on broadleaf trees, especially oaks; widely distributed in the Northeast, North Central, and South regions; year-round.

EDIBILITY: Inedible.

REMARKS: Pathogenic, causing a white heartrot of living broadleaf trees. The epithet *everhartii* honors American mycologist Benjamin Matlack Everhart (1818–1904).

Fulvifomes everhartii

Fulvifomes robiniae (Murrill) Murrill

= *Fomes robiniae* (Murrill) Sacc.
= *Phellinus robiniae* (Murrill) A. Ames
= *Pyropolyporus robiniae* Murrill

COMMON NAME: Cracked-cap Polypore
MACROSCOPIC FEATURES: FRUITBODY perennial, sessile, up to 40 cm wide, hoof-shaped to shelflike, hard and woody. UPPER SURFACE finely tomentose, azonate, and yellowish brown when young, becoming encrusted, sulcate, deeply cracked, glabrous, and blackish in age, sometimes coated with algae or mosses; margin rounded, often lobed or fissured, yellowish brown when actively growing, blackish on older specimens. FERTILE SURFACE yellow-brown to reddish brown, quickly staining dark reddish brown when scratched or bruised. PORES circular, 7–8 per mm; tubes up to 5 mm deep. FLESH up to 2.5 cm thick, azonate, hard and woody, dull yellow-brown to pale reddish brown; odor and taste not distinctive.
MICROSCOPIC FEATURES: Spores 5–6 × 4.5–5 µm, ovoid to subglobose, smooth, reddish brown; setae lacking; hyphal system dimitic, clamp connections absent.

OCCURRENCE: Solitary or in overlapping groups on standing or fallen black locust trees and a few other broadleaf species; widely distributed in the Northeast, North Central, and South region; year-round.
EDIBILITY: Inedible.
REMARKS: Pathogenic, causing a white rot. The epithet *robiniae* means "growing on black locust." *Fulvifomes merrillii* (not illustrated) is similar but grows on conifers, especially hemlock, and has been reported from Tennessee and Florida. The shelflike to hoof-shaped fruitbody is perennial, sessile, up to 10 cm wide and 5 cm thick. The upper surface is roughened, shallowly sulcate, reddish brown at first, and becomes blackened and deeply cracked in age. It has a yellowish brown, rounded margin that is narrowly sterile below. The fertile surface is dull purplish brown, glancing and lustrous, with circular pores that measure 7–10 per mm. It has concentrically zonate, yellowish brown, lustrous flesh, up to 2 cm thick.

Fulvifomes robiniae

Fuscoporia gilva (Schwein.) T. Wagner & M. Fisch.

= *Hapalopilus gilvus* (Schwein.) Murrill
= *Phellinus gilvus* (Schwein.) Pat.

COMMON NAME: Mustard-yellow Polypore
MACROSCOPIC FEATURES: FRUITBODY annual or perennial, sessile, 3–12 cm wide, up to 3 cm thick at the point of attachment, fan- to shell-shaped or semicircular. UPPER SURFACE nearly glabrous, usually uneven, wrinkled or rough, azonate or faintly zonate, brownish yellow to bright rusty yellow when young, soon becoming dark yellowish brown to rusty brown; margin sharp, somewhat velvety and yellow at first, becoming brown in age. FERTILE SURFACE reddish brown at first, becoming dark purplish brown as it ages. PORES variable, round to angular or irregular, 5–8 per mm; tubes up to 1 cm deep. FLESH up to 5–20 mm thick, mustard yellow to bright yellowish brown, staining black with KOH; odor and taste not distinctive.

MICROSCOPIC FEATURES: Spores 4–5 × 3–4 µm, ellipsoid to ovoid, hyaline, smooth, inamyloid; hymenial setae abundant, 20–30 × 5–6 µm, subulate, sharp, thick-walled, dark reddish brown in KOH; hyphal system dimitic, clamp connections absent.

OCCURRENCE: Solitary, in groups, or in overlapping clusters on living or dead broadleaf trees, especially oak; widely distributed in the Northeast, North Central, and South regions; year-round.

EDIBILITY: Inedible.

REMARKS: Pathogenic and saprotrophic, causing a heartrot of living trees and a white rot of decaying wood. The epithet *gilva* means "pale yellow."

Fuscoporia gilva

Fuscoporia viticola (Schwein.) Murrill

= *Phellinus viticola* (Schwein.) Donk
= *Polyporus viticola* Schwein.

MACROSCOPIC FEATURES: FRUITBODY perennial, effused-reflexed or sometimes sessile and shelflike or entirely resupinate, often laterally fused, up to 6 cm wide and 1 cm thick. UPPER SURFACE tomentose or glabrous, uneven and sulcate, reddish brown or sometimes blackish in age; margin sharp or rounded, usually paler brown. FERTILE SURFACE reddish brown. PORES circular to angular, 4–7 per mm, with thick, entire dissepiments; tubes up to 5 mm deep, reddish brown, often whitish within. FLESH up to 4 mm thick, fibrous, reddish brown; odor and taste not distinctive.

MICROSCOPIC FEATURES: Spores 5–8 × 1.5–2 μm, cylindric, often curved, smooth, hyaline, inamyloid; hymenial setae abundant, 25–80 × 5–9 μm, narrowly subulate, sharp, thick-walled, dark reddish brown in KOH; hyphal system dimitic, clamp connections absent.

OCCURRENCE: On dead branches and logs of conifers or broadleaf trees; widely distributed in the Northeast, North Central, and South regions; year-round.

EDIBILITY: Inedible.

REMARKS: Saprotrophic, causing a white rot. The epithet *viticola* means "growing on grape vines." Entirely resupinate specimens may be up to 35 cm. The long narrow setae and narrow cylindric spores are diagnostic.

Fuscoporia viticola

Fuscopostia fragilis (Fr.) B. K. Cui, L. L. Shen & Y. C. Dai

= *Oligoporus fragilis* (Fr.) Gilb. & Ryvarden
= *Postia fragilis* (Fr.) Jülich
= *Tyromyces fragilis* (Fr.) Donk

COMMON NAME: Staining Cheese Polypore
MACROSCOPIC FEATURES: FRUITBODY annual, sessile, soft and spongy, up to 6 cm wide, shelf-like, semicircular, broadly convex to somewhat flattened, attached to wood. UPPER SURFACE tomentose to glabrous, azonate, whitish to buff, staining reddish brown when bruised or drying; margin sharp, wavy. FERTILE SURFACE whitish to buff, staining reddish brown when bruised or drying. PORES circular to angular, 5–6 per mm; tubes up to 4 mm deep. FLESH up to 1.5 cm thick, fibrous, azonate, white; odor and taste not distinctive.
MICROSCOPIC FEATURES: Spores 4–5 × 1–1.5 μm, allantoid to cylindrical, smooth, hyaline, inamyloid; hyphal system monomitic, clamp connections present.

OCCURRENCE: Solitary, in groups, or in overlapping clusters on decaying conifers, rarely on aspen; widely distributed in the Northeast, North Central, and South regions; summer–early winter.
EDIBILITY: Inedible.
REMARKS: Saprotrophic on decaying conifer wood. The epithet *fragilis* means "easily broken or marked." *Postia leucomallella* = *Oligoporus leucomallellus* (not illustrated), widely distributed in the Northeast and North Central regions, is similar. It forms an effused-reflexed, narrow, elongated fruitbody along the upper edge of a decurrent tube layer. The upper surface is white to creamy white and becomes straw-colored or dirty brownish as it ages or dries. It has a white to dark creamy white fertile surface with angular pores, 3–4 per mm, and white flesh. Microscopically, it has rare to abundant light yellow, cylindrical to clavate and obtuse gloeocystidia in the subhymenium that measure 10–35 × 4–8 μm. It grows on dead conifers, especially larch, pine, and spruce.

Fuscopostia fragilis

Ganoderma applanatum (Pers.) Pat.

= *Fomes applanatus* (Pers.) Fr.
= *Polyporus applanatus* (Pers.) Wallr.

COMMON NAME: Artist's Conk

MACROSCOPIC FEATURES: FRUITBODY perennial, 5–65 cm wide, up to 10 cm or more thick, sessile, shelflike or rarely hoof-shaped, thickened at the point of attachment. UPPER SURFACE covered with a thin crust that is typically too tough to fracture using thumb or fingernail pressure, concentrically sulcate, dull brown to blackish brown or grayish, finely cracked and roughened in age, sometimes appearing dusty when coated with a thick layer of brown spores; margin thin or thick, rounded, white when actively growing. FERTILE SURFACE white, staining brown when bruised. PORES circular, 4–6 per mm; tubes up to 15 mm deep per layer. FLESH corky to woody, reddish brown; odor and taste not distinctive.

MICROSCOPIC FEATURES: Spores 6–9 × 4.5–6 µm, ovoid, with a truncate apex and germ pore, smooth but appearing roughened, light brown; wall two-layered with interwall pillars; hyphal system trimitic, clamp connections present.

OCCURRENCE: Solitary, in groups, or in overlapping clusters on a wide variety of broadleaf trees; widely distributed in the Northeast, North Central, and South regions; year-round.

EDIBILITY: Inedible.

REMARKS: Pathogenic, causing a white rot. *Ganoderma* means "having a shiny or lustrous skin." The epithet *applanatum* means "flattened and shelflike." It is called the Artist's Conk because drawings can be made on the fresh white fertile surface when etched with a sharp instrument. When bruised, the white fertile surface turns permanently brown. The fertile surface is sometimes attacked by a parasitic ascomycete, the Golden-mouthed Spore-eating Fungus, *Sporophagomyces chrysostomus* (not illustrated). It is a radiating, feathery mat of mycelium that is white at first and becomes brown from trapped spores. Compare with *Ganoderma megaloma*, which may be a distinct species or just a morphological variant.

Ganoderma applanatum

Ganoderma colossus (Fr.) C. F. Baker

= *Tomophagus colossus* (Fr.) Murrill

COMMON NAME: Elephant's Foot

MACROSCOPIC FEATURES: FRUITBODY annual, sessile, up to 30 cm wide and long, up to 10 cm thick, semicircular to elongated or variously irregular, soft and spongy when fresh. UPPER SURFACE glabrous, covered with a thin crust that is soft and easily dented, somewhat glossy or dull, yellow to pale brown; margin blunt, whitish to yellow. FERTILE SURFACE white to cream when fresh, ochraceous to pale brown when dry. PORES angular to rounded, 2–4 per mm, moderately thick-walled; tubes concolorous with fertile surface, pale brown, up to 3 cm deep. FLESH up to 10 cm thick, creamy white to pale buff, soft, fibrous-spongy, azonate, homogeneous; odor and taste not distinctive.

MICROSCOPIC FEATURES: Spores 14–19 × 8–12 μm, ellipsoid to ovoid, with a truncate apex and germ pore, smooth but appearing roughened, pale brown; wall two-layered with interwall pillars; chlamydospores scattered through the flesh, 18–23 μm, spherical, thick-walled, with a coarsely reticulate surface and blunt, cylindrical projections, reddish brown; hyphal system dimitic, clamp connections present.

OCCURRENCE: Solitary or in groups on decaying wood or woodchips of various broadleaf trees, also reported on southern hackberry and on Australian pine woodchips; distributed in the Gulf Coast states, rare; late fall–winter.

EDIBILITY: Unknown.

REMARKS: Pathogenic, causing white rot and butt rot. It is a pantropical species that also occurs in Florida. It is easy to recognize because of the pale flesh with a thin yellow to pale brown crust. The epithet *colossus* means "gigantic."

Ganoderma colossus

Ganoderma curtisii (Berk.) Murrill

= *Polyporus curtisii* (Berk.) Cooke

MACROSCOPIC FEATURES: FRUITBODY annual, 3–20 cm wide, fan- to kidney-shaped. UPPER SURFACE roughened and uneven, with concentric zones and shallow furrows, covered with a thin, shiny crust and appearing varnished, glabrous, creamy white when very young, becoming ochre or reddish brown and retaining these colors well into maturity, sometimes becoming partly dull brown when coated with spores; margin acute or obtuse, yellow to ochre. FERTILE SURFACE whitish to yellowish, becoming brownish in age, staining brown when bruised. PORES circular or nearly so, 4–6 per mm; tubes up to 2 cm deep. STALK 3–12 cm long, 1–3 cm thick, lateral to subcentral, varnished, shiny, dark ochre to dark reddish brown and darker than the cap. FLESH up to 1.5 cm thick, leathery to corky when fresh, becoming tough and rigid when dry, creamy white to buff, with black, shiny resinous deposits present; odor and taste not distinctive.

MICROSCOPIC FEATURES: Spores 9–13 × 5–7 µm, ovoid, with a truncate apex and germ pore, smooth but appearing roughened, light brown; wall two-layered with interwall pillars; hyphal system trimitic, clamp connections present.

OCCURRENCE: Solitary, in groups, or in overlapping clusters on stumps, roots, and trunks of broadleaf trees, sometimes on the ground attached to buried wood; widely distributed in the Northeast, North Central, and South regions; year-round.

EDIBILITY: Inedible.

REMARKS: Opportunistic pathogen, causing a white rot. The epithet *curtisii* honors American mycologist Moses Ashley Curtis (1808–1872). *Ganoderma ravenelii* (not illustrated) is nearly identical and grows on broadleaf trees or on the ground, but it has creamy white to buff flesh that lacks black, shiny, resinous deposits, and its spores measure 11.7–14.5 × 5–6.5 µm. *Ganoderma curtisii* f.sp. *meredithiae* is very similar but grows on pine stumps or on the ground at the base of pine trees. *Ganoderma lucidum* is not known to occur in North America, except for northern Utah and northern California, where it is thought to have been introduced by people cultivating it. Molecular analysis has demonstrated that it is a nearly identical species that occurs in Europe and Asia.

Ganoderma curtisii

Ganoderma curtisii **f.sp.** *meredithiae* Adask. & Gilb.

COMMON NAME: Pine Varnish Conk

MACROSCOPIC FEATURES: FRUITBODY annual, 5–16 cm wide, circular to kidney-shaped. UPPER SURFACE dry, covered with a thin, shiny crust and appearing varnished, glabrous, creamy white to yellowish buff at first, becoming reddish brown at maturity, concentrically zoned and shallowly sulcate; margin somewhat blunt. FERTILE SURFACE creamy white at first, becoming pale pinkish cream at maturity. PORES circular to angular, 4–6 per mm; tubes up to 2 cm deep. STALK 3–10 cm long, 1–3 cm thick, nearly equal or tapered in either direction, central or lateral, colored like the cap, coated with a thin, shiny, varnished crust, sometimes rudimentary or absent. FLESH up to 2 cm thick, corky to fibrous-tough, light buff near the upper surface, grading to pale purplish brown toward the tubes; odor and taste not distinctive.

MICROSCOPIC FEATURES: Spores 9.5–11.5 × 5.5–7 μm, ellipsoid with a truncate apex and germ pore; wall two-layered with interwall pillars, appearing roughened, pale brown; hyphal system trimitic, clamp connections present.

OCCURRENCE: Solitary, scattered, or in groups at the base of living pine trees or on dead pines or stumps; widely distributed in the South region; year-round.

EDIBILITY: Inedible.

REMARKS: Opportunistic pathogen, causing a white rot. This species was named in honor of mycologist Dr. Meredith Blackwell of Louisiana State University. All other similar species grow on broadleaf trees. The designation "f.sp." is used for infraspecific categories (below the species level), in this case because of growth on pines instead of broadleaf wood.

Ganoderma curtisii f.sp. *meredithiae*

Ganoderma lobatoideum Steyaert

MACROSCOPIC FEATURES: FRUITBODY perennial, reviving and producing new growth below the older growth from the previous year, up to 20 cm wide, sessile or with a rudimentary stalk, shelflike, semicircular or fan-shaped, sometimes lobed. UPPER SURFACE covered with a thin crust, uneven, knobby and rough, dull to slightly shiny, sometimes concentrically sulcate, yellowish brown to reddish brown or dark brown; margin white in growing specimens, usually with a yellow-ochre rim. FERTILE SURFACE yellowish buff at first, soon becoming dull reddish brown to purplish brown. PORES 4–7 per mm; tubes up to 15 mm deep. FLESH up to 2 cm thick, corky, reddish brown; odor and taste not distinctive.

MICROSCOPIC FEATURES: Spores 6.5–9 × 4–6.5 μm, obovate to obpyriform, with a truncate apex and germ pore, smooth but appearing roughened, pale brown; wall two-layered with interwall pillars; hyphal system trimitic, clamp connections present.

OCCURRENCE: Solitary or in groups on decaying broadleaf wood or on the ground attached to roots; widely distributed in the South region; year-round.

EDIBILITY: Inedible.

REMARKS: Opportunistic pathogen, causing a white rot of broadleaf trees. The epithet *lobatoideum* means "resembling *Ganoderma lobatum*." *Ganoderma lobatum* is nearly identical, but much more widely distributed. It has a thick white margin when actively growing, lacks the yellow-ochre rim, and has slightly larger spores that measure 7.5–11 × 5–7 μm.

Ganoderma lobatoideum

Ganoderma lobatum (Cooke) G. F. Atk.

= *Fomes lobatus* Cooke
= *Polyporus lobatus* Schwein.

MACROSCOPIC FEATURES: FRUITBODY perennial, reviving and producing new growth below the older growth from the previous year, up to 20 cm wide, sessile or with a rudimentary stalk, shelflike, semicircular or fan-shaped, sometimes lobed. UPPER SURFACE glabrous, dull to slightly shiny, often concentrically zoned or sulcate with pale yellow to darker orange-yellow bands, coated with a thin crust that is easily broken with thumb or fingernail pressure, rusty brown to tawny or dull brown, becoming rough, uneven, cracked and darker brown in age; margin rounded, even, thick and white when actively growing, sometimes lobed. FERTILE SURFACE creamy white to yellowish buff at first, becoming dull purplish brown. PORES 4–7 per mm; tubes up to 15 mm deep.

FLESH up to 2 cm thick, corky, brown; odor and taste not distinctive.

MICROSCOPIC FEATURES: Spores 7.5–11 × 5–7 μm, broadly ellipsoid to ovoid, with a truncate apex and germ pore, smooth but appearing roughened, pale brown; wall two-layered with interwall pillars; hyphal system trimitic, clamp connections present.

OCCURRENCE: Solitary or in groups on decaying broadleaf wood or on the ground attached to roots; widely distributed in the Northeast, North Central, and South regions; year-round.

EDIBILITY: Inedible.

REMARKS: Opportunistic pathogen, causing a white rot of broadleaf trees. The epithet *lobatum* means "having lobes." *Ganoderma lobatoideum*, reported only from the South region, is nearly identical, but it has slightly smaller spores that measure 6.5–9 × 4–6.5 μm.

Ganoderma lobatum

Ganoderma martinicense Welti & Courtec.

MACROSCOPIC FEATURES: FRUITBODY annual, 6–30 cm wide, kidney-shaped to semicircular. UPPER SURFACE uneven, with wide concentric bumps and radial folds, covered with a thin, shiny crust that appears varnished, glabrous, thin and easily compressed by finger pressure, reddish brown, becoming orange-brown toward the margin, then ochre and finally creamy white at the margin when actively growing; margin uneven, wavy, sometimes lobed. FERTILE SURFACE white, staining brown when bruised. PORES circular to irregular, 4–5 per mm; tubes up to 1 cm deep, dark reddish brown. STALK 3–12 cm long, up to 3 cm thick, typically central, tapered down-

Ganoderma martinicense (A)

ward, appearing varnished, dark brown to blackish. FLESH up to 1 cm thick, with resinous bands, dark reddish brown; odor described as resembling brioche bread.

MICROSCOPIC FEATURES: Spores 9.5–12 × 5–7 μm, broadly almond-shaped to oblong-ovoid, with a truncate apex and germ pore, smooth but appearing roughened, pale brown; wall two-layered with interwall pillars; hyphal system trimitic, clamp connections present.

OCCURRENCE: Solitary or in groups, sometimes fused laterally, on the roots or lower trunks of broadleaf trees, including oaks and the *Albizia* silk tree; reported from the Gulf Coast states to as far north as Illinois; year-round in the South region.

EDIBILITY: Inedible.

REMARKS: Opportunistic pathogen, causing a white rot. The epithet *martinicense* refers to Martinique, where this polypore was first collected and described.

Ganoderma martinicense (B)

Ganoderma megaloma (Lév.) Bres.

= *Elfvingia megaloma* (Lév.) Murrill
= *Polyporus megaloma* Lév.

MACROSCOPIC FEATURES: FRUITBODY perennial, 5–35 cm or more wide, up to 5 cm or more thick, sessile, shelflike or rarely hoof-shaped, semicircular, thickened at the point of attachment. UPPER SURFACE covered with a thin crust, concentrically sulcate, finely cracked and roughened in age, whitish or light to medium gray, sometimes brownish when coated with spores; margin usually thick, rounded, sterile below, entire or wavy, whitish when actively growing. FERTILE SURFACE white, staining brown when bruised. PORES circular, 4–6 per mm; tubes up to 15 mm deep per layer. FLESH corky to woody, reddish brown to dark brown; odor and taste not distinctive.

MICROSCOPIC FEATURES: Spores 7–8 × 5–6 µm, ovoid, with a truncate apex and germ pore, smooth but appearing roughened, light brown; wall two-layered with interwall pillars; hyphal system trimitic, clamp connections present.

OCCURRENCE: Solitary, in groups, or in overlapping clusters on a wide variety of broadleaf trees; widely distributed in the Northeast, North Central, and South regions; year-round.

EDIBILITY: Inedible.

REMARKS: Pathogenic, causing a white rot. Various sources do not agree as to whether *Ganoderma megaloma* is a distinct species or a morphological variant of *Ganoderma applanatum*. Molecular analysis will be needed to resolve this issue. Of note, Lee Overholts, in *The Polyporaceae of the United States, Alaska, and Canada*, includes *Polyporus megaloma* as a synonym of *Fomes applanatus* = *Ganoderma applanatum*.

Ganoderma megaloma

Ganoderma parvulum Murrill

= *Fomes parvulus* (Murrill) Sacc. & D. Sacc.
= *Ganoderma stipitatum* (Murrill) Murrill
= *Ganoderma subamboinense* (Henn.) Bazzalo &
J. E. Wright ex Moncalvo & Ryvarden

MACROSCOPIC FEATURES: FRUITBODY annual, 6.5–15 cm wide, projecting 4.5–8 cm, semi-circular to fan-shaped or shell-shaped, sessile or with a stalk, corky-woody. UPPER SURFACE covered with a thin, shiny crust that appears varnished, radially wrinkled or concentrically sulcate, sometimes weakly zonate, reddish brown to violet-brown, sometimes gradually paler toward the margin with a whitish to yellowish or yellow-orange band. FERTILE SURFACE white to whitish or yellowish, grayish yellow on drying, staining dark brown when bruised. PORES mostly angular, 4–5 per mm; tubes up to 6 mm deep. STALK absent or 1.5–4.5(8) cm long and 5–30 mm thick, lateral, sometimes forming a cylindrical base when multiple fruitbodies are growing together, varnished, colored like the upper surface. FLESH 3–24 mm thick, fibrous, tough, grayish yellow to grayish orange near the upper surface, brownish below; odor not distinctive.

MICROSCOPIC FEATURES: Spores 6–9.5 × 4.8–7 µm, ovoid, with a truncate apex, yellowish, wall two-layered with interwall pillars; chlamydospores

Ganoderma parvulum (A)

sometimes present in the flesh, 7–13 × 6–12 μm, spherical to ellipsoid; hyphal system dimitic, clamp connections present.

OCCURRENCE: Solitary or sometimes growing together and forming several fused fruitbodies on Burdekin plum, *Pleiogynium timoriense*, in South Florida. It also grows on a variety of other host plants in the Neotropics; fall–winter.

EDIBILITY: Inedible.

REMARKS: Opportunistic pathogen, causing a white rot. The epithet *parvulum* means "small and pretty," a reference to the small stature of this species. *Ganoderma weberianum* (not illustrated) is thought to have a worldwide tropical distribution. It is sometimes reported from Florida and has been described as a similar taxon distinct from *Ganoderma parvulum*, but molecular analysis has demonstrated that it is a complex of species.

Ganoderma parvulum (B)

Ganoderma sessile Murrill

MACROSCOPIC FEATURES: FRUITBODY 3–25 cm wide, semicircular or fan- to kidney-shaped or irregular, usually sessile but sometimes with a rudimentary or short stalk. UPPER SURFACE roughened and uneven, often with a few zones or shallowly sulcate, covered with a thin, shiny crust and appearing varnished, glabrous, dark red to reddish brown, becoming ochraceous outward, with a broad white margin. FERTILE SURFACE white at first, becoming yellowish then dull brown in age, staining brown when bruised. PORES more or less circular, 4–6 per mm; tubes up to 2 cm deep. STALK when present, 2–6 cm long, 1–3 cm thick, lateral or subcentral, often twisted, varnished, shiny, dark reddish brown. FLESH up to 3 cm thick, leathery to corky when fresh, becoming tough and rigid when dry, often zonate when thick, typically brown but sometimes yellowish; odor and taste not distinctive.

MICROSCOPIC FEATURES: Spores 9–12 × 5.5–8 µm, ellipsoid, with a truncate apex and germ pore; wall two-layered with interwall pillars, smooth but appearing roughened, brown; hyphal system trimitic, clamp connections present.

OCCURRENCE: Solitary, in groups, or in overlapping clusters on stumps, roots, or on the ground at the base of standing broadleaf trees; widely distributed in the Northeast, North Central, and South regions; year-round.

EDIBILITY: Inedible.

REMARKS: Opportunistic pathogen, causing a white rot. The epithet *sessile* means "attached without a stalk."

Ganoderma sessile

Ganoderma tsugae Murrill

= *Fomes tsugae* (Murrill) Sacc. & D. Sacc.
= *Polyporus tsugae* (Murrill) Overh.

COMMON NAME: Hemlock Varnish Shelf
MACROSCOPIC FEATURES: FRUITBODY annual, 6–31 cm wide, fan- to kidney-shaped. UPPER SURFACE smooth or wrinkled, concentrically zoned and shallowly sulcate, covered with a thin, shiny crust and appearing varnished, glabrous, brownish red to mahogany or reddish orange, often bright orange-yellow near the margin, rarely blue to bluish green; margin bright creamy white. FERTILE SURFACE white to creamy white, becoming brown in age or when bruised. PORES circular to angular, 4–6 per mm; tubes up to 1.5 cm deep. STALK 3–15 cm long, 1–4 cm thick, typically

Ganoderma tsugae (A)

lateral, varnished, brownish red to mahogany or reddish orange. FLESH up to 5 cm thick, corky or tough, whitish; odor and taste not distinctive.

MICROSCOPIC FEATURES: Spores 13–15 × 7.5–8.5 μm, ellipsoid, with a truncate apex and germ pore; wall two-layered with interwall pillars, smooth but appearing roughened, brown; hyphal system trimitic, clamp connections present.

OCCURRENCE: Solitary or in groups on several genera of living and decaying conifer wood, especially hemlock and fir; widely distributed and fairly common in the Northeast and North Central regions, occasionally reported in the South region; year-round.

EDIBILITY: Inedible.

REMARKS: Opportunistic pathogen, causing a white rot. The epithet *tsugae* refers to hemlock, the host tree on which it grows. *Ganoderma sessile* and *Ganoderma curtisii* grow on broadleaf trees. *Ganoderma curtisii* f.sp. *meredithiae* grows exclusively on pines and has smaller spores.

Ganoderma tsugae (B)

Ganoderma tuberculosum Murrill

= *Ganoderma oerstedii* (Fr.) Torrend

MACROSCOPIC FEATURES: FRUITBODY perennial, 7–30 cm wide, up to 4 cm thick, rigid, shelf-like, semicircular to kidney-shaped, sessile. UPPER SURFACE shallowly sulcate, typically radially wrinkled, warty and deeply cracked on older specimens, often umbonate near the point of attachment, covered with a thin, shiny crust and appearing varnished, glabrous, reddish brown to chestnut-colored, becoming dull dark brown in age; margin blunt, creamy white when actively growing, becoming reddish brown at maturity. FERTILE SURFACE creamy white at first, becoming brownish in age. PORES circular, 3–4 per mm; tubes up to 3.5 cm deep. FLESH corky when young, becoming tough and woody in age, pale yellowish brown to reddish brown; odor and taste not distinctive.

MICROSCOPIC FEATURES: Spores 8 × 6 μm, ovoid, with a truncate apex and germ pore; wall two-layered with interwall pillars, smooth but appearing roughened, dark brown; hyphal system trimitic, clamp connections present.

OCCURRENCE: Solitary or in groups on decaying conifer or broadleaf trees; widely distributed in the Gulf Coast states; year-round.

EDIBILITY: Inedible.

REMARKS: Opportunistic pathogen, causing a white rot. This is a pantropical species that also occurs along the Gulf Coast states. The epithet *tuberculosum* means "roughened with wartlike projections," a reference to the cap surface.

Ganoderma tuberculosum (A)

Ganoderma tuberculosum (B)

Ganoderma zonatum Murrill

= *Fomes zonatus* (Murrill) Sacc. & D. Sacc.
= *Ganoderma sulcatum* Murrill

COMMON NAME: Palm Trunk Conk
MACROSCOPIC FEATURES: FRUITBODY annual, up to 20 cm wide, shelflike, hard and woody, sessile or with a rudimentary stalk. UPPER SURFACE distinctly zonate when mature, smooth or concentrically sulcate, covered with a thin, shiny crust and appearing varnished, glabrous, becoming dull when covered with spores or algae or in age, often variously colored with a mixture of reddish orange, wood brown to dark purplish brown or mahogany; margin thick, rounded or blunt and white when actively growing, becoming brown in age. FERTILE SURFACE white to creamy white at first, becoming purplish brown in age or when bruised. PORES circular to angular, 5–6 per mm; tubes up to 1.5 cm deep. FLESH up to 4 cm thick, dark purplish brown, concentrically zonate, soft-fibrous.

MICROSCOPIC FEATURES: Spores 11–13 × 5–6 μm, narrowly ellipsoid to cylindrical-ellipsoid, with a truncate apex and germ pore; wall two-layered with interwall pillars, smooth but appearing roughened, brown; hyphal system trimitic, clamp connections present.

OCCURRENCE: Solitary, in groups, or in overlapping clusters on the trunks of palm trees; widely distributed in the South region, especially the Gulf Coast states; year-round.

EDIBILITY: Inedible.

REMARKS: Pathogenic, causing canopy collapse, or white butt and root rot of palmettos and other palms. The epithet *zonatum* means "having distinct zones."

Ganoderma zonatum

Globifomes graveolens (Schwein.) Murrill

= *Fomes graveolens* (Schwein.) Cooke
= *Polyporus graveolens* (Schwein.) Fr.

Sweet Knot

FRUITBODY annual or sometimes perennial, up to 20 cm wide, 25 cm long, and 15 cm deep, sessile, composed of small, overlapping caps in a rounded to hoof-shaped or columnar mass. CAP 2–5 cm wide, petal-like, laterally fused, with a long overhanging margin. UPPER SURFACE radially wrinkled, dull yellow-brown with a tan margin when young, becoming dark brown to grayish black, hard and crustose in age; margin rounded, sometimes wavy. FERTILE

Globifomes graveolens (A)

SURFACE purplish gray when young, becoming dark grayish brown. PORES circular, 3–6 per mm; tubes up to 2.5 mm deep. FLESH up to 6 mm thick, tough, yellowish brown; odor sweet, resembling apples or green fodder, or not distinctive; taste not distinctive.

MICROSCOPIC FEATURES: Spores 10–14 × 3–4.5 µm, cylindrical, smooth, hyaline, inamyloid; sclerids present in the flesh, thick-walled, irregular, sometimes lobed or branched, reddish brown in KOH; hyphal system trimitic, clamp connections present.

OCCURRENCE: Solitary or in groups on broadleaf trees, especially oaks; widely distributed in the Northeast, North Central, and South regions; year-round.

EDIBILITY: Inedible.

REMARKS: Pathogenic, causing a white rot in the heartwood of living broadleaf trees. The epithet *graveolens* means "strong-smelling," a reference to the odor of the cut flesh.

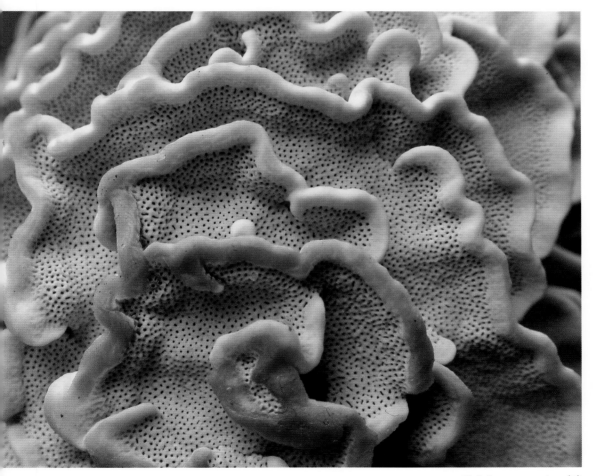

Globifomes graveolens (B)

Gloeophyllum sepiarium (Wulfen) P. Karst.

= *Daedalea sepiaria* (Wulfen) Fr.
= *Lenzites sepiaria* (Wulfen) Fr.

COMMON NAMES: Rusty-gilled Polypore, Yellow-red Gill Polypore

MACROSCOPIC FEATURES: FRUITBODY annual to perennial, 2.5–10 cm wide, semicircular to kidney-shaped, slightly convex or flat, sessile, tough. UPPER SURFACE covered with short, stiff hairs that become appressed in age, concentrically zonate and sulcate, bright yellowish red to reddish brown, becoming grayish or blackish in age; margin orange-yellow to brownish yellow or whitish, sometimes with tufts of tiny hairs. FERTILE SURFACE golden brown to rusty brown. PORES fairly thick, elongated and labyrinthine, 1–2 per mm; tubes up to 7 mm deep. FLESH up to 6 mm thick, tough, yellow-brown to rusty brown; odor and taste not distinctive.

MICROSCOPIC FEATURES: Spores 9–13 × 3–5 μm, cylindrical, smooth, hyaline, inamyloid; hymenial cystidia 25–95 × 3–7 μm, subulate to obtuse, smooth, hyaline; hyphal system trimitic, clamp connections present.

OCCURRENCE: Solitary, in groups, or in overlapping rosette-shaped clusters on decaying wood, usually conifers; widely distributed in the Northeast, North Central, and South regions; year-round.

EDIBILITY: Inedible.

REMARKS: Saprotrophic, causing a brown rot of decaying wood. The epithet *sepiarium* means "reddish brown." All parts stain black with KOH. *Gloeophyllum trabeum* has a smooth, weakly zonate to azonate, sessile fruitbody that is reddish brown to dark brown and becomes grayish in age, and its fertile surface has a combination of small pores, 2–4 per mm, and labyrinthine or lamellate pores.

Gloeophyllum sepiarium

Gloeophyllum striatum (Fr.) Murrill

= *Daedalea striata* Fr.

COMMON NAME: Zoned Gilled Polypore
MACROSCOPIC FEATURES: FRUITBODY annual, up to 8 cm wide and 5 mm thick at the base, semicircular to fan-shaped, flexible, fibrous-tough. UPPER SURFACE finely velvety at first, becoming glabrous in age, rough and uneven, conspicuously zonate, sometimes shallowly sulcate, pale yellowish brown to darker brown, paler in age or when dry; margin thin, sharp, wavy. FERTILE SURFACE brown to dark brown, becoming grayish brown in age. PORES lamellate, sometimes forking and anastomosing, or splitting and becoming teethlike in age, 0.5–1 per mm; tubes 1–5 mm deep. STALK a thickened rudimentary point of attachment, or absent. FLESH up to 1.5 mm thick, fibrous-tough, yellowish brown to dark rusty brown; odor and taste not distinctive.

MICROSCOPIC FEATURES: Spores 6–10 × 2.5–3.5 μm, oblong-ellipsoid to cylindrical, smooth, hyaline, inamyloid; hymenial cystidia 30–60 × 5–7 μm, fusoid, smooth, hyaline; hyphal system dimitic, clamp connections present.
OCCURRENCE: Solitary, scattered, or in overlapping or fused and rosette-shaped clusters on decaying broadleaf wood, more rarely on conifers, especially juniper and cypress; widely distributed in the South region and extending northward along the Atlantic Coast to Maryland; year-round.
EDIBILITY: Inedible.
REMARKS: Saprotrophic, causing a brown rot of decaying wood. The epithet *striatum* means "having stripes or zones." Addition of KOH to the flesh produces a black reaction.

Gloeophyllum striatum

Gloeophyllum trabeum (Pers.) Murrill

= *Daedalea trabea* (Pers.) Fr.

MACROSCOPIC FEATURES: FRUITBODY annual or perennial, up to 8 cm wide, sessile, semicircular to fan-shaped or elongated and laterally fused, leathery and tough. UPPER SURFACE weakly zonate, sometimes shallowly sulcate, finely velvety to appressed-tomentose at first, becoming more or less glabrous in age, sometimes slightly roughened, reddish brown to dark brown, becoming grayish in age, creamy white to yellow along the margin when actively growing; margin thin, wavy. FERTILE SURFACE ochre to yellow-brown, becoming dark brown. PORES highly variable and irregular, often partly lamellate and partly poroid, thin- or thick-walled, often 2–4 per mm; tubes up to 4 mm deep. FLESH up to 4 mm thick, reddish brown to dark brown; odor and taste not distinctive.

MICROSCOPIC FEATURES: Spores 6.5–9.5 × 3–4.5 µm, cylindrical, smooth, hyaline, inamyloid; hymenial cystidia 20–30 × 4–6 µm, fusoid to slightly clavate, hyaline; hyphal system dimitic, clamp connections present.

OCCURRENCE: Solitary, in groups, or in overlapping clusters on broadleaf trees or conifers, often elongated along cracks in wood; widely distributed in the Northeast, North Central, and South regions; year-round.

EDIBILITY: Inedible.

REMARKS: Saprotrophic, causing a brown rot of decaying wood. The epithet *trabeum* means "beam or timbers," a reference to the substrates on which it often occurs. It is one of the major causes of decay in structural timbers.

Gloeophyllum trabeum (A)

Gloeophyllum trabeum (B)

Gloeoporus dichrous (Fr.) Bres.

= *Gelatoporia dichroa* (Fr.) Ginns
= *Polyporus dichrous* Fr.
= *Vitreoporus dichrous* (Fr.) Zmitr.

COMMON NAMES: Bubble Gum Polypore, Gelatinous-pored Polypore

MACROSCOPIC FEATURES: FRUITBODY annual, composed of sessile, fused caps in rows or overlapping clusters. CAP up to 10 cm wide and 5 mm thick at the base, variable from effused-reflexed to resupinate or shelflike. UPPER SURFACE finely tomentose to nearly glabrous, somewhat zonate, white to creamy white, becoming ochraceous or grayish ochre in age; margin acute, undulating. FERTILE SURFACE orange-brown to pinkish brown or purplish brown, with a whitish margin when actively growing, gelatinous and stretchable when fresh, drying hard and resinous. PORES round to angular, 4–6 per mm; tubes up to 1 mm deep. FLESH up to 4 mm thick, soft and fibrous or cottony, white; odor and taste not distinctive.

MICROSCOPIC FEATURES: Spores 3.5–5.5 × 0.5–1.5 μm, allantoid to cylindrical, hyaline, smooth, inamyloid; hyphal system monomitic, clamp connections present.

OCCURRENCE: In overlapping fused groups on decaying broadleaf wood, sometimes on conifers, or on old, woody polypores; widely distributed in the Northeast, North Central, and South regions; spring–early winter, sometimes year-round in the South region.

EDIBILITY: Inedible.

REMARKS: Saprotrophic, causing a white rot of decaying broadleaf trees or sometimes conifers. The epithet *dichrous* means "having two colors." The fertile surface and tubes are stretchable and separable from the flesh, hence the common name.

Gloeoporus dichrous

Grifola frondosa (Dicks.) Gray

COMMON NAMES: Hen of the Woods, Maitake

MACROSCOPIC FEATURES: FRUITBODY annual, up to 60 cm wide, a dense cluster of overlapping and partially fused caps attached to branches arising from a short and thick common stalk. CAP 2–8 cm wide, fan- to petal-shaped, laterally attached. UPPER SURFACE glabrous or finely tomentose, zonate, gray to brownish gray, becoming dark brown in age; margin thin, wavy. FERTILE SURFACE white to creamy white. PORES angular, 1–3 per mm, white; tubes up to 5 mm deep. STALK 2–4.5 cm long, up to 10 cm thick, repeatedly branched, white. FLESH up to 6 mm thick, firm, white; odor and taste not distinctive.

MICROSCOPIC FEATURES: Spores 5–7 × 3.5–5 µm, oval to elliptic, smooth, hyaline; hyphal system dimitic, clamp connections present.

OCCURRENCE: Solitary or in groups on the ground at the base of broadleaf trees, especially oak; widely distributed in the Northeast, North Central, and South regions; late summer–fall.

EDIBILITY: Edible.

REMARKS: Pathogenic, causing a white rot. The epithet *frondosa* means "full of leaves," a reference to the numerous caps. *Meripilus sumstinei* has thicker, shelflike caps and a white fertile surface that stains black. The circular caps found in *Polyporus umbellatus* are attached centrally to branches of the common stalk.

Grifola frondosa

Gyrodontium sacchari (Spreng.) Hjortstam

= *Hydnum clavarioides* Berk. & M. A. Curtis

MACROSCOPIC FEATURES: FRUITBODY annual, effused-reflexed, consisting of sessile caps attached to wood; CAP up to 8 cm wide, often laterally fused and spreading up to 18 cm or more, shelflike. UPPER SURFACE woolly to slightly velvety, soft and sticky when young, whitish to orangish yellow, darkening in age. FERTILE SURFACE consisting of flattened or conical spines, 5–10 mm long, easily removed from the flesh, olive-green to yellow, becoming reddish brown from maturing spores. FLESH 3–6 mm thick, soft and spongy, white with yellowish tints; odor not distinctive.

MICROSCOPIC FEATURES: Spores 4–6 × 2.25–3.5 µm, elliptical, smooth, thick-walled, yellowish brown, dextrinoid; hyphal system monomitic, clamp connections absent.

OCCURRENCE: Solitary or in overlapping groups on decaying broadleaf wood; distributed along the Gulf Coast states; fall–early winter.

EDIBILITY: Inedible.

REMARKS: Saprotrophic on decaying broadleaf wood. It is a pantropical species and has been reported from Africa, Asia, Europe, and Mexico.

Gyrodontium sacchari

Hapalopilus croceus (Pers.) Donk

= *Aurantiporus croceus* (Pers.) Murrill

MACROSCOPIC FEATURES: FRUITBODY annual, sessile, 5–20 cm wide, convex, fan-shaped to semi-circular, thickened toward the point of attachment. UPPER SURFACE velvety, azonate, soft and watery when fresh, bright orange, becoming brownish orange and smooth or rough with tufts of agglutinated hyphae as it ages; margin thick, blunt. FERTILE SURFACE bright reddish orange, becoming brownish as it dries. PORES angular, 2–3 per mm; tubes up to 3 cm deep at the base. FLESH 1–3 cm thick, soft and watery when fresh, becoming corky and brittle, bright orange when fresh, becoming dark orange to brownish in age; odor not distinctive, taste slightly bitter.

MICROSCOPIC FEATURES: Spores 4–7 × 3–4.5 μm, broadly ellipsoid, smooth, hyaline, inamyloid; hyphal system monomitic, clamp connections present.

OCCURRENCE: Solitary or in groups on oak or chestnut; widely distributed in the Northeast, North Central, and South regions; late spring–early winter.

EDIBILITY: Inedible and possibly deadly poisonous.

REMARKS: Pathogenic, causing a white rot in heartwood. *Hapalopilus* means "having a soft, tender fruitbody." The epithet *croceus* means "saffron yellow." The upper surface of the fruitbody stains red to carmine with KOH.

Hapalopilus croceus

Hapalopilus rutilans (pers.) Murrill

= *Hapalopilus nidulans* (Fr.) P. Karst.

COMMON NAME: Tender Nesting Polypore
MACROSCOPIC FEATURES: FRUITBODY annual, sessile, 3–15.5 cm wide, convex, fan-shaped to semicircular, thickened at the point of attachment, soft and watery when fresh, becoming corky and brittle when dry. UPPER SURFACE finely tomentose at first, becoming nearly smooth in age, sometimes with one or more shallow concentric furrows, pinkish brown to reddish brown or pale brown, sometimes with ochraceous tints when dry; margin sharp, curved, concolorous. FERTILE SURFACE ochraceous to cinnamon-brown. PORES angular, 2–4 per mm; tubes up to 1 cm deep. FLESH 1–3 cm thick at the base, soft and watery when fresh, pale cinnamon; odor not distinctive, taste slightly bitter or not distinctive.

MICROSCOPIC FEATURES: Spores 3.5–5 × 2–3 μm, ellipsoid to cylindrical, hyaline, smooth, inamyloid; hyphal system monomitic, clamp connections present.
OCCURRENCE: Solitary or in groups on decaying broadleaf wood, very rarely reported on conifers; widely distributed in the Northeast and North Central regions, occasionally reported from the South region; late spring–early winter.
EDIBILITY: Deadly poisonous.
REMARKS: Saprotrophic, causing a white rot of decaying broadleaf trees. The epithet *rutilans* means "reddish or ruddy." The upper surface of the fruitbody stains bright violet to purplish with KOH. This polypore is very popular with those who dye wool because it produces a rich, dark purple color.

Hapalopilus rutilans

Heterobasidion irregulare Garbel. & Otrosina

= *Polyporus irregularis* Underw.

COMMON NAME: Conifer-base Polypore

MACROSCOPIC FEATURES: FRUITBODY perennial, sessile, 2.5–25 cm wide, variable from shelf-like to spreading in rows, semicircular to irregular, sometimes fused. UPPER SURFACE uneven and roughened with shallow furrows, indistinctly zoned, velvety or glabrous, becoming encrusted, brown, then blackish in age; margin rounded, wavy. FERTILE SURFACE ivory to pinkish cream, smooth, glancing. PORES circular to angular or irregular, 4–5 per mm; tubes up to 3 mm deep. FLESH up to 1 cm thick, corky, azonate, ivory to pinkish cinnamon; odor and taste not distinctive.

MICROSCOPIC FEATURES: Spores 4.5–6.5 × 3.5–4.5 μm, subglobose, finely warty, hyaline, with oil drops. Few, if any, spores are found in most microscopic examinations; hyphal system dimitic, clamp connections absent.

OCCURRENCE: Solitary or in groups on stumps, roots, or trunks of conifers, especially pine and hemlock, or sometimes on the ground attached to buried roots; widely distributed in the Northeast, North Central, and South regions; year-round.

EDIBILITY: Inedible.

REMARKS: Pathogenic, causing tree root rot known as *Heterobasidion* root disease. This is a major pathogen of North American conifers, especially loblolly and slash pine. Once infected, the trees are susceptible to butt rot, windthrow, decreased growth, and ultimately death. *Heterobasidion* means "having different or variable basidia." The epithet *irregulare* means "irregular," a reference to the shape of the pores. *Heterobasidion annosum* (not illustrated) is a European species that does not occur in North America.

Heterobasidion irregulare

Hexagonia cucullata (Mont.) Murrill

= *Favolus cucullatus* Mont.
= *Pseudofavolus cucullatus* (Mont.) Pat.

MACROSCOPIC FEATURES: FRUITBODY annual, consisting of a sessile cap attached to wood by a small whitish disk. CAP 2–8 cm wide, acutely convex to convex, fan- to kidney-shaped. UPPER SURFACE glabrous, smooth, azonate, whitish to ochraceous when young, soon becoming ochre and darkening in age; margin incurved, wavy, often with a dark reddish tint. FERTILE SURFACE dark ochraceous to dull reddish brown. PORES hexagonal to angular, 1–3 per mm; tubes up to 2 mm deep. FLESH up to 2 mm thick, tough, straw-colored to pale ochraceous; odor and taste not distinctive.

MICROSCOPIC FEATURES: Spores 11.5–16 × 4–6 μm, cylindrical, smooth, hyaline, inamyloid; hyphal system dimitic, clamp connections present.

OCCURRENCE: Solitary, scattered, or in overlapping groups on decaying broadleaf wood; widely distributed in the South region; year-round.

EDIBILITY: Inedible.

REMARKS: Saprotrophic, causing a white rot of decaying broadleaf trees. *Hexagonia* means "with hexagonal or six-sided pores." The epithet *cucullata* means "hooded."

Hexagonia cucullata

Hexagonia hydnoides (Sw.) M. Fidalgo

= *Cerrena hydnoides* (Sw.) Zmitr.
= *Pogonomyces hydnoides* (Sw.) Murrill
= *Trametes hydnoides* (Sw.) Fr.

COMMON NAME: Hairy Hexagonia

MACROSCOPIC FEATURES: FRUITBODY annual, sessile, 3–20 cm wide, convex to nearly flat, fan-shaped to semicircular, sometimes laterally fused, flexible when fresh, becoming rigid when dry. UPPER SURFACE covered with conspicuous erect, stiff hairs that fall off in age, zonate after the hairs fall off, not sulcate, dark brown to blackish; margin thin, acute. FERTILE SURFACE fulvous to dark brown with a distinct grayish tint when fresh, staining dark brown when bruised. PORES round to somewhat irregular, 3–5 per mm; tubes 1–8 mm deep. FLESH up to 1.5 cm thick but typically much thinner, cinnamon-brown to dark brown; odor and taste not distinctive.

MICROSCOPIC FEATURES: Spores 11–14 × 3.5–5 μm, cylindrical, smooth, hyaline, inamyloid; hyphal system trimitic, clamp connections present.

OCCURRENCE: Solitary, in groups, or in overlapping clusters on decaying broadleaf wood, especially oaks; widely distributed in the South region; year-round.

EDIBILITY: Inedible.

REMARKS: Saprotrophic, causing a white rot of decaying broadleaf trees. The epithet *hydnoides* means that it resembles species in the genus *Hydnum*, which have spines or teeth on their fertile surfaces. The taxonomic disposition of this species is uncertain at this time.

Hexagonia hydnoides

Hexagonia papyracea Berk.

= *Cerrena papyracea* (Berk.) Zmitr.

= *Hexagonia variegata* Berk.

= *Trametes variegata* (Berk.) Zmitr., Wasser & Ezhov

MACROSCOPIC FEATURES: FRUITBODY annual, sessile, 3–15 cm wide, 1–3 mm thick, semicircular to fan-shaped or kidney-shaped, leathery and flexible. UPPER SURFACE soft and velvety at first, becoming nearly glabrous in age, distinctly zonate with light to dark brown or purplish brown zones, sometimes slightly grayish green when coated with algae, often radially wrinkled when mature; margin thin, wavy. FERTILE SURFACE grayish brown when actively growing, later dark brown, purplish brown, or brown near the margin. PORES hexagonal to angular, becoming elongated to sinuous in age, 1–2 per mm; tubes up to 1 mm deep. FLESH 1–2 mm thick, dark brown; odor and taste not distinctive.

MICROSCOPIC FEATURES: Spores 9–14 × 4.5–5.5 μm, cylindrical, thin-walled, hyaline, inamyloid; hyphal system trimitic, clamp connections present.

OCCURRENCE: Solitary or in overlapping groups on stumps and logs of numerous broadleaf species, especially oak; widely distributed along the Gulf Coast states; fall–winter.

EDIBILITY: Inedible.

REMARKS: Saprotrophic on broadleaf trees, causing a white rot. The epithet *papyracea* means "resembling parchment or paper," a reference to the thin, leathery, flexible fruitbody. All parts of this polypore stain black with the application of KOH.

Hexagonia papyracea (A)

Hexagonia papyracea (B)

Hydnopolyporus palmatus (Hook.) O. Fidalgo

= *Hydnopolyporus fimbriatus* (Cooke) D. A. Reid
= *Polyporus palmatus* (Hook.) Berk
= *Polystictus fimbriatus* Cooke

MACROSCOPIC FEATURES: FRUITBODY annual, up to 20 cm wide, consisting of numerous fan-shaped to spatula-like caps with rudimentary stalks, usually forming a rosette cluster. CAP up to 2.5 cm wide, 1.5–3 mm thick, erect, flexible, fibrous or tough. UPPER SURFACE somewhat velvety, becoming glabrous in age, azonate or faintly concentrically zoned, smooth or radially striate, white to pale tan, becoming darker when dried; margin thin, wavy, entire or fimbriate to irregularly split; FERTILE SURFACE variable, from nearly smooth, warty, reticulate, with flattened teeth, to distinctly poroid; white. PORES angular to sinuous, 2–5 per mm; tubes up to 2 mm deep. STALK rudimentary on each cluster. FLESH thin, fibrous-tough, white; odor and taste not distinctive.

MICROSCOPIC FEATURES: Spores 3.5–5 × 2.5–3.5 µm, broadly ellipsoid to subglobose, smooth, hyaline, inamyloid, often with one large oil drop; hyphal system monomitic, clamp connections absent.

OCCURRENCE: In clusters or groups, sometimes solitary, on the ground arising from buried wood or on stumps of broadleaf trees; widely distributed in the South region; late spring–early winter.

EDIBILITY: Reported to be edible, but somewhat tough.

REMARKS: Saprotrophic, causing a white rot of decaying broadleaf trees. *Hydnopolyporus* means "having tubes that split and become teethlike." The epithet *palmatus* means "lobed or divided like a hand with fingers." Compare with *Podoscypha aculeata*, which has a rough and uneven fertile surface that lacks pores or flattened teeth.

Hydnopolyporus palmatus

Hydnoporia corrugata (Fr.) K. H. Larss. & Spirin

= *Hymenochaete corrugata* (Fr.) Lév.
= *Hymenochaetopsis corrugata* (Fr.) S. H. He &
  Jiao Yang

COMMON NAME: Glue Crust Fungus
MACROSCOPIC FEATURES: FRUITBODY annual or
sometimes perennial, several centimeters to deci-
meters wide, up to 0.2 mm thick, forming fully resupinate crustose patches that are tightly attached
to wood. FERTILE SURFACE hard, brittle, azonate, uneven, rough, warty, and conspicuously
cracked, with bristlelike setae visible when viewed
with a hand lens, reddish brown to grayish brown.
MICROSCOPIC FEATURES: Spores 4.5–6 × 1.8–
2.3 μm, cylindrical-elliptic, somewhat curved at the
apiculus, smooth, hyaline, inamyloid; setae 40–
70 × 6–10 μm, thick-walled, subulate, dark brown,
typically with pale and finely encrusted tips; hyphal system monomitic, clamp connections absent.
OCCURRENCE: On twigs, small branches, and
trunks of standing or fallen broadleaf trees; widely
distributed in the Northeast, North Central, and
South regions; summer–early winter.

EDIBILITY: Inedible.
REMARKS: Pathogenic, causing glue crust disease
of broadleaf twigs and branches. The epithet *corrugata* means "coarsely wrinkled or ridged." The
common name was chosen because this fungus
glues together twigs and small branches that are
in contact with each other. *Hymenochaete fuligi-
nosa* (not illustrated) is also fully resupinate and
forms crustose patches on the underside of logs
and branches of spruce and pine, usually at higher
elevations. The fertile surface is reddish brown to
dark gray-brown, slightly roughened and sometimes fissured. It has slender, subulate setae that
measure 45–80 × 6.5–8.5 μm. *Hymenochaete cinnamomea* (not illustrated) is also fully resupinate and
forms crustose patches on decaying trunks and
branches of broadleaf trees, rarely on conifers. It
has a smooth, velvety, rusty red to cinnamon-ochre
fertile surface and long, slender setae that measure 55–95 × 5–7 μm. Also compare with *Hydnoporia tabacina*, which is zonate and not conspicuously
cracked.

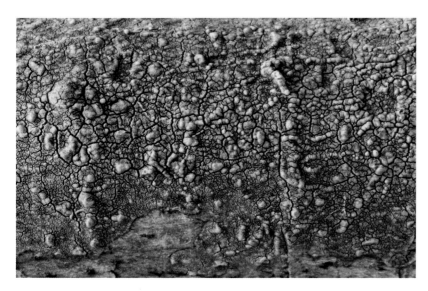

Hydnoporia corrugata

Hydnoporia olivacea (Schwein.) Teixeira

= *Hydnochaete olivacea* (Schwein.) Banker

= *Hymenochaetopsis olivacea* (Schwein.) S. H. He & Jiao Yang

= *Irpex cinnamomeus* Fr.

COMMON NAME: Brown-toothed Crust

MACROSCOPIC FEATURES: FRUITBODY annual or persisting, a resupinate crustlike mass extending up to 30 cm or more on wood. FERTILE SURFACE dry, leathery, consisting of jagged teethlike projections, flattened to cylindrical, dull yellowish brown to reddish brown, up to 2 mm long, with bristlelike setae visible when viewed with a handlens. FLESH up to 3 mm thick, leathery, brown; odor and taste not distinctive.

MICROSCOPIC FEATURES: Spores 5.5–7 × 1–1.5 μm, cylindrical to allantoid, smooth, hyaline, inamyloid; setae abundant on the fertile surface, 30–150 × 9–15 μm, subulate to ventricose, thick-walled, with a membranous sheath, dark reddish brown in KOH; hyphal system dimitic, clamp connections absent.

OCCURRENCE: On the underside of fallen broadleaf branches, especially oaks; widely distributed in the Northeast, North Central, and South regions; year-round.

EDIBILITY: Inedible.

REMARKS: Saprotrophic on decaying broadleaf wood. The epithet *olivacea* means "olive-colored."

Hydnoporia olivacea

Hydnoporia tabacina (Sowerby) Spirin, Miettinen & K. H. Larss.

= *Hymenochaete tabacina* (Sowerby) Lév.
= *Hymenochaetopsis tabacina* (Sowerby) S. H. He & Jiao Yang
= *Stereum tabacinum* (Sowerby) Fr.

COMMON NAME: Willow Glue

MACROSCOPIC FEATURES: FRUITBODY annual or sometimes perennial, a thin spreading crust with small, shelflike, semicircular to fan-shaped, sessile caps, growing on wood. CAP 1–2 cm wide, often laterally fused and extending 20–30 cm or more, projecting 6–10 mm from the substrate, leathery, flexible, able to be torn. UPPER SURFACE dry, densely matted and woolly, becoming nearly glabrous in age, concentrically zonate with bands of yellowish brown to orange-brown and dark brown; margin orange-yellow to bright golden yellow. FERTILE SURFACE smooth or uneven, often cracked when dry, dull brown, with numerous dark brown, spiny setae (use a hand lens). FLESH thin, fibrous-tough, dull brown; odor and taste not distinctive.

MICROSCOPIC FEATURES: Spores 4.5–7 × 1.5–2.5 μm, allantoid to nearly cylindrical, smooth, hyaline, inamyloid; setae 60–92(105) × 7–12 μm, subulate, thick-walled, reddish brown, sometimes finely encrusted toward the apex; hyphal system monomitic, clamp connections absent.

OCCURRENCE: In overlapping clusters on decaying broadleaf wood; widely distributed in the Northeast, North Central, and South regions; year-round.

EDIBILITY: Inedible.

REMARKS: Saprotrophic on broadleaf wood. The epithet *tabacina* means "colored like tobacco." The cap surface immediately stains black with KOH. *Hymenochaete rubiginosa* is similar but has a dark reddish brown to blackish brown upper surface with rounded concentric ridges, a paler brown margin, and smaller subulate setae that measure 40–60 × 5–7 μm. *Hydnoporia corrugata* is very similar but is resupinate and conspicuously cracked.

Hydnoporia tabacina

Hymenochaete iodina (Mont.) Baltazar & Gibertoni

= *Cyclomyces iodinus* (Mont.) Pat.
= *Cycloporellus iodinus* (Mont.) Murrill
= *Polyporus iodinus* Mont.

MACROSCOPIC FEATURES: FRUITBODY annual, sessile, 1–6 cm wide, 1–3 mm thick, often 10 cm or more when laterally fused, semicircular to fan-shaped, flexible. UPPER SURFACE finely velvety, with numerous narrow, concentric zones that are bright to dark rusty brown; margin thin, incurved, often lobed or incised. FERTILE SURFACE dark cinnamon to rusty brown. PORES angular to irregular, 3–5 per mm, typically elongating and forming sinuous, concentrically arranged ridges on mature specimens, sometimes incised or teethlike in age; tubes up to 1 mm deep. FLESH up to 1 mm thick, but usually less than 0.5 mm thick, firm, rusty brown, separated from the upper surface by a black zone; odor and taste not distinctive.

MICROSCOPIC FEATURES: Spores 3.5–4.5 × 2–2.5 μm, oblong-ellipsoid, smooth, hyaline; setae 23–60 × 4–7 μm, subulate, with a bent base, dark brown, abundant; hyphal system monomitic, clamp connections absent.

OCCURRENCE: Overlapping and laterally confluent on dead, downed broadleaf logs and trunks, especially oak; widely distributed along the Gulf Coast states from Florida to Texas; year-round.

EDIBILITY: Inedible.

REMARKS: Saprotrophic, causing a white rot of dead oaks and other broadleaf trees. The epithet *iodina* means "having the dark brown color of iodine," a reference to the fertile surface. All parts of the fruitbody stain black with KOH.

Hymenochaete iodina

Hymenochaete rubiginosa (Dicks.) Lév.

MACROSCOPIC FEATURES: FRUITBODY perennial, effused-reflexed, often fused laterally and overlapping, 1–4 cm wide, up to 1 mm thick and projecting 1–4 cm from the substrate. UPPER SURFACE uneven, with rounded concentric ridges, finely tomentose or nearly glabrous, ochre-brown to dark reddish brown or blackish brown; margin sharp, wavy, somewhat paler brown, often somewhat scalloped. FERTILE SURFACE uneven, warty or bumpy or sometimes nearly smooth, lacking pores, dark brown to grayish brown, with an orange-brown to reddish brown marginal area. FLESH thin, brown; odor and taste not distinctive. MICROSCOPIC FEATURES: Spores 4.5–6 × 2.5–3 µm, elliptical, smooth, hyaline, inamyloid; setae 40–60 × 5–7 µm, thick-walled, subulate, dark brown; hyphal system monomitic, clamp connections absent.

OCCURRENCE: Solitary or in groups on decaying broadleaf wood; widely distributed in the Northeast, North Central, and South regions; year-round.

EDIBILITY: Inedible.

REMARKS: Saprotrophic on decaying broadleaf wood. The epithet *rubiginosa* means "rusty or rust-colored." *Hydnoporia tabacina* has a densely matted and woolly upper surface that becomes nearly glabrous in age and is concentrically zonate with bands of yellowish brown to orange-brown and dark brown. It has an orange-yellow to bright golden yellow margin and larger subulate setae that measure 60–92(105) × 7–12 µm.

Hymenochaete rubiginosa

Inocutis dryophila (Berk.) Fiasson & Niemelä

= *Inonotus dryophilus* (Berk.) Murrill

MACROSCOPIC FEATURES: FRUITBODY annual, sessile, 4–22 cm wide and 2.5–12 cm thick, triangular to hoof-shaped. UPPER SURFACE tomentose to hirsute when young, becoming rough, uneven and appressed-fibrillose to nearly glabrous when mature, often zonate, not sulcate, becoming cracked; whitish to buff at first, becoming golden brown to reddish brown and finely grayish brown to blackish as it ages; margin rounded, concolorous. FERTILE SURFACE rough, buff at first, becoming dark reddish brown. PORES angular, 1–3 per mm, becoming lacerated; tubes up to 3 cm deep. FLESH up to 11 cm thick, consisting mainly of a hard, granular core, up to 8 cm thick, of inter-mixed brown and whitish hyphae with a thinner outer fibrous layer up to 3 cm thick; odor and taste not distinctive.

MICROSCOPIC FEATURES: Spores 6–8 × 4.5–6 μm, ellipsoid to ovoid, smooth, brownish, inamyloid; setae lacking; hyphal system monomitic, clamp connections absent.

OCCURRENCE: Usually solitary, sometimes in groups, on broadleaf trees, especially oaks; widely distributed in the Northeast, North Central, and South regions; year-round.

EDIBILITY: Inedible.

REMARKS: Pathogenic, causing a white rot of heartwood of oaks. The epithet *dryophila* means "oak loving."

Inocutis dryophila

Inocutis ludoviciana (Pat.) T. Wagner & M. Fisch.

= *Inonotus ludovicianus* (Pat.) Bondartsev & Singer

MACROSCOPIC FEATURES: FRUITBODY annual, sessile to substipitate, consisting of a cluster or rosette of overlapping caps, up to 50 cm wide when fully developed, attached to wood. CAP 10–30 cm wide and 1–2.5 cm thick, fan-shaped, sappy and tough when fresh, brittle when dry. UPPER SURFACE often zonate, wrinkled, warty, and radially lined, becoming appressed-tomentose toward the margin, not sulcate and not covered with a hard crust at any stage, rusty red to rusty brown; margin thin, sharp, buff to pale yellow when actively growing. FERTILE SURFACE buff, becoming cinnamon to chestnut brown, darkening in age, quickly staining dark brown when bruised, sometimes glancing. PORES angular, thin-walled and becoming lacerated, 2–3 per mm, sometimes up to 1 mm wide; tubes up to 1 cm deep. FLESH 0.5–2 cm thick, fibrous, rusty brown; odor and taste not distinctive.

MICROSCOPIC FEATURES: Spores 5–7 × 3.5–4.5 μm, ellipsoid to bean-shaped with one side flattened, smooth, rusty brown; hyphal system monomitic, clamp connections absent, setae lacking.

OCCURRENCE: Typically a cluster of overlapping caps, growing at the base of oak, sweet gum, or tupelo trees; widely distributed in the South region; late spring–fall.

EDIBILITY: Inedible.

REMARKS: Pathogenic, causing a white pocket rot in the butt and roots of living broadleaf trees. The epithet *ludoviciana* means "of Louisiana," a reference to where this polypore was collected and described. Handling the fertile surface of this polypore sometimes stains fingers dark brown. All parts stain black with KOH.

Inocutis ludoviciana

Inocutis rheades (Pers.) Fiasson & Niemelä

= *Inonotus rheades* (Pers.) Bondartsev & Singer
= *Polyporus rheades* Pers.

MACROSCOPIC FEATURES: FRUITBODY annual, effused-reflexed or resupinate, usually forming overlapping caps from the resupinate portion that are fibrous-tough and flexible when fresh and rigid when dry. CAP 5–11 cm wide, sessile, fan-shaped to semicircular or irregular, broadly convex. UPPER SURFACE coated with a dense layer of fibrils that become matted in age, azonate, pale yellow-brown at first, darkening in age, often becoming rusty brown from deposited spores; margin thin, incurved, wavy. FERTILE SURFACE pale yellowish brown when young, becoming dark reddish brown in age. PORES angular, often lacerated, 1–3 per mm; tubes up to 1 cm deep. FLESH up to 2 cm thick, shiny, bright yellow at first, becoming dark rusty brown; odor and taste not distinctive.

MICROSCOPIC FEATURES: Spores 5–6 × 3.5–4 μm, ovoid to broadly ellipsoid, often flattened on one side, smooth, pale brown; sclerids present in the flesh, highly variable, thick-walled; hyphal system dimitic, clamp connections absent.

OCCURRENCE: Solitary, in groups, or in overlapping clusters on aspen; widely distributed in the Northeast and North Central regions; late spring–early winter.

EDIBILITY: Inedible.

REMARKS: Pathogenic, causing a white rot in heartwood of living or dead aspen.

Inocutis rheades

Inocutis texana (Murrill) Seb. Martínez

= *Inonotus texanus* Murrill
= *Polyporus texanus* (Murrill) Sacc. & Trotter

MACROSCOPIC FEATURES: FRUITBODY annual, sessile, 3–8 cm wide, up to 5 cm thick, shelflike or hoof-shaped. UPPER SURFACE finely tomentose and pale yellowish brown at first, soon becoming glabrous and reddish brown, often blackish brown and cracking radially and concentrically in age; margin thick, rounded. FERTILE SURFACE yellowish brown at first, becoming dark brown or blackening in age. PORES circular to angular, 1–3 per mm; tubes up to 3.5 cm deep. FLESH up to 1 cm thick, fibrous, yellowish brown, with a granular core of intermixed white and brown tissue; odor and taste not distinctive.

MICROSCOPIC FEATURES: Spores 7–10 × 4.5–6 μm, ovoid to broadly ellipsoid, yellowish brown,

Inocutis texana (A)

smooth, inamyloid; setae absent, sclerids present in the granular core; hyphal system dimitic, clamp connections absent.

OCCURRENCE: Solitary or in groups on living mesquite and acacia; known only from Texas and Arizona; fall–winter.

EDIBILITY: Inedible.

REMARKS: Pathogenic, causing a white rot of living acacia and mesquite. The epithet *texana* means "of Texas." Compare with *Fulvifomes badius*, which has smaller, circular to angular pores, that measure 4–6 per mm. *Inocutis porrecta = Inonotus porrectus* (not illustrated), known only from the Gulf Coast states, has a fan-shaped to circular fruitbody, up to 5 cm wide and 5–15 mm thick, with a narrowed base. It has a zonate, finely tomentose, bright yellowish brown upper surface; a dull purplish brown decurrent fertile surface; circular to angular pores 5–6 per mm; and lustrous, concentrically zonate, bright golden brown flesh. Spores are 4.5–6 × 3.5–4.5 μm, broadly ellipsoid to ovoid, reddish brown, smooth; it lacks setae and grows at the base of live oaks.

Inocutis texana (B)

Inonotus amplectens Murrill

= *Polyporus amplectens* (Murrill) Sacc. & Trotter

COMMON NAME: Pawpaw Polypore

MACROSCOPIC FEATURES: FRUITBODY annual, 1–4 cm wide, 1–2.5 cm thick, hemispherical, clasping, sessile. UPPER SURFACE soft, velvety, dark yellowish orange to dark brown; margin obtuse, entire, straw-colored, becoming thin, undulating or toothed, decurved and concolorous in age. FERTILE SURFACE concave, honey yellow at first, becoming reddish brown at maturity, covered by a yellowish membrane when young. PORES nearly round, 2–4 per mm, larger when fused, splitting into irregular teethlike plates in age; tubes 2–4 mm long. FLESH soft, spongy-fibrous, rusty brown; odor and taste not distinctive.

MICROSCOPIC FEATURES: Spores 5–6.5 × 3.5–4 µm, ellipsoid, smooth, with one or two oil drops, hyaline; inamyloid; hyphal system monomitic, clamp connections absent.

OCCURRENCE: Solitary or in groups encircling living twigs of pawpaw (*Asimina* species); widely distributed in the North Central and South regions, occasionally reported from the Northeast region; year-round.

EDIBILITY: Inedible.

REMARKS: Pathogenicity status unknown. The epithet *amplectens* means "encircling," a reference to its growth habit. *Phylloporia fruticum* = *Inonotus fruticum* (not illustrated) forms fruitbodies 1–5 cm wide, semicircular to round, soft and spongy, golden yellow to rusty brown, attached to or encircling twigs or branches of various shrubs and trees, especially oleander and orange. It has a rusty brown to cinnamon brown fertile surface that becomes very dark brown in age.

Inonotus amplectens (A)

Inonotus amplectens (B)

Inonotus cuticularis (Bull.) P. Karst.

= *Inonotus perplexus* (Peck) Murrill
= *Polyporus cuticularis* (Bull.) Fr.

COMMON NAME: Clustered Bracket

MACROSCOPIC FEATURES: FRUITBODY annual, sessile, typically growing in large, overlapping clusters on wood, 4–16 cm wide, shelflike, semicircular to fan- or shell-shaped. UPPER SURFACE conspicuously woolly-tomentose or radially fibrillose, uneven and knobby or warty, weakly to distinctly zonate with rusty brown and yellowish brown zones as it matures, occasionally very shallowly sulcate, spongy, often with moisture drops when fresh, especially along the margin, becoming dark brown to blackish and sometimes finely cracked in age; margin acute, undulating, sometimes lobed, color variable, whitish to yellowish or rusty brown to dull brown. FERTILE SURFACE glancing, whitish to dull brownish yellow when very young, soon brown to dark grayish brown, often with moisture drops when fresh, especially near the margin, rapidly staining dark brown when bruised. PORES angular, 3–5 per mm; tubes 2–10 mm deep. FLESH 2–10 mm thick, fibrous-tough, bright yellowish brown to rusty brown; odor and taste not distinctive.

MICROSCOPIC FEATURES: Spores 5.5–8 × 4–5.5 µm, broadly ellipsoid to ovoid or subglobose, smooth, yellowish brown; setal hyphae conspicuous and abundant on the cap surface, thick-walled, with a highly variable, spiny branching pattern, reddish brown; setae usually not abundant, embedded and inconspicuous, 15–30 × 5–11 µm, subulate to ventricose, frequently hooked, sometimes absent; hyphal system monomitic, clamp connections absent.

OCCURRENCE: Overlapping clusters on standing, dead broadleaf trees or from wounds on living trees, especially oaks; widely distributed in the Northeast, North Central, and South regions; year-round.

EDIBILITY: Inedible.

REMARKS: Saprotrophic, causing a white rot of decaying broadleaf trees. The spore deposit is bright yellowish brown. The fresh cap surface stains purple with KOH. *Inonotus* means "ear-shaped." The epithet *cuticularis* means "pertaining to the cuticle."

Inonotus cuticularis

Inonotus glomeratus (Peck) Murrill

= *Polyporus glomeratus* Peck

MACROSCOPIC FEATURES: FRUITBODY annual, effused-reflexed or resupinate, often forming overlapping caps from the resupinate portion that may extend up to 2 meters on fallen trees. CAP up to 10 cm wide and 1.5 cm thick, sessile, fibrous-tough. UPPER SURFACE finely tomentose to glabrous, azonate, yellow-brown, often covered with a bright yellow mass of spores, sometimes forming a sterile black, cracked, and crusty conk; margin wavy, concolorous or yellow-ochre when actively growing. FERTILE SURFACE grayish brown, glancing. PORES angular, 3–5 per mm, becoming lacerated in age; tubes up to 7 mm deep. FLESH up to 1 cm thick, fibrous to corky, faintly zonate, golden brown to dark yellowish brown, shiny on cut surfaces.

MICROSCOPIC FEATURES: Spores 5–7 × 4–6 µm, broadly ellipsoid to ovoid, smooth, yellowish, inamyloid; hymenial setae 16–28 × 5–9 µm, subulate to ventricose, thick-walled, not hooked, abundant; hyphal system monomitic, clamp connections absent.

OCCURRENCE: In overlapping clusters or groups, sometimes solitary, on broadleaf trees, especially maple and beech, usually on trunks or stumps; widely distributed in the Northeast and North Central regions; fall–early spring.

EDIBILITY: Inedible.

REMARKS: Pathogenic, causing a white rot of living or dead broadleaf trees. The epithet *glomeratus* means "closely gathered together." This polypore does not fruit on living trees but often produces sterile conks. It fruits profusely on fallen trees and stumps.

Inonotus glomeratus

Inonotus hispidus (Bull.) P. Karst.

= *Polyporus hispidus* (Bull.) Fr.

COMMON NAMES: Shaggy Bracket, Shaggy Polypore

MACROSCOPIC FEATURES: FRUITBODY annual, sessile, shelflike or sometimes hoof-shaped, 10–30 cm wide, convex, semicircular to fan-shaped, soft or tough, broadly attached. UPPER SURFACE azonate, covered with stiff, bright reddish orange hairs that become reddish brown to blackish in age; margin rounded and blunt, bright sulfur yellow when young. FERTILE SURFACE uneven, yellow at first, becoming yellow-ochre then yellowish brown or blackish in age, staining darker brown when bruised. PORES angular to irregularly rounded, 1–3 per mm, sometimes exuding clear droplets when moist and fresh; tubes up to 1.5 cm deep. FLESH up to 7.5 cm thick, azonate or somewhat zonate, soft or tough, yellow to ochre near the margin and upper portion, dark rusty brown near the tubes, sometimes uniformly dark rusty brown throughout, immediately staining brownish when exposed; odor somewhat fruity and pleasant or not distinctive, taste not distinctive.

MICROSCOPIC FEATURES: Spores 8–11 × 6–8 µm, subglobose to ovoid, thick-walled, smooth, brown; setal hyphae lacking in the trama; setae sometimes present, 20–30 × 6–8 µm, dark brown; hyphal system monomitic, clamp connections absent.

OCCURRENCE: Solitary or in groups on broadleaf trees, especially oak and walnut; widely distributed in the Northeast, North Central, and South regions; summer–early winter.

EDIBILITY: Inedible.

REMARKS: Pathogenic, causing a white rot of broadleaf trees, especially oaks. The epithet *hispidus* means "having stiff hairs." The flesh of mature or older specimens is often infested with small, pinkish larvae. *Inonotus quercustris* has a tomentose to appressed-tomentose, golden yellow to orange cap that becomes rusty brown in age and has conspicuous setal hyphae in its trama.

Inonotus hispidus

Inonotus obliquus (Fr.) Pilát

= *Polyporus obliquus* Fr.

COMMON NAMES: Birch Canker, Chaga, Clinker Polypore

MACROSCOPIC FEATURES: PSEUDO-FRUITBODY perennial, sessile, 10–40 cm wide and long, a conspicuous, irregularly shaped, rough, sterile conk resembling charred wood or a cankerlike growth on living trees. OUTER PORTION black or dark brown to reddish brown, hard and brittle, deeply cracked. INNER PORTION corky, bright yellow-brown to rusty brown.

OCCURRENCE: Solitary or in groups, usually on standing birch, sometimes on other broadleaf trees including beech, elm, and hop hornbeam; widely distributed in the Northeast and North Central regions, sometimes reported from the upper South region; year-round.

EDIBILITY: Can be ground and steeped to make a refreshing hot or cold drink called Chaga tea.

REMARKS: Pathogenic, causing a white rot of heartwood of living broadleaf trees. The epithet *obliquus* means "slanting sidewise." The reproductive fruitbody is seldom observed. It develops beneath the bark, closely attached to the outer layer of wood, and eventually ruptures the bark. The fertile surface becomes dark reddish brown, and the pores are circular, 6–8 per mm. It produces broadly elliptic, smooth, hyaline to pale yellow spores that measure 8–10 × 5–7 μm. The hyphal system is monomitic and clamp connections are absent.

Inonotus obliquus (A)

Inonotus obliquus (B)

Inonotus quercustris M. Blackw. & Gilb.

MACROSCOPIC FEATURES: FRUITBODY annual, sessile, 10–20 cm wide, convex, shelflike or sometimes hoof-shaped, soft at first, becoming tough at maturity. UPPER SURFACE moist or dry, azonate, tomentose to appressed-tomentose, golden yellow to orange when young, becoming rusty brown with darker areas in age; margin rounded to acute. FERTILE SURFACE yellow to golden yellow, with a bright golden luster when viewed obliquely, becoming brownish in age, staining darker brown when bruised. PORES angular, 3–5 per mm, sometimes exuding clear droplets when moist and fresh; tubes up to 1 cm deep. FLESH moist, soft and spongy at first, becoming dry, firm and tough at maturity, dark reddish brown with faint concentric zones, immediately staining brownish when exposed; odor and taste not distinctive.

MICROSCOPIC FEATURES: Spores 7.5–10 × 5.5–8 μm, ellipsoid, thick-walled, smooth, pale yellow; setal hyphae present in trama, up to 200 μm long, 3–10 μm wide, conspicuous, thick-walled, tapered to a point, dark reddish brown; hymenial setae absent; hyphal system monomitic, clamp connections absent.

OCCURRENCE: Solitary or in overlapping clusters on oaks, especially water oak, *Quercus nigra*; widely distributed in the Northeast, North Central, and South regions; year-round.

EDIBILITY: Inedible.

REMARKS: The epithet *quercustris* means "occurring on oaks." *Inonotus hispidus* has conspicuous stiff hairs on the upper surface and lacks setal hyphae.

Inonotus quercustris

Inonotus rickii (Pat.) D. A. Reid

= *Polyporus rickii* (Pat.) Sacc. & Trotter

MACROSCOPIC FEATURES: FRUITBODY annual, up to 20 cm wide, initially a sessile, cushiony mass of soft and fleshy, moist, and velvety brown tissue that exudes clear droplets from the entire surface. Within a few weeks the cushiony mass becomes firm, shelflike to hoof-shaped, and eventually crumbly and dusty with elongated, aggregated, stringy masses of hyphae. UPPER SURFACE tomentose, azonate, golden brown at first, becoming rough and dark rusty brown in age. FERTILE SURFACE brown. PORES angular, 2–3 per mm; tubes up to 8 mm deep. FLESH up to 6 cm thick, conspicuously concentrically zonate, firm then eventually crumbling into a mass of powdery chlamydospores.

MICROSCOPIC FEATURES: Basidiospores 6–8.5 × 4.5–5.5 μm, ovoid to broadly ellipsoid, smooth, reddish brown; chlamydospores 10–30 μm wide, thick-walled, globose to ellipsoid, mostly with an elongated cylindrical appendage, smooth, dark reddish brown in KOH, abundant in the flesh; hymenial cystidia 15–20 × 4–6 μm, subulate to ventricose, thick-walled, dark brown in KOH, not hooked, frequent; hyphal system monomitic, clamp connections absent.

OCCURRENCE: Solitary or in overlapping groups on wax myrtle and oaks, occasionally on silver maple or other broadleaf trees; widely distributed in southeastern Georgia and along the Gulf Coast states; late spring–fall.

EDIBILITY: Inedible.

REMARKS: Pathogenic, causing a white rot of heartwood. This uncommon polypore is easy to recognize when it becomes crumbly and dusty with elongated, aggregated, stringy masses of hyphae.

Inonotus rickii

Irpex lacteus (Fr.) Fr.

= *Polyporus tulipiferae* (Schwein.) Overh.

COMMON NAME: Milk-white Toothed Polypore
MACROSCOPIC FEATURES: FRUITBODY annual, an effused-reflexed, spreading crust of overlapping fused caps on decaying wood. CAP 1–3 cm wide, shell-shaped to semicircular, convex to nearly flat, typically laterally fused, stiff. UPPER SURFACE dry, azonate to faintly zoned, tomentose, white to creamy white; margin acute. FERTILE SURFACE white to creamy white, poroid near the margin. PORES angular, 2–3 per mm; tubes up to 3 mm deep, tubes soon splitting and becoming jagged or teethlike; teeth up to 3 mm long. FLESH up to 1.5 mm thick, tough, white to buff.
MICROSCOPIC FEATURES: Spores 5–7 × 2–3 μm, oblong to cylindrical, straight or curved, smooth, hyaline, inamyloid; cystidia 50–110 × 5–10 μm, thick-walled, heavily encrusted apically, conspicuous, abundant; hyphal system dimitic, clamp connections absent.
OCCURRENCE: In spreading, overlapping clusters on decaying broadleaf wood, sometimes on conifers; widely distributed in the Northeast, North Central, and South regions; year-round.
EDIBILITY: Inedible.
REMARKS: Saprotrophic, causing a white rot of decaying wood. *Irpex* means "a rake with iron teeth." The epithet *lacteus* means "milk," a reference to the

Irpex lacteus

color of the fruitbody. *Xylodon paradoxus* is similar, but its fruitbody is a white to creamy white spreading crust that is flat or somewhat projecting, bracketlike, and darkens in age. It usually has small nodules on the upper surface, tiny hairs on the margin, and the creamy white fertile surface is labyrinthine with irregular and angular elongated pores that sometimes form teethlike projections. Clamp connections are present on all septa. Also compare with *Spongipellis pachyodon*, which has much larger teeth.

Ischnoderma benzoinum (Wahlenb.) P. Karst.

= *Polyporus benzoinus* (Wahlenb.) Fr.

COMMON NAMES: Benzoin Bracket, Conifer Resinous Polypore

MACROSCOPIC FEATURES: FRUITBODY annual, sessile, shelflike, often growing in overlapping clusters, 4–20 cm wide, fan-shaped to semicircular, convex to nearly flattened, fleshy and sappy when young and fresh, becoming tough or brittle in age. UPPER SURFACE concentrically and radially furrowed and wrinkled, faintly to distinctly zoned, tomentose at first, becoming glabrous in age, dark red-brown to blackish brown, paler toward the margin; margin undulating, white when actively growing, becoming ochre to brown as it matures, sometimes exuding drops of amber resinlike fluid when fresh. FERTILE SURFACE white to ochraceous, rapidly staining dark brown when bruised, becoming pale brown in age. PORES circular, 4–6 per mm; tubes 5–8 mm deep. FLESH 1–2 cm thick, soft, whitish to pale yellow in immature specimens, becoming straw-colored to ochraceous or dull yellow as it matures; odor and taste not distinctive.

MICROSCOPIC FEATURES: Spores 5–6 × 2–2.5 μm, cylindrical to allantoid, smooth, hyaline, inamyloid; hyphal system dimitic, clamp connections present.

Ischnoderma benzoinum (A)

Ischnoderma benzoinum (B)

OCCURRENCE: Solitary, in groups, or in overlapping clusters, narrowly or broadly attached to decaying conifers; widely distributed in the Northeast and North Central regions; year-round.

EDIBILITY: Edible.

REMARKS: Saprotrophic, causing a white rot of decaying wood. *Ischnoderma* means "having wrinkled skin." The epithet *benzoinum* means "exuding resinous drops." The upper surface stains black in KOH. Compare with *Ischnoderma resinosum*, which has a wider distribution, a paler upper surface, and grows on broadleaf trees. Some authors treat *Ischnoderma benzoinum* and *I. resinosum* as synonyms. Molecular analysis is needed to clarify this issue.

Ischnoderma resinosum (Schrad.) P. Karst.

= *Ischnoderma fuliginosum* (Scop.) Murrill
= *Polyporus resinosus* (Schrad.) Fr.

COMMON NAMES: Resinous Polypore, Steak of the Woods

MACROSCOPIC FEATURES: FRUITBODY annual, sessile, shelflike, often growing in overlapping clusters, 7–26 cm wide, up to 3 cm thick at the base, fan-shaped to semicircular, convex to flattened, fleshy and sappy when young and fresh, becoming tough or brittle in age. UPPER SURFACE concentrically and radially furrowed, faintly to distinctly zoned, velvety at first, covered with a thin, glossy, resinous crust on mature specimens, dull brownish orange to dark brown; margin thick, rounded, whitish to ochre, frequently exuding drops of amber, resinlike fluid when fresh. FERTILE SURFACE white, rapidly staining dark brown when bruised, becoming pale brown in age. PORES angular to circular, 4–6 per mm, sometimes up to 2 mm wide on older specimens; tubes up to 1 cm deep. FLESH up to 2.5 cm thick, soft or tough, straw-colored to dull yellow, with a darker brown zone near the tubes; odor and taste not distinctive.

MICROSCOPIC FEATURES: Spores 4.5–7 × 1.5–2.5 μm, cylindrical to allantoid, smooth, hyaline, inamyloid; hyphal system dimitic, clamp connections present.

OCCURRENCE: Solitary, in groups, or in overlapping clusters, broadly attached to decaying broadleaf trees; widely distributed in the Northeast, North Central, and South regions; year-round.

EDIBILITY: Edible.

REMARKS: Saprotrophic, causing a white rot of decaying wood. The white rot usually produces a strong anise odor. *Ischnoderma* means "having wrinkled skin." The epithet *resinosum* means "having resin," a reference to the amber, resinlike fluid. The upper surface stains black in KOH. At the end of the growing season this polypore sometimes forms a large mass with distorted, overlapping, effused-reflexed caps. Compare with *Ischnoderma benzoinum*, which has a more northern distribution, a darker upper surface, and grows on conifers. Some authors treat *Ischnoderma benzoinum* and *I. resinosum* as synonyms. Molecular analysis is needed to clarify this issue.

Ischnoderma resinosum

Jahnoporus hirtus (Cooke) Nuss

= *Albatrellus hirtus* (Cooke) Donk
= *Polyporus hirtus* Quél.
= *Scutiger hispidellus* (Peck) Murrill

COMMON NAME: Bitter Iodine Polypore
MACROSCOPIC FEATURES: FRUITBODY annual, 4–15 cm wide, 5–20 mm thick, circular or sometimes deformed, convex, solitary or several from a branching stalk base. UPPER SURFACE azonate, wrinkled or smooth, covered with short, stiff, erect hairs at first, becoming nearly glabrous in age, grayish brown to pale purplish brown; margin thin, wavy, often torn. FERTILE SURFACE white to creamy white, drying yellowish. PORES nearly round at first, becoming angular to irregular, 1–2 per mm, often lacerated and teethlike in age; tubes 2–6 mm deep. STALK up to 10 cm long, up to 4 cm thick, simple or branched, typically lateral, sometimes central, tomentose or glabrous, tan to yellowish brown or pale purplish brown. FLESH 3–20 mm thick, white; odor not distinctive, taste very bitter.
MICROSCOPIC FEATURES: Spores 12–17 × 4.5–6 μm, fusiform, smooth, hyaline, inamyloid; basidia

Jahnoporus hirtus (A)

Jahnoporus hirtus (B)

4-sterigmate, sterigmata swollen, up to 2.5 μm thick; hyphal system monomitic, clamp connections present.

OCCURRENCE: Solitary or in groups on the ground around conifer trees or stumps, attached to buried wood or on the roots of uptorn trees; Northeast and North Central regions; summer–early winter.

EDIBILITY: Inedible.

REMARKS: Saprotrophic, causing a white rot of decaying wood. The epithet *hirtus* means "rough, with stiff hairs." This is a rare polypore that is more commonly found in the western United States and Canada.

Laeticutis cristata (Schaeff.) Audet

= *Albatrellus cristatus* (Schaeff.) Kotl. & Pouzar
= *Polyporus cristatus* (Schaeff.) Fr.
= *Scutiger cristatus* (Schaeff.) Bondartsev & Singer

COMMON NAME: Crested Polypore

MACROSCOPIC FEATURES: FRUITBODY annual, consisting of a cap and stalk, growing on the ground with broadleaf trees, rarely conifers. CAP 5–20 cm wide, up to 2 cm thick, convex to slightly depressed, irregularly rounded to fan-shaped. UPPER SURFACE azonate, finely tomentose, often forming coarse scales or cracks, especially at the center, yellowish green to olive or brown; margin thin, incurved, wavy, and often lobed. FERTILE SURFACE decurrent, white to yellowish or greenish yellow. PORES circular to angular, 2–4 per mm, becoming lacerated in age; tubes up to 6 mm deep. STALK 2.5–10 cm long, 1–2.5 cm thick, central or eccentric, simple or sometimes branched, smooth, whitish to greenish or olive-brown. FLESH up to 1 cm thick, tough, whitish, staining yellowish green; odor not distinctive, taste bitter or not distinctive.

MICROSCOPIC FEATURES: Spores 5–7 × 4–5 μm, broadly elliptic to subglobose, smooth, hyaline, weakly amyloid; hyphal system monomitic, clamp connections absent.

OCCURRENCE: Solitary or in fused clusters on the ground in broadleaf or mixed woods, especially with oaks, rarely with conifers; widely distributed in the Northeast, North Central, and South regions; summer–early winter.

EDIBILITY: Inedible.

REMARKS: Mycorrhizal, not a wood-rotting fungus. The epithet *cristata* means "crested." *Scutiger pescaprae* has a woolly to scaly, reddish brown to dark brown cap with yellow flesh showing between the scales.

Laeticutis cristata

Laetiporus cincinnatus (Morgan) Burds., Banik & T. J. Volk

= *Polyporus cincinnatus* Morgan

COMMON NAME: White-pored Sulphur Shelf

MACROSCOPIC FEATURES: FRUITBODY annual, up to 55 cm wide, a large rosette of convex to nearly flat, laterally fused caps attached to a central branching stalk. CAP 3–25 cm wide, fan- to petal-shaped, soft when young, becoming tough in age. UPPER SURFACE velvety, radially wrinkled, bright orange to pinkish orange; margin blunt, wavy, sometimes lobed, white to pinkish cream. FERTILE SURFACE white to pale cream, bruising pale brown. PORES circular, 3–4 per mm; tubes up to 4 mm deep. STALK 4–9 cm long, 2–5 cm thick, whitish, sometimes poorly defined. FLESH up to 2 cm thick, fleshy to fibrous, white; odor and taste not distinctive.

MICROSCOPIC FEATURES: Spores 4.5–5.5 × 3.5–4 µm, oval to elliptic, smooth, hyaline, inamyloid; hyphal system dimitic, clamp connections absent.

OCCURRENCE: On the ground attached to roots at the base of oak trees or stumps, rarely with other broadleaf trees, sometimes on standing trees or stumps; widely distributed in the Northeast, North Central, and South regions; summer–early winter, sometimes year-round.

EDIBILITY: Edible when young and thoroughly cooked. Although this mushroom is not toxic, reports of allergic reactions are even more common for it than for *Laetiporus sulphureus*. Use caution when eating it for the first time.

REMARKS: Pathogenic, causing a brown rot. The epithet *cincinnatus* refers to Cincinnati, Ohio, which is near the location where the type specimen was collected.

Laetiporus cincinnatus

Laetiporus gilbertsonii **var.** *pallidus* Burds.

COMMON NAMES: Dixie Chick, Southern Chicken
MACROSCOPIC FEATURES: FRUITBODY a cluster
of overlapping shelflike caps growing on oak trees.
CAP up to 20 cm wide, fan- to hoof-shaped or an
irregular mass, broadly convex or somewhat flattened, fleshy and soft when young and fresh, becoming tough or brittle in age. UPPER SURFACE
glabrous, smooth, light orange to pale orange, becoming zonate, nearly white then dark brown in
age; margin thick, rounded and blunt at first, acute
in age. FERTILE SURFACE bumpy, uneven, and
orange to pale orange when young, becoming
cream to whitish then brown as it ages. PORES circular to angular, 2–4 per mm; tubes up to 6 mm
deep. STALK lateral and rudimentary, narrowed
to the point of attachment. FLESH up to 2 cm
thick, pale yellow to whitish; odor and taste not
distinctive.
MICROSCOPIC FEATURES: Spores 5–6.5 × 3.5–
4.5 µm, broadly ovoid, smooth, hyaline, inamyloid;
hyphal system dimitic, clamp connections absent.
OCCURRENCE: In overlapping clusters or sometimes solitary, on standing trunks or logs of oaks,
especially live oak, *Quercus virginiana*; widely distributed in the South region; fall–winter, sometimes year-round.
EDIBILITY: Edible. Although not toxic, this mushroom is reported to cause allergic reactions even

Laetiporus gilbertsonii var. *pallidus*

more commonly than *Laetiporus sulphureus*. Use
caution when eating it for the first time.
REMARKS: Pathogenic, causing a brown rot. The epithet *gilbertsonii* honors American mycologist Robert Lee Gilbertson (1925–2011); *pallidus* means
"pale," a reference to the pale colors of the cap and
fertile surface.

Laetiporus huroniensis Burds. & Banik

MACROSCOPIC FEATURES: FRUITBODY annual, up to 40 cm wide or more, a large, overlapping cluster of convex to nearly flat, laterally fused caps broadly attached to wood. CAP 5–25 cm wide, up to 3 cm thick, shelflike, semicircular to fan-shaped, soft when young, becoming tough in age. UPPER SURFACE somewhat velvety, dry, often wrinkled and roughened, bright to dull orange, fading to orange-yellow then whitish in age; margin blunt, wavy, often lobed, pale orange. FERTILE SURFACE decurrent, lemon yellow, becoming bright creamy yellow in age. PORES circular to angular, 2–4 per mm; tubes up to 5 mm deep. STALK lateral and rudimentary or absent. FLESH up to 3 cm thick, often thicker at the point of attachment, pale yellow; odor and taste not distinctive.

MICROSCOPIC FEATURES: Spores 5–7 × 4.2–5 μm, broadly ovoid, smooth, hyaline, inamyloid; hyphal system dimitic, clamp connections absent.

OCCURRENCE: In overlapping clusters or long rows, sometimes solitary, on the trunks of mature or overmature conifers, especially hemlock; Northeast and North Central regions; summer–early winter.

EDIBILITY: Unknown, possibly toxic.

REMARKS: Pathogenic, causing a brown cubical rot. The epithet *huroniensis* refers to the Huron Mountains in the Upper Peninsula of Michigan, where this species is commonly found. *Laetiporus sulphureus* is very similar but grows on broadleaf trees, especially oaks.

Laetiporus huroniensis

Laetiporus persicinus (Berk. & M. A. Curtis) Gilb.

= *Meripilus persicinus* (Berk. & M. A. Curtis) Ryvarden
= *Polyporus persicinus* Berk. & M. A. Curtis

MACROSCOPIC FEATURES: FRUITBODY annual, a large cap with a central stalk usually attached to the roots of oak trees. CAP 10–26 cm wide, circular to fan-shaped, soft and fleshy when young, becoming tough in age. UPPER SURFACE dry, tomentose, azonate to faintly zoned, smooth at first, becoming uneven with wartlike bumps in age, pinkish brown with a whitish to pinkish cream margin when young, becoming darker brown with a blackish brown margin in age; margin blunt, wavy, sometimes lobed. FERTILE SURFACE whitish to pinkish cream at first, becoming pale pinkish yellow then pale brown at maturity, quickly staining dark brown when bruised,

Laetiporus persicinus (A)

sometimes exuding amber droplets, decurrent at least half the length of the stalk. PORES circular, 3–4 per mm; tubes up to 8 mm deep. STALK up to 10 cm long, 3–7 cm thick, solid, central, sometimes branched, dry, pinkish brown, often binding leaves and soil at the base. FLESH up to 2 cm thick, soft, whitish; odor variously described as resembling ham or bacon, or not distinctive; taste unpleasant or not distinctive.

MICROSCOPIC FEATURES: Spores 6.5–8 × 4–5 μm, ovoid to ellipsoid, smooth, hyaline, inamyloid; hyphal system dimitic, clamp connections absent.

OCCURRENCE: Solitary, scattered, or in overlapping clusters, attached to buried or aboveground roots at or near the base of living oak or pine trees; widely distributed in the South region; year-round.

EDIBILITY: Edible. The taste is variously described as sour, like fermented ham, or delicious.

REMARKS: Pathogenic, causing a brown root and butt rot of living trees. The epithet *persicinus* means "peach," a reference to the color of the fertile surface. Molecular analysis indicates that this species does not belong in the genus *Laetiporus*. Additional research is required to resolve this issue.

Laetiporus persicinus (B)

Laetiporus sulphureus (Bull.) Murrill

= *Polyporus sulphureus* (Bull.) Fr.

COMMON NAMES: Chicken Mushroom, Chicken of the Woods, Sulphur Shelf

MACROSCOPIC FEATURES: FRUITBODY annual, up to 50 cm wide or more, a large rosette or overlapping cluster of convex to nearly flat, laterally fused caps broadly attached to wood. CAP 5–30 cm wide, shelflike, semicircular to fan-shaped, soft when young, becoming tough in age. UPPER SURFACE somewhat velvety, dry, often wrinkled and roughened, bright to dull orange, fading to orange-yellow then whitish in age; margin blunt, wavy, often lobed, pale orange. FERTILE SURFACE bright sulfur yellow. PORES angular, 3–4 per mm; tubes up to 4 mm deep. STALK lateral and rudimentary or absent. FLESH up to 2 cm thick, tender to fibrous when fresh, becoming tough and brittle in age, white; odor nutty or not distinctive, taste not distinctive.

MICROSCOPIC FEATURES: Spores 5–8 × 3.5–5 µm, oval to elliptic, smooth, hyaline, inamyloid; hyphal system dimitic, clamp connections absent.

OCCURRENCE: In overlapping clusters, rosettes, or long rows, sometimes solitary, on broadleaf trees, especially oaks; widely distributed in the Northeast, North Central, and South regions; summer–early winter, sometimes year-round.

EDIBILITY: Edible when young and thoroughly cooked. It has been reported to cause gastrointestinal upset when gathered from cherry trees, if undercooked, if too old, or when consumed with alcohol. Use caution when eating for the first time.

REMARKS: Pathogenic, causing a brown cubical rot. The epithet *sulphureus* refers to the sulfur yellow color of the fertile surface. *Laetiporus cincinnatus* forms large rosettes of bright orange to pinkish orange caps with a white to pale pinkish cream margin and a white fertile surface. It grows on the ground attached to roots at the base of oak trees or stumps, rarely on other species, from summer through early winter. Although *L. cincinnatus* is not toxic, reports of allergic reactions to it are even more common than reports on *Laetiporus sulphureus*. Use caution when eating either mushroom for the first time. Compare with *Laetiporus huroniensis* which grows on conifers.

Laetiporus sulphureus

Lentinus arcularius (Batsch) Zmitr.

= *Polyporus arcularius* (Batsch) Fr.

COMMON NAME: Spring Polypore

MACROSCOPIC FEATURES: FRUITBODY annual, consisting of a cap and prominent stalk attached to wood. CAP 1.5–7.5 cm wide, circular or nearly so, broadly convex to shallowly funnel-shaped. UPPER SURFACE dry, covered with small radiating scales, ochre-brown to dark yellow-brown; margin fringed with short hairs. FERTILE SURFACE white to cream, darkening in age. PORES angular to hexagonal and radially arranged like a honeycomb, decurrent, 1–2 per mm; tubes up to 2 mm deep. STALK up to 4 cm long, 2–5 mm thick, nearly equal or sometimes with an enlarged base, central, solid, scurfy, colored like the cap. FLESH up to 1 mm thick, tough to leathery, creamy white; odor and taste not distinctive.

MICROSCOPIC FEATURES: Spores 7–11 × 2–3 μm, cylindrical, smooth, hyaline, inamyloid; hyphal system monomitic, clamp connections present.

OCCURRENCE: In groups or clusters on fallen branches, logs, and stumps of decaying broadleaf trees; widely distributed in the Northeast, North Central, and South regions; spring–early summer.

EDIBILITY: Inedible.

REMARKS: Saprotrophic, causing a white rot of decaying broadleaf trees. The epithet *arcularius* means "having chambers or vaults," a reference to the honeycomb structure of the fertile surface. *Neofavolus alveolaris* has an orange-yellow to reddish orange cap and a short lateral stalk.

Lentinus arcularius

Lentinus brumalis (Pers.) Zmitr.

= *Polyporus brumalis* (Pers.) Fr.

COMMON NAME: Winter Polypore

MACROSCOPIC FEATURES: FRUITBODY annual, consisting of a cap and prominent stalk attached to wood. CAP 2.5–7.5 cm wide and 8 mm thick, convex to nearly flat or centrally depressed. UPPER SURFACE finely hairy to minutely scaly, sometimes obscurely zonate, yellow-brown to gray-brown or blackish; margin incurved, often crenulate and appearing finely fringed. FERTILE SURFACE decurrent, glancing, white to creamy white. PORES angular to irregular, 2–4 per mm, becoming lacerated; tubes up to 2 mm deep. STALK 1.2–5 cm long, up to 5 mm thick, central or slightly eccentric, nearly equal or enlarged at the point of attachment, smooth or finely hairy, colored like the cap or paler. FLESH up to 3 mm thick, tough, corky, white; odor and taste not distinctive.

MICROSCOPIC FEATURES: Spores 6–8 × 2–2.5 μm, cylindrical to slightly curved, smooth, hyaline, inamyloid; hyphal system monomitic, clamp connections present.

OCCURRENCE: Solitary, in groups, or in clusters on decaying broadleaf wood; widely distributed in the Northeast, North Central, and upper South regions; late winter–spring.

EDIBILITY: Inedible.

REMARKS: Saprotrophic, causing a white rot of decaying broadleaf trees. The epithet *brumalis* means "occurring in winter." *Lentinus arcularius* is similar but has a paler cap surface and larger pores that are radially aligned.

Lentinus brumalis

Lentinus crinitus (L.) Fr.

= *Panus crinitus* (L.) Singer

MACROSCOPIC FEATURES: FRUITBODY annual, consisting of a cap and prominent stalk attached to wood. CAP 2.5–7.5 cm wide, convex with a depressed center, often funnel-shaped. UPPER SURFACE dry, covered with dense, long, pale yellowish brown to dark reddish brown radiating hairs, silky and shiny at the center; margin incurved at first, becoming somewhat elevated and wavy at maturity, usually adorned with loose, projecting hairs. FERTILE SURFACE deeply decurrent, whitish to creamy white. PORES distinctly lamellate, close to crowded; edges finely serrate. STALK 2–4 cm long, 2–6 mm thick, nearly equal or tapered in either direction, solid, dry, scurfy, colored like the cap but usually paler, especially toward the apex. FLESH thin, tough and leathery, white to buff; odor and taste not distinctive.

MICROSCOPIC FEATURES: Spores 5.5–8 × 1.8–3 μm, elliptic, smooth, hyaline, inamyloid; hyphal system monomitic, clamp connections present.

OCCURRENCE: Scattered, in groups, or in clusters on decaying broadleaf wood; widely distributed in the South region; year-round.

EDIBILITY: Inedible.

REMARKS: Saprotrophic on decaying broadleaf wood. The epithet *crinitus* means "having long hairs." *Lentinus berteroi*, a tropical species found throughout Mexico, Central and South America, and along the Gulf Coast states, is very similar to *Lentinus crinitus* but has conspicuous hairs on the stalk, a darker stalk base, and a more yellow, lamellate fertile surface. It is a saprotrophic species that grows on decaying wood or tree roots. Photographs of *Lentinus berteroi* are shown on the next page.

Lentinus crinitus

Lentinus berteroi (A)

Lentinus berteroi (B)

Lentinus tigrinus (Bull.) Fr.

= *Panus tigrinus* (Bull.) Singer

COMMON NAME: Tiger Sawgill, Tiger-spot Lentinus

MACROSCOPIC FEATURES: FRUITBODY annual, consisting of a cap and prominent stalk attached to wood. CAP 2–10 cm wide, convex to broadly convex with a depressed center. UPPER SURFACE dry, covered by small brown to grayish brown scales over a whitish to yellowish ground color; margin incurved at first, often wavy or split in age. FERTILE SURFACE decurrent, whitish to buff. PORES distinctly lamellate, crowded, with a serrate margin. STALK 2–8 cm long, 4–8 mm thick, central, nearly equal, dry, with brown scales over a whitish ground color, scaly to densely hairy near the base, sometimes rooting on decaying wood. FLESH up to 3 mm thick, fibrous-tough, white; odor somewhat resinous, taste not distinctive.

MICROSCOPIC FEATURES: Spores 6.5–12 × 2.5–3.5 µm, narrowly elliptic, smooth, hyaline, inamyloid; hyphal system monomitic, clamp connections present.

OCCURRENCE: Solitary, in groups, or in clusters on decaying broadleaf wood; widely distributed in the Northeast, North Central, and South regions; spring–early winter.

EDIBILITY: Inedible.

REMARKS: Saprotrophic on decaying broadleaf wood. The epithet *tigrinus* means "spotted cat," a reference to the pattern of the cap.

Lentinus tigrinus

Lentinus tricholoma (Mont.) Zmitr.

= *Leucoporus tricholoma* (Mont.) Pat.
= *Polyporus tricholoma* Mont.

MACROSCOPIC FEATURES: FRUITBODY annual, consisting of a cap and prominent stalk attached to wood. CAP 1–4 cm wide, 0.5–2 mm thick, flat or centrally depressed. UPPER SURFACE smooth, glabrous or with scattered hairs, creamy white to pale tan or pale brown; margin with hairs up to 4 mm long that agglutinate or disappear in age. FERTILE SURFACE whitish at first, becoming ochraceous to pale brown. PORES circular to angular, 2–5(6) per mm; tubes up to 1 mm deep. STALK up to 4 cm long, 1–3 mm thick, central, nearly equal, finely scurfy, pale tan to reddish brown. FLESH up to 1 mm thick, whitish to tan; odor and taste not distinctive.

MICROSCOPIC FEATURES: Spores 6–7 × 2–3 μm, cylindrical, hyaline, inamyloid; hyphal system dimitic, clamp connections present.

OCCURRENCE: Solitary or in groups on decaying broadleaf wood; distributed along the Gulf Coast states; late spring–early winter.

EDIBILITY: Inedible.

REMARKS: Saprotrophic on broadleaf trees. The epithet *tricholoma* means "having a hairy border or margin."

Lentinus tricholoma (A)

Lentinus tricholoma (B)

Lenzites betulinus (L.) Fr.

= *Trametes betulina* (L.) Pilát

COMMON NAMES: Gilled Bracket, Multicolor Gill
Polypore

MACROSCOPIC FEATURES: FRUITBODY annual,
3–10 cm wide, sessile, kidney-shaped to semicircular, nearly flat, tough and flexible. UPPER SUR-
FACE velvety to hairy, with distinct multicolored
concentric zones of variable color, often white,
pink, gray, yellow, orange, or brown, sometimes
green when covered with algae; margin acute.
FERTILE SURFACE white to creamy white.
PORES thin, conspicuously lamellate, sometimes
forking, occasionally with elongated pores near the
margin. FLESH up to 2 mm thick, tough, white;
odor and taste not distinctive.

MICROSCOPIC FEATURES: Spores 4–6 × 2–3 µm, cylindrical to allantoid, smooth, hyaline, inamyloid;
hyphal system trimitic, clamp connections present.

OCCURRENCE: Solitary or in groups on decaying
broadleaf wood, especially birch, oak, and willow,
rarely on conifers; widely distributed in the Northeast, North Central, and South regions; summer–
early winter, sometimes year-round.

EDIBILITY: Inedible.

REMARKS: Saprotrophic, causing a white rot of decaying broadleaf trees. The epithet *betulinus* means
"associated with birch trees." It was originally described as growing on birch but is now known to
grow on many broadleaf species. *Lenzites betulina* is a variant spelling that occurs in some field
guides. *Daedaleopsis septentrionalis* also grows on
decaying birch wood, but its fruitbody has a glabrous upper surface, grayish lamellate pores, and
much larger spores that measure 7–12 × 2–3.5 µm.
Gloeophyllum species have brown lamellate pores.

Lenzites betulinus

Leptoporus mollis (Pers.) Quél.

= *Leptoporus erubescens* (Fr.) Bourdot & Galzin
= *Polyporus mollis* (Pers.) Fr.
= *Tyromyces mollis* (Pers.) Kotl. & Pouzar

COMMON NAME: Pink Sherbet Polypore

MACROSCOPIC FEATURES: FRUITBODY annual, effused-reflexed or sessile, up to 12 cm wide, rounded to semicircular or elongated, flat or slightly convex, fibrous-tough. UPPER SURFACE tomentose to nearly glabrous, wrinkled in age, azonate, white to pale pink or pale reddish purple at first, becoming darker pink then purplish brown in age; margin concolorous or creamy white. FERTILE SURFACE white to pink or pale reddish purple when young, becoming dark purplish brown in age, staining purplish brown when bruised. PORES circular to angular, 3–4 per mm; tubes up to 1 cm deep. FLESH up to 7 mm thick, soft to fibrous-tough, white to pinkish buff at first, becoming pale pinkish brown; odor and taste not distinctive.

MICROSCOPIC FEATURES: Spores 5–6 × 1.5–2 μm, allantoid, smooth, hyaline, inamyloid; hyphal system monomitic, clamp connections absent.

OCCURRENCE: Solitary, in groups, or in fused clusters, sometimes resupinate or effused-reflexed, on decaying conifer wood; widely distributed in the Northeast, North Central, and South regions; year-round.

EDIBILITY: Inedible.

REMARKS: Pathogenic, causing a brown cubical rot of conifers. *Leptoporus* means "having slender or small pores." The epithet *mollis* means "soft." The upper surface stains violet in KOH.

Leptoporus mollis

Loweomyces fractipes (Berk. & M. A. Curtis) Jülich

= *Abortiporus fractipes* (Berk. & M. A. Curtis) Gilb. & Ryvarden
= *Polyporus fractipes* Berk. & M. A. Curtis

MACROSCOPIC FEATURES: FRUITBODY annual, highly variable, consisting of a cap and stalk attached to wood. CAP 1–6 cm wide, 1–5 mm thick, semicircular to fan- or kidney-shaped, soft when fresh, brittle when dry. UPPER SURFACE white when fresh, becoming ochraceous to straw-colored in age, azonate, often somewhat wrinkled, finely tomentose to nearly glabrous, becoming conspicuously appressed-fibrous when dried. FERTILE SURFACE white to creamy white. PORES angular, 4–5 per mm, typically decurrent and sharply delimited; tubes up to 3 mm deep. STALK up to 4 cm long, sometimes rudimentary, narrowed downward, round to flattened, central or lateral. FLESH white, duplex with a hard lower layer and a looser, sometimes agglutinated or fibrous upper layer.

MICROSCOPIC FEATURES: Spores 4.5–6 × 4–5 μm, ovoid to globose, many with a single large guttule, smooth, hyaline; hyphal system monomitic, clamp connections present.

OCCURRENCE: Solitary, scattered, or in groups on various broadleaf trees, often from buried wood or roots; widely distributed in the Northeast, North Central, and South regions; summer–early winter.

EDIBILITY: Inedible.

REMARKS: Pathogenic, causing a white rot of broadleaf trees. The epithet *fractipes* means "with a broken foot," possibly a reference to the highly variable stalk.

Loweomyces fractipes

Meripilus sumstinei (Murrill) M. J. Larsen & Lombard

= *Grifola sumstinei* Murrill

COMMON NAME: Black-staining Polypore

MACROSCOPIC FEATURES: FRUITBODY annual, a large, dense cluster of overlapping, shelflike caps up to 50 cm wide, attached to a short, thick, common stalk. CAP 6–20 cm wide, fan- to spoon-shaped, fleshy-fibrous. UPPER SURFACE glabrous to slightly velvety, grayish tan to pale dull orange with black stains when young, becoming yellowish brown or grayish to blackish brown when mature, often somewhat concentrically zonate; margin thin, wavy, staining black when bruised or in age. FERTILE SURFACE white, bruising dark brown or blackish. PORES angular, 3–6 per mm; tubes up to 8 mm deep. STALK 1–3 cm long, up to 12 cm thick at the point of attachment, brownish orange to brownish. FLESH up to 1.6 cm thick, fleshy-fibrous, white; odor and taste not distinctive.

MICROSCOPIC FEATURES: Spores 6–7 × 4.5–6 μm, oval to subglobose, smooth, hyaline, inamyloid; hyphal system monomitic, clamp connections absent.

OCCURRENCE: Solitary or in groups at the base of broadleaf trees and stumps; widely distributed in the Northeast, North Central, and South regions; summer–fall.

EDIBILITY: Edible when young.

REMARKS: Pathogenic, causing a white rot of broadleaf trees. The epithet *sumstinei* honors American educator and mycologist David Ross Sumstine (1870–1965). It was previously called *Meripilus giganteus*, a species we now know only occurs in Europe. *Grifola frondosa* has gray to brownish gray caps, thinner flesh, and a white fertile surface that does not stain black.

Meripilus sumstinei

Metuloidea fragrans (A. David & Tortič) Miettinen

= *Antrodiella fragrans* (A. David & Tortič)
  A. David & Tortič
= *Trametes fragrans* A. David & Tortič

MACROSCOPIC FEATURES: FRUITBODY annual, consisting of sessile caps broadly attached to wood and usually overlapping, sometimes effused-reflexed, with a sweet odor resembling the scent of vanilla or cinnamon. CAP up to 5 cm wide and 1 cm thick at the base, tough and flexible when fresh. UPPER SURFACE finely velvety, zonate or somewhat sulcate, grayish or pale brown to cinnamon with orange tints; margin wavy or sometimes lobed, white to pale yellow. FERTILE SURFACE pale to dark brown with a shiny grayish tint. PORES round, 6–7 per mm; tubes up to 5 mm deep. FLESH up to 5 mm thick, pale orange to brown.

MICROSCOPIC FEATURES: Spores 3–4 × 2–3 μm, ovoid, smooth, hyaline, inamyloid; hyphal system trimitic, clamp connections present.

OCCURRENCE: Solitary or in overlapping groups on dead hardwoods, especially oak; widely distributed in the Northeast, North Central, and South regions; year-round.

Metuloidea fragrans (A)

Metuloidea fragrans (B)

EDIBILITY: Inedible.

REMARKS: Saprotrophic, causing a white rot. The epithet *fragrans* refers to the distinctive sweet odor. The fruitbody of *Steccherinum subrawakense* is very similar, and it has a cinnamon scent, but its fertile surface consists of short, crowded teeth. The cap of *Antrodiella canadensis* = *Antrodiella overholtsii* (not illustrated) has a velvety to tomentose upper surface, white then soon dull brown or gray, with radial lines of tufted hyphae. It occurs in the upper Northeast and upper North Central regions. The fruitbody of *Antrodiella semisupina* has a sessile cap or is sometimes effused-reflexed or rarely resupinate. The upper surface is appressed-velvety, azonate, white at first, then ochraceous to pale straw-colored. It usually grows in laterally fused, overlapping groups on dead broadleaf or conifer wood in the Northeast, North Central, and upper South regions.

Microporellus dealbatus (Berk. & M. A. Curtis) Murrill

= *Polyporus dealbatus* Berk. & M. A. Curtis

MACROSCOPIC FEATURES: FRUITBODY annual, consisting of a cap and stalk on the ground attached to buried wood. CAP 2–16 cm wide, circular to fan-shaped or kidney-shaped, tough at first, becoming hard and woody. UPPER SURFACE dry, somewhat velvety to nearly glabrous, distinctly zonate with a mixture of buff to brown, pale grayish brown, or pale smoky gray colors; margin thin, acute, whitish. FERTILE SURFACE white, becoming creamy white and finally ochraceous at maturity, sometimes wrinkled. PORES angular to irregularly rounded, minute, 6–9 per mm; tubes up to 3 mm deep. STALK 3–10 cm long, 3–12 mm thick, typically central, rarely lateral, nearly equal or tapered in either direction, often twisted, dry, rigid, colored like the cap or paler. FLESH up to 4 mm thick, tough, white; odor and taste not distinctive.

MICROSCOPIC FEATURES: Spores 4.5–6 × 3.5–4.5 μm, ellipsoid to lacrimoid, smooth, hyaline, inamyloid to weakly dextrinoid; hyphal system dimitic, clamp connections present.

OCCURRENCE: Solitary, scattered, or in groups on the ground or well-decayed stumps in broadleaf or mixed woods; widely distributed in the South region, occasionally reported from the lower Northeast and North Central regions; year-round.

EDIBILITY: Inedible.

REMARKS: *Microporellus* means "having very small pores." The epithet *dealbatus* means "off-white." *Microporellus obovatus* grows on wood, has a lateral stalk, a paler spoon-shaped cap, and slightly smaller subglobose to ellipsoid spores.

Microporellus dealbatus

Microporellus obovatus (Jungh.) Ryvarden

= *Polyporus obovatus* (Jungh.) P. Karst.

MACROSCOPIC FEATURES: FRUITBODY annual, consisting of a cap and typically lateral stalk attached to wood. CAP 2–7 cm wide, spoon- to fan-shaped, sometimes kidney-shaped to nearly circular, tough, becoming hard and brittle. UPPER SURFACE finely velvety then nearly glabrous in age, white when young, becoming creamy white to ochraceous, sometimes zonate with darker grayish or brownish zones; margin thin, acute. FERTILE SURFACE white at first, becoming creamy white to pale straw-colored. PORES angular, minute, 6–8 per mm; tubes up to 3 mm deep. STALK up to 7 cm long, 2–6 mm thick, lateral or sometimes eccentric, occasionally rudimentary, typically colored like the cap. FLESH up to 3 mm thick, tough, white; odor and taste not distinctive.

MICROSCOPIC FEATURES: Spores 3.5–5 × 2–4.5 μm, subglobose to ellipsoid, smooth, hyaline, inamyloid; hyphal system dimitic, clamp connections present.

OCCURRENCE: Solitary or in small groups or clusters attached to dead wood in broadleaf or mixed woods; widely distributed in the South region, occasionally reported from the lower Northeast and North Central regions; year-round.

EDIBILITY: Inedible.

REMARKS: Saprotrophic on decaying broadleaf wood. The epithet *obovatus* means "egg-shaped with the broad end up." *Microporellus dealbatus* has a central or rarely lateral stalk and a more concentrically zoned darker cap; it grows on the ground or on well-decayed stumps and has slightly larger ellipsoid to lacrimoid spores.

Microporellus obovatus

Mycorrhaphium adustum (Schwein.) Maas Geest.

= *Hydnum adustum* Schwein.
= *Steccherinum adustum* (Schwein.) Banker

COMMON NAME: Kidney-shaped Tooth

MACROSCOPIC FEATURES: FRUITBODY annual, 2.5–7.5 cm wide, kidney- to fan-shaped, sometimes circular, broadly convex to nearly flat. UPPER SURFACE finely roughened to somewhat velvety, whitish to tan, staining smoky gray when bruised; margin thin, wavy, weakly zonate, slowly staining black when bruised, sometimes blackish in age. FERTILE SURFACE distinctly spiny, white at first, becoming smoky gray to pinkish brown at maturity, slowly staining black when bruised; spines up to 3 mm long, somewhat flattened, typically fused and appearing forked at their tips.

STALK 2–3 cm long, 1–2 cm thick, sometimes rudimentary, lateral, somewhat velvety, whitish to dull creamy white. FLESH thin, fibrous-tough, white; odor and taste not distinctive.

MICROSCOPIC FEATURES: Spores 2.5–4 × 1–1.5 μm, cylindrical, smooth, hyaline, inamyloid; hyphal system dimitic, clamp connections present.

OCCURRENCE: Solitary, scattered, or in groups, often fused or overlapping on decaying broadleaf logs and branches, especially oak; widely distributed in the Northeast, North Central, and South regions; year-round.

EDIBILITY: Inedible.

REMARKS: Saprotrophic on decaying broadleaf wood. The epithet *adustum* means "scorched," a reference to the smoky gray colors of the fruitbody.

Mycorrhaphium adustum

Neoalbatrellus caeruleoporus (Peck) Audet

= *Albatrellus caeruleoporus* (Peck) Pouzar
= *Polyporus caeruleoporus* Peck

COMMON NAMES: Blue Albatrellus, Blue-pored Polypore

MACROSCOPIC FEATURES: FRUITBODY annual, consisting of a cap and stalk, growing on the ground with conifers. CAP 2.5–12 cm wide, convex to nearly flat, circular to kidney-shaped, sometimes depressed at the center. UPPER SURFACE smooth to slightly scurfy, becoming cracked at maturity, azonate, grayish blue to dull gray, brownish in age; margin acute or rounded, incurved and wavy. FERTILE SURFACE decurrent, blue to grayish blue. PORES angular, 2–3 per mm, becoming thin and lacerated; tubes up to 5 mm thick. STALK 2.5–7 cm long, 6–25 mm thick, central to eccentric, nearly equal or tapered downward, pitted on the upper half, smooth below, blue to grayish blue. FLESH up to 1 cm thick, firm, whitish; odor and taste not distinctive.

MICROSCOPIC FEATURES: Spores 4–6 × 3–5 µm, subglobose, smooth, hyaline, inamyloid; hyphal system monomitic, clamp connections present.

OCCURRENCE: Solitary or in groups on the ground, usually with hemlock; widely distributed but uncommon in the Northeast and North Central Regions; summer–fall.

EDIBILITY: Edible.

REMARKS: Mycorrhizal, not a wood-rotting fungus; The epithet *caeruleoporus* means "having a dark blue fertile surface." The blue color of fresh fruitbodies fades on drying and often becomes reddish orange to brownish.

Neoalbatrellus caeruleoporus

Neoantrodia serialiformis (Kout & Vlasák) Audet

= *Antrodia serialiformis* Kout & Vlasák

MACROSCOPIC FEATURES: FRUITBODY perennial, effused-reflexed with small, sessile caps in the upper part, often elongated 20 cm or more on the substrate. CAP up to 2 cm wide, very tough; margin narrow, sharp, white. UPPER SURFACE slightly tomentose to glabrous, azonate or faintly zonate, uniformly dark brown. FERTILE SURFACE white, becoming sordid brown in age. PORES round, 3–4 per mm; tubes up to 5 mm deep. FLESH up to 1 mm thick, white; odor and taste not distinctive.

MICROSCOPIC FEATURES: Spores 4.5–6 × 2–2.5 μm, ellipsoid to subfusiform, hyaline; hyphal system dimitic, clamp connections present.

OCCURRENCE: On decorticated oak trunks and logs; widely distributed in the Northeast, North Central, and South regions; fall–spring, sometimes year-round.

EDIBILITY: Inedible.

REMARKS: Saprotrophic, causing a white rot of oaks. *Neoantrodia serialis* forms a resupinate to effused-reflexed fruitbody. Its upper surface is finely tomentose to glabrous, faintly zonate, and ochraceous to pale cinnamon-brown; the fertile surface is white to buff; and the spores are larger. It usually grows on conifers, but sometimes on broadleaf trees, especially aspen, and is widely distributed in the Northeast, North Central, and higher elevations of the upper South regions.

Neoantrodia serialiformis

Neoantrodia serialis (Fr.) Audet

= *Antrodia serialis* (Fr.) Donk

COMMON NAMES: Serried Crust, Tinder Mushroom

MACROSCOPIC FEATURES: FRUITBODY annual to biennial, resupinate at first, becoming effused-reflexed, in groups or dense clusters of overlapping caps attached to wood. CAP 2–10 mm wide, knobby or rounded, sloped forward. UPPER SURFACE faintly zonate, finely tomentose at first, becoming glabrous in age, ochraceous to pale cinnamon-brown; margin rounded and curved downward, white. FERTILE SURFACE white to cork-colored or buff, becoming more sordid brown as it ages. PORES more or less rounded, thick-walled, 2–3 per mm; tubes up to 5 mm deep. FLESH 1–4 mm thick, tough, white to ochre.

MICROSCOPIC FEATURES: Spores 6.3–8(10) × 2.2–4 μm, subfusiform to cylindrical, smooth, hyaline, inamyloid; hyphal system dimitic, clamp connections present.

OCCURRENCE: In groups or dense clusters of overlapping caps on conifers or sometimes broadleaf trees, especially aspen; widely distributed in the Northeast, North Central, and higher elevations of the upper South regions; late spring–fall.

EDIBILITY: Inedible.

REMARKS: Saprotrophic, causing a brown cubical rot. The epithet *serialis* means "arranged in rows." Older fruitbodies are often attacked by insects that leave brownish granules on the upper and fertile surfaces, sometimes attached to thin, cobwebby threads. *Neoantrodia variiformis* is similar and also grows on conifers, but it has larger pores, 1–2 per mm, and somewhat larger spores that measure 8–12 × 3–4.5 μm.

Neoantrodia serialis

Neoantrodia variiformis (Peck) Audet

= *Antrodia variiformis* (Peck) Donk
= *Polyporus variiformis* Peck

MACROSCOPIC FEATURES: FRUITBODY annual, narrowly effused-reflexed, rarely resupinate, typically with several sessile caps on the upper portion. CAP up to 4 cm wide, elongated, narrow, tough and flexible when fresh, harder when dry. UPPER SURFACE finely tomentose and cinnamon-brown, in narrow, often slightly sulcate zones, becoming more grayish and glabrous with some scattered tufts of agglutinated hyphae in age. FERTILE SURFACE white or whitish, becoming pale brown in age. PORES round to angular, sometimes irregular to labyrinthine, 1–2 per mm; tubes 1–3 mm deep. FLESH less than 1 mm thick, duplex, whitish on the outer portion, gradually becoming cinnamon on the inner portion, often with a thin black zone near the substrate.

MICROSCOPIC FEATURES: Spores 8–12 × 3–4.5 μm, cylindrical, hyaline; hyphal system dimitic, clamp connections present.

OCCURRENCE: On conifer logs and trunks, also reported on birch and oak; widely distributed in the Northeast and North Central regions, rarely reported from the upper South region; summer–early spring.

EDIBILITY: Inedible.

REMARKS: Pathogenic, causing a brown rot in conifers. *Neoantrodia serialis* is similar and also grows on conifers, but it has smaller pores, 2–3 per mm, and somewhat smaller spores that measure 6.3–8(10) × 2.2–4 μm.

Neoantrodia variiformis

Neofavolus alveolaris (DC.) Sotome & T. Hatt.

= *Favolus canadensis* Klotzsch
= *Hexagonia alveolaris* (DC.) Murrill
= *Polyporus alveolaris* (DC.) Bondartsev & Singer
= *Polyporus mori* (Pollini) Fr.

COMMON NAME: Hexagonal-pored Polypore

MACROSCOPIC FEATURES: FRUITBODY annual, consisting of a cap and short stalk attached to wood. CAP 2–6.5 cm wide, convex, often centrally depressed, circular to fan- or kidney-shaped. UPPER SURFACE appressed-scaly to radially fibrillose, azonate, orange-yellow to reddish orange, fading to pale yellow or tan in age; margin inrolled when young, somewhat fringed when mature. FERTILE SURFACE decurrent, creamy white to pale yellow or tan. PORES angular to hexagonal and radially arranged, 1–2 per mm, becoming lacerated with age; tubes up to 5 mm deep. STALK up to 2 cm long but typically shorter, 3–7 mm thick, lateral or sometimes central, nearly equal, solid, whitish. FLESH tough, creamy white to buff; odor and taste not distinctive.

MICROSCOPIC FEATURES: Spores 11–14.5 × 4–5 μm, cylindrical, smooth, hyaline, inamyloid; hyphal system dimitic, clamp connections present.

OCCURRENCE: Solitary or in groups on fallen branches of broadleaf trees, especially beech and oak; widely distributed in the Northeast, North Central, and South regions; spring–late fall.

EDIBILITY: Edible but tough.

REMARKS: Saprotrophic on decaying broadleaf wood. The epithet *alveolaris* means "having small pits or hollows." *Lentinus arcularius* has a darker brownish cap and a longer stalk.

Neofavolus alveolaris

Neofavolus suavissimus (Fr.) J. S. Seelan, Justo & Hibbitt

= *Lentinus suavissimus* Fr.
= *Panus suavissimus* (Fr.) Singer

MACROSCOPIC FEATURES: FRUITBODY annual, consisting of a cap and stalk attached to wood. CAP 1–5 cm wide, fan- to kidney-shaped or nearly circular, depressed to somewhat funnel-shaped at maturity. UPPER SURFACE smooth to radially fibrillose, dry or moist, often translucent-striate when young and fresh, pale yellow to ochraceous; margin incurved at first, becoming wavy and up-turned in age. FERTILE SURFACE white to dull white. PORES deeply decurrent, distinctly lamel-late, close to crowded, edges finely serrate. STALK 1–2 cm long, 3–6 mm thick, central to eccentric or sometimes lateral, with a slightly swollen base, gla-brous except woolly near the point of attachment, concolorous with the cap or paler. FLESH tough, white to pale cream; odor sweet, aniselike; taste not distinctive.

MICROSCOPIC FEATURES: Spores 6–9 × 2–4 μm, cylindrical, smooth, hyaline, inamyloid; hyphal system dimitic, clamp connections present.

OCCURRENCE: Scattered or in groups on decay-ing wood of poplar and willow; widely distributed in the Northeast and North Central regions, occa-sionally reported from the upper South region; late spring–fall.

EDIBILITY: Inedible.

REMARKS: Saprotrophic on decaying wood. The ep-ithet *suavissimus* means "sweet or agreeable." The tough consistency of the flesh, lamellate pores with serrate edges, and aniselike odor are the distinctive features. *Lenzites betulinus* is somewhat similar, but it has an odorless, zonate, sessile fruitbody.

Neofavolus suavissimus

Neolentinus lepideus (Fr.) Redhead & Ginns

= *Lentinus lepideus* (Fr.) Fr.

COMMON NAMES: Scaly Lentinus, Train Wrecker
MACROSCOPIC FEATURES: FRUITBODY annual, with a cap and prominent stalk attached to wood. CAP 5–20 cm wide, circular, convex to nearly flat or slightly depressed. UPPER SURFACE slightly viscid or dry, with conspicuous brownish scales over a whitish to yellowish ground color. FERTILE SURFACE distinctly lamellate, decurrent, broad, subdistant, serrated in age, white to yellowish; partial veil present on immature specimens, leaving a scaly or membranous ring on the stalk that usually disappears. STALK 4–12 cm long, 1–3 cm thick, central to eccentric, dry, whitish with brownish scales or hairs. FLESH thick, tough, white, slowly becoming yellowish in age; odor variously reported as fragrant, pungent, disagreeable, or not distinctive; taste not distinctive.
MICROSCOPIC FEATURES: Spores 9–12 × 4–5 μm, cylindrical, smooth, hyaline, inamyloid; hyphal system monomitic, clamp connections present.
OCCURRENCE: Solitary or in groups or clusters on decaying conifer wood, fence posts, and railroad ties, rarely on broadleaf trees; widely distributed in the Northeast, North Central, and South regions; late spring–early winter.
EDIBILITY: Edible when young and tender.
REMARKS: Saprotrophic on decaying wood. The epithet *lepideus* means "scaly."

Neolentinus lepideus

Nigroporus vinosus (Berk.) Murrill

= *Polyporus vinosus* Berk.

COMMON NAME: Dark Violet Polypore
MACROSCOPIC FEATURES: FRUITBODY annual, sessile, shelflike, 2–12 cm wide, up to 1 cm thick, semicircular to fan- or kidney-shaped, tough or leathery, becoming brittle as it dries. UPPER SURFACE velvety to nearly glabrous, typically zonate and shallowly sulcate, violet to vinaceous brown at first, becoming purplish brown to dark violet at maturity; margin sharp, whitish when actively growing. FERTILE SURFACE purplish brown to dark violet. PORES irregularly rounded, 7–8 per mm; tubes up to 4 mm deep. FLESH up to 6 mm thick, vinaceous brown or paler; odor and taste not distinctive.
MICROSCOPIC FEATURES: Spores 3.5–4.5 × 1–1.5 μm, allantoid to cylindrical, smooth, hyaline, inamyloid; hyphal system dimitic, clamp connections present.
OCCURRENCE: Solitary, in groups, or in overlapping clusters on broadleaf trees or sometimes conifers; widely distributed in the South region, occasionally reported in the lower Northeast and North Central regions; late spring–early winter.
EDIBILITY: Inedible.
REMARKS: Saprotrophic on decaying wood. *Nigroporus* means "having a dark fertile surface." The epithet *vinosus* means "wine-red." *Nigrofomes melanoporus* (not illustrated), known only from the Gulf Coast states, has a very hard, shelflike, semicircular fruitbody up to 20 cm wide and 5 cm thick. It has a finely velvety or glabrous, dull, encrusted, sulcate, warty and slightly cracked, dark brown upper surface that becomes purplish black in age. The fertile surface is dark brown to purplish black, with very small circular pores, 6–9 per mm, and hard, dark chestnut to purplish black flesh up to 1 cm thick. Its spores are broadly ellipsoid, hyaline, and inamyloid, measuring 4–5 × 3–3.5 μm. It lacks clamp connections, and it grows on decaying broadleaf wood.

Nigroporus vinosus

Niveoporofomes spraguei (Berk. & M. A. Curtis) B. K. Cui, M. L. Han & Y. C. Dai

= *Fomitopsis spraguei* (Berk. & M. A. Curtis) Gilb. & Ryvarden

= *Polyporus spraguei* Berk. & M. A. Curtis

COMMON NAMES: Sprague's Plague, Sprague's Polypore

MACROSCOPIC FEATURES: FRUITBODY annual, sessile, shelflike, firm and tough, 5–12 cm wide, up to 5 cm thick, semicircular to fan-shaped or irregular and spreading. UPPER SURFACE azonate, appressed-strigose to tomentose, becoming nearly glabrous in age, smooth or roughened, white to ivory or pale ochraceous, developing greenish blue to grayish blue stains, especially along the margin, as it ages; margin rounded or acute. FERTILE SURFACE white to buff or pale brown. PORES circular to angular, 3–6 per mm; tubes up to 6 mm deep. FLESH up to 4 cm thick, corky or tough, white to pale ochraceous; odor not distinctive, taste variously described as slightly acidic, bitter, or not distinctive.

MICROSCOPIC FEATURES: Spores 5.5–7 × 4–5 μm, ovoid to broadly ellipsoid, smooth, hyaline, inamyloid; hyphal system trimitic, clamp connections present.

OCCURRENCE: Solitary or in groups on decaying broadleaf wood; widely distributed in the Northeast, North Central, and South regions; late spring–early winter.

EDIBILITY: Inedible.

REMARKS: Pathogenic, causing a brown rot of broadleaf trees. The epithet *spraguei* honors C. J. Sprague, who collected it as an undescribed species. The fruitbody of *Postia livens* also often stains blue, but it is smaller and has a softer, spongy texture.

Niveoporofomes spraguei

Onnia circinata (Fr.) P. Karst.

= *Inonotus circinatus* (Fr.) Teng

MACROSCOPIC FEATURES: FRUITBODY annual, up to 20 cm wide and 2 cm thick, usually sessile, semicircular to fan-shaped or nearly circular. UPPER SURFACE tomentose or glabrous, light buff to tan or reddish brown, azonate or faintly zonate; margin blunt, wavy, sometimes lobed. FERTILE SURFACE buff to yellowish brown, becoming darker brown when bruised or in age. PORES angular, 3–4 per mm; tubes up to 1 cm deep. STALK, when present, variable, rudimentary, often lateral, sometimes central, tomentose, ochraceous to dark rusty brown. FLESH up to 1 cm thick, spongy or firm and corky, brown.

MICROSCOPIC FEATURES: Spores 5–7 × 3–4 µm, ellipsoid to ovoid, smooth, hyaline, inamyloid; setae 50–80 × 12–20 µm, subulate, mostly hooked, scattered, frequent; hyphal system monomitic, clamp connections absent.

OCCURRENCE: Solitary or sometimes in groups on conifer trunks or stumps, especially pines, sometimes on the ground at the base of trees; widely distributed in the Northeast, North Central, and South regions; year-round.

EDIBILITY: Inedible.

REMARKS: Pathogenic, causing a white pocket rot of heartwood in the roots and butt of living conifers. The epithet *circinata* means "curled inward or hooked," a reference to the setae. *Onnia tomentosa* is very similar, except its fruitbody is slightly thinner and it has straight setae.

Onnia circinata

Onnia tomentosa (Fr.) P. Karst.

= *Inonotus tomentosus* (Fr.) Teng
= *Polyporus tomentosus* Fr.

COMMON NAME: Woolly Velvet Polypore
MACROSCOPIC FEATURES: FRUITBODY annual, a circular to fan-shaped or irregular cap with a short stalk, usually growing on the ground. CAP 4–17 cm wide, up to 1 cm thick, sometimes lobed or fused, tough. UPPER SURFACE dry, velvety or tomentose, wrinkled and uneven or sometimes smooth, azonate or faintly zonate, tan to ochraceous or rusty brown; margin blunt, wavy to irregular when mature, usually paler than the disk. FERTILE SURFACE buff at first, soon becoming grayish brown to dark brown. PORES angular, 2–4 per mm; tubes up to 4 mm deep. STALK 2–5 cm long, 6–20 mm thick, sometimes rudimentary, central to lateral, velvety, ochraceous to dark rusty brown. FLESH up to 6 mm thick, tough, yellowish brown to rusty brown.

MICROSCOPIC FEATURES: Spores 5–6 × 3–4 μm, elliptic, smooth, yellowish; setae abundant, 50–140 × 7–11 μm, subulate to ventricose, thick-walled, straight; hyphal system monomitic, clamp connections absent.
OCCURRENCE: Solitary, in groups, or in fused clusters on the ground, duff, roots or decaying wood of conifers; widely distributed in the Northeast, North Central, and South regions; summer–early winter.
EDIBILITY: Inedible.
REMARKS: Pathogenic, causing a white rot. The epithet *tomentosa* means "covered with matted short hairs." The flesh stains black in KOH. *Onnia circinata* is very similar, except its fruitbody is slightly thicker and it has hooked setae. *Phaeolus schweinitzii* is similar but it has a larger, dull orange to ochre or rusty brown cap, up to 26 cm wide, and a yellowish to greenish yellow fertile surface that stains darker brown when bruised or in age.

Onnia tomentosa

Osmoporus mexicanus (Mont.) Y. C. Dai & S. H. He

= *Gloeophyllum mexicanum* (Mont.) Ryvarden
= *Gloeophyllum protractum* (Fr.) Imazeki
= *Lenzites mexicana* Mont.

MACROSCOPIC FEATURES: FRUITBODY annual or perennial, 3–10 cm wide, sessile, fan-shaped, often laterally fused and elongated along the substrate, broadly attached, tough to woody. UPPER SURFACE finely tomentose when young, especially along the margin, soon becoming glabrous and roughened, often shallowly furrowed, grayish at first, developing concentric zones of dull brown to rusty brown, gray or blackish; margin thin, acute, often undulating. FERTILE SURFACE ochraceous to reddish brown. PORES distinctly lamellate and labyrinthine, fairly thick-walled and sometimes forked, occasionally rounded near the margin, 0.5–1.2 per mm, up to 1 cm deep. FLESH 2–6 mm thick, leathery, tough, yellow-brown to pale rusty brown; odor and taste not distinctive.

MICROSCOPIC FEATURES: Spores 9–12.5 × 3.5–4 µm, cylindrical, slightly curved, smooth, hyaline, inamyloid; hymenial cystidia 20–60 × 3.5–6 µm, subulate to obtuse, hyaline to pale brown, walls thicker toward the base; hyphal system trimitic, clamp connections present.

OCCURRENCE: Solitary, in groups, or in overlapping clusters on decaying conifer wood, especially pines, often on processed timbers including posts, poles, and railway ties; widely distributed in the Northeast, North Central, and South regions; year-round.

EDIBILITY: Inedible.

REMARKS: Saprotrophic, causing a brown rot of decaying conifers. The epithet *mexicanus* refers to Mexico, where this polypore was first collected and described.

Osmoporus mexicanus

Osteina obducta (Berk.) Donk

= *Oligoporus obductus* (Berk.) Gilb. & Ryvarden
= *Polyporus obductus* Berk.

MACROSCOPIC FEATURES: FRUITBODY annual, tough, up to 13 cm wide and 2 cm deep, semicircular to fan-shaped. UPPER SURFACE azonate, glabrous, smooth or wrinkled, sometimes cracked in age, white to buff, grayish or dark grayish brown; margin concolorous, often wavy or split. FERTILE SURFACE white to yellowish. PORES angular, 3–5 per mm; tubes up to 3 mm deep. STALK up to 5 cm long and 3 cm thick, usually lateral with a narrowed base, whitish to grayish or pale gray-ish brown. FLESH up to 2.5 cm thick, tough, brittle when dry, white; odor and taste not distinctive.

MICROSCOPIC FEATURES: Spores 5–6.5 × 2–2.5 μm, cylindrical, smooth, hyaline, inamyloid; hyphal system monomitic, clamp connections present.

OCCURRENCE: Solitary or in overlapping clusters on decaying conifer wood, rarely on broadleaf trees; uncommon, widely distributed in the Northeast and North Central regions; summer–fall.

EDIBILITY: Inedible.

REMARKS: Saprotrophic on decaying conifers. The epithet *obducta* means "covered over or overspread."

Osteina obducta

Oxyporus populinus (Schumach.) Donk

= *Polyporus populinus* (Schumach.) Fr.
= *Rigidoporus populinus* (Schumach.) Pouzar

COMMON NAME: Mossy Maple Polypore
MACROSCOPIC FEATURES: FRUITBODY perennial, sessile, shelflike, 3–20 cm wide, fan- to kidney-shaped, convex, often overlapping and laterally fused, fibrous-tough. UPPER SURFACE tomentose, becoming nearly glabrous in age, white to creamy white or buff, darkening in age, often covered with mosses near the base or nearly overall on mature specimens; margin sharp or rounded. FERTILE SURFACE white to creamy white or buff. PORES circular to angular, 4–7 per mm; tubes up to 5 mm deep per layer, stratified and separated by thin layers of flesh on mature specimens. FLESH up to 2 cm thick, corky to fibrous-tough, white to buff; odor not distinctive, taste acidic or not distinctive.

MICROSCOPIC FEATURES: Spores 3.5–4.5 × 2.5–4 μm, subglobose, smooth, hyaline, inamyloid; hyphal system monomitic, clamp connections absent.

OCCURRENCE: Solitary, in groups, or in overlapping clusters on standing broadleaf trees, especially maple; widely distributed in the Northeast, North Central, and South regions; year-round.

EDIBILITY: Inedible.

REMARKS: Pathogenic, causing a white rot of broadleaf trees. *Oxyporus* means "acidic-tasting pores." The epithet *populinus* means "on poplar trees," somewhat of a misnomer since this fungus typically occurs on maple.

Oxyporus populinus

Panellus pusillus (Pers. ex Lév.) Burds. & O. K. Mill.

= *Dictyopanus pusillus* (Pers. ex Lév.) Singer
= *Gloeoporus pusillus* Pers. ex Lév.

MACROSCOPIC FEATURES: FRUITBODY annual, a small cap with an eccentric to lateral stalk attached to decaying broadleaf wood. CAP 3–16 mm wide, convex, semicircular to kidney- or fan-shaped. UPPER SURFACE moist or dry, glabrous or finely pubescent, smooth or finely wrinkled, sometimes with one or two very shallow concentric furrows, white to whitish when young, soon becoming pinkish buff to pale salmon; margin incurved, sometimes sulcate or splitting. FERTILE SURFACE whitish to pale pinkish buff. PORES angular, somewhat radially aligned, 2–5 per mm; tubes up to 1 mm deep. STALK up to 6 mm long, 1–2 mm thick, enlarged downward or nearly equal, finely pubescent, colored like the cap. FLESH up to 2 mm thick, firm, white; odor and taste not distinctive.

MICROSCOPIC FEATURES: Spores 4.5–6 × 2–3 µm, oblong to ellipsoid, smooth, hyaline, amyloid; hyphal system monomitic, clamp connections present.

OCCURRENCE: In dense groups and overlapping clusters on decaying broadleaf branches, logs, stumps, and trunks; widely distributed in the Northeast, North Central, and South regions; summer–fall, year-round in the lower South region.

EDIBILITY: Unknown.

REMARKS: Saprotrophic on decaying broadleaf wood. The epithet *pusillus* means "very small." This fungus is bioluminescent.

Panellus pusillus

Panus conchatus (Bull.) Fr.

= *Lentinus torulosus* (Pers.) Lloyd

COMMON NAMES: Lilac Oysterling, Smooth Panus, Twisted Lentinus

MACROSCOPIC FEATURES: FRUITBODY annual, consisting of a cap and prominent stalk attached to wood. CAP 2.5–13 cm wide, circular to fan- or shell-shaped, convex when young, becoming broadly convex, sometimes depressed at the center or broadly funnel-shaped. UPPER SURFACE dry, glabrous, smooth, violet to purplish at first, soon fading to pale yellowish brown or tan, sometimes cracking and forming tiny scales in age; margin uplifted and wavy or lobed in age. FERTILE SURFACE distinctly lamellate, decurrent, longitudinally striate well down on the stalk, close to crowded, purplish, fading to buff or tan. STALK 1–4 cm long, 5–25 mm thick, central to eccentric, dry, velvety to fuzzy at least when young, violet at first, fading to buff or tan. FLESH tough, white; odor and taste not distinctive.

MICROSCOPIC FEATURES: 5–6.5 × 2.5–3.5 μm, elliptic to cylindrical, smooth, hyaline, inamyloid; hyphal system monomitic, clamp connections present.

OCCURRENCE: Solitary, in groups, or in clusters on decaying broadleaf logs and stumps; widely distributed in the Northeast, North Central, and South regions; spring–late fall.

EDIBILITY: Edible but tough.

REMARKS: Saprotrophic on decaying broadleaf wood. The epithet *conchatus* means "shell-shaped." It is sometimes difficult to identify once the distinctive purplish colors have faded.

Panus conchatus

Panus lecomtei (Fr.) Corner

= *Lentinus strigosus* Fr.
= *Panus neostrigosus* Drechsler-Santos &
  Wartchow

COMMON NAMES: Hairy Panus, Ruddy Panus
MACROSCOPIC FEATURES: FRUITBODY annual, consisting of a cap and short stalk attached to wood. CAP 2–7.5 cm wide, semicircular to fan-shaped or broadly funnel-shaped. UPPER SURFACE dry, densely hairy, purplish when young, becoming pinkish tan to reddish brown especially over the disk; margin inrolled to incurved, often lobed. FERTILE SURFACE distinctly lamellate, decurrent, close, narrow, white to tan. STALK 1–4 cm long, sometimes rudimentary, ec-centric to lateral, dry, solid, densely hairy, colored like the fertile surface. FLESH thin, tough, white; odor not distinctive, taste slightly bitter or not distinctive.
MICROSCOPIC FEATURES: Spores 4.5–7 × 2.5–4 µm, elliptic, smooth, hyaline, inamyloid; hyphal system monomitic, clamp connections present.
OCCURRENCE: Solitary, in groups, or in clusters on broadleaf logs and stumps; widely distributed in the Northeast, North Central, and South regions; spring–late fall.
EDIBILITY: Edible but typically tough and bitter.
REMARKS: Saprotrophic on decaying broadleaf wood. Compare with *Panus conchatus*, which has a smooth, cracked, or scaly, but not hairy, cap.

Panus lecomtei

Panus tephroleucus (Mont.) T. W. May & A. E. Wood

= *Lentinus siparius* Berk. & M. A. Curtis
= *Lentinus tephroleucus* Mont.
= *Panus siparius* (Berk. & M. A. Curtis) Singer

MACROSCOPIC FEATURES: FRUITBODY annual, consisting of a cap and stalk attached to sclerotium and buried wood. CAP 1–4 cm wide, convex, deeply depressed to funnel-shaped. UPPER SURFACE dry, covered with short, erect bundles of hairs that become somewhat scalelike toward the margin, dark purple at first, fading and becoming reddish brown to grayish brown, often radially striate; margin inrolled on young specimens, becoming nearly plane at maturity. FERTILE SURFACE deeply decurrent, creamy white. PORES distinctly lamellate, close to crowded, narrow; edges entire. STALK 2–10 cm long, 1.5–12 mm thick, nearly equal or enlarged at either end, central or eccentric, dry, solid, uniformly velvety to distinctly hairy, colored like the cap. FLESH up to 1.5 mm thick, leathery, creamy white; odor and taste not distinctive.

MICROSCOPIC FEATURES: Spores 6–8 × 2.5–4 μm, oblong-cylindrical to lacrimoid, smooth, hyaline, inamyloid; hyphal system monomitic, clamp connections present.

OCCURRENCE: Solitary, scattered, or in groups on the ground arising from a sclerotium and buried wood in oak and pine woods, often partially buried in sand; widely distributed along the Gulf Coast from Florida to Texas; spring–fall.

EDIBILITY: Inedible.

REMARKS: Saprotrophic on decaying wood.

Panus tephroleucus

Pappia fissilis (Berk. & M. A. Curtis) Zmitr.

= *Aurantiporus fissilis* (Berk. & M. A. Curtis) H. Jahn ex Ryvarden
= *Polyporus fissilis* Berk. & M. A. Curtis
= *Tyromyces fissilis* (Berk. & M. A. Curtis) Donk

MACROSCOPIC FEATURES: FRUITBODY annual, sessile, broadly attached to wood, up to 20 cm wide, 4–13 cm thick at the base, shelflike to hoof-shaped, sappy to waxy and tough when fresh. UPPER SURFACE tomentose to pubescent, typically rough and tufted, uneven and undulating, white at first, becoming creamy white to ochraceous, sometimes with a pinkish tinge; margin variable, thick or thin, rounded or sharp. FERTILE SURFACE white at first, becoming creamy white, sometimes with a pinkish tint, often splitting when mature. PORES round to angular, 2–3 per mm; tubes up to 2.5 cm deep, pale brown. FLESH up to 5 cm thick, thicker at the base, white to creamy white or with a pinkish tint, often with fine radial zones, sometimes staining yellow when cut, then slowly fading to brownish; odor slightly sweet or not distinctive, taste not distinctive.

MICROSCOPIC FEATURES: Basidiospores 4–6 × 3–4 µm, ellipsoid to subglobose, smooth, hyaline, inamyloid; chlamydospores present in the flesh, 4–10 µm, globose, slightly thick-walled, smooth, inamyloid; hyphal system monomitic, clamp connections present.

OCCURRENCE: Solitary or in overlapping clusters along a common base, usually on living broadleaf trees, especially oak, not known to occur on locust trees; widely distributed in the Northeast, North Central, and South regions; late spring–fall, year-round in the South region.

EDIBILITY: Inedible.

REMARKS: Pathogenic, causing a white rot of broadleaf trees. The epithet *fissilis* means "tending to split." *Tyromyces humeanus* (not illustrated) has a white to pale gray cap that is soft and sappy, velvety to glabrous, up to 10 cm wide, becoming ochraceous to pale yellowish brown in age, with a strong odor of anise. The white fertile surface stains beige to pale brown when bruised, with 2–4 angular to slightly irregular pores per mm. It grows on broadleaf trees and has been reported only from Florida. *Vanderbylia robiniophila* is similar but usually grows on black locust and has larger spores. *Loweomyces subgiganteus* = *Tyromyces subgiganteus* (not illustrated) has a sessile fruitbody, up to 6 cm wide and 8 mm thick, that is shelflike or semicircular to fan-shaped and sappy when fresh. The upper surface is azonate, white to creamy white, and velvety when young, becoming appressed-velvety as it ages. The fertile surface is white to pale straw-colored, with pores round to irregular, 3–5 per mm, and the white flesh is up to 5 mm deep. Spores are subglobose, thin-walled, smooth, hyaline, inamyloid, measuring 5–5.5 × 4–4.5 µm. It grows on living or dead broadleaf trees in the Northeast, North Central, and upper South regions. All of these similar species lack chlamydospores in their flesh.

Pappia fissilis

Perenniporia fraxinophila (Peck) Ryvarden

= *Fomes fraxinophilus* (Peck) Sacc.
= *Polyporus fraxinophilus* Peck

COMMON NAME: Ash Tree Polypore
MACROSCOPIC FEATURES: FRUITBODY perennial, up to 9 cm wide and 7 cm thick, sessile, hoof-shaped or sometimes effused-reflexed, hard and woody. UPPER SURFACE glabrous, reddish brown to brown when young, becoming grayish brown to blackish as it matures, often covered with algae or moss, cracked and sulcate in age; margin thick, rounded, whitish when actively growing. FERTILE SURFACE creamy white to buff. PORES circular to angular, 3–5 per mm; tubes up to 5 mm deep per layer. FLESH up to 1 cm thick, corky to woody, buff to pale yellowish brown; odor and taste not distinctive.

MICROSCOPIC FEATURES: Spores 9–11 × 6.5–8 μm, ellipsoid to subglobose, truncate at the apex, thick-walled, with a germ pore, smooth, hyaline, dextrinoid; hyphal system dimitic, clamp connections present.
OCCURRENCE: Solitary, in groups, or in overlapping clusters, usually well above ground, on living or dead ash trees; widely distributed in the Northeast and North Central regions, sometimes reported from the upper South region; year-round.
EDIBILITY: Inedible.
REMARKS: Pathogenic, causing a white heartrot of living or dead ash trees. *Perenniporia* means "a polypore with a perennial fruitbody." The epithet *fraxinophila* means "loving ash trees." Compare with *Vanderbylia fraxinea*, which is also pathogenic on ash trees but has smaller, nontruncate spores.

Perenniporia fraxinophila (A)

Perenniporia fraxinophila (B)

Phaeolus schweinitzii (Fr.) Pat.

= *Polyporus schweinitzii* Fr.

COMMON NAMES: Dye Maker's Polypore, Dyer's Polypore

MACROSCOPIC FEATURES: FRUITBODY annual, 4–26 cm wide, circular to fan-shaped, nearly flat. UPPER SURFACE dry, tomentose, faintly to distinctly zonate, dull orange, becoming rusty brown to dark brown in age; margin sharp, wavy or lobed, yellowish to brownish orange. FERTILE SURFACE decurrent, yellow to greenish yellow or orange, staining brown when bruised, becoming yellowish brown to dark rusty brown in age. PORES angular, 0.5–2 per mm; tubes up to 1.5 cm deep. STALK 2–7 cm long, up to 5 cm thick, enlarged upward, pale to dark brown. FLESH up to 3 cm thick, tough, yellowish to reddish brown; odor and taste not distinctive.

MICROSCOPIC FEATURES: Spores 6–9 × 2.5–5 μm, ellipsoid to ovoid, smooth, hyaline, inamyloid; cystidia 20–90 × 7–13 μm, cylindrical, yellowish, frequent; hyphal system monomitic, clamp connections absent.

OCCURRENCE: Solitary or sometimes in rosettes on conifer roots or on the ground attached to buried roots; widely distributed in the Northeast, North Central, and South regions; year-round.

EDIBILITY: Inedible.

REMARKS: Pathogenic, causing a brown cubical rot of conifers. All parts stain black in KOH. The epithet *schweinitzii* honors German-American botanist and mycologist Lewis David de Schweinitz (1780–1834). Preliminary molecular analysis has demonstrated that *Phaeolus schweinitzii* is a complex of five species that occur in North America.

Phaeolus schweinitzii

Phellinopsis conchata (Pers.) Y. C. Dai

= *Phellinus conchatus* (Pers.) Quél.
= *Polyporus conchatus* (Pers.) Fr.

MACROSCOPIC FEATURES: FRUITBODY peren-
nial, sessile, up to 15 cm wide and 4 cm thick, shell-
shaped to semicircular or irregular, thickened at
the point of attachment, hard and woody. UP-
PER SURFACE glabrous, encrusted, azonate, sulcate, rough and uneven, color variable, yellowish
to grayish or rusty brown, sometimes blackish, especially as it ages, often a mixture of these colors,
usually coated with moss or algae; margin moderately thick, rounded, rusty yellow to yellow-brown.
FERTILE SURFACE often depressed from the
margin, yellowish brown to dark brown, intensify-
ing to darker brown when bruised. PORES circular, 5–6 per mm; tubes up to 2 mm deep per layer,
concolorous with the flesh. FLESH up to 5 mm
thick, azonate, woody, rusty brown; odor and taste
not distinctive.

MICROSCOPIC FEATURES: Spores $5–6.5 \times 4–4.5$ µm,
ovoid to subglobose, smooth, hyaline, inamyloid;
hyphal system dimitic, clamp connections absent; setae $20–50 \times 7–9$ µm, subulate to ventricose,
thick-walled, dark brown in KOH, sometimes deformed, abundant.

OCCURRENCE: Solitary or in overlapping groups
on a wide variety of broadleaf trees, especially ash,
birch, hawthorn, and oak; widely distributed in
the Northeast, North Central, and South regions;
year-round.

EDIBILITY: Inedible.

REMARKS: Saprotrophic on decaying broadleaf
trunks and stumps. The epithet *conchata* means
"shell-shaped." All parts stain black in KOH. The
Cushion Bracket, *Phellinus pomaceus* = *Fomes
pomaceus* (not illustrated), has a hard and woody
fruitbody, hoof- to cushion-shaped, perennial, and
sessile, up to 10 cm wide and 5 cm thick. The upper surface is light grayish brown at first, becomes
blackish and cracked as it matures, and is often
coated with algae, lichens, or mosses. It has a light
yellowish brown to reddish brown fertile surface
that may stain darker brown when bruised, 7–9 circular pores per mm, and woody, zonate, shiny, yellowish brown to reddish brown flesh. The spores
are ovoid to broadly ellipsoid, smooth, inamyloid,
and measure $4–5 \times 3–4.5$ µm. The setae are rare,
thick-walled, subulate to ventricose, measuring 14–
$17 \times 4.5–7$ µm, and it lacks clamp connections. It
grows on cherry, peach, or plum trees and is widely
distributed in the Northeast, North Central, and
South regions.

Phellinopsis conchata

Phellinus igniarius (L.) Quél.

= *Fomes igniarius* (L.) Fr.
= *Phellinus alni* (Bondartsev) Parmasto
= *Polyporus igniarius* (L.) Fr.

COMMON NAMES: False Tinder Polypore, Flecked-flesh Polypore, Willow Bracket
MACROSCOPIC FEATURES: FRUITBODY perennial, sessile, hoof-shaped to shelflike, up to 20 cm wide and 8 cm thick. UPPER SURFACE glabrous and smooth at first, becoming sulcate, encrusted and deeply cracked in age, gray or blackish; margin thick and rounded, concolorous or yellowish- to reddish-brown. FERTILE SURFACE pale cinnamon-brown to dark purplish brown. PORES circular, 5–6 per mm; tubes up to 4 mm deep. FLESH up to 2 cm thick, hard and woody, zonate, dark reddish brown with white flecks of tissue intermixed; odor and taste not distinctive.
MICROSCOPIC FEATURES: Spores 5–6.5 × 4.5–6 μm, broadly ovoid to subglobose, thick-walled, smooth, hyaline, inamyloid; setae 14–17 × 4–6 μm, ventricose to subulate, thick-walled, abundant to rare; hyphal system dimitic, clamp connections absent.
OCCURRENCE: Solitary or in groups on many different genera of broadleaf trees; widely distributed in the Northeast, North Central, and upper South regions; year-round.
EDIBILITY: Inedible.
REMARKS: Pathogenic, causing a white rot of the heartwood of broadleaf trees. The epithet *igniarius* means "pertaining to fire," a reference to the appearance of the fruitbody's upper surface. Compare with *Fomitiporia calkinsii*, which has shiny yellowish brown flesh with white radial streaks near the tubes and point of attachment. The pores are smaller, 6–8 per mm, and it has a yellowish brown to rusty brown fertile surface and dextrinoid spores that measure 5–7 × 5–6 μm.

Phellinus igniarius

Phellinus lundellii Niemelä

= *Ochroporus lundellii* (Niemelä) Niemelä

COMMON NAME: Lundell's Polypore
MACROSCOPIC FEATURES: FRUITBODY perennial, sessile, resupinate at first, becoming effused-reflexed on vertical surfaces, fused laterally, typically up to 18 cm wide, 8 cm thick, and spreading vertically or horizontally, but sometimes very large when growing in old-growth forests. UPPER SURFACE glabrous, encrusted, shallowly sulcate, smooth or cracked, dark brown to blackish; margin often wavy. FERTILE SURFACE pale brown when fresh, staining darker brown when bruised, becoming darker reddish brown in age. PORES circular, 5–6 per mm; tubes up to 1 cm deep, stratified on older specimens, pale brown, often stuffed with white mycelium, with very thick dissepiments. FLESH usually less than 1 cm thick but may be up to 4 cm, fibrous-tough, readily splitting, dull yellow to yellow-brown at first, becoming dark reddish brown in age; odor and taste not distinctive.

MICROSCOPIC FEATURES: Spores 4.5–6 × 4–5 μm, ovoid to broadly ellipsoid, with thickened walls, smooth, hyaline, inamyloid; setae 8–20 × 4–7 μm, subulate to slightly ventricose, thick-walled, usually abundant; hyphal system dimitic, clamp connections absent.

OCCURRENCE: In groups or overlapping clusters on standing or downed broadleaf trees, especially alder and birch; widely distributed but uncommonly reported in the Northeast, North Central, and upper South regions; year-round.

EDIBILITY: Inedible.

REMARKS: Saprotrophic on decaying broadleaf wood.

Phellinus lundellii

Phellinus tremulae (Bondartsev) Bondartsev & P. N. Borisov

= *Fomes tremulae* (Bondartsev) P. N. Borisov

= *Ochroporus tremulae* (Bondartsev) Fiasson & Niemelä

COMMON NAME: Aspen Bracket, Aspen Polypore, False Tinder Fungus

MACROSCOPIC FEATURES: FRUITBODY perennial, sessile, up to 24 cm wide and 15 cm thick, hoof-shaped, hard and woody. UPPER SURFACE finely tomentose and pale brown at first, becoming glabrous, dark grayish brown then blackish, encrusted and cracked as it ages; margin whitish to pale brown when actively growing, often deeply fissured. FERTILE SURFACE light brown to purplish brown, staining darker brown when fresh specimens are bruised. PORES circular, 5–7 per mm; tubes up to 3 mm deep. FLESH hard and woody, dark reddish brown with white flecks; odor and taste not distinctive.

MICROSCOPIC FEATURES: Spores 4.5–5 × 4.5–5 μm, subglobose, with thickened walls at maturity, smooth, hyaline, inamyloid; setae 12–30 × 6–8 μm, ventricose to subulate, thick-walled, few to numerous; hyphal system dimitic, clamp connections absent.

OCCURRENCE: Solitary or in overlapping groups on branch scars or wounds of standing aspen, *Populus* species; widely distributed in the Northeast and North Central regions; year-round.

EDIBILITY: Inedible.

REMARKS: Pathogenic, causing a white trunk rot of living aspen trees. The epithet *tremulae* means "growing on quaking aspen, *Populus tremuloides*."

Phellinus tremulae

Phellinus wahlbergii (Fr.) D. A. Reid

= *Fuscoporia wahlbergii* (Fr.) T. Wagner & M. Fisch.

= *Polyporus wahlbergii* (Fr.) Lloyd

MACROSCOPIC FEATURES: FRUITBODY perennial, sessile, 5–20 cm wide, shelflike, semicircular to somewhat elongated. UPPER SURFACE reddish brown to umber, tomentose, narrowly banded with sulcate to flat zones; margin somewhat blunt and rounded, concolorous. FERTILE SURFACE grayish brown to brown. PORES circular, minute, 5–9 per mm; tubes up to 15 mm deep. FLESH up to 5 mm thick, reddish brown; odor and taste not distinctive.

MICROSCOPIC FEATURES: Spores 4–5 × 3.5–4.5 μm, subglobose, thin-walled, hyaline to very pale yellowish; setae 15–35 × 6–9 μm, mostly hooked, sometimes straight, thick-walled, sharp, dark brown; hyphal system dimitic, clamp connections absent.

OCCURRENCE: Sometimes solitary but more commonly in overlapping clusters on decaying broadleaf wood; widely distributed in the South region; year-round.

EDIBILITY: Inedible.

REMARKS: Saprotrophic, causing a white rot of decaying broadleaf trees. This is a pantropical species that occurs as far north as South Carolina. Positive identification may require microscopic examination to reveal the conspicuous hooked setae, which are most distinctive. Other similar species have nonhooked setae.

Phellinus wahlbergii

Phlebia radiata Fr.

= *Phlebia aurantiaca* (Sow.) Karst.
= *Xylodon carneus* (Fr.) Kuntze

COMMON NAME: Radiating Phlebia, Wrinkled Crust

MACROSCOPIC FEATURES: FRUITBODY annual, 1–4 cm wide, resupinate or slightly effused-reflexed at the margin, firmly attached to the substrate, circular, often radially furrowed from the point of attachment and fused laterally to form extensive rows. FERTILE SURFACE uneven, warty, color highly variable, orange-red to coral-red, pinkish gray, or tan with an orangish margin, typically paler and fringed on the edges. FLESH up to 1 mm thick, soft, waxy to gelatinous when fresh, tough when dry; odor not distinctive.

MICROSCOPIC FEATURES: Spores 3.5–5.5 × 1.5–2 μm, allantoid to elliptical, usually with two or more oil drops, smooth, hyaline; hyphal system monomitic, clamp connections present.

OCCURRENCE: On decaying broadleaf or conifer logs, stumps, and trunks; widely distributed in the Northeast, North Central, and South regions; summer–early winter.

EDIBILITY: Inedible.

REMARKS: Saprotrophic on decaying wood. The epithet *radiata* means "having spokelike grooves." The fungus is highly variable in color and form, often appearing to be different species.

Phlebia radiata (A)

Phlebia radiata (B)

Phlebia tremellosa (Schrad.) Nakasone & Burds.

= *Merulius tremellosus* Schrad.

COMMON NAME: Trembling Merulius
MACROSCOPIC FEATURES: FRUITBODY annual, a sessile, spreading, often coalescing crust with caps that project 2–4 cm from the substrate and up to 5 mm thick. UPPER SURFACE finely velvety, bright white, becoming pale yellow with a pinkish tint and appearing translucent and gelatinous in age. FERTILE SURFACE consisting of reticulate ridges and shallow pits, orange, yellow, or pinkish orange, becoming dark orange when old. FLESH thin, gelatinous to cartilaginous, nearly hyaline or with an orange tint; odor and taste not distinctive.

MICROSCOPIC FEATURES: Spores 3–4 × 0.5–1.5 μm, allantoid, smooth, hyaline, inamyloid; hyphal system monomitic, clamp connections present.
OCCURRENCE: On logs, branches, or stumps of broadleaf trees, especially oak; widely distributed in the Northeast, North Central, and South regions; summer–early winter.
EDIBILITY: Inedible.
REMARKS: Saprotrophic on broadleaf trees. The genus name *Phlebia* means "having veins," a reference to the pattern of ridges and pits on the fertile surface. The epithet *tremellosa* means "trembling," referring to the gelatinous condition of older fruitbodies.

Phlebia tremellosa

Phlebiopsis crassa (Lév.) Floudas & Hibbett

= *Hjortstamia crassa* (Lév.) Boidin & Gilles
= *Laxitextum crassum* (Lév.) Lentz
= *Phanerochaete crassa* (Lév.) Burds.
= *Porostereum crassum* (Lév.) Hjortstam & Ryvarden

MACROSCOPIC FEATURES: FRUITBODY annual, a resupinate to effused-reflexed, spreading crust. UPPER SURFACE velvety to matted and woolly, sometimes warty and uneven or cracking in age, lacking pores, brownish with purplish tints or bright purple to nearly dark violet; margin often partially reflexed, whitish when actively growing. FLESH thin, brown.

MICROSCOPIC FEATURES: Spores 5.5–7.5 × 3–4 µm, ellipsoid, smooth, hyaline, inamyloid; cystidia 50–120 × 8–20 µm, cylindrical with a subulate apex, smooth or strongly encrusted, thick-walled, hyaline to pale brown.

OCCURRENCE: Closely attached and spreading on decaying broadleaf branches and logs; widely distributed in the Northeast, North Central, and South regions; fall–early spring.

EDIBILITY: Inedible.

REMARKS: The epithet *crassa* means "thick or heavy." The color of the upper surface is highly variable and frequently changes as it ages. Compare with *Ceriporia purpurea* and *Skeletocutis lilacina*, which are similarly colored but have pores.

Phlebiopsis crassa

Picipes admirabilis (Peck) J. L. Zhou & B. K. Cui

= *Cerioporus admirabilis* (Peck) Zmitr. & Kovalenko
= *Polyporus admirabilis* Peck

MACROSCOPIC FEATURES: FRUITBODY annual, consisting of large, lobed caps that often form rosettes up to 36 cm wide, arising from a stalk. CAP up to 17 cm wide, fan-shaped to circular or semicircular and slightly depressed to funnel-shaped. UPPER SURFACE dry, glabrous, azonate, smooth or cracking concentrically, bright white, becoming creamy white to pale buff in age; margin rounded, narrowly sterile below. FERTILE SURFACE white to pale buff, PORES decurrent, circular to angular, 3–4 per mm. STALK 2.5–8 cm long or sometimes rudimentary, up to 3.5 cm thick, central to lateral, with a narrowed base, white becoming pale buff to yellowish brown or almost black on the lower portion. FLESH up to 4 cm thick, firm to fibrous-tough, white to creamy white or pale buff; odor strong and unpleasant to sickeningly sweet, taste not distinctive.

MICROSCOPIC FEATURES: Spores 7–9 × 3–3.5 μm, cylindrical, smooth, hyaline, inamyloid; hyphal system dimitic, clamp connections present.

OCCURRENCE: Solitary, on decaying broadleaf stumps and trunks; Northeast region; rare; summer–early winter.

EDIBILITY: Inedible.

REMARKS: Pathogenic, causing a white heartrot. The epithet *admirabilis* means "becoming wonderful or strange." MycoBank currently lists *Polyporus lowei* as a synonym of *Picipes admirabilis*, a designation we believe to be incorrect. We are proposing *Picipes lowei* as a nom. prov. *Picipes lowei* has pale gray caps, not white, and a distinctive odor of anise.

Picipes admirabilis

Picipes badius (Pers.) Zmitr. & Kovalenko

= *Polyporus badius* (Pers.) Schwein.
= *Royoporus badius* A. B. De

COMMON NAMES: Bay-brown Polypore, Pitch-colored Polypore

MACROSCOPIC FEATURES: FRUITBODY annual, consisting of a cap and prominent stalk attached to wood. CAP 4–20 cm wide, circular to irregular, convex or centrally depressed to funnel-shaped, tough. UPPER SURFACE glabrous, smooth, shiny or dull, pale reddish brown with a darker center when young, becoming reddish brown with a blackish brown center in age; margin incurved at first, thin, wavy or lobed at maturity. FERTILE SURFACE decurrent, white to pale buff. PORES circular to angular, 5–7 per mm; tubes up to 1 cm or more. STALK 1–3 cm long, 3–16 mm thick, nearly equal or tapered downward, central or slightly eccentric, smooth, reddish brown near the apex, black below. FLESH up to 1.5 cm thick, corky, azonate, pale buff; odor and taste not distinctive.

MICROSCOPIC FEATURES: Spores 6–10 × 3–5 μm, cylindrical, smooth, hyaline, inamyloid; hyphal system dimitic, clamp connections present.

OCCURRENCE: Solitary, scattered, or in groups on decaying broadleaf wood; late spring–early winter.

EDIBILITY: Inedible.

REMARKS: Saprotrophic on decaying broadleaf wood. The epithet *badius* means "reddish brown."

Picipes badius

Picipes lowei Burdsall & Lombard nom. prov.

MACROSCOPIC FEATURES: FRUITBODY annual, consisting of large, lobed caps arising from a stalk. CAP up to 25 cm wide, semicircular to fan-shaped and usually depressed near the point of attachment. UPPER SURFACE moist or dry, glabrous, azonate, pale gray at first, with grayish to brownish radiating streaks, becoming brownish yellow in age; margin rounded, inrolled to incurved, thin on older specimens, even or narrowly sterile below. FERTILE SURFACE white when young, becoming buff to pale yellow, drying tan to pale caramel brown. PORES decurrent, circular to angular, 4–5 per mm. STALK 2.5–7.5 cm long or sometimes rudimentary, 2–5 cm thick, lateral, with a narrowed base, sometimes fused, pale brown at first, soon becoming dark brown to nearly black on the lower portion. FLESH up to 1.5 cm thick, tough and flexible, white, tan in older specimens; odor of anise with hints of sweet almond, strong when fresh, persisting in dried collections; taste not distinctive.

MICROSCOPIC FEATURES: Spores 6.5–9 × 2.5–4 µm, broadly cylindrical, smooth, hyaline, inamyloid; hyphal system dimitic, clamp connections present on the generative hyphae of the tube trama, but difficult to observe.

OCCURRENCE: Solitary, in groups, or in overlapping clusters like rosettes on decaying broadleaf wood, especially sugar maple and oak; reported from Michigan and North Carolina, distribution limits yet to be determined; rare; summer–fall.

EDIBILITY: Unknown.

REMARKS: Saprotrophic on decaying broadleaf wood. The epithet *lowei* honors American mycologist Josiah L. Lowe (1905–1997), who specialized in the study of polypores. Burdsall and Lombard published *Polyporus lowei* as a new species

Picipes lowei (A)

in the February 1989 issue of *Memoirs of the New York Botanical Garden*. The description was based on collections by H. H. Burdsall, J. Ammirati, and A. H. Smith. The name *Polyporus lowei* is already occupied; therefore, we are proposing *Picipes lowei* as a nom. prov. MycoBank currently lists *Polyporus lowei* as a synonym of *Picipes admirabilis*, a designation we believe to be incorrect based on personal communication with H. H. Burdsall and examination of fresh specimens. *Picipes admirabilis* has white caps, not pale gray, lacks a distinctive odor, and occurs only in the upper northeastern United States.

Picipes lowei (B)

Picipes melanopus (Pers.) Zmitr. & Kovalenko

= *Polyporus melanopus* (Pers.) Fr.

COMMON NAME: Black-footed Polypore

MACROSCOPIC FEATURES: FRUITBODY annual, consisting of a cap and prominent stalk attached to buried wood. CAP up to 10 cm wide, circular to kidney-shaped or irregular, convex or centrally depressed to funnel-shaped. UPPER SURFACE finely scurfy, azonate or faintly zoned, tan to pale grayish brown or reddish brown; margin thin, often wavy or lobed, typically incurved. FERTILE SURFACE decurrent, white to creamy white then dull yellow and staining brown. PORES circular to angular, 6–8 per mm; tubes 1–3 mm deep. STALK up to 7 cm long and 2 cm thick, central, white on the upper portion, rusty to dark brown below, with a rootlike underground extension. FLESH up to 5 mm thick, azonate, firm, white; odor and taste not distinctive.

MICROSCOPIC FEATURES: Spores 7–9 × 3–3.5 μm, cylindrical, smooth, hyaline, inamyloid; hyphal system dimitic, clamp connections present.

OCCURRENCE: Solitary or in groups on the ground attached to buried conifer or broadleaf wood; widely distributed in the Northeast, North Central, and South regions; summer–early winter.

EDIBILITY: Inedible.

REMARKS: Saprotrophic on decaying wood. The epithet *melanopus* means "having a dark or black foot." The wispy grayish cast on the cap of some of the specimens in the photograph is caused by *Lecanicillium fungicola* = *Verticillium fungicola*, a parasitic mold that often attacks this polypore species.

Picipes melanopus

Picipes tubaeformis (P. Karst.) Zmitr. & Kovalenko

= *Polyporus picipes* f. *tubaeformis* (P. Karst.) Domański, Orloś & Skirg.

COMMON NAME: Trumpet Saddle

MACROSCOPIC FEATURES: FRUITBODY annual, consisting of a cap and prominent stalk attached to wood. CAP up to 10 cm wide, circular, depressed and funnel- to trumpet-shaped. UPPER SURFACE glabrous or nearly so, inconspicuously zonate, faintly striate, pale grayish brown; margin thin, incurved and remaining so well into maturity. FERTILE SURFACE strongly decurrent, somewhat uneven and wrinkled, white. PORES circular to angular, 4–7 per mm; tubes 1–2 mm deep. STALK up to 7 cm long and 1 cm wide, central, velvety at first, becoming glabrous, initially reddish brown, darkening to blackish in age. FLESH up to 5 mm thick, azonate, firm, white; odor and taste not distinctive.

MICROSCOPIC FEATURES: Spores 7–9 × 3–4 µm, cylindrical, smooth, hyaline, inamyloid; hyphal system dimitic, clamp connections present.

OCCURRENCE: Solitary or in groups on decaying broadleaf wood; widely distributed but not commonly collected; Northeast and North Central regions; year-round.

EDIBILITY: Inedible.

REMARKS: Saprotrophic on decaying wood. The epithet *tubaeformis* means "trumpet-shaped."

Picipes tubaeformis

Piptoporellus species, South region

COMMON NAME: Mystery Chick

MACROSCOPIC FEATURES: FRUITBODY annual, up to 30 cm wide and 3.5 cm thick, attached to wood. CAP convex to nearly flat, often laterally fused, 5–15 cm wide, shelflike, semicircular to fan-shaped, soft when young, becoming tough in age. UPPER SURFACE dry, often wrinkled, roughened and pitted, somewhat zonate with lighter and darker bands, bright orange, fading to orange-yellow then whitish and finally brown in age; margin inrolled at first, blunt, wavy, often lobed, becoming markedly distorted as it ages, pale to dark orange. FERTILE SURFACE pale orange, becoming whitish when mature. PORES circular to angular, 4–5 per mm, sometimes becoming lacerate and teethlike in age; tubes less than 1 mm deep. STALK up to 6 cm long and 4 cm wide, colored like the cap. FLESH up to 2.5 cm thick, woody or tough, pale salmon, darkest toward the margin; odor sweet or not distinctive, taste tart and astringent.

MICROSCOPIC FEATURES: Spores 3.5–5.5 × 2.5–3.5 μm ellipsoid, smooth, hyaline, inamyloid; hyphal system dimitic, clamp connections not observed.

OCCURRENCE: Solitary, in groups, or in overlapping clusters on decorticated logs and stumps of broadleaf trees, especially live oak, *Quercus virginiana*; widely distributed in the South region; year-round.

EDIBILITY: Unknown.

REMARKS: Saprotrophic on decaying wood. At the time of this writing, a description of this species has not been formally published. It commonly occurs throughout the Gulf Coast states. For comparison, the specimen on the left in our photograph is *Laetiporus sulphureus*, which has a bright sulfur yellow fertile surface, tubes up to 4 mm deep, white flesh, and larger spores that measure 5–8 × 3.5–5 μm. Also compare with *Laetiporus gilbertsonii* var. *pallidus*, which has a light orange to pale orange cap surface, pale yellow to whitish flesh, and larger pores with deeper tubes.

Piptoporellus species, South region

Plicaturopsis crispa (Pers.) D. A. Reid

= *Trogia crispa* (Pers.) Fr.

COMMON NAME: Crimped Gill

MACROSCOPIC FEATURES: FRUITBODY 1–2.5 cm wide, consisting of fan- to shell-shaped caps. UPPER SURFACE dry, finely tomentose, faintly concentrically zonate, yellow-orange to reddish brown or yellow-brown; margin incurved to inrolled, undulating, sometimes scalloped or lobed, whitish to pale yellow. FERTILE SURFACE consisting of gill-like folds, crimped, often forked and vein-like, frequently anastomosing, moderately distant, narrow, whitish to grayish. STALK rudimentary, a narrow central extension of the cap, sometimes absent. FLESH thin, flexible when moist, hard and brittle when dry; odor and taste not distinctive.

MICROSCOPIC FEATURES: Spores 3–4 × 1–1.5 μm, allantoid to elliptic, smooth, hyaline, often containing two oil drops.

OCCURRENCE: In overlapping clusters or groups on branches and trunks of broadleaf trees, especially beech and birch; widely distributed in the Northeast, North Central, and upper South regions; year-round.

EDIBILITY: Inedible.

REMARKS: The epithet *crispa* means "wavy or folded." This fungus has a white spore deposit.

Plicaturopsis crispa (A)

Plicaturopsis crispa (B)

Podoscypha aculeata (Berk. & M. A. Curtis) Boidin

= *Cotylidia aculeata* (Berk. & M. A. Curtis) Lentz

MACROSCOPIC FEATURES: FRUITBODY annual, up to 25 cm wide and 20 cm high, consisting of a rosette cluster of tightly packed, wide and flattened branches arising from a common base. UPPER SURFACE rough and uneven, whitish to creamy white, becoming grayish, pinkish, or brownish in age; margin fringed. FERTILE SURFACE rugged, folded, and often torn, whitish to creamy white, becoming grayish, pinkish, or brownish in age. FLESH thin, tough, leathery, white.

MICROSCOPIC FEATURES: Spores 4.5–7 × 4–5 μm, smooth, ellipsoid to ovate, inamyloid; clamp connections present.

OCCURRENCE: Solitary or in groups on the ground with broadleaf trees; found in the North Central and South regions; fall–early winter.

EDIBILITY: Unknown.

REMARKS: Saprotrophic or possibly mycorrhizal with broadleaf trees. It is a rare fungus, reported to date from southern Indiana and Missouri, South Carolina, Mississippi, and Brazil. Compare with *Hydnopolyporus palmatus*, which has pores or flattened teeth on its fertile surface.

Podoscypha aculeata (A)

Podoscypha aculeata (B)

Polyporoletus sublividus Snell

= *Albatrellus sublividus* (Snell) Pouzar
= *Polyporus sublividus* (Snell) J. Lowe
= *Scutiger sublividus* (Snell) Singer, Snell &
   W. L. White

MACROSCOPIC FEATURES: FRUITBODY annual, consisting of a cap and lateral to central stalk, growing on the ground. CAP up to 18 cm wide and 2.5 cm thick, circular to kidney-shaped or lobed. UPPER SURFACE azonate, tomentose to fibrillose, sometimes with fibrils becoming appressed in a reticulate pattern or becoming nearly glabrous, uneven or cracked in age, dark purplish gray, fading to cinnamon-buff or olivaceous tawny. FERTILE SURFACE purplish gray to olive-buff or pale tan. PORES decurrent, circular to angular, becoming elongated or torn near the stalk, 1–2 per mm; tubes up to 1 cm deep, tube layer not separable. STALK up to 10 cm long and 4 cm thick, lateral to central, cylindrical, with a somewhat bulbous base and white basal mycelium, reticulate, tomentose to finely hispid, pale brown to olivaceous. FLESH up to 1.5 cm thick, soft, azonate, pinkish buff to pale brownish salmon.

MICROSCOPIC FEATURES: Spores 10–12 × 8–10 µm, subglobose to broadly ellipsoid, with a large spherical oil drop, appearing slightly rough, with a double wall separated by interwall partitions, hyaline, inamyloid. The outer wall of some spores may slough off, allowing them to appear smooth; hyphal system monomitic, clamp connections present.

Polyporoletus sublividus

OCCURRENCE: Solitary or in groups on the ground with broadleaf trees, especially oak; northern areas of the South region; rare; late spring–fall.
EDIBILITY: Unknown.
REMARKS: Mycorrhizal, not a wood-rotting fungus. This unusual polypore resembles species in the genera *Albatrellus* and *Boletus*. The genus name *Polyporoletus* is a combination of *Polyporus* and *Boletus*. The epithet *sublividus* means "somewhat bluish."

Polyporus radicatus Schwein.

COMMON NAME: Rooting Polypore

MACROSCOPIC FEATURES: FRUITBODY annual, consisting of a cap and deeply rooting stalk attached to buried roots. CAP 3–20 cm wide, 3–15 mm thick, circular, convex to nearly flat or slightly depressed, fibrous-tough. UPPER SURFACE velvety to finely scaly, dry, sometimes finely cracked and roughened, azonate, yellowish brown to reddish brown; margin incurved when young, uplifted and wavy in age. FERTILE SURFACE decurrent, white to creamy yellow. PORES angular, 2–3 per mm; tubes up to 5 mm deep. STALK 5–16 cm long, 6–25 mm thick, central, scurfy, yellowish brown, enlarged downward, then tapered below as a black, underground rootlike base that extends up to 30 cm or more. FLESH up to 1 cm thick, fibrous-tough, white; odor and taste not distinctive.

MICROSCOPIC FEATURES: Spores 12–15 × 6–8 μm, oblong to elliptic, smooth, hyaline, inamyloid; hyphal system dimitic, clamp connections present.

OCCURRENCE: Solitary, scattered, or in groups on the ground attached to buried roots, usually in broadleaf woods; widely distributed in the Northeast, North Central, and South regions; summer–early winter.

EDIBILITY: Inedible.

REMARKS: Pathogenic, causing a white rot of broadleaf trees. The epithet *radicatus* means "rooting."

Polyporus radicatus

Polyporus umbellatus (Pers.) Fr.

= *Cladomeris umbellata* (Pers.) Quél.
= *Dendropolyporus umbellatus* (Pers.) Jülich.
= *Grifola umbellata* (Pers.) Pilát

COMMON NAME: Umbrella Polypore
MACROSCOPIC FEATURES: FRUITBODY annual, up to 50 cm wide, a compound cluster with numerous rounded caps arising from a strongly branched stalk. CAP 2–4 cm wide, circular, each with a separate stalk branch. UPPER SURFACE depressed over the center, glabrous or radially fibrillose to finely scaly, pale grayish brown to light yellow-brown or sometimes dull white. FERTILE SURFACE decurrent, white to creamy white. PORES angular, elongated near the stalk, 1–3 per mm; tubes up to 2 mm deep. STALK central to eccentric, cylindrical or irregularly shaped, extensively branched, brownish or colored like the fertile surface, attached at the base to a buried sclerotium. FLESH up to 1 mm thick, soft to somewhat fibrous, whitish; odor and taste not distinctive.

MICROSCOPIC FEATURES: Spores 7–10 × 3–4 μm, cylindrical, smooth, hyaline, inamyloid; hyphal system dimitic, clamp connections present.

OCCURRENCE: Solitary or in groups on the ground, often near stumps, in broadleaf and mixed woods, usually with beech or oak; widely distributed in the Northeast, North Central, and South regions; spring–fall.

EDIBILITY: Edible.

REMARKS: Pathogenic, causing a white rot of broadleaf trees. The epithet *umbellatus* means "with umbrellas," a reference to the circular stalked caps.

Polyporus umbellatus

Porodaedalea chrysoloma (Fr.) Fiasson & Niemelä

= *Phellinus chrysoloma* (Fr.) Donk
= *Phellinus piceinus* (Peck) Pat.
= *Polyporus chrysoloma* Fr.

COMMON NAME: Spruce Polypore

MACROSCOPIC FEATURES: FRUITBODY perennial or sometimes annual, sessile, up to 15 cm wide, shelf-like, semicircular to elongated, arising from a resupinate or effused-reflexed, bright yellowish brown base. UPPER SURFACE tomentose to hispid, sulcate, zonate, dull reddish brown; margin sharp or somewhat rounded, usually wavy, slightly lobed, narrowly sterile below, bright yellowish brown or sometimes creamy white when actively growing. FERTILE SURFACE glancing, bright yellowish brown at first, darkening in age. PORES slightly labyrinthine to angular, 1–3 per mm; tubes up to 1 cm deep. FLESH up to 4 mm thick, fibrous-tough, reddish brown; odor and taste not distinctive.

MICROSCOPIC FEATURES: 4–5.5 × 4–5 μm, ovoid to subglobose, smooth, hyaline, inamyloid; setae 25–60 × 7–10 μm, subulate, thick-walled, straight, abundant; hyphal system dimitic, clamp connections absent.

OCCURRENCE: In overlapping clusters on standing conifer trees and stumps, or in rows on fallen trees; widely distributed in the Northeast and North Central regions; summer–late fall.

EDIBILITY: Inedible.

REMARKS: Pathogenic, causing a white pocket rot of living and decaying conifers. The epithet *chrysoloma* means "having a golden margin." All parts stain black in KOH. *Porodaedalea pini* is similar and also grows on conifers. It is larger, distinctly shelflike or hoof-shaped, often blackish when mature, and has shorter, wider setae.

Porodaedalea chrysoloma

Porodaedalea pini (Brot.) Murrill

= *Phellinus pini* (Brot.) Pilát

COMMON NAME: Ochre-orange Hoof Polypore
MACROSCOPIC FEATURES: FRUITBODY perennial, sessile, up to 15 cm wide and 8 cm thick, at first resupinate, becoming shelflike to irregular and finally hoof-shaped, corky to woody. UPPER SURFACE tomentose near the margin or nearly overall when young, light reddish brown at first, becoming dark brown to blackish as it matures, concentrically zonate and finally crusty, rough, sulcate, and sometimes cracked in age; margin thick, rounded, reddish brown when actively growing, older specimens sometimes coated with lichens, mosses, or algae. FERTILE SURFACE ochre to ochre-orange or yellow-brown. PORES circular to angular or labyrinthine, 1–3 per mm; tubes up to 6 mm deep. FLESH up to 3 cm thick, corky to woody, reddish brown to yellowish brown, lustrous, usually with one or more thin black layers.

MICROSCOPIC FEATURES: Spores 4.5–7 × 3.5–5 μm, ovoid, smooth, hyaline, inamyloid; setae 40–50 × 10–14 μm, subulate to ventricose, thick-walled, abundant; hyphal system dimitic, clamp connections absent.
OCCURRENCE: Solitary, in groups, or in overlapping clusters on living conifers; widely distributed in the Northeast, North Central, and South regions; year-round.
EDIBILITY: Inedible.
REMARKS: Pathogenic, causing a white pocket rot in the heartwood of living conifers. The epithet *pini* means "growing on pines." All parts stain black in KOH. *Porodaedalea chrysoloma* is similar and also grows on conifers. It is smaller, typically effused-reflexed, with the upper surface dull reddish brown, and it has longer, narrower setae. It also has a more northern distribution.

Porodaedalea pini

Porodisculus pendulus (Fr.) Murrill

= *Dictyopanus pendulus* (Fr.) Teng
= *Polyporus pendulus* (Fr.) Ellis

COMMON NAMES: Pendulous-disk Polypore
MACROSCOPIC FEATURES: FRUITBODY annual,
1–5 mm wide, circular, pendant from a stalklike
base, attached to wood. UPPER SURFACE azonate, granular to powdery, whitish to pale brown;
margin rounded, incurved to inrolled. FERTILE
SURFACE convex, granular to powdery, whitish
to pale brown. PORES rounded, minute, somewhat obscured, 8–10 per mm; tubes up to 1 mm
deep. BASE stalklike, 3–5 mm long, dorsal or lateral, tapered toward the point of attachment.
FLESH up to 1.5 mm thick, firm, corky, whitish;
odor and taste not distinctive.
MICROSCOPIC FEATURES: Spores 3.5–4.5 × 0.8–
1.2 µm, allantoid, smooth, hyaline, inamyloid; hyphal system monomitic, clamp connections absent.
OCCURRENCE: In large groups on freshly dead
twigs, branches, and logging slash of broadleaf
trees, especially oaks; widely distributed in the
Northeast, North Central, and South regions;
summer–early winter.
EDIBILITY: Inedible.
REMARKS: Saprotrophic on decaying broadleaf
wood. *Porodisculus* means "little poroid disk." The
epithet *pendulus* means "hanging down." It is the
world's smallest polypore.

Porodisculus pendulus (A)

Porodisculus pendulus (B)

Poronidulus conchifer (Schwein.) Murrill

= *Trametes conchifer* (Schwein.) Pilát

COMMON NAME: Little Nest Polypore
MACROSCOPIC FEATURES: FRUITBODY annual, sessile, at first a small cup- to fan-shaped sterile structure, which develops one or more circular caps. CUP up to 1.6 cm wide, glabrous, smooth, concentrically zoned, brown at first, then white and brown. CAP 1–5 cm wide, fan- to kidney-shaped, flattened, fibrous-tough. UPPER SURFACE slightly velvety, smooth to radially wrinkled, concentrically zoned, with zones of contrasting colors, white to grayish white, yellowish, or pale brown, sometimes forming secondary cups; margin thin, wavy. FERTILE SURFACE white to yellowish tan. PORES angular, 2–4 per mm; tubes up to 2 mm deep. FLESH less than 1 mm thick, fibrous-tough, white; odor and taste not distinctive.
MICROSCOPIC FEATURES: Spores 5–7 × 1.5–2.5 μm, cylindrical, smooth, hyaline, inamyloid; hyphal system monomitic, clamp connections absent.
OCCURRENCE: In groups on decaying broadleaf branches; widely distributed in the Northeast, North Central, and South regions; late spring–early winter.
EDIBILITY: Inedible.
REMARKS: Saprotrophic on decaying broadleaf branches. The epithet *conchifer* means "shell-bearing," a reference to the tiny cups in the caps.

Poronidulus conchifer

Postia livens Miettinen & Vlasák

COMMON NAME: Blue Cheese Polypore

MACROSCOPIC FEATURES: FRUITBODY annual, sessile, 2–8 cm wide, shell-shaped to shelf-like, broadly convex to somewhat flattened, soft and spongy, attached to wood. UPPER SURFACE tomentose to strigose, or sometimes glabrous, smooth, whitish, typically with bluish tints, sometimes bruising intensely blue; margin sharp. FERTILE SURFACE whitish to pale gray, usually staining blue. PORES angular, sometimes split or torn, 4–6 per mm; tubes 1–6 mm deep. FLESH up to 1.5 cm thick, soft, spongy, watery when fresh, white, becoming yellowish or grayish in age; odor fragrant or not distinctive, taste not distinctive.

MICROSCOPIC FEATURES: Spores 4.1–5.7(7) × 1–1.7 μm, cylindrical to allantoid, smooth, hyaline, inamyloid; hyphal system monomitic, clamp connections present.

OCCURRENCE: Solitary or in groups on conifers or broadleaf trees; widely distributed in the Northeast, North Central, and South regions; summer–early winter.

EDIBILITY: Inedible.

REMARKS: Saprotrophic on decaying conifers and broadleaf trees. The epithet *livens* means "grayish bluish." *Postia caesia* is a European species that does not occur in North America. A recent publication by Miettinen et al. (2018) demonstrates that what has been called *Postia caesia* in eastern North America is a complex of at least four macroscopically similar species. *Postia livens* may be the most commonly occurring member of this complex. *Postia simulans* (not illustrated) has a white to creamy white, matted or almost glabrous upper surface, rarely pubescent, that occasionally turns blue, grayish, or ochraceous. It has (4)5–7 pores per mm, spores that measure 4.1–6.3(8.1) × 1.2–1.9 μm and grows on conifers and broadleaf trees. *Postia caesiosimulans* (not illustrated) has a more or less glabrous, white to creamy white upper surface when young that becomes grayish to pale ochraceous, rarely with bluish flecks. It has 5–7 pores per mm, spores that measure 4.1–5.5(7) × 1–1.6 μm, and grows on broadleaf trees. *Postia populi* (not illustrated) is nearly identical to *Postia caesiosimulans*, but it has a wrinkled margin when mature, 5–8 pores per mm, and usually grows on fallen logs and branches of aspen, cottonwood, and poplar. *Niveoporofomes spraguei* has a firm and tough fruitbody, whitish to ivory, usually with greenish blue stains, corky to tough flesh, and it grows on broadleaf wood.

Postia livens

Postia tephroleuca (Fr.) Jülich

= *Oligoporus tephroleucus* (Fr.) Gilb. & Ryvarden

COMMON NAME: Grayling Bracket

MACROSCOPIC FEATURES: FRUITBODY annual, effused-reflexed or resupinate, 2–14 cm wide and 1–4 cm thick, triangular to semicircular or fan-shaped, soft and watery when fresh, attached to wood. UPPER SURFACE strigose or velvety, frequently glabrous in age, creamy white to grayish, often with a brownish tinge. FERTILE SURFACE whitish when fresh, becoming yellowish in age or when drying. PORES angular, 2–4 per mm, dissepiments entire or becoming finely lacerate and dentate; tubes up to 1.5 cm deep. FLESH up to 1 cm thick, soft, whitish, usually concentrically zonate; odor and taste not distinctive.

MICROSCOPIC FEATURES: Spores 3.5–6 × 1–2 μm, cylindric to allantoid, smooth, hyaline, inamyloid; hyphal system monomitic, clamp connections present.

OCCURRENCE: On a wide variety of conifer and broadleaf trees; widely distributed in the Northeast, North Central, and upper South regions; year-round.

EDIBILITY: Inedible.

REMARKS: Saprotrophic, causing a brown cubical rot of dead conifer or broadleaf wood. The epithet *tephroleuca* means "grayish and white."

Postia tephroleuca (A)

Postia tephroleuca (B)

Pseudofistulina radicata (Schwein.) Burds.

= *Fistulina radicata* (Schwein.) Schwein.

MACROSCOPIC FEATURES: FRUITBODY annual, consisting of a cap and long, radicating stalk attached to broadleaf trees. CAP 3–7.5 cm wide, rounded to kidney-shaped or irregularly lobed. UPPER SURFACE densely tomentose, azonate, yellowish brown, darkening in age; margin acute, sometimes incised. FERTILE SURFACE white to cream-colored at first, becoming pinkish buff to ochraceous. PORES circular, 5–7 per mm; tubes up to 3 mm deep. STALK 4–10 cm long, up to 1 cm thick, distinctly lateral, usually tapered downward, typically radicating, colored like the cap or whitish, tomentose on the upper portion, sometimes whitish toward the base. FLESH up to 7 mm thick, fibrous-tough, white when fresh, becoming pale buff when dry; odor and taste not distinctive.

MICROSCOPIC FEATURES: Spores 3–4 × 2–3 μm, ovoid, smooth, hyaline, inamyloid; hyphal system monomitic, clamp connections absent.

OCCURRENCE: Solitary or scattered on the ground attached to buried broadleaf roots, or sometimes on decaying broadleaf logs and stumps; widely distributed but uncommon in the Northeast, North Central, and South regions; late spring–early winter.

EDIBILITY: Inedible.

REMARKS: Saprotrophic on decaying wood. The epithet *radicata* means "rooted."

Pseudofistulina radicata

Pseudoinonotus dryadeus (Pers.) T. Wagner & M.Fisch.

= *Inonotus dryadeus* (Pers.) Murrill

COMMON NAME: Weeping Polypore

MACROSCOPIC FEATURES: FRUITBODY annual, sessile, 13–36 cm wide and up to 15 cm thick, shelf-like or top-shaped to somewhat rounded, convex, sometimes laterally fused, attached to wood. UPPER SURFACE smooth, azonate, becoming finely cracked in age, whitish when very young, soon buff to brown, typically exuding amber droplets when fresh; margin blunt, concolorous or ivory. FERTILE SURFACE buff at first, becoming dark brown. PORES circular to angular, 4–6 per mm; tubes up to 3 cm deep. FLESH up to 15 cm thick, soft or tough, zonate, bright yellowish brown at first, becoming reddish brown in age, distinctly mottled with whitish streaks when cut; odor and taste not distinctive.

MICROSCOPIC FEATURES: Spores 6–8 × 5–7 µm, sub-globose, smooth, hyaline, becoming thick-walled, dextrinoid; setae 25–40 × 9–16 µm, ventricose, often hooked, thick-walled, rare or frequent; hyphal system monomitic, clamp connections absent.

OCCURRENCE: Solitary, in groups, or in overlapping clusters usually at the base of oak trees, sometimes on stumps or on the ground attached to buried roots; widely distributed in the Northeast, North Central, and South regions; year-round.

EDIBILITY: Inedible.

REMARKS: Pathogenic, causing a white rot of heartwood in oaks; The epithet *dryadeus* means "associated with oak trees."

Pseudoinonotus dryadeus

Punctularia strigosozonata (Schwein.) P. H.B. Talbot

= *Merulius strigosozonatus* Schwein.

= *Phlebia strigosozonata* (Schwein.) Lloyd

COMMON NAMES: Bacon Strips, Tree Bacon, Zoned Phlebia

MACROSCOPIC FEATURES: FRUITBODY annual, effused-reflexed, 1–4.5 cm wide, often laterally fused up to 15 cm wide and spreading, semicircular, nearly flat to convex or upturned, flexible, leathery-waxy. UPPER SURFACE matted tomentose to densely hairy, dark reddish brown to grayish brown, sometimes with blackish zones, becoming uneven, pitted, zonate, and sulcate as it ages; margin wavy, creamy white to yellowish orange when actively growing. FERTILE SURFACE smooth at first, soon developing radially elongated, crowded wrinkles and warts, weakly to distinctly concentrically zonate, reddish brown, becoming grayish brown to blackish brown in age. FLESH up to 0.5 mm thick, glistening, sometimes gelatinous, reddish brown to purplish black; odor and taste not distinctive.

MICROSCOPIC FEATURES: Spores 6–8 × 3.5–4 µm, elliptical to ovate, smooth, hyaline to pale brown; clamp connections present.

OCCURRENCE: In overlapping clusters on decaying broadleaf wood, especially beech, oak, and poplar; widely distributed in the Northeast, North Central, and South regions; year-round.

EDIBILITY: Inedible.

REMARKS: Saprotrophic on decaying broadleaf wood.

Punctularia strigosozonata

Pycnoporellus alboluteus (Ellis & Everh.) Kotl. & Pouzar

= *Aurantiporellus alboluteus* (Ellis & Everh.) Murrill

= *Fomes alboluteus* Ellis & Everh.

= *Phaeolus alboluteus* (Ellis & Everh.) Pilát

= *Polyporus alboluteus* (Ellis & Everh.) Ellis & Everh.

COMMON NAME: Orange Sponge Polypore
MACROSCOPIC FEATURES: FRUITBODY annual, sessile, up to 15 cm or more wide, resupinate at first, becoming effused-reflexed and crustlike to cushion-shaped, soft and spongy when fresh. UPPER SURFACE dry, azonate, loosely hairy to fibrous-scaly, bright orange. FERTILE SURFACE bright orange to yellow-orange, becoming dull yel-

Pycnoporellus alboluteus (A)

low and eventually weathering or fading to white as it ages. PORES angular, 1–3 mm wide, soon splitting and becoming teethlike or jagged with white edges in age; tubes up to 2 cm deep. FLESH up to 3 mm thick, soft, pale orange; odor and taste not distinctive.

MICROSCOPIC FEATURES: Spores 6–10 × 2.5–4 μm, cylindrical, smooth, hyaline, inamyloid; cystidia 60–120 × 5–10 μm, cylindrical, thin to moderately thick-walled, hyaline; hyphal system monomitic, clamp connections absent.

OCCURRENCE: Solitary or in groups spreading along the lower sides of decaying conifer logs and branches, especially spruce and pine; widespread but uncommon in the Northeast and North Central regions; spring–fall.

EDIBILITY: Inedible.

REMARKS: Saprotrophic on decaying conifers. The epithet *alboluteus* means "a combination of white and yellow." All tissues quickly stain cherry red in KOH.

Pycnoporellus alboluteus (B)

Pycnoporellus fulgens (Fr.) Donk

= *Hydnum fulgens* Fr.
= *Polyporus aurantiacus* Peck
= *Polyporus fibrillosus* P. Karst.

COMMON NAME: Splendid Polypore
MACROSCOPIC FEATURES: FRUITBODY annual, sessile, 4–12 cm wide, shelflike, fan-shaped to semi-circular, convex to somewhat flattened, soft and spongy when fresh, fibrous-tough and rigid when dry. UPPER SURFACE often zonate, dry, tomentose or nearly glabrous at first, soon becoming fibrillose to conspicuously hairy; pale orange at first, becoming pale to dark orange-brown or rusty brown in age; margin thin, sometimes wavy or lobed. FERTILE SURFACE whitish at first then pale to dark orange or orange-brown. PORES circular to angular, sometimes sinuous, often unequal, 1.5–2.5 per mm, frequently lacerated in age; tubes up to 6 mm deep. FLESH up to 2 cm thick, corky to fibrous-tough, pale orange to rusty red; odor and taste not distinctive.

MICROSCOPIC FEATURES: Spores 5–9 × 2.5–4(5) µm, cylindrical to oblong, smooth, hyaline, inamyloid; cystidia 45–60 × 4–6 µm, narrowly cylindrical, thin-walled, hyaline; hyphal system monomitic, clamp connections absent.

OCCURRENCE: Solitary, scattered in groups, or in overlapping clusters on decaying conifer logs and slash, sometimes on broadleaf trees; widely distributed in the Northeast, North Central, and upper South regions; year-round.

EDIBILITY: Inedible.

REMARKS: Saprotrophic, usually on conifers but sometimes on broadleaf trees. The epithet *fulgens* means "shining or glowing." The upper surface and flesh stains reddish then quickly black in KOH.

Pycnoporellus fulgens

Pyrofomes juniperinus (H. Schrenk) Vlasák & Spirin

= *Fomes juniperinus* (H. Schrenk) Sacc. & P. Syd.
= *Polyporus juniperinus* H. Schrenk
= *Pyropolyporus juniperinus* (H. Schrenk) Murrill

MACROSCOPIC FEATURES: FRUITBODY perennial, sessile, hard and woody, up to 12 cm wide, projecting up to 10 cm, hemispherical at first, becoming hoof-shaped, broadly attached to wood. UPPER SURFACE with conspicuous annular layers, indistinctly hispid, dull gray, becoming darker gray and nearly glabrous in age, occa-sionally finely cracked, sometimes green when coated with algae; margin blunt, yellowish brown when actively growing. FERTILE SURFACE yellowish brown to ochraceous brown, glancing, soft and smooth. PORES circular to slightly elongated, 2.5–4 per mm; combined tube layers up to 6 cm deep. FLESH up to 1 cm thick, hard corky to woody, rusty brown; odor and taste not distinctive.

MICROSCOPIC FEATURES: Spores 5–8.2 × 3.7–6.6 µm, broadly ellipsoid to subglobose, smooth,

Pyrofomes juniperinus (A)

Pyrofomes juniperinus (B)

thick-walled, truncate, brownish; hyphal system dimitic, clamp connections present.

OCCURRENCE: Solitary or in groups on standing trunks of junipers; widely distributed in the North Central region and lower portion of the South region; year-round.

EDIBILITY: Inedible.

REMARKS: Pathogenic on living junipers. The epithet *juniperinus* means "occurring on junipers." *Pyrofomes demidoffii* has been reported from Europe, Middle Asia, East Africa, and North America; following recent DNA-based studies, however, North American specimens are now called *Pyrofomes ju-*niperinus. *Inonotus juniperinus* (not illustrated) is also pathogenic on junipers, usually attacking the roots. It has an annual, sessile, semicircular to fan-shaped fruitbody, 3–7 cm wide and 5–20 mm thick, that is soft and flexible when fresh. The upper surface is often zonate or wrinkled, rusty to umber brown, becoming dark brownish black in age. The fertile surface is deep rusty to umber brown, with angular to irregular pores, 3–5 per mm. The flesh is up to 1 cm thick and deep rusty to umber brown. It lacks setae, and the spores are 5–6 × 4–5.5 μm, broadly ellipsoid to subglobose. It is known only from Texas.

Radulomyces copelandii (Pat.) Hjortstam & Spooner

= *Hydnum copelandii* Pat.
= *Radulodon copelandii* (Pat.) N. Maek.
= *Sarcodontia copelandii* (Pat.) Imazeki

COMMON NAME: Asian Beauty

MACROSCOPIC FEATURES: FRUITBODY annual, resupinate to very slightly effused-reflexed, spreading up to 30 cm long, consisting of spines arising from the resupinate base. UPPER SURFACE thin, uneven, granular, white to yellowish; margin up to 2 mm thick, dense, white. FERTILE SURFACE consisting of white to yellowish spines that become buff to brownish in age; spines densely crowded, up to 1.4 cm long. FLESH up to 1 mm thick, fibrous to horny; odor not distinctive, taste not reported.

MICROSCOPIC FEATURES: Spores 6–7.2 × 5.4–6.6 μm, subglobose, smooth, hyaline, inamyloid; hyphal system monomitic, clamp connections present.

OCCURRENCE: Solitary, in groups, or in overlapping clusters on decaying trunks and logs of broadleaf trees, especially oak and maple; widely distributed in the Northeast region, also occasionally reported from the North Central and South regions; year-round.

EDIBILITY: Inedible.

REMARKS: Saprotrophic on decaying broadleaf wood. This Asian fungus was first reported from Massachusetts in 2009. The spine tips appear fimbriate under 10× magnification. *Radulodon americanus* (not illustrated), reported from across Canada, the northern United States, and Colorado, is similar but grows on species of poplar. It is dimitic and has globose to subglobose spores that measure 4.5–6.5 × 4–5.8 μm. Compare with *Sarcodontia setosa*, a sulfur yellow, resupinate, spreading crust with crowded spines, which grows under the bark of decaying apple trees. Also compare with *Spongipellis pachyodon*, which forms conspicuous caps.

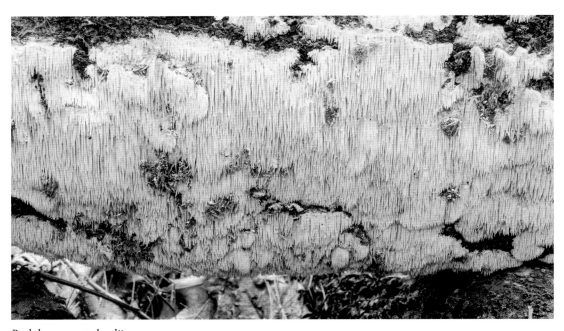

Radulomyces copelandii

Rhodofomes cajanderi (P. Karst.) B. K. Cui, M. L. Han, & Y. C. Dai

= *Fomes subroseus* (Weir) Overh.

= *Fomitopsis cajanderi* (P. Karst.) Kotl. & Pouzar

COMMON NAME: Rosy Polypore

MACROSCOPIC FEATURES: FRUITBODY perennial, sessile, 3–14(20) cm wide, convex to nearly flat, semicircular to fan-shaped or irregular, tough, becoming corky or brittle when dry. UPPER SURFACE appressed-fibrillose, smooth or somewhat roughened, typically faintly zonate, pinkish brown to reddish brown or grayish brown; margin fairly sharp, typically whitish when young. FERTILE SURFACE rosy pink to pinkish brown. PORES circular to angular, 3–5 per mm; tubes 1–3 mm deep per season. FLESH 2–15 mm thick, tough, rosy pink, becoming pinkish brown in age; odor and taste not distinctive.

MICROSCOPIC FEATURES: Spores 4–7 × 1.5–2 μm, allantoid, smooth, hyaline, inamyloid; hyphal system dimitic, clamp connections present.

OCCURRENCE: Solitary, scattered, or in clusters on decaying conifer wood, especially pine and hemlock, rarely on broadleaf trees; widely distributed in the Northeast, North Central, and South regions; year-round.

EDIBILITY: Inedible.

REMARKS: Saprotrophic, causing a brown cubical rot of conifers. The epithet *cajanderi* honors A. K. Cajander, who first submitted a collection as an unknown species. *Rhodofomes roseus* is similar but appears to be restricted to boreal areas and has cylindrical spores. *Rhodofomitopsis feei* = *Fomitopsis feei* (not illustrated), known only from Florida, is very similar to *Rhodofomes cajanderi*. It differs by growing on decaying broadleaf wood and having more cylindrical to oblong spores that measure 5–6.5 × 2.5–3 μm.

Rhodofomes cajanderi

Rhodofomes roseus (Alb. & Schwein.) Vlasák

= *Fomes roseus* (Alb. & Schwein.) Fr.
= *Fomitopsis rosea* (Alb. & Schwein.) P. Karst.

COMMON NAME: Pink Polypore
MACROSCOPIC FEATURES: FRUITBODY perennial, sessile, up to 12 cm wide, shelflike to hoof-shaped, tough and woody. UPPER SURFACE at first tomentose and pale rose pink, becoming glabrous, crustose, cracked, and darkening to brownish black in age; margin rounded, concolorous. FERTILE SURFACE pale rose pink, becoming pinkish brown when mature, staining dark pink when bruised. PORES circular to angular, 3–5 per mm; tubes 0.5–3 mm deep per season. FLESH up to 3 cm thick, fibrous-tough or woody, azonate, pinkish brown.

MICROSCOPIC FEATURES: Spores 5.5–7.5 × 2–2.5 μm, cylindrical, smooth, hyaline, inamyloid; hyphal system dimitic, clamp connections present.

OCCURRENCE: Solitary or in groups on conifers, especially fir and spruce; Northeast region; year-round.

EDIBILITY: Inedible.

REMARKS: Saprotrophic on decaying conifers. The epithet *roseus* means "rosy pink." *Rhodofomes cajanderi* is similar but much more widely distributed, and it has allantoid spores.

Rhodofomes roseus

Rigidoporus microporus (Sw.) Overeem

= *Polyporus microporus* (Sw.) Fr.

COMMON NAME: White Root Rot Polypore
MACROSCOPIC FEATURES: FRUITBODY annual or sometimes perennial, up to 22 cm wide and 2 cm thick, shelflike, semicircular or fan-shaped, broadly attached. UPPER SURFACE slightly velvety and orange-brown to reddish brown at first, soon becoming glabrous, concentrically zonate and sulcate, uneven, dull or slightly shiny, fading to pale brown or tinted greenish when coated with algae; margin thin, sometimes curved downward, white or concolorous. FERTILE SURFACE pale orange to brownish orange, fading to ochraceous or darkening in age, staining dull orange when bruised. PORES circular to angular, 6–9 per mm; tubes up to 1 cm deep. FLESH up to 1 cm thick, white to creamy white or very pale brown; odor and taste not distinctive.

MICROSCOPIC FEATURES: Spores 3.5–5 × 3.5–4 μm, subglobose, smooth, hyaline, inamyloid; hyphal system dimitic, clamp connections absent.
OCCURRENCE: Solitary, in overlapping groups or clusters on broadleaf trees, especially magnolia and oaks; widely distributed along the Gulf Coast states; year-round.
EDIBILITY: Inedible.
REMARKS: Pathogenic, causing white root rot of broadleaf trees. It is a major pathogen of tropical crop plants including bamboo, cacao, coconut, coffee, and tea. The epithet *microporus* means "having very small pores." *Rigidoporus lineatus* (not illustrated) is nearly identical and is also widely distributed along the Gulf Coast states. It has clavate, thick-walled, smooth to strongly encrusted cystidia partly embedded in the trama. Microscopic examination of sectioned tubes is required to positively identify these two species.

Rigidoporus microporus

Rigidoporus ulmarius (Sowerby) Imazeki

= *Fomes geotropus* (Cooke) Cooke
= *Polyporus ulmarius* (Sowerby) Fr.

MACROSCOPIC FEATURES: FRUITBODY perennial, sessile, up to 30 cm wide and 6 cm thick, effused-reflexed or shelflike to hoof-shaped, typically enlarged to substipitate at the point of attachment. UPPER SURFACE appressed-tomentose to nearly glabrous, very rough and uneven, azonate, whitish to pale buff or pale ochraceous, sometimes green when coated with algae; margin rounded or somewhat sharp, sterile below, pale buff. FERTILE SURFACE pale orange to pinkish buff when fresh, becoming brownish pink in age or when drying, staining darker orange to pinkish brown when bruised. PORES angular to circular, 5–6 per mm; tubes up to 4 cm deep, indistinctly stratified in older specimens. FLESH up to 5 cm thick at the base, thinner outward, fibrous, azonate, pinkish or pale buff; odor and taste not distinctive.

MICROSCOPIC FEATURES: Spores 7–11 × 6.5–10 µm, globose to subglobose, smooth, hyaline, inamyloid; hyphal system monomitic, clamp connections absent.

OCCURRENCE: Solitary or in groups on several species of broadleaf trees, also on bald cypress; widely distributed in the South region; year-round.

EDIBILITY: Inedible.

REMARKS: Pathogenic, causing a yellowish, stringy root and butt rot of living trees. The epithet *ulmarius* means "growing on elm."

Rigidoporus ulmarius

Sarcodontia setosa (Pers.) Donk

= *Hydnum setosum* Pers.

MACROSCOPIC FEATURES: FRUITBODY annual, a resupinate, spreading, sulfur yellow crust, up to 20 cm or more long, irregular in outline and tightly attached to wood. FERTILE SURFACE consisting of crowded, pale to bright yellow spines that erratically discolor wine-red when bruised or in age; spines 5–15 mm long with tapered tips, tough, waxy. FLESH tough, waxy, yellow; odor fruity but unpleasant, taste not distinctive.

MICROSCOPIC FEATURES: Spores 5–6 × 3.5–4 μm, subglobose to teardrop-shaped, smooth, thick-walled, hyaline, inamyloid; hyphal system monomitic, clamp connections present.

OCCURRENCE: Elongated patches on the underside of decaying branches or logs, in knotholes, or under the bark of decaying apple or possibly other fruit trees; widely distributed in the Northeast and North Central regions, but rarely collected; summer–fall.

EDIBILITY: Inedible.

REMARKS: Saprotrophic on decaying fruit trees. *Sarcodontia* means "having fleshy teeth." The epithet *setosa* means "bristly."

Sarcodontia setosa

Schizophyllum commune Fr.

COMMON NAME: Common Split Gill

MACROSCOPIC FEATURES: CAP 1–4.5 cm wide, fan- to shell-shaped, thin, flexible. UPPER SURFACE densely covered with tiny hairs; surface dry, white to grayish white; margin incurved to inrolled when young, often becoming wavy and torn in age. GILLS subdistant, white to pinkish gray, split lengthwise along the free edge, usually serrated or torn. STALK absent or rudimentary. FLESH thin, flexible, whitish to grayish, sometimes with brownish tinges; odor and taste not distinctive.

MICROSCOPIC FEATURES: Spores 5–7.5 × 2–3 µm, cylindric, smooth, hyaline; cystidia absent.

OCCURRENCE: Solitary, scattered or in overlapping clusters on decaying broadleaf wood; widely distributed in the Northeast, North Central, and South regions; year-round.

EDIBILITY: Inedible.

REMARKS: *Schizophyllum commune* means "split gills growing in groups." This fungus has a white spore deposit. It can be found on all continents except Antarctica and is a rare cause of fungal sinusitis or lung disease.

Schizophyllum commune

Schizophyllum fasciatum Pat.

= *Schizophyllum mexicanum*

MACROSCOPIC FEATURES: CAP 2–6 cm wide, semi-circular to kidney- or fan-shaped, thin, flexible, entire or lobed. UPPER SURFACE densely covered with fine, long hairs, radiately sulcate near the margin, concentrically zonate with alternate light and dark zones of grayish and pale or darker brown, often white on the margin or at the point of attachment, when actively growing. GILLS subdistant, pale gray to pinkish gray or pinkish brown, split lengthwise along the free edge. STALK absent or rudimentary. FLESH thin, flexible, whitish to grayish, sometimes with brownish tinges; odor and taste not distinctive.

MICROSCOPIC FEATURES: Spores 7 × 2 μm, elongate-ellipsoid, smooth, hyaline; cystidia 36–54 × 3.5–4.5 μm, awl-shaped, hyaline.

OCCURRENCE: Solitary, scattered, or in groups, sometimes overlapping, on decaying broadleaf wood; widely distributed in the South region; year-round.

EDIBILITY: Inedible.

REMARKS: In this genus of six species from the Western Hemisphere, this is the only one that has cystidia.

Schizophyllum fasciatum (A)

Schizophyllum fasciatum (B)

Scutiger pes-caprae (Pers.) Bondartsev & Singer

= *Albatrellus pes-caprae* (Pers.) Pouzar
= *Polyporus pes-caprae* Pers.

COMMON NAME: Goat's Foot

MACROSCOPIC FEATURES: FRUITBODY annual, consisting of a cap and stalk growing on the ground, usually with conifers. CAP 2.5–20 cm wide, irregular or kidney-shaped to somewhat circular, convex at first, then expanding. UPPER SURFACE dry, woolly to scaly, reddish brown, olive-brown, dark yellow-brown, or blackish brown, somewhat yellowish between the scales; margin lobed. FERTILE SURFACE short-decurrent, white to yellowish or pinkish, bruising grayish yellow or pale greenish yellow. PORES large, angular to hexagonal, 1–2 mm wide; tubes up to 3 mm deep. STALK 2.5–7.5 cm long, 1–6 cm thick, simple or sometimes branched, eccentric or lateral, rarely central, cylindrical, often with an enlarged base, smooth or somewhat roughened with minute scales, white to yellowish or orangish. FLESH soft when fresh, creamy white, staining pinkish when exposed; odor usually pleasant like hazelnuts, or not distinctive, taste not distinctive.

MICROSCOPIC FEATURES: Spores 8–11 × 6–8 μm, broadly elliptic with a distinct apiculus, smooth, hyaline, inamyloid; hyphal system monomitic, clamp connections present.

OCCURRENCE: Solitary or in groups on the ground arising from buried wood, in conifer or mixed conifer and broadleaf forests; widely distributed in the Northeast and South regions; late spring–early winter.

EDIBILITY: Edible.

REMARKS: Mycorrhizal, not a wood-rotting fungus. It is superficially like a bolete, but its pore layer is not readily separable from the cap flesh. The epithet *pes-caprae* means "foot of a goat." Compare with *Laeticutis cristata*, which usually grows with broadleaf trees and has smaller spores that measure 5–7 × 4–5 μm.

Scutiger pes-caprae

Sistotrema confluens Pers.

= *Hydnotrema confluens* (Pers.) Link
= *Irpex confluens* (Pers.) P. Kumm.

COMMON NAME: Confluent Sistotrema

MACROSCOPIC FEATURES: FRUITBODY annual, resupinate or consisting of a cap and stalk, growing on the ground with mats of conifer needles. CAP up to 2 cm wide, fanlike to funnel-shaped; margin thin, typically uneven or lobed. UPPER SURFACE finely tomentose at first, becoming nearly glabrous, irregularly ridged and pitted or nearly smooth, slightly viscid, white, becoming creamy white to buff or very pale brown. FERTILE SURFACE decurrent, initially composed of anastomosing ridges or poroid, soon becoming distinctly teethlike, white to buff. STALK up to 1 cm long and 3 mm wide, lateral, tapered downward, glabrous, pale buff, with stringy white mycelium. FLESH about 1 mm thick, soft, fibrous, white; odor not distinctive, taste sweetish woody.

MICROSCOPIC FEATURES: Spores 3.8–5.5 × 1.8–2.5 μm, short-cylindrical to oblong, smooth, hyaline, inamyloid; hyphal system monomitic, clamp connections present.

OCCURRENCE: In groups or confluent clusters on the ground with conifer needles; widely distributed in the Northeast, North Central, and upper South regions; summer–fall.

EDIBILITY: Inedible.

REMARKS: Mycorrhizal with conifers. The epithet *confluens* means "occurring together or growing as one."

Sistotrema confluens

Skeletocutis lilacina A. David & Jean Keller

MACROSCOPIC FEATURES: FRUITBODY annual, resupinate, tightly attached to the substrate, forming irregular porose patches up to 6 cm or more long and 1 mm thick, marginal portions sometimes projecting or effused-reflexed, brownish on the upper surface, elastic and soft when fresh, hard and brittle when dry; margin distinctly demarcated, sterile and white when immature. FERTILE SURFACE lilac with a grayish tint. PORES rounded to angular, 5–6 per mm; tubes 0.5–1 mm long.

MICROSCOPIC FEATURES: Spores 3–4 × 0.8–1 µm, strongly allantoid, smooth, hyaline, inamyloid; hyphal system dimitic, clamp connections present.

OCCURRENCE: On decaying broadleaf trunks and branches; widely distributed in the Northeast, North Central, and South regions; year-round.

EDIBILITY: Inedible.

REMARKS: The epithet *lilacina* means "lilac." Compare with *Ceriporia purpurea*, which is similarly colored but has 3–5 pores per mm and larger spores. Also compare with *Phlebiopsis crassa*, which is similarly colored but lacks pores.

Skeletocutis lilacina (A)

Skeletocutis lilacina (B)

Sparassis americana R. H. Petersen

COMMON NAME: American Cauliflower Mushroom

MACROSCOPIC FEATURES: FRUITBODY 15–30 cm high and wide, a rounded, lettucelike cluster of flattened branches attached to a common, partially buried, stalklike base; branches densely arranged, with leaf- to fanlike, curly, flexible lobes, margin often incised. UPPER AND LOWER SURFACES smooth, azonate, whitish, creamy white to pale yellow or tan. FLESH thin, white; odor fragrant or not distinctive, taste not distinctive.

MICROSCOPIC FEATURES: Spores 5–7 × 3–4 µm, oval, smooth, hyaline; hyphal system monomitic, clamp connections present.

OCCURRENCE: Solitary or in groups on the ground in conifer or mixed woods, sometimes on well-decayed conifer logs and stumps; widely distributed in the Northeast, North Central, and South regions; summer–early winter.

EDIBILITY: Edible.

REMARKS: Saprotrophic or possibly parasitic on the ground with conifers. *Sparassis* means "torn," a reference to the numerous individual branches of the fruitbody. The epithet *americana* means "American." This fungus has been previously identified as *Sparassis crispa*, but molecular studies have shown that *Sparassis crispa* is a European species that does not occur in North America.

Sparassis americana

Sparassis spathulata (Schwein.) Fr.

= *Sparassis herbstii* Peck

COMMON NAMES: Cauliflower Mushroom, Eastern Cauliflower Mushroom

MACROSCOPIC FEATURES: FRUITBODY up to 35 cm high and wide, a rounded, lettucelike cluster of flattened, undulating branches attached to a buried, branching central base; branches densely arranged, spoon-shaped to spadelike, somewhat flexible, widest at the tips and tapered downward, margin entire. UPPER AND LOWER SURFACES smooth, distinctly zonate, whitish, creamy white to pale yellow or tan. FLESH thin, white; odor fragrant or not distinctive, taste not distinctive.

MICROSCOPIC FEATURES: Spores 5.9–8 × 4.7–5.8 μm, elliptical, smooth, hyaline; hyphal system monomitic, clamp connections present.

OCCURRENCE: Solitary or in groups on the ground at the base of oak or pine trees; widely distributed in the Northeast, North Central, and South regions; summer–fall.

EDIBILITY: Edible.

REMARKS: Saprotrophic or parasitic on the ground at the base of oak or pine trees. The epithet *spathulata* means "little spade or blade," a reference to the individual branches.

Sparassis spathulata

Spongipellis pachyodon (Pers.) Kotl. & Pouzar

= *Sarcodontia pachyodon* (Pers.) Spirin

COMMON NAMES: Marshmallow Polypore, Spongy Toothed Polypore

MACROSCOPIC FEATURES: FRUITBODY a leathery to tough spreading crust of effused-reflexed overlapping caps on wood. CAP 2–5 cm wide, fan-shaped, convex. UPPER SURFACE azonate, nearly glabrous, white to creamy white, becoming ochraceous to brownish in age; margin acute and somewhat incurved. FERTILE SURFACE white to creamy white, darkening in age, often lamellate or poroid near the margin but not always readily apparent, even on young specimens, soon breaking up and forming conspicuous flattened teeth up to 1.5 cm long. FLESH 3–8 mm thick, leathery to tough, white to pale cream; odor and taste not distinctive.

MICROSCOPIC FEATURES: Spores 5–7 × 5–6.5 µm, subglobose, thick-walled, smooth, hyaline, inamyloid, with a large oil drop, cyanophilous in cotton blue; hyphal system monomitic, clamp connections present.

OCCURRENCE: Solitary, in groups, or in overlapping clusters on living broadleaf trees, especially oak; widely distributed in the Northeast, North Central, and South regions; year-round.

EDIBILITY: Inedible.

REMARKS: Pathogenic, causing a white trunk rot in living broadleaf trees. The epithet *pachyodon* means "thick teeth." Compare with *Irpex lacteus*, which has much smaller teeth, up to 3 mm long.

Spongipellis pachyodon

Spongipellis unicolor (Fr.) Murrill

= *Sarcodontia unicolor* (Fr.) Zmitr. & Spirin

MACROSCOPIC FEATURES: FRUITBODY annual, a thick sessile cap attached to wood. CAP up to 18 cm wide, 8–12 cm thick, shelflike and semicircular or hoof-shaped. UPPER SURFACE azonate, with stiff, erect hairs or tomentose, becoming nearly glabrous in age, smooth or longitudinally uneven and roughened, sometimes with tufts of agglutinated hairs, soft to somewhat fibrous when fresh, becoming hard and brittle when mature; creamy white to pale buff, becoming cinnamon-buff to ochraceous tawny in age; margin rounded, concolorous. FERTILE SURFACE pale buff at first, becoming ochraceous to ochraceous orange as it ages. PORES circular to angular then weakly labyrinthine, sometimes arranged in more or less concentric rows, 1–2 per mm, dissepiments often splitting and becoming somewhat teethlike on older specimens; tubes up to 2 cm deep. FLESH up to 8 cm thick, zonate, soft and spongy on the upper portion, fibrous-tough below, pale buff.
MICROSCOPIC FEATURES: Spores 7–9 × 6–7 µm, ovoid to ellipsoid, smooth, hyaline, inamyloid, cyanophilous in cotton blue; hyphal system monomitic, clamp connections present.
OCCURRENCE: Solitary or sometimes in groups on broadleaf trees, especially oaks; widely distributed in the Northeast, North Central, and South regions; year-round.
EDIBILITY: Inedible.
REMARKS: Pathogenic, causing a white rot of broadleaf trees. The epithet *unicolor* means "of one color." *Spongipellis delectans* = *Sarcodontia delectans* (not illustrated) has an annual, sessile, soft, shelflike or hoof-shaped fruitbody up to 15 cm wide and 3–4 cm thick. The upper surface is azonate, tomentose to nearly glabrous, white, becoming pale brown or streaked reddish brown as it dries. Its fertile surface is white to pale buff or ochraceous and has circular to angular or sometimes labyrinthine pores, with thin dissepiments that become lacerated and teethlike in age and measure 1–2 per mm or sometimes larger on older specimens. The tubes are up to 1 cm deep, and the teeth may be up to 1 cm long. The flesh is soft and white to ochraceous. It has broadly ellipsoid to subglobose, hyaline, inamyloid spores that measure 7–9 × 5–7 µm, and clamp connections are present. It grows on living or decaying broadleaf trees and is widely distributed in the Northeast, North Central, and South regions, summer–early winter. *Spongipellis spumeus* = *Sarcodontia spumea* (not illustrated) is very similar but has round and entire pores, and the dissepiments do not break up and form teeth.

Spongipellis unicolor (A)

Spongipellis unicolor (B)

Steccherinum ochraceum (Pers.) Gray

= *Climacodon ochraceus* (Pers.) P. Karst.
= *Irpex ochraceous* (Pers.) Kotir. & Saaren

MACROSCOPIC FEATURES: FRUITBODY annual, forming resupinate patches 5–25 cm long or becoming effused-reflexed and forming fan-shaped to semicircular fruitbodies up to 7.5 cm wide on decaying wood. UPPER SURFACE zonate, grooved, with erect velvety hairs, dull white or ochraceous to pale grayish orange, greenish when covered with algae; margin rounded, wavy, lobed, whitish when actively growing. FERTILE SURFACE consisting of orange to salmon spines 1–3 mm long, crowded, sometimes fused. FLESH thin, dry, fibrous-tough, white; odor and taste not distinctive.

MICROSCOPIC FEATURES: Spores 3–5 × 2–2.5 μm, oval to oblong-ellipsoid, smooth, hyaline, inamyloid, with one oil drop; cystidia on the spines, thick-walled, projecting beyond the basidia, hyaline, typically encrusted; hyphal system dimitic, clamp connections present.

Steccherinum ochraceum (A)

Steccherinum ochraceum (B)

OCCURRENCE: In overlapping clusters or spreading patches on decaying broadleaf trunks, logs, and branches, often on the underside; widely distributed in the Northeast, North Central, and South regions; year-round.

EDIBILITY: Inedible.

REMARKS: Saprotrophic on decaying broadleaf wood. The epithet *ochraceum* means "pale brownish orange-yellow." The application of KOH is negative on all surfaces. Compare with *Climacodon pulcherrimus*. *Irpex lacteus* is similar but has a white to creamy white fruitbody.

Steccherinum oreophilum Lindsey & Gilb.

= *Irpex oreophilus* (Lindsey & Gilb.) Niemelä

MACROSCOPIC FEATURES: FRUITBODY annual, effused-reflexed, semicircular or laterally fused and elongated up to 5 cm or more, with conspicuous teethlike projections, growing on wood. UPPER SURFACE with erect or matted hairs, azonate, white to creamy white; margin thin, often fringed, whitish to ochraceous. FERTILE SURFACE poroid near the margin, soon splitting and becoming teethlike; teeth up to 7 mm long, somewhat flattened, minutely fringed, white to creamy white, developing ochraceous or brownish tints in age. FLESH usually less than 1 mm thick, tough, fibrous, white; odor and taste not distinctive.

MICROSCOPIC FEATURES: Spores 6–8 × 3–4 μm, short, cylindrical to oblong, smooth, hyaline, inamyloid; cystidia 8–10 μm wide, cylindrical, thick-walled, encrusted over the apical portion; hyphal system dimitic, clamp connections present.

OCCURRENCE: On decaying broadleaf wood, especially oaks; in Texas and the desert Southwest, also reported from Alberta and the Northwest Territories, Canada; year-round.

EDIBILITY: Inedible.

REMARKS: Saprotrophic, causing a white rot. The epithet *oreophilum* means "loving mountains," a reference to the high-elevation habitat in the desert Southwest, where this species was originally collected and described.

Steccherinum oreophilum

Steccherinum subrawakense Murrill

= *Hydnum subrawakense* (Murrill) Murrill
= *Irpex subrawakensis* (Murrill) Saaren & Kotir.

MACROSCOPIC FEATURES: FRUITBODY annual, consisting of a stalkless cap attached to decaying wood. CAP up to 6 cm wide, shell- to fan-shaped or semicircular. UPPER SURFACE uneven, with small, rounded bumps, whitish to grayish and sulcate at first, becoming conspicuously zonate with bands of tan, ochre, buff, and brown; margin thin, sterile, entire, wavy or slightly lobed. FERTILE SURFACE consisting of crowded teeth, 2–10 mm long, firm and tough, rounded or flat, pointed, simple or divided at the tip, yellow-brown or grayish brown, staining darker brown when bruised.

FLESH 2–4 mm thick, tough, yellowish brown to brown; odor of cinnamon or black cherries, especially when drying or placed on a dehydrator; taste not distinctive.

MICROSCOPIC FEATURES: Spores 2.5–3 × 1–1.5 μm, ellipsoid, smooth, hyaline, with one oil drop.

OCCURRENCE: In groups or overlapping clusters, often fused laterally, on broadleaf branches and logs, especially oaks; widely distributed in the Northeast, North Central, and South regions; fall–early winter.

EDIBILITY: Inedible.

REMARKS: Saprotrophic on decaying wood. It was first collected by E. West and W. A. Murrill near Gainesville, Florida, in 1938.

Steccherinum subrawakense

Stereum complicatum complex (Fr.) Fr.

= *Thelephora complicata* Fr.

COMMON NAME: Crowded Parchment
MACROSCOPIC FEATURES: FRUITBODY annual, a spreading crust of sessile or effused-reflexed caps, often laterally fused, narrowly attached to wood. CAP up to 2 cm wide and 0.4 mm thick, fan-shaped, flexible. UPPER SURFACE coated with whitish, silky hairs that are appressed toward the margin and erect toward the point of attachment (use a hand lens), zonate, sometimes with shallow radial grooves, variously colored from yellow-orange to grayish orange or brownish, shiny when dry; margin often wavy, crimped or incised, typically creamy buff or orangish. FERTILE SURFACE smooth or conspicuously cracked, bright yellow-orange to pale orange when fresh, becoming pale orange-brown when dry, sometimes staining red when cut or bruised, but not exuding red juice. FLESH very thin, tough, whitish; odor and taste not distinctive.
MICROSCOPIC FEATURES: Spores 5–7.5 × 2–3 µm, cylindrical, smooth, hyaline, inamyloid; hyphal system dimitic, clamp connections absent.
OCCURRENCE: In groups or dense overlapping clusters on twigs, branches, logs, stumps, and standing trunks of decaying conifers or broadleaf trees, especially oak; widely distributed in the Northeast, North Central, and South regions; year-round.
EDIBILITY: Inedible.
REMARKS: Saprotrophic on decaying wood. The epithet *complicatum* means "folded back on itself." Compare with *Stereum gausapatum* and *Stereum hirsutum*. Some authors consider *Stereum complicatum*, *Stereum gausapatum*, and *Stereum hirsutum* to be different forms of the same species.

Stereum complicatum complex

Stereum gausapatum complex (Fr.) Fr.

= *Stereum quercinum* Potter
= *Thelephora gausapata* Fr.

COMMON NAME: Bleeding Oak Crust

MACROSCOPIC FEATURES: FRUITBODY annual or perennial, sometimes resupinate but usually effused-reflexed, consisting of caps that are broadly attached to wood. CAP up to 6 cm wide and 1–2 mm thick, flexible, fan-shaped, often laterally fused and sometimes forming extensive rows. UPPER SURFACE appressed-tomentose, becoming nearly glabrous, zonate, variously colored with yellow, orange, beige, rusty brown, or dark brown bands, sometimes with greenish tints when coated with algae; margin sharp, white when actively growing, sometimes becoming wavy, curly, or lobed. FERTILE SURFACE uneven, warty, pinkish buff to pale grayish brown or pale ochre-brown, sometimes with a grayish overcast in places if fresh, staining dark red when cut or bruised.

FLESH thin, leathery, tough, whitish to buff; odor and taste not distinctive.

MICROSCOPIC FEATURES: Spores 6.5–9 × 3–4 μm, elliptic-cylindrical, smooth, hyaline, inamyloid; hyphal system dimitic, clamp connections absent.

OCCURRENCE: In groups or overlapping clusters on decaying oaks, rarely on other broadleaf trees; widely distributed in the Northeast, North Central, and South regions; year-round.

EDIBILITY: Inedible.

REMARKS: Saprotrophic on broadleaf trees, especially oaks. The epithet *gausapatum* means "resembling a woolen cloth." *Stereum sanguinolentum*, widely distributed in the Northeast and North Central regions, is similar, and its fertile surface also stains dark red, but it grows exclusively on conifers. Compare also with *Stereum complicatum* and *Stereum hirsutum*. Some authors consider *Stereum complicatum*, *Stereum gausapatum*, and *Stereum hirsutum* to be different forms of the same species.

Stereum gausapatum complex

Stereum hirsutum complex (Willd.) Pers.

= *Thelephora hirsuta* Willd.

COMMON NAME: Hairy Parchment

MACROSCOPIC FEATURES: FRUITBODY annual, a dense cluster of sessile caps, narrowly attached to wood, CAP up to 3 cm wide and 1.5 mm thick, fan- or shell-shaped, often laterally fused, flexible. UPPER SURFACE covered with short, coarse, stiff, whitish to grayish hairs (use a hand lens), occasionally with shallow radial grooves, concentrically zonate with reddish brown, yellow-orange, and grayish bands, sometimes with dark brown bands, occasionally green when coated with algae, dull when dry; margin wavy, sometimes incised, creamy yellow. FERTILE SURFACE smooth or warty, yellowish to reddish brown or grayish brown, sometimes staining darker yellow when cut or bruised. FLESH up to 1 mm thick, yellowish; odor and taste not distinctive.

MICROSCOPIC FEATURES: Spores 5–8 × 2–3.5 μm, elliptic-cylindrical, smooth, hyaline, inamyloid; hyphal system dimitic, clamp connections absent.

OCCURRENCE: In dense overlapping clusters on branches, logs, and stumps of decaying conifers or broadleaf trees; widely distributed in the Northeast, North Central, and South regions; year-round.

EDIBILITY: Inedible.

REMARKS: Saprotrophic on conifers or broadleaf trees. The epithet *hirsutum* means "covered with stiff hairs." It is sometimes attacked by a parasitic jelly fungus called the Golden Ear, *Tremella aurantia* = *Naematelia aurantia*. Compare with *Stereum complicatum* and *Stereum gausapatum*. Some authors consider *Stereum complicatum*, *Stereum gausapatum* and *Stereum hirsutum* to be different forms of the same species.

Stereum hirsutum complex

Stereum ostrea complex (Blume & T. Nees) Fr.

COMMON NAME: False Turkey-tail

MACROSCOPIC FEATURES: FRUITBODY annual, consisting of sessile caps attached to wood. CAP up to 8 cm wide, thin, leathery, fan- to oyster shell-shaped, overlapping or sometimes laterally fused. UPPER SURFACE covered with fine silky hairs, typically concentrically zoned with reddish brown, gray, yellow, and orange bands, often whitish along the margin. FERTILE SURFACE smooth, reddish brown to reddish buff or buff, not staining when cut or bruised. FLESH thin, leathery, tough, whitish to buff; odor and taste not distinctive.

MICROSCOPIC FEATURES: Spores 5–7.5 × 2–3 μm, cylindrical, smooth, hyaline, inamyloid; hyphal system dimitic, clamp connections absent.

OCCURRENCE: In groups, rows, or dense clusters on decaying broadleaf branches, logs, and stumps; widely distributed in the Northeast, North Central, and South regions; year-round.

EDIBILITY: Inedible.

REMARKS: Saprotrophic on broadleaf trees. The epithet *ostrea* means "resembling an oyster." It is often misidentified as the Turkey-tail, *Trametes versicolor*, a polypore with many tiny pores on its white fertile surface. *Stereum subtomentosum* is nearly identical, but its fertile surface stains yellow when cut or bruised. Considerable confusion about identification differences, if any, between *Stereum ostrea* and *Stereum subtomentosum* in North America exists in the literature. Some individuals think that the cut fertile surface of fresh specimens of *Stereum ostrea* sometimes stains yellow. It is also possible that what has been identified as *Stereum ostrea* in North America may actually be *Stereum subtomentosum*.

Stereum ostrea complex

Stereum sanguinolentum (Alb. & Schwein.) Fr.

= *Stereum balsameum* Peck

COMMON NAMES: Bleeding Conifer Parchment, Bleeding Stereum

MACROSCOPIC FEATURES: FRUITBODY annual, resupinate to effused-reflexed, 5–25 mm wide, often coalescing and forming crustose to elastic and leathery patches up to 30 cm or more in diameter. UPPER SURFACE finely hirsute or tomentose, undulating, indistinctly zonate, yellowish red to brownish red; margin whitish. FERTILE SURFACE uneven, wrinkled and warty or sometimes nearly smooth, grayish yellow-brown or ochre, sometimes with a pale violet tint; marginal portion paler, quickly staining blood-red when cut or bruised. FLESH very thin, yellowish red; odor and taste not distinctive.

MICROSCOPIC FEATURES: Spores 6–11 × 2.5–4 µm, elliptic-cylindric, smooth, hyaline.

OCCURRENCE: In groups or overlapping clusters on conifer wood, especially spruce, pine, and larch, often on the underside of the substrate; widely distributed in the Northeast and North Central regions; year-round.

EDIBILITY: Inedible.

REMARKS: Pathogenic, causing a red heartrot of conifers, especially spruce. It is sometimes attacked by *Tremella encephala*, a parasitic jelly fungus that forms brainlike, cushion-shaped or nearly round fruitbodies, up to 2 cm wide or more, that are whitish to yellowish or pale pinkish brown with a rather hard white core surrounded by brownish gelatinized tissue.

Stereum sanguinolentum (A)

Stereum sanguinolentum (B)

Stereum striatum (Fr.) Fr.

COMMON NAME: Silky Parchment

MACROSCOPIC FEATURES: FRUITBODY annual, a spreading crust of sessile, fan-shaped to shell-shaped caps that are often laterally fused; CAP up to 1.5 cm wide, rounded, somewhat flattened, attached to the substrate at a central point. UPPER SURFACE dry, shiny, pale gray to silvery or buff, with radiating silky fibers. FERTILE SURFACE smooth, buff to yellowish or brownish at first, becoming whitish in age, not staining when cut or bruised. FLESH very thin and tough, whitish; odor and taste not distinctive.

MICROSCOPIC FEATURES: Spores 6–8.5 × 2–3.5 μm, cylindrical, smooth, hyaline, inamyloid; hyphal system dimitic, clamp connections absent.

OCCURRENCE: In groups or clusters on decaying twigs and branches of broadleaf trees, especially American hornbeam, *Carpinus caroliniana*; widely distributed in the Northeast, North Central, and South regions; year-round.

EDIBILITY: Inedible.

REMARKS: Saprotrophic on broadleaf trees. The epithet *striatum* means "having minute radiating furrows or lines," a reference to the radiating silky fibers on the upper surface of the cap.

Stereum striatum

Stereum subtomentosum complex Pouzar

MACROSCOPIC FEATURES: FRUITBODY annual, sessile, 3–7 cm wide, thin, leathery, semicircular to fan-shaped, overlapping or sometimes laterally fused, attached to wood by a narrowed base. UPPER SURFACE concentrically zonate, slightly appressed-tomentose, becoming nearly glabrous in age, grayish to grayish orange or ochre-yellowish, sometimes greenish when coated with algae; margin paler to whitish. FERTILE SURFACE smooth to slightly warty, cracked when dry, yellowish to grayish yellow or ochraceous when fresh, becoming grayish ochre when dry, staining yellow when cut or bruised. FLESH very thin, elastic and tough when fresh, leathery when dry, reddish buff; odor and taste not distinctive.

MICROSCOPIC FEATURES: Spores 5.5–6.5 × 2–3 μm, elliptic-cylindrical, smooth, hyaline, inamyloid; hyphal system dimitic, clamp connections absent.

OCCURRENCE: In groups or overlapping clusters on decaying broadleaf wood; widely distributed in the Northeast, North Central, and upper South regions; year-round.

EDIBILITY: Inedible.

REMARKS: Saprotrophic on broadleaf trees. The epithet *subtomentosum* means "nearly tomentose," a reference to the upper surface. *Stereum ostrea* is nearly identical, but its fertile surface does not stain yellow when cut or bruised. Considerable confusion about identification differences, if any, between *Stereum ostrea* and *Stereum subtomentosum* in North America exists in the literature. Some individuals think that the cut fertile surface of fresh specimens of *Stereum ostrea* sometimes stains yellow. It is also possible that what has been identified as *Stereum ostrea* in North America may actually be *Stereum subtomentosum*.

Stereum subtomentosum complex

Thelephora cuticularis Berk.

MACROSCOPIC FEATURES: FRUITBODY annual, 1–3 cm wide, shelflike, irregularly fan-shaped to semicircular, broadly attached to the substrate, sometimes effused-reflexed or laterally fused. UPPER SURFACE dry, appressed-fibrillose to nearly glabrous, zonate or azonate, becoming radially wrinkled, dark brown to blackish; margin wavy, often lobed, somewhat rounded, soft, white. FERTILE SURFACE smooth, dark brown to blackish with purplish tints. FLESH 2–3 mm thick, tough, brown to blackish; odor not distinctive.

MICROSCOPIC FEATURES: Spores 8–12 × 5–9 μm, subangular to irregular, echinulate, pale brown; hyphae of the subhymenium stain greenish blue to blue in KOH; clamp connections absent.

OCCURRENCE: Solitary, scattered, or in overlapping groups on decaying broadleaf wood, especially oaks, also on the ground attached to buried wood; widely distributed in the Northeast, North Central, and South regions; fall–early winter.

EDIBILITY: Inedible.

REMARKS: Mycorrhizal, not a wood-rotting fungus.

Thelephora cuticularis

Thelephora terrestris Ehrh.

= *Thelephora crustosa* Lloyd

COMMON NAMES: Common Fiber Vase, Earth Fan
MACROSCOPIC FEATURES: FRUITBODY annual, 1.3–7 cm wide, 2–5 cm high, partially erect and spreading, composed of circular to fan-shaped stalkless caps in overlapping clusters, often laterally fused and forming patches up to 30 cm or more in diameter. UPPER SURFACE covered with short, stiff hairs, often matted and woolly or scaly, somewhat concentrically zonate, rusty brown to grayish brown, becoming blackish brown in age; margin woolly, coarsely torn, often with small, fan-shaped outgrowths, white or brown. FERTILE SURFACE somewhat wrinkled and finely warty, pinkish brown or darker brown. FLESH thin, leathery, watery brown; odor somewhat earthy or not distinctive, taste not distinctive.

MICROSCOPIC FEATURES: Spores 8–12 × 6–9 μm, angularly oval to elliptic, nearly smooth to warty or spiny, purplish.

OCCURRENCE: Solitary or in overlapping clusters attached to roots, branches, seedlings, or mosses, or on the ground, in conifer or mixed woods; widely distributed in the Northeast, North Central, and South regions; year-round.

EDIBILITY: Inedible.

REMARKS: Mycorrhizal. The epithet *terrestris* means "on the ground." This fungus has a purple-brown spore deposit. It is the most common species of *Thelephora* in eastern North America. Compare with *Thelephora terrestris* f. *concrescens*.

Thelephora terrestris

Thelephora terrestris f. *concrescens* S. Lundell

MACROSCOPIC FEATURES: FRUITBODY 1.3–7 cm wide, partially erect and enveloping the stems and branches of host plants, composed of circular to fan-shaped or funnel-shaped stalkless caps in overlapping clusters, sometimes laterally fused and forming patches up to 25 cm or more in diameter. UPPER SURFACE covered with short, stiff hairs, often matted and woolly or scaly, somewhat concentrically zoned, rusty brown to dark brown or grayish brown, becoming blackish brown in age; margin wavy or sometimes lobed, white to grayish when fresh. FERTILE SURFACE somewhat wrinkled and finely warty to nearly smooth, grayish to pinkish brown when young, becoming darker brown in age. FLESH thin, leathery, brown; odor somewhat earthy or not distinctive, taste not distinctive.

MICROSCOPIC FEATURES: Spores 8–12 × 6–9 μm, angularly oval to elliptic, warty and spiny, brown.

OCCURRENCE: In overlapping clusters that envelop and clasp plant stems and branches in broadleaf and mixed woods; widely distributed in the Northeast, North Central, and South regions; year-round.

EDIBILITY: Inedible.

REMARKS: Mycorrhizal. *Concrescens* means "fused together." This fungus has a purplish brown spore deposit. *Thelephora terrestris* grows on the ground attached to roots, branches, seedlings, and mosses in conifer or mixed woods, but does not envelop the substrate.

Thelephora terrestris f. *concrescens*

Thelephora vialis Schwein.

= *Thelephora tephroleuca* Berk. & M. A. Curtis

COMMON NAME: Vase Thelephore

MACROSCOPIC FEATURES: FRUITBODY annual, up to 15 cm wide and 2.5–10 cm high, a semierect rosette of caps arising from a central stalk, often highly variable. CAP funnel-shaped or fused and somewhat vase-shaped. UPPER SURFACE minutely scaly, grayish purple, sometimes dull yellow; margin wavy, whitish to yellowish. FERTILE SURFACE wrinkled and colored like the upper surface. STALK 1–5 cm long, 5–40 mm thick, enlarged downward, solid, whitish to grayish.

FLESH thick, leathery, whitish to grayish; odor faintly sharp and disagreeable or not distinctive, taste unpleasant or not distinctive.

MICROSCOPIC FEATURES: Spores 4.5–8 × 4.5–6.5 µm, angular, warty, minutely spiny, olive-buff; clamp connections present.

OCCURRENCE: Solitary, scattered, or in groups with broadleaf trees, especially oaks; widely distributed in the Northeast, North Central, and South regions; summer–early winter.

EDIBILITY: Inedible.

REMARKS: Mycorrhizal. It is sometimes collected for dyeing silk or wool.

Thelephora vialis

Trametella trogii (Berk.) Domański

= *Cerrena trogii* (Berk.) Zmitr.
= *Coriolopsis trogii* (Berk.) Domański
= *Funalia trogii* (Berk.) Bondartsev & Singer
= *Trametes trogii* Berk.

COMMON NAME: Trog's Tramete
MACROSCOPIC FEATURES: FRUITBODY annual, sessile or effused-reflexed, rarely resupinate, up to 12 cm wide and 2 cm thick, semicircular, flexible when fresh. UPPER SURFACE covered with a dense layer of ochraceous, brownish, tan, or tawny hairs, becoming grayish in age but not blackish, faintly zonate or azonate; margin thin, sharp, uneven. FERTILE SURFACE whitish to ochraceous buff, often with a a grayish or lavender tint when actively growing. PORES angular, 1–2 per mm, becoming labyrinthine and up to 11 mm long, sometimes lacerated; tubes up to 9 mm deep. FLESH up to 5 mm thick, fibrous, white to creamy buff; odor and taste not distinctive.
MICROSCOPIC FEATURES: Spores 8–10(12) × 2.5–4 µm, cylindrical, hyaline, smooth, inamyloid; hyphal system trimitic, clamp connections present.

Trametella trogii (A)

OCCURRENCE: Solitary or in groups, sometimes overlapping, on decaying broadleaf wood, especially poplar and willow; widely distributed in the Northeast and North Central regions; fall–early winter.

EDIBILITY: Inedible.

REMARKS: Saprotrophic, causing a white rot. The epithet *trogii* honors Swiss mycologist Jacob Gabriel Trog (1781–1865). The Brownflesh Bracket, *Trametella gallica* = *Coriolopsis gallica* (not illustrated), is very similar, but it has a brown to grayish fertile surface, brown flesh, and spores are 10–16 × 3–5 μm. *Phylloporia ribis* (not illustrated), widely distributed in the Northeast and North Central regions, grows on living broadleaf shrubs, especially currants, rose bushes, and honeysuckles. It forms perennial, semicircular, overlapping caps, 3–15 cm wide, that often enclose the stems on which they are growing. A soft and spongy tomentum on the upper surface is separated from the flesh by a distinct black line that is absent near the margin. The upper surface is distinctly zonate and sulcate, rusty brown to dark brown, greenish tinted when coated with algae, and has a broad, yellow-brown to rusty brown margin. The fertile surface is yellow-brown to rusty brown and has round pores, 6–7 per mm. The spores are broadly ellipsoid, yellowish, and measure 3–4.5 × 2.5–3 μm. *Phylloporia chrysites* (not illustrated) is nearly identical to *Phylloporia ribis* but has subglobose spores, 2.5–3.5 μm, and is known only from Florida and the tropics.

Trametella trogii (B)

Trametes aesculi (Fr.) Justo

MACROSCOPIC FEATURES: FRUITBODY annual to perennial, 5–35 cm wide, up to 3 cm thick, shelflike, semicircular to fan- or kidney-shaped, corky when fresh, becoming rigid when dry, attached to wood by a short, stalklike, thickened base. UPPER SURFACE finely tomentose, soon becoming glabrous, smooth or concentrically sulcate, often slightly uneven and warty, azonate or faintly zonate, white to creamy white, buff or grayish, becoming ochraceous to dull orange or brown on older specimens, often partially covered from the base outward with green algae; margin thin, bent downward, even or lobed. FERTILE SURFACE white to creamy white. PORES highly variable, often with circular, labyrinthine, or lamellate components present from the base to the margin, 1–2 per mm; tubes up to 6 mm deep. FLESH up to 1.5 cm thick, tough to woody, white to creamy white; odor and taste not distinctive.

MICROSCOPIC FEATURES: Spores 5–7 × 2–3 µm, cylindrical to allantoid, smooth, hyaline, inamyloid; hyphal system trimitic, clamp connections present.

OCCURRENCE: Solitary or in groups on decaying broadleaf wood; widely distributed in the Northeast, North Central, and South regions; year-round.

EDIBILITY: Inedible.

REMARKS: Saprotrophic on decaying broadleaf wood. The highly variable fertile surface, which changes from the base to the margin, is an excellent field identification feature. *Trametes gibbosa* is very similar, but it has a conspicuously uneven and warty upper surface that is distinctly velvety or fuzzy when observed with a hand lens, and it has smaller spores that measure 4–5.5 × 2–2.5 µm. *Trametes elegans* (not illustrated) is a somewhat similar species that does not occur in the United States or Canada. It does occur in Central and South America, Africa, Australia, and Southeast Asia.

Trametes aesculi

Trametes cinnabarina (Jacq.) Fr.

= *Polyporus cinnabarinus* (Jacq.) Fr.
= *Pycnoporus cinnabarinus* (Jacq.) P. Karst.

COMMON NAME: Cinnabar-red Polypore

MACROSCOPIC FEATURES: FRUITBODY annual, sessile, tough, 3–14 cm wide, up to 2 cm thick, convex to nearly flat, semicircular to kidney-shaped. UPPER SURFACE dry, azonate, glabrous, roughened or wrinkled, sometimes smooth, bright or dull orange-red, sometimes mixed with yellow or brownish tints; margin sharp or rounded. FERTILE SURFACE pale or dark orange-red. PORES circular to angular, sometimes elongated, 2–4 per mm; tubes 1–4 mm deep. FLESH up to 1.5 cm thick, corky or tough, reddish orange; odor and taste not distinctive.

MICROSCOPIC FEATURES: Spores 4.5–8 × 2.5–4 µm, cylindrical to slightly allantoid, smooth, hyaline, inamyloid; hyphal system trimitic, clamp connections present.

OCCURRENCE: Solitary or in groups on decaying broadleaf logs and branches, rarely on conifers; widely distributed in the Northeast, North Central, and South regions; year-round.

EDIBILITY: Inedible.

REMARKS: Saprotrophic, causing a white rot of decaying broadleaf trees, rarely conifers. The epithet *cinnabarina* means "orange-red." *Trametes sanguinea* has a smaller and thinner fruitbody, typically less than 5 mm thick, an orange-red fertile surface, and its spores measure 5–6 × 2–2.5 µm. It grows exclusively on broadleaf trees, especially oak.

Trametes cinnabarina

Trametes ectypa (Berk. & M. A. Curtis) Gilb. & Ryvarden

= *Polyporus ectypus* Berk. & M. A. Curtis

MACROSCOPIC FEATURES: FRUITBODY annual, sessile or with a short lateral contracted base, rigid and corky, up to 12 cm wide, up to 8 mm thick at the point of attachment, semicircular. UPPER SURFACE finely velvety or nearly glabrous, multizonate and sulcate, tan to dingy pale yellowish brown at first, becoming reddish brown from the base outward, color variable from zone to zone; margin thin, sharp, sometimes uneven and roughened, sterile. FERTILE SURFACE creamy white, becoming brownish when dry. PORES round to angular, 4–6 per mm; tubes up to 4 mm deep, white, darker toward the margin. FLESH up to 5 mm thick, dense, white; odor and taste not distinctive.

MICROSCOPIC FEATURES: Spores 4.5–6 × 2–2.5 µm, cylindrical, smooth, hyaline, inamyloid; hyphal system trimitic, clamp connections present.

OCCURRENCE: Solitary or in overlapping clusters on decaying broadleaf wood; widely distributed in the South region; year-round.

EDIBILITY: Inedible.

REMARKS: Saprotrophic, causing a white rot on dead broadleaf trees. The epithet *ectypa* means "carved or worked in relief," a reference to the multizonate upper surface. *Trametes subectypa* = *Trametes subectypus*, an orthographic variant reported from Georgia and the Gulf Coast states, is nearly identical. It differs by having an azonate to faintly zonate, white to straw-colored upper surface. It may be just a color variant of *Trametes ectypa*; molecular analysis is needed to resolve the issue.

Trametes ectypa

Trametes gibbosa (Pers.) Fr.

= *Daedalea gibbosa* (Pers.) Pers.

COMMON NAME: Lumpy Bracket

MACROSCOPIC FEATURES: FRUITBODY annual to perennial, 5–20 cm wide, up to 3 cm thick, shelf-like, semicircular to fan- or kidney-shaped, corky when fresh, becoming rigid when dry, attached to wood by a short, stalklike, thickened base. UPPER SURFACE warty and uneven, distinctly velvety or fuzzy, especially when observed with a hand lens, often concentrically zoned or sulcate, sometimes nearly smooth near the margin, white to cream, buff, or very pale ochraceous, occasionally developing gray tints as it ages, often covered from the base outward with green algae; margin thin, acute, even or lobed, whitish or brownish. FERTILE SURFACE whitish to cream-colored, becoming grayish ochre in age. PORES radially elongated and sometimes labyrinthine or nearly lamellate, especially near the margin, 1–3 per mm; tubes up to 5 mm deep. FLESH up to 1.5 cm thick, tough to woody, white to pale cream; odor and taste not distinctive.

MICROSCOPIC FEATURES: Spores 4–5.5 × 2–2.5 µm, elliptic-cylindrical, smooth, hyaline, inamyloid; hyphal system trimitic, clamp connections present.

OCCURRENCE: Solitary, scattered, or in groups on decaying broadleaf wood; widely distributed in the Northeast, North Central, and South regions; year-round.

EDIBILITY: Inedible.

REMARKS: *Trametes aesculi* is very similar, but its upper cap surface is typically finely tomentose, soon becoming glabrous; its fertile surface is highly variable, and it has larger spores that measure 5–7 × 2–3 µm.

Trametes gibbosa

Trametes hirsuta (Wulfen) Lloyd

= *Polyporus hirsutus* (Wulfen) Fr.

COMMON NAME: Hairy Bracket

MACROSCOPIC FEATURES: FRUITBODY annual, sessile, 2–10 cm wide, shelflike, semicircular, leathery and flexible when fresh. UPPER SURFACE covered with coarse hairs, zonate and often concentrically sulcate, sometimes bumpy and uneven, pale gray or brown, occasionally with yellowish tints, usually with darker or paler bands, sometimes distinctly greenish gray when coated with algae; margin thin, typically pale gray or yellowish brown. FERTILE SURFACE white to tan, becoming grayish in age. PORES circular to angular, 3–4 per mm; tubes up to 6 mm deep. FLESH up to 8 mm thick, duplex, upper layer soft-fibrous, gray-ish, separated from the lower layer by a thin black line at least at the base; lower layer corky, whitish; often with a pronounced anise odor when fresh, disappearing when dry; taste not distinctive.

MICROSCOPIC FEATURES: Spores 5–9 × 2–2.5 μm, cylindrical, smooth, hyaline, inamyloid; hyphal system trimitic, clamp connections present.

OCCURRENCE: Solitary or in overlapping clusters on decaying broadleaf wood, rarely on conifers; widely distributed in the Northeast, North Central, and South regions; year-round.

EDIBILITY: Inedible.

REMARKS: Saprotrophic on decaying broadleaf wood. The epithet *hirsuta* means "having coarse hairs." The flesh of *Trametes pubescens* is not duplex and lacks a thin black line.

Trametes hirsuta

Trametes lactinea (Berk.) Sacc.

= *Leiotrametes lactinea* (Berk.) Welti & Courtec
= *Polyporus lactineus* Berk.

MACROSCOPIC FEATURES: FRUITBODY annual, 5–25 cm wide, shelflike, semicircular to fan- or kidney-shaped, sometimes forming rosettes of overlapping caps, sessile. UPPER SURFACE uneven and conspicuously warty or sometimes nearly smooth, glabrous, usually concentrically zoned and often shallowly furrowed, highly variable with pale to dark brown or grayish bands on a whitish to grayish ground color, sometimes whitish or grayish nearly overall; margin variable, fairly thick and blunt or rounded on some specimens, thin on others, especially thin when growing on conifers, brown or whitish. FERTILE SURFACE white to creamy white, becoming dull pale yellow to brownish in age. PORES initially round, becoming angular at maturity, 2–3 per mm; tubes up to 1.5 cm deep. FLESH 0.5–2.5 cm thick, corky, white to yellowish; odor and taste not distinctive.

MICROSCOPIC FEATURES: Spores 5–7 × 2.5–3.2 µm, oblong-elliptical to cylindrical, smooth, hyaline, inamyloid; hyphal system trimitic, clamp connections present.

OCCURRENCE: Solitary, in groups, or in overlapping clusters, broadly attached to trunks, logs, and stumps of decaying broadleaf trees or pines, sometimes on the ground arising from buried wood; widely distributed in the Northeast, North Central, and South regions; year-round.

EDIBILITY: Inedible.

REMARKS: Saprotrophic on decaying wood. Overlapping and fused clusters of this polypore may be up to 60 cm or wider. Numerous publications and internet postings have mistaken this species for *Trametes cubensis* (not illustrated), which has 5–7 pores per mm. *Trametes lactinea* has also been confused with the less commonly encountered *Trametes aesculi*, which usually has circular, labyrinthine, and lamellate components present from the base to the margin of its fertile surface.

Trametes lactinea

Trametes nivosa (Berk.) Murrill

= *Fomitopsis nivosa* (Berk.) Gilb. & Ryvarden
= *Polyporus nivosus* Berk.

MACROSCOPIC FEATURES: FRUITBODY annual to biennial, sessile, 5–16 cm wide, shelflike, fan-shaped or semicircular, fibrous-tough when moist and fresh, woody when dry. UPPER SURFACE white at first, becoming pale brown and eventually developing a dark, resinous, cuticular layer that spreads from the base outward in older specimens, glabrous, slightly roughened to nearly smooth, azonate; margin acute. FERTILE SURFACE whitish at first, becoming brownish gray to grayish brown, usually glancing. PORES circular to angular, 6–8 per mm; tubes up to 1 cm deep. FLESH up to 2 cm thick, zonate, white to creamy white, tough to woody; odor and taste not distinctive.

MICROSCOPIC FEATURES: Spores 6–9 × 2–3 μm, cylindrical, thin-walled, frequently collapsed, smooth, hyaline, inamyloid; hyphal system trimitic, clamp connections present.

OCCURRENCE: Solitary, scattered, or in overlapping clusters on broadleaf trees, especially fruit trees; widely distributed along the Gulf Coast states from Florida to Texas; year-round.

EDIBILITY: Inedible.

REMARKS: Saprotrophic on decaying broadleaf wood. The epithet *nivosa* means "full of snow," a reference to the color of young fruitbodies. The formation of a dark, resinous, cuticular layer in older specimens is a key identification feature. Compare with *Fomitella supina*, which has ochraceous to brown flesh.

Trametes nivosa

Trametes ochracea (Pers.) Gilb. & Ryvarden

= *Polyporus ochraceous* (Pers.) Sommerf.

MACROSCOPIC FEATURES: FRUITBODY annual, sessile, 2–8 cm wide, fan- to kidney-shaped or sometimes effused-reflexed, thin, tough, flexible, flattened, sometimes laterally fused and forming rows. UPPER SURFACE finely tomentose to nearly glabrous, somewhat zonate, variously colored, typically yellowish buff with darker zones of reddish brown, dark brown, and grayish; margin thin, sharp, wavy, sometimes folded or lobed. FERTILE SURFACE creamy white to grayish. PORES circular, 3–4 per mm; tubes up to 4 mm deep. FLESH up to 5 mm thick, fibrous-tough, azonate, creamy white, lacking a thin brown to blackish layer between the upper surface and the flesh; odor and taste not distinctive.

MICROSCOPIC FEATURES: Spores 6–8 × 2–2.5 μm, cylindrical, slightly curved, smooth, hyaline, inamyloid; hyphal system trimitic, clamp connections present.

OCCURRENCE: In groups or overlapping clusters on decaying broadleaf wood, rarely on conifers; widely distributed in the Northeast, North Central, and South regions; year-round.

EDIBILITY: Inedible.

REMARKS: Saprotrophic, causing a white rot of broadleaf trees. The epithet *ochracea* means "ochre-colored, yellowish buff." Compare with *Trametes versicolor*, which has a thin brown to blackish layer between the upper surface and the flesh, is more colorful and more distinctly zonate.

Trametes ochracea

Trametes pavonia (Hook.) Ryvarden

= *Polyporus pavonius* (Hook.) Fr.

MACROSCOPIC FEATURES: FRUITBODY annual, sessile, up to 10 cm wide and 3 mm thick at the base, semicircular to fan-shaped, often fused laterally, leathery and flexible when fresh. UPPER SURFACE persistently tomentose, multizonate, white to ochraceous at first, becoming buff to pale dull brown, slightly shiny, often green at the base when covered with algae; margin thin, wavy. FERTILE SURFACE white to pale ochraceous. PORES circular to angular, sometimes slightly elongated radially on older specimens, 5–6 per mm; tubes up to 1 mm deep. FLESH 1–2 mm thick, fibrous, white; odor and taste not distinctive.

MICROSCOPIC FEATURES: Spores 5–6 × 3–4 µm, ellipsoid, hyaline, smooth, inamyloid; hyphal system trimitic, clamp connections present.

OCCURRENCE: Solitary or in overlapping clusters on broadleaf trees; widely distributed along the Gulf Coast states from Florida to Texas; year-round.

EDIBILITY: Inedible.

REMARKS: Saprotrophic on decaying broadleaf wood. The epithet *pavonia* means "pertaining to peacocks." Compare with *Trametes villosa*, which is similar but has much larger pores. *Trametes membranacea* (not illustrated), widely distributed in the South region, is very similar and also grows on broadleaf trees. It is up to 8 cm wide, semicircular to fan-shaped with a contracted base, and the upper surface is zonate, velvety when young, and soon becomes glabrous. Both the upper and fertile surfaces are dull white at first and soon become creamy white to pale tan. The angular pores, 5–6 per mm, often become lacerated, and the spores measure 4.5–6 × 2–2.5 µm.

Trametes pavonia

Trametes pubescens (Schumach.) Pilát

= *Polyporus pubescens* (Schumach.) Fr.

MACROSCOPIC FEATURES: FRUITBODY annual, sessile, up to 9 cm wide, semicircular, thin, leathery. UPPER SURFACE tomentose to finely velvety, becoming nearly glabrous, azonate or faintly zonate, creamy white to buff, sometimes green when covered with algae. FERTILE SURFACE creamy white to light ochraceous-buff or darker in age, sometimes becoming grayish. PORES angular to somewhat elongated, 3–5 per mm; tubes up to 4 mm deep. FLESH up to 5 mm thick, uniformly fibrous-tough, not duplex, lacking a thin black line, white to creamy white; odor and taste not distinctive.

MICROSCOPIC FEATURES: Spores 5–7 × 1.5–2 μm, cylindrical to slightly allantoid, smooth, hyaline, inamyloid; hyphal system trimitic, clamp connections present.

OCCURRENCE: Solitary or in overlapping clusters on broadleaf trees, rarely on conifers; widely distributed in the Northeast, North Central, and South regions; year-round.

EDIBILITY: Inedible.

REMARKS: Saprotrophic on decaying broadleaf wood. The epithet *pubescens* means "having downy hairs." The uniformly creamy white to buff, typically azonate and finely velvety cap, and the creamy white to ochraceous-buff fertile surface are good field identification characters. The tubes and pores of fresh specimens are frequently occupied by insect larvae (use a hand lens). The flesh of *Trametes hirsuta* is duplex with a thin black line that separates the upper and lower portions.

Trametes pubescens

Trametes sanguinea (L.) Lloyd

= *Polyporus sanguineus* (L.) Fr.
= *Pycnoporus sanguineus* (L.) Murrill

COMMON NAMES: Cinnabar Bracket, Orange Polypore

MACROSCOPIC FEATURES: FRUITBODY annual, sessile, tough, up to 8 cm wide, typically less than 5 mm thick, convex to nearly flat and shelflike, semicircular. UPPER SURFACE dry, usually zonate, finely tomentose to nearly glabrous, roughened or wrinkled, sometimes smooth, orange-red to orange, becoming salmon-buff in age; margin sharp, pale orange or whitish when actively growing. FERTILE SURFACE orange-red, dark brown in age. PORES circular, 5–6 per mm; tubes up to 2 mm deep. FLESH up to 3 mm thick, fibrous-tough, zonate or azonate, orange-buff; odor and taste not distinctive.

MICROSCOPIC FEATURES: Spores 5–6 × 2–2.5 µm, cylindrical to slightly allantoid, smooth, hyaline, inamyloid; hyphal system trimitic, clamp connections present.

OCCURRENCE: Solitary or in groups on broadleaf logs and branches, or sometimes on conifers, especially pines; widely distributed in the South region, northern distribution limits yet to be determined; year-round.

EDIBILITY: Inedible.

REMARKS: Saprotrophic, causing a white rot of decaying broadleaf trees. The epithet *sanguinea* means "blood red." *Trametes cinnabarina* has a larger and thicker fruitbody, up to 2 cm thick, and larger spores that measure 4.5–8 × 2.5–4 µm.

Trametes sanguinea

Trametes suaveolens (L.) Fr.

= *Polyporus suaveolens* (L.) Fr.

COMMON NAME: Sweet Trametes

MACROSCOPIC FEATURES: FRUITBODY annual, sessile, up to 14 cm wide and 1.4 cm thick, semicircular or elongated, corky. UPPER SURFACE finely tomentose to nearly glabrous, azonate, smooth, creamy white to buff; margin rounded. FERTILE SURFACE creamy white at first, becoming pale brown in age. PORES circular to angular, 2–3 per mm; tubes up to 1 cm deep. FLESH up to 3.5 mm thick, zonate, soft corky, white to creamy white; odor pleasant, aniselike; taste not distinctive.

MICROSCOPIC FEATURES: Spores 9–12 × 4–4.5 μm, cylindrical, smooth, thin-walled, hyaline, inamyloid; hyphal system trimitic, clamp connections present.

OCCURRENCE: Usually solitary on broadleaf trees, especially birch, poplar, and willow, also reported on balsam fir; widely distributed in the Northeast, North Central, and South regions; year-round.

EDIBILITY: Inedible.

REMARKS: Pathogenic, causing a white rot of broadleaf trees. The epithet *suaveolens* means "sweet-smelling."

Trametes suaveolens

Trametes versicolor (L.) Lloyd

= *Polyporus versicolor* (L.) Fr.

COMMON NAME: Turkey-tail
MACROSCOPIC FEATURES: FRUITBODY annual, sessile, 2–10 cm wide, fan- to kidney-shaped, thin, tough, flexible, flattened, sometimes laterally fused and forming extensive rows. UPPER SURFACE covered with silky to velvety, delicate, soft hairs; conspicuously zonate with various colors, often with shades of orange, green, blue, brown, or gray; margin thin, sharp, wavy, sometimes folded or lobed. FERTILE SURFACE white to buff or sometimes pale grayish. PORES circular to angular, 4–5 per mm, often becoming slightly jagged as they age; tubes up to 3 mm deep. FLESH up to 3 mm thick, tough, white to creamy white, with a thin brown to blackish layer between the upper surface and the flesh that can be seen when the specimen is cut or torn; odor and taste not distinctive.

MICROSCOPIC FEATURES: Spores 5–6 × 1.5–2 µm, cylindrical to allantoid, smooth, hyaline; hyphal system trimitic, clamp connections present.

OCCURRENCE: Solitary, in groups, or in overlapping clusters, rows, or rosettes on wood; widely distributed in the Northeast, North Central, and South regions; year-round.

EDIBILITY: Inedible.

REMARKS: Pathogenic, causing white rot, as well as paperbark and sapwood rot syndrome on apple

Trametes versicolor (A)

Trametes versicolor (B)

trees. The epithet *versicolor* means "of various colors." It is sometimes used to make a tea. *Trametes ochracea* is similar, but it lacks a thin brown to blackish layer between the upper surface and the flesh, is less colorful and less distinctly zonate. *Trametes hirsuta* has a conspicuously hairy cap, and its fertile surface becomes grayish in age. *Trametes pubescens* has a finely hairy to smooth, creamy white to yellowish buff, azonate or faintly zoned cap. *Stereum* species lack pores on the lower surface. The upper surface of *Trametes versicolor* may have Fairy Pins, fruitbodies of *Phaeocalicium polyporaeum* (see p. 355), which resemble miniature matchsticks, dark olive-brown to blackish. See the Remarks section of *Trichaptum biforme* for additional information.

Trametes villosa (Sw.) Kreisel

= *Polyporus pinsitus* Fr.
= *Polyporus villosus* (Sw.) Fr.

MACROSCOPIC FEATURES: FRUITBODY annual, sessile, up to 8 cm wide and 1–2 mm thick, semicircular to fan-shaped, often fused laterally, flexible. UPPER SURFACE covered with coarse, elongated, upright or somewhat flattened hairs, becoming tomentose but not glabrous in age, distinctly zonate, white to grayish or brown; margin thin, wavy or lobed. FERTILE SURFACE white to cream, becoming smoky brown to blackish in age. PORES angular, thin-walled, 1–3 per mm, frequently breaking up and becoming finely incised and teethlike in age, often slightly elongated radially, but not labyrinthine; tubes up to 1 mm deep. FLESH 1.5–3 mm thick, tough, flexible, white; odor and taste not distinctive.

MICROSCOPIC FEATURES: Spores 5.5–8.5 × 2.5–3.5 μm, cylindrical to allantoid, smooth, hyaline, inamyloid; hyphal system trimitic, clamp connections present.

OCCURRENCE: In groups or clusters on decaying conifers or broadleaf trees; widely distributed in the Northeast, North Central, and South regions; year-round.

EDIBILITY: Inedible.

REMARKS: Saprotrophic on decaying conifers and broadleaf trees. The epithet *villosa* means "hairy or shaggy." This fungus is usually easy to recognize because of the thin, flexible fruitbody with a hairy cap and large pores that become teethlike in age. *Trametes hirsuta* has thicker and larger caps with smaller pores. Compare with *Trametopsis cervina*, which is larger, thicker, and has angular to irregular pores that become conspicuously labyrinthine, then coarsely teethlike.

Trametes villosa (A)

Trametes villosa (B)

Trametes villosa (C)

Trametopsis cervina (Schwein.) Tomšovský

= *Trametes cervina* (Schwein.) Bres.

MACROSCOPIC FEATURES: FRUITBODY annual, sessile, 3–15 cm wide, shell- to fan-shaped or hoof-shaped, often laterally fused, leathery to stiff. UPPER SURFACE covered with short, coarse hairs, zonate or sometimes faintly zonate, pinkish buff, brownish orange, pinkish cinnamon, or darker cinnamon; margin thin, incurved, usually white when actively growing, sometimes darker purplish brown and finely incised as it dries or in age. FERTILE SURFACE cinnamon-buff to tan at first, then cinnamon or darker brown in age. PORES angular to irregular when young, becoming conspicuously labyrinthine, then breaking up and becoming coarsely teethlike with pale tips, 1–3 per mm; tubes up to 8 mm deep. FLESH typically less than 5 mm thick, soft and flexible, becoming tough and rigid when dry, white to buff; odor and taste not distinctive.

MICROSCOPIC FEATURES: Spores 7–10 × 2–3 µm, elliptic to slightly allantoid, smooth, hyaline, inamyloid; hyphal system trimitic, clamp connections present.

OCCURRENCE: In large, overlapping clusters on decaying broadleaf wood, rarely on conifers; widely distributed in the Northeast, North Central, and South regions; year-round.

EDIBILITY: Inedible.

REMARKS: Saprotrophic on decaying wood. The epithet *cervina* means "pertaining to deer," a reference to the colors of this polypore. *Cerrena unicolor* is similar but has a distinctly zonate upper surface, a thin dark zone separating the upper surface from the flesh, and a gray to smoky gray or grayish brown fertile surface when mature. Also compare with *Trametes villosa*, which is smaller, thinner, and more flexible and has angular pores that do not become labyrinthine or coarsely teethlike.

Trametopsis cervina

Trichaptum abietinum (Pers.) Ryvarden

= *Polyporus abietinus* (Pers.) Fr.

COMMON NAME: Fir Polypore

MACROSCOPIC FEATURES: FRUITBODY annual, effused-reflexed or sessile, 1–6 cm wide, up to 2 mm thick, semicircular to kidney-shaped or fan-shaped, convex to nearly flat, often laterally fused, flexible or stiff. UPPER SURFACE distinctly zonate and variously colored, white to grayish or reddish brown, sometimes green when covered with algae, especially on older specimens; margin thin, wavy, typically violet. FERTILE SURFACE violet to purple-brown, usually fading to buff in age. PORES angular, 3–4 per mm, splitting and becoming teethlike or jagged in age but remaining poroid along the margin; tubes up to 1.5 mm deep. FLESH up to 1.5 mm thick, white to pale buff, duplex, upper layer soft, lower layer fibrous-tough; odor and taste not distinctive.

MICROSCOPIC FEATURES: Spores 6–8 × 2.5–3.5 μm, cylindrical to slightly allantoid, smooth, hyaline, inamyloid; cystidia abundant, 18–30 × 3–7 μm, fusoid, apically encrusted, slightly thick-walled; hyphal system dimitic, clamp connections present.

OCCURRENCE: Solitary or in overlapping clusters on conifers; widely distributed in the Northeast, North Central, and South regions; year-round.

EDIBILITY: Inedible.

REMARKS: Saprotrophic on decaying conifers. The epithet *abietinum* means "occurring on fir trees." Compare with *Trichaptum fuscoviolaceum*, which is nearly identical, but the gill-like pores on its fertile surface are radially elongated and lacerated before splitting into teeth. *Trichaptum biforme* is very similar but grows on broadleaf trees. The upper surface of *Trichaptum abietinum* may have Fairy Pins, the dark olive-brown to blackish fruitbodies of *Phaeocalicium polyporaeum*, which resemble miniature matchsticks (see p. 355).

Trichaptum abietinum

Trichaptum biforme (Fr.) Ryvarden

= *Polyporus biformis* Fr.

COMMON NAMES: Parchment Bracket, Violet Toothed Polypore

MACROSCOPIC FEATURES: FRUITBODY annual, sessile, 2–9 cm wide and up to 3 mm thick, semicircular to kidney-shaped or fan-shaped, convex to nearly flat, often laterally fused, flexible or stiff. UPPER SURFACE distinctly zonate and variously colored, appressed-fibrillose to finely velvety at first, becoming nearly glabrous in age, white to grayish or reddish brown, sometimes green when covered with algae, especially on older specimens; margin thin, wavy, typically violet. FERTILE SURFACE violet to purple-brown, sometimes drying dark purple-brown, but usually fading to buff in age. PORES angular, 2–5 per mm, splitting and becoming teethlike or jagged in age; tubes up to 2 mm deep. FLESH up to 1.5 mm thick, azonate, tough, fibrous, pale buff; odor and taste not distinctive.

MICROSCOPIC FEATURES: Spores 5–8 × 2–2.5 μm, cylindrical to slightly allantoid, smooth, hyaline, inamyloid; cystidia abundant, 20–35 × 3–5 μm, fusoid, apically encrusted, slightly thick-walled; hyphal system dimitic, clamp connections present.

Trichaptum biforme

OCCURRENCE: In overlapping clusters on decaying broadleaf wood; widely distributed in the Northeast, North Central, and South regions; year-round.

EDIBILITY: Inedible.

REMARKS: Saprotrophic, causing a white pocket rot in sapwood of decaying broadleaf trees. *Trichaptum abietinum* is very similar but grows on conifer wood. The upper surface, especially when colonized by green algae, may have Fairy Pins, the dark olive-brown to blackish fruitbodies of *Phaeocalicium polyporaeum*, which resemble miniature matchsticks (use a hand lens). They are the sexual reproductive structures of a parasitic, nonlichenized fungus. They also grow on fruitbodies of *Trichaptum abietinum* and the Turkey-tail, *Trametes versicolor*.

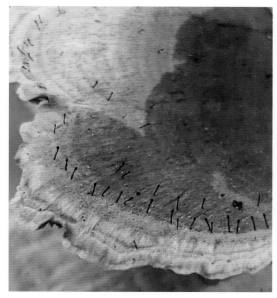

Phaeocalicium polyporaeum

Trichaptum fuscoviolaceum (Ehrenb.) Ryvarden

= *Irpex fuscoviolaceus* (Ehrenb.) Fr.

COMMON NAME: Violet Fungus

MACROSCOPIC FEATURES: FRUITBODY annual, up to 8 cm wide, typically effused-reflexed, rarely sessile or resupinate, often laterally fused. UPPER SURFACE dry, tomentose to slightly hirsute, azonate, white to gray, sometimes greenish when coated with algae; margin white to pale brown. FERTILE SURFACE with gill-like pores that are radially elongated and lacerated and become irregular along the margin before splitting and forming teeth; violet to purplish when fresh, fading to ochraceous or pale brown in age or when drying. FLESH less than 1 mm thick, typically duplex, with a cottony, white upper layer and pale brown to purplish lower layer; odor and taste not distinctive.

MICROSCOPIC FEATURES: Spores 6–7.5 × 2.5–3 µm, cylindric to slightly curved, smooth, hyaline, inamyloid; cystidia abundant, 15–28 × 4–7 µm, broadly fusoid, apically encrusted, thick-walled; hyphal system dimitic, clamp connections present.

OCCURRENCE: In groups or overlapping clusters on decaying conifers, especially pine, spruce, and hemlock; widely distributed but not common in the Northeast, North Central, and upper South regions; summer–fall.

EDIBILITY: Inedible.

REMARKS: The epithet *fuscoviolaceum* means "brownish violet or dusky violet." Compare with *Trichaptum abietinum*, which is nearly identical but has angular pores and its fertile surface does not form teeth near the margin. *Trichaptum byssogenum* (not illustrated) has a small, up to 3 cm wide, resupinate, effused-reflexed, or sessile fruitbody. The upper surface is hispid or strigose with grayish to pale brown hairs that are not forked. It has a purplish fertile surface, 1–2 circular to angular pores per mm, abundant encrusted fusoid cystidia, and grows on decaying conifer or broadleaf wood in the South region.

Trichaptum fuscoviolaceum

Trichaptum laricinum (P. Karst.) Ryvarden

= *Lenzites laricinus* P. Karst.

MACROSCOPIC FEATURES: FRUITBODY annual, sessile, 1–4 cm wide, up to 4 mm thick, semicircular to kidney-shaped or fan-shaped, convex to nearly flat, rigid. UPPER SURFACE covered with coarse hairs, faintly zonate, gray to purplish gray or tan, greenish if coated with algae; margin thin. FERTILE SURFACE with distinct stiff radial lamellae that are forked, sometimes poroid near the margin, purplish to purple-brown; lamellae up to 3 mm deep. FLESH up to 1 mm thick, leathery, azonate, pale purplish brown.

MICROSCOPIC FEATURES: Spores 6–7 × 2–2.5 µm, allantoid, smooth, hyaline, inamyloid; cystidia abundant, 15–25 × 4–6 µm, broadly fusoid, apically encrusted, thick-walled; hyphal system dimitic, clamp connections present.

OCCURRENCE: Solitary or in groups on wood of various conifer species; widely distributed in the Northeast and North Central regions; year-round.

EDIBILITY: Inedible.

REMARKS: Saprotrophic on decaying conifer wood. The epithet *laricinum* means "occurring on larch."

Trichaptum laricinum (A)

Trichaptum laricinum (B)

Trichaptum perrottetii (Lév.) Ryvarden

= *Trametes perrottetii* Lév.

MACROSCOPIC FEATURES: FRUITBODY annual, sessile, up to 15 cm wide and 8 mm thick, shelflike, semicircular to elongated, usually broadly attached. UPPER SURFACE covered with a dense layer of coarse, stiff, erect or flattened, forked hairs that are brownish or grayish and darkest near the point of attachment, weakly zonate or sometimes azonate; margin sharp, entire. FERTILE SURFACE violet at first, becoming brown as it dries. PORES angular or circular, splitting, coalescing, and becoming sinuous to labyrinthine and teethlike in age, 2–3 per mm; tubes 2–5 mm deep. FLESH typically less than 1 mm thick, azonate, dark ochraceous to brown; odor and taste not distinctive.

MICROSCOPIC FEATURES: Spores 5–7 × 2–3.5 μm, cylindrical to oblong-ellipsoid, smooth, hyaline, inamyloid; cystidia 10–18 μm, clavate to ventricose, with a tapered apex, smooth or with an apical crown of crystals, abundant in the hymenium; hyphal system dimitic, clamp connections present.

OCCURRENCE: In overlapping groups or clusters on decaying broadleaf wood, especially oaks, also on old, creosote-treated railroad ties used to make garden beds; reported from southern Georgia and Florida; fall–winter.

EDIBILITY: Inedible.

REMARKS: Saprotrophic, causing a white rot of broadleaf trees. The forked hairs are distinctive and a key identification feature.

Trichaptum perrottetii

Trichaptum sector (Ehrenb.) Kreisel

= *Polyporus sector* (Ehrenb.) Fr.

MACROSCOPIC FEATURES: FRUITBODY annual, sessile, up to 10 cm wide and 1–4 mm thick, semicircular to fan-shaped, broadly attached, often fused laterally, leathery and flexible. UPPER SURFACE tomentose to velvety, zonate, becoming glabrous in zones, white to ochraceous-buff; margin thin, wavy or curled, sometimes fimbriate. FERTILE SURFACE gray or dark purplish brown to nearly black. PORES angular, 3–6 per mm, often slightly toothed on mature specimens; tubes up to 1 mm deep. FLESH 1–3 mm thick, duplex, upper layer white to gray, lower layer grayish to purplish brown; odor and taste not distinctive.

MICROSCOPIC FEATURES: Spores 6–7 × 2–2.5 μm, cylindrical-oblong to ellipsoid, smooth, hyaline, inamyloid; cystidia abundant, 15–20 × 4–7 μm, clavate to fusiform, apically encrusted, thick-walled; hyphal system trimitic, clamp connections present.

OCCURRENCE: Solitary or in overlapping clusters on broadleaf trees; widely distributed in the South region; year-round.

EDIBILITY: Inedible.

REMARKS: Saprotrophic on decaying broadleaf wood. The epithet *sector* means "one who cuts off."

Trichaptum sector

Trichaptum subchartaceum (Murrill) Ryvarden

= *Coriolus subchartaceus* Murrill
= *Polyporus subchartaceus* (Murrill) Overh.

MACROSCOPIC FEATURES: FRUITBODY annual, sessile, up to 6 cm wide and 1 cm thick, semicircular or elongated, often laterally fused. UPPER SURFACE covered with coarse hairs, faintly zonate, pale buff to pale gray, often with yellowish tints as it dries; margin rounded, typically purple to violaceus. FERTILE SURFACE purple to violaceous, fading to buff. PORES circular to angular, 3–4 per mm, becoming teethlike in age; tubes up to 3 mm deep. FLESH up to 7 mm thick, duplex, azonate, pale buff, upper layer soft and fibrous, lower layer corky; odor and taste not distinctive.

MICROSCOPIC FEATURES: Spores 7.5–11 × 2–3 μm, cylindrical to slightly allantoid, smooth, hyaline, inamyloid; cystidia abundant, 20–30 × 5–7 μm, cylindrical, apically encrusted, slightly thick-walled; hyphal system dimitic, clamp connections present.

OCCURRENCE: Solitary or in overlapping clusters on aspen, cottonwood, and poplar; widely distributed in the northern portions of the Northeast and North Central regions; year-round.

EDIBILITY: Inedible.

REMARKS: Saprotrophic on decaying broadleaf wood. The epithet *subchartaceum* means "somewhat like paper."

Trichaptum subchartaceum

Trullella polyporoides (Ryvarden & Iturr.) Zmitr.

= *Trulla polyporoides* (Ryvarden & Iturr.) Miettinen & Ryvarden

= *Tyromyces polyporoides* Ryvarden & Iturr.

MACROSCOPIC FEATURES: FRUITBODY annual, 2–7 cm wide, up to 8 mm thick, pileate, rounded to somewhat spoon-shaped, soft and flexible when fresh, easily broken into pieces when dry, attached to wood by a stalk. UPPER SURFACE distinctly zonate, smooth, glabrous, slightly shiny or dull, light yellowish brown to ochraceous with lighter and darker zones; margin sharp and wavy. FERTILE SURFACE white to grayish, becoming ochraceous as it matures, staining brown. PORES circular, 7–8 per mm; tubes up to 2 mm deep, white to creamy white. STALK up to 1.5 cm long and thick, enlarged downward or nearly equal, lateral, rounded, glabrous, smooth, colored like the upper surface or more ochraceous-orange. FLESH up to 4 mm thick at the base, dense, white; odor not distinctive.

MICROSCOPIC FEATURES: Spores 4–4.5 × 1–1.5 µm, allantoid, thin-walled, smooth, hyaline, inamyloid; hyphal system dimitic, flesh generative, hyphae wide and thick-walled, clamp connections present.

OCCURRENCE: Solitary, in groups, or in clusters on the bark of dead, fallen wood of *Lysiloma latisiliquum* (false tamarind, wild tamarind); in the eastern United States, reported only from Everglades National Park, Florida; late fall–spring.

EDIBILITY: Inedible.

REMARKS: Saprotrophic on decaying wood. *Trullella* means "resembling a small ladle or spoon," a reference to the shape of the fruitbody. The epithet *polyporoides* means "resembling a polypore."

Trullella polyporoides (A)

Trullella polyporoides (B)

Truncospora mexicana Vlasák, Spirin & Kout

MACROSCOPIC FEATURES: FRUITBODY perennial, sessile, 5–20 mm wide, semicircular. UPPER SURFACE indistinctly striate and zonate, whitish to creamy white at first, becoming pale ochraceous, especially toward the margin, on mature specimens; margin somewhat thick and blunt, fertile, even. FERTILE SURFACE pale creamy white when young, becoming pale ochraceous to brownish. PORES circular to angular then partly sinuous, 5–7 per mm; tubes up to 13 mm deep, indistinctly stratified, creamy white to brownish. FLESH up to 2 mm thick, creamy white to brownish; odor not distinctive.

MICROSCOPIC FEATURES: Spores 10.4–14 × 6.5–9.3 μm, ellipsoid to broadly ellipsoid, often truncate, smooth, hyaline, dextrinoid; hyphal system di-trimitic, clamp connections present.

OCCURRENCE: Solitary or in groups on decaying broadleaf branches and logs; found in Texas and Mexico; fall–winter.

EDIBILITY: Inedible.

REMARKS: Saprotrophic on broadleaf trees, especially oaks. The epithet *mexicana* means "of Mexico." *Truncospora floridana* (not illustrated), known only from Key Largo, Florida, also grows on decaying broadleaf wood. It is nearly identical but has slightly thicker flesh, up to 3 mm, and slightly smaller spores, 9.8–12.1 × 6–8.4 μm. *Truncospora tropicalis* (not illustrated) also grows on decaying broadleaf wood in the Florida Keys. Nearly identical, it has the same size spores as *Truncospora floridana* but slightly larger pores, 4–5(6) per mm, that tend to be radially arranged.

Truncospora mexicana

Truncospora ohiensis (Berk.) Pilát

= *Fomes ohiensis* (Berk.) Murrill
= *Fomitopsis ohiensis* (Berk.) Bondartsev & Singer
= *Perenniporia ohiensis* (Berk.) Ryvarden
= *Trametes ohiensis* Berk.

MACROSCOPIC FEATURES: FRUITBODY perennial, sessile, up to 8 cm wide and 2.5 cm thick, semicircular. UPPER SURFACE azonate to faintly zonate, shallowly sulcate, glabrous, creamy white to pale yellowish brown when young, becoming darker brown to blackish in age; margin rounded, creamy white when actively growing. FERTILE SURFACE creamy white, usually slowly staining pale ochraceous to brownish when bruised or in age. PORES circular, 5–7 per mm; tubes up to 4 mm deep. FLESH up to 5 mm thick, firm and corky, white to tan; odor and taste not distinctive.

MICROSCOPIC FEATURES: Spores 13–16 × 7–10 μm, ellipsoid to ovoid, thick-walled, truncate, smooth, hyaline, dextrinoid; hyphal system dimitic, clamp connections present.

OCCURRENCE: Solitary or in groups on decaying broadleaf wood, especially oak; widely distributed in the Northeast and North Central regions, sometimes reported from the upper South region and Texas; year-round.

EDIBILITY: Inedible.

REMARKS: Saprotrophic on decaying broadleaf wood. The epithet *ohiensis* means "of Ohio." *Truncospora wisconsinensis* (not illustrated), known only from Wisconsin, has a white, semicircular fruitbody up to 2.5 cm wide and 1.2 cm thick at the center. The upper surface is glabrous, weakly concentrically sulcate, and the margin is sharp. The pore surface is white with circular pores, 3–5 per mm, and tubes up to 5 mm deep. It has white to creamy white flesh, up to 7 mm thick, and ellipsoid, truncate, hyaline, strongly dextrinoid spores that measure 8–11.5 × 5.5–8 μm. It grows on decaying oak.

Truncospora ohiensis

Tyromyces chioneus (Fr.) P. Karst.

= *Polyporus albellus* Peck
= *Tyromyces albellus* (Peck) Bondartsev & Singer

COMMON NAME: White Cheese Polypore
MACROSCOPIC FEATURES: FRUITBODY annual, sessile, 2–10 cm wide, semicircular, convex to nearly flat, broadly attached, soft and spongy when fresh, easily detached. UPPER SURFACE slightly velvety to appressed-fibrillose, becoming nearly glabrous as it dries or in age, azonate, dry or moist, sometimes uneven or warty, white at first, becoming pale yellow to pale gray in age; margin thin, fairly sharp, sometimes uneven. FERTILE SURFACE white to creamy white, becoming darker yellowish to ochraceous when dry. PORES angular to circular, 3–5 per mm; tubes up to 8 mm deep. FLESH up to 2 cm thick, soft, spongy, white; odor fragrant when fresh, taste not distinctive.
MICROSCOPIC FEATURES: Spores 4–5 × 1.5–2 μm, cylindrical to slightly allantoid, smooth, hyaline, inamyloid; hyphal system dimitic, clamp connections present.

OCCURRENCE: Solitary or in groups on broadleaf trees; widely distributed in the Northeast, North Central, and South regions; summer–early winter.
EDIBILITY: Inedible.
REMARKS: Saprotrophic on decaying broadleaf wood. *Tyromyces* means "having a cheesy consistency." The epithet *chioneus* means "snow white." A significant amount of water can be squeezed out of fresh specimens. *Tyromyces humeanus* (not illustrated), reported only from Florida, has a similarly colored upper surface and grows on broadleaf trees, but its flesh has a strong odor of anise, its white fertile surface stains beige to pale brown when bruised, it has 2–4 angular to slightly irregular pores per mm, and ellipsoid to oval spores that measure 3.5–5 × 2.5–3.5 μm.

Tyromyces chioneus

Tyromyces fumidiceps G. F. Atk.

= *Leptoporellus fumidiceps* (G. F. Atk.) Spirin
= *Oligoporus fumidiceps* (G. F. Atk.) Teixeira
= *Polyporus fumidiceps* (G. F. Atk.) Sacc. & Trotter

COMMON NAME: Smoky Cheese Polypore
MACROSCOPIC FEATURES: FRUITBODY annual, sessile, semicircular to fan-shaped, broadly attached, 2–6 cm wide, soft and watery when fresh, becoming more rigid when dry, easily detached. UPPER SURFACE convex, azonate, covered with stiff or matted hairs, becoming roughened or tufted especially near the base in age, grayish to buff, creamy tan or pale grayish brown; margin thin, fairly sharp, sometimes uneven. FERTILE SURFACE dull white to ochraceous buff, with a pale olive tint when mature. PORES angular, 4–6 per mm; tubes up to 1 cm deep. FLESH up to 2 cm thick, easily crumbled, white; odor fragrant, taste not distinctive.

MICROSCOPIC FEATURES: Spores 3–4 × 2–3 μm, ellipsoid to ovoid with an attenuated base, smooth, hyaline, inamyloid; hyphal system monomitic, clamp connections present.

OCCURRENCE: Solitary or in overlapping groups on decaying broadleaf wood, usually close to the ground on tree trunks and stumps; widespread in the Northeast, North Central, and South regions; summer–early winter.

EDIBILITY: Inedible.

REMARKS: Saprotrophic, causing a white rot. The epithet *fumidiceps* means "having smoky heads or caps."

Tyromyces fumidiceps

Tyromyces galactinus (Berk.) J. Lowe

= *Polyporus galactinus* Berk.

MACROSCOPIC FEATURES: FRUITBODY annual, sessile, up to 12 cm wide and 3 cm thick, semicircular, broadly attached, watery and sappy when fresh, rigid when dry, easily detached. UPPER SURFACE covered with coarse hairs or distinctly tomentose, azonate, white to pale gray, becoming more yellow to pale ochraceous in age or as it dries. FERTILE SURFACE white to creamy white. PORES angular, 4–6 per mm, becoming lacerated or teethlike in age; tubes up to 1 cm deep; teeth up to 1 cm long. FLESH up to 2 cm thick, white to creamy white; odor slightly fragrant, taste not distinctive.

MICROSCOPIC FEATURES: Spores 2.5–3×2–2.5 μm, ellipsoid to oval, smooth, hyaline, inamyloid; hyphal system monomitic, clamp connections present.

OCCURRENCE: Solitary or in overlapping groups on broadleaf trees; widely distributed in the Northeast, North Central, and South regions; year-round.

EDIBILITY: Inedible.

REMARKS: Saprotrophic on decaying broadleaf wood. The epithet *galactinus* means "milky white." *Amylosporus campbellii* = *Tyromyces graminicola* (not illustrated) consists of a cluster of caps on the ground in grassy areas attached to roots, or on woody substrates, especially citrus, juniper, or bamboo. Caps are up to 15 cm wide, semicircular to fan-shaped, sessile or with a rudimentary central or lateral stalk, and soft and spongy when fresh. The upper and fertile surfaces are creamy white to buff, sometimes with ochraceous tints or darker brown spots in age or when dry. It has circular to angular pores, 2–4 per mm, that become somewhat lacerate or sinuous in age, and white flesh that darkens to buff or ochraceous in age and has an unpleasant odor as specimens mature. The spores are ellipsoid, hyaline, amyloid, and smooth, or have scattered amyloid granules and measure 4.5–5.5×2.5–4 μm. Generative hyphae in the flesh sometimes have double or multiple clamp connections. It is possibly parasitic on grass roots.

Tyromyces galactinus

Tyromyces kmetii (Bres.) Bondartsev & Singer

= *Leptoporellus kmetii* (Bres.) Spirin
= *Polyporus kmetii* Bres.

MACROSCOPIC FEATURES: FRUITBODY annual, sessile, up to 12 cm wide and 2.5 cm thick, shelflike, semicircular, broadly attached, fleshy and sappy when fresh. UPPER SURFACE finely velvety at first, soon becoming uneven and slightly warty or roughened with small, projecting, pointed fascicles of white to bright orange hairs over a pale orange to whitish ground color. The fascicles become agglutinated in age or when dry and fade to apricot orange, pale ochraceous, or creamy white; margin thin, slightly wavy. FERTILE SURFACE pale orange-buff to creamy white or light straw-colored.

PORES angular, 3–4 per mm, sometimes enlarging when the tubes begin to dry; tubes up to 1 cm deep. FLESH up to 1.5 cm thick, soft and watery when fresh, white; odor and taste not distinctive.

MICROSCOPIC FEATURES: Spores 4–4.5 × 2–3 μm, broadly ellipsoid, smooth, hyaline, inamyloid; hyphal system monomitic, clamp connections present.

OCCURRENCE: Solitary or overlapping on broadleaf trees; widely distributed along the Gulf Coast states and also reported from Ontario; year-round.

EDIBILITY: Inedible.

REMARKS: Pathogenic, causing a white rot of broadleaf trees. It is considered a rare species.

Tyromyces kmetii (A)

Tyromyces kmetii (B)

Vanderbylia fraxinea (Bull.) D. A. Reid

= *Perenniporia fraxinea* (Bull.) Ryvarden

MACROSCOPIC FEATURES: FRUITBODY perennial, sessile, up to 16 cm wide and 8 cm thick, shelf-like, semicircular to fan-shaped, often somewhat hoof-shaped, convex, broadly attached, corky to firm and rigid. UPPER SURFACE velvety at first, becoming glabrous, slightly zonate, often with small warts or thin ridges, ochraceous when young, becoming unevenly brown to gray, sometimes with reddish spots, finally gray to blackish, with a very thin crust; margin rounded. FERTILE SURFACE pale tan to wood-colored. PORES circular to somewhat angular, 4–6 per mm; tubes 2–10 mm deep per layer. FLESH up to 3 cm thick at the base, corky, yellowish buff to creamy white or pale tan; odor and taste not distinctive.

MICROSCOPIC FEATURES: Spores 6–8 × 5–6.5 μm, subglobose to teardrop-shaped, smooth, hyaline, variably dextrinoid; hyphal system dimitic, clamp connections present.

OCCURRENCE: Solitary or in overlapping clusters on living trunks of broadleaf trees, especially ash trees, sometimes on stumps; widely distributed in the Northeast, North Central, and South regions; year-round.

Vanderbylia fraxinea

EDIBILITY: Inedible.

REMARKS: Pathogenic, causing a white root and butt rot of broadleaf trees. The epithet *fraxinea* means "pertaining to ash trees." Compare with *Perenniporia fraxinophila*, which is also pathogenic on ash trees but has larger, truncate spores.

Vanderbylia robiniophila (Murrill) B. K. Cui & Y. C. Dai

= *Perenniporia robiniophila* (Murrill) Ryvarden
= *Polyporus robiniophilus* (Murrill) Lloyd
= *Trametes robiniophila* Murrill

MACROSCOPIC FEATURES: FRUITBODY perennial, sessile, shelflike, up to 20 cm wide and 5 cm thick, semicircular to triangular, watery and soft when fresh, corky when dry. UPPER SURFACE usually uneven, rough and warty, azonate, white to creamy white when fresh, becoming ochraceous to brownish or grayish as it dries; margin usually thick and rounded. FERTILE SURFACE white to grayish or pale brown. PORES round to angular, 5–7 per mm; tubes up to 2 cm deep. FLESH up to 3 cm thick, cottony or tough, white to ochraceous; odor and taste not distinctive.

MICROSCOPIC FEATURES: Spores subglobose to ovoid, smooth, thick-walled, hyaline, dextrinoid, 5–9 × 5–7 μm; hyphal system dimitic, clamp connections present.

OCCURRENCE: In groups or clusters, often vertically oriented and overlapping, or sometimes solitary, on broadleaf trees, especially black locust; widely distributed in the Northeast, North Central, and South regions; year-round.

EDIBILITY: Inedible.

REMARKS: Pathogenic, causing a white heartrot of broadleaf trees. The epithet *robiniophila* means "loving black locust."

Vanderbylia robiniophila (A)

Vanderbylia robiniophila (B)

Xanthoporia andersonii (Ellis & Everh.) Murrill

= *Inonotus andersonii* (Ellis & Everh.) Černý
= *Mucronoporus andersonii* Ellis & Everh.

MACROSCOPIC FEATURES: FRUITBODY annual, widely resupinate up to 60 cm or more, soft and spongy when fresh, becoming hard and brittle when dry. FERTILE SURFACE typically rough and uneven, sometimes cracked, bright yellow to yellow-brown. PORES round to angular, of highly variable size, 1–6 per mm, dissepiments thick when young, often split or torn on older specimens. FLESH up to 1 mm thick, yellowish to reddish brown; odor not distinctive.

MICROSCOPIC FEATURES: Spores 5.5–8 × 4–5 μm, broadly ellipsoid, thick-walled, smooth, yellowish, inamyloid; hymenial setae 20–48 × 8–12 μm, subulate to ventricose; hyphal system dimitic, clamp connections absent.

OCCURRENCE: Under the bark or outer layers of sapwood of broadleaf trees, usually oak or hickory, eventually rupturing the bark; widely distributed in the Northeast, North Central, and South regions; year-round.

EDIBILITY: Inedible.

REMARKS: Pathogenic, causing a white rot of living trees.

Xanthoporia andersonii (A)

Xanthoporia andersonii (B)

Xanthoporia radiata (Sowerby) Ṭura, Zmitr., Wasser, Raats & Nevo

= *Inonotus radiatus* (Sowerby) P. Karst.

COMMON NAME: Alder Bracket
MACROSCOPIC FEATURES: FRUITBODY annual, up to 5 cm wide and 1.5 cm thick, effused-reflexed or sessile, semicircular. UPPER SURFACE finely tomentose at first, becoming appressed-tomentose to nearly glabrous, sometimes concentrically zon- ate, not sulcate; bright ochraceous orange at first, soon becoming golden brown to yellowish brown or reddish brown, blackening in age; margin rounded, sometimes radially wrinkled. FERTILE SURFACE pale yellowish brown when young, becoming dark brown as it ages. PORES angular, 2–5 per mm, with thin dissepiments that become lacerate and develop tiny hairs that are best ob-

Xanthoporia radiata (A)

served at an oblique angle using a lens; tubes up to 7 mm deep, whitish within. FLESH up to 1 cm thick, lustrous, faintly zonate, yellowish brown and reddish brown; odor and taste not distinctive. MICROSCOPIC FEATURES: Spores 5–6.5 × 3–4.5 µm, narrowly ellipsoid to ovoid, smooth, hyaline; hymenial setae 14–50 × 7–12 µm, mostly ventricose but sometimes subulate, thick-walled, straight or sometimes hooked at the tip, reddish brown; hyphal system monomitic, flesh hyphae 3–7 µm wide, clamp connections absent.

OCCURRENCE: Usually in groups or overlapping clusters, but sometimes solitary, on broadleaf trees, especially alder and oaks; widely distributed in the Northeast, North Central, and South regions; spring–fall, sometimes year-round.
EDIBILITY: Inedible.
REMARKS: Saprotrophic, causing a white rot of decaying broadleaf trees. The epithet *radiata* means "having radiating markings." Compare with *Fuscoporia viticola*.

Xanthoporia radiata (B)

Xylobolus subpileatus (Berk. & M. A. Curtis) Boidin

= *Stereum frustulatum* var. *subpileatum* (Berk. & M. A. Curtis) A. L. Welden

COMMON NAME: Bacon of the Woods

MACROSCOPIC FEATURES: FRUITBODY perennial, 1–6 cm wide, up to 1.5 mm thick, corky to very hard, drying rigid, effused-reflexed and forming a semicircular to fan-shaped cap that is often laterally fused. UPPER SURFACE typically undulating, zonate, sometimes concentrically sulcate, tomentose, grayish orange to pale brown at first, becoming reddish brown to dark cinnamon-brown in age, sometimes green when coated with mosses or algae; margin even, whitish or brownish. FERTILE SURFACE smooth or slightly velvety, often deeply cracked in age, whitish to pale orange, light buff, or pinkish buff. FLESH up to 1 mm thick, pale orange; odor and taste not distinctive.

MICROSCOPIC FEATURES: Spores 4–5 × 2–3 µm, cylindrical, smooth, hyaline, inamyloid; hyphal system dimitic, clamp connections absent.

OCCURRENCE: Scattered, in groups, or in clusters on logs, stumps, and trunks of broadleaf trees, especially oak; widely distributed in the Northeast, North Central, and South regions; year-round.

EDIBILITY: Inedible.

REMARKS: Saprotrophic on broadleaf trees. The epithet *subpileatus* means "having partially developed caps." The contrasting pale lower surface and dark upper surface helps to identify this species.

Xylobolus subpileatus

Xylodon paradoxus (Schrad.) Chevall.

= *Hydnum paradoxum* Schrad.
= *Poria versipora* (Pers.) Sacc.
= *Schizopora paradoxa* (Schrad.) Donk

COMMON NAME: Split Pore Crust

MACROSCOPIC FEATURES: FRUITBODY annual, resupinate, effused, 1–5 mm thick, consisting of uneven, rounded, nodular mounds of various length and width. FERTILE SURFACE poroid at first, white to creamy white or grayish, becoming darker gray or brownish in age. PORES highly variable in size and shape, angular, irregular or labyrinthine, becoming split and irregularly teethlike as it ages. TEETH up to 3 mm long, flattened. FLESH up to 2 mm thick, tough, whitish to buff; odor and taste not distinctive.

MICROSCOPIC FEATURES: Spores 5.5–6.5 × 3.5–4.5 μm, ellipsoid, smooth, usually with one oil drop, hyaline, inamyloid; hyphal system dimitic, clamp connections present on all septa.

OCCURRENCE: On decaying broadleaf branches, logs, and stumps; widely distributed in the Northeast, North Central, and South regions; summer–early winter.

EDIBILITY: Inedible.

REMARKS: Saprotrophic, causing a white rot in decaying broadleaf trees. The epithet *paradoxus* means "strange or contrary to expectation." Compare with *Irpex lacteus*, which has a white to creamy white fertile surface that is poroid near the margin with split tubes that become jagged or teethlike. It lacks clamp connections.

Xylodon paradoxus

APPENDIX A

Microscopic Examination of Polypores

Many polypore species can be identified using only macroscopic features; others, however, require microscopic examination for accurate identification. Spore size and morphology, cystidia, setae, hyphal system composition, and the presence or absence of clamp connections are some of the features that require microscopic examination in these cases. An in-depth discussion of microscopy is beyond the scope of this book, but we have included information on basic equipment, its care, and microscopic techniques necessary for those interested.

Equipment

A good-quality light microscope equipped with a sub-stage condenser, a built-in light source, and superior lenses is vital for the microscopic examination of polypores. The microscope should have at least three objective lenses—10×, 40×, and an oil-immersion 100×—as well as one or two ocular lenses. An optional fourth objective lens, 4×, is often very useful. To make accurate measurements of microscopic features, an ocular micrometer is required. Some ocular lenses have an ocular micrometer already inserted; others do not, and a micrometer must be bought separately. The magnification of each combination of lenses (ocular plus objective) is different; therefore, the ocular micrometer needs to be calibrated using a tiny glass ruler called a stage micrometer. Most microscope dealers, as well as college and university biology departments, have stage micrometers and may be willing to assist you with the calibration procedure.

Additional useful items include glass slides, cover slips (22 mm square), box of single-edged razor blades, fine-tip jeweler's forceps, type A immersion oil, a pair of dissecting needles, and dropper bottles for chemical reagents. Also, because care and maintenance of the microscope is essential, lens paper and cleaning fluid are strongly recommended. Never leave oil on the 100× objective lens. Clean it using lens paper and cleaning fluid. Do not place the other objective lenses in the oil; it could permanently damage them. All of the above items can be purchased using online sources.

Techniques

Spores may be obtained for examination from four sources: from a naturally occurring spore deposit that is sometimes present on the upper surface of the fruit-body or on the surrounding leaf litter or wood where the polypore is growing (fig. 9), from a spore deposit made in your home or laboratory as described in appendix C, from fresh polypores, or from dried specimens. An advantage of using fresh or dried material from the polypore itself is that it allows for the examination of microscopic structures such as cystidia, setae, hyphae, or clamp connections.

If you are using a naturally occurring spore deposit or other spore deposit as your source, scrape off a minute amount of the deposit using a single-edged razor blade or knife. Place the spores into a small drop of water or another mounting medium (e.g., a 2–5 percent KOH solution) and gently mix to distribute them evenly in the medium. Carefully place a cover slip over the mixture and gently apply pressure to it using a pencil eraser to remove air bubbles and excess fluid.

When using fresh material for examination of spores, gently scrape off small pieces of the fertile surface, place them in the mounting medium of your

FIGURE 9. Naturally occurring spore deposit

choice, add the cover slip, and gently apply pressure as noted above. When using dried specimens, gently scrape a few very small pieces of the fertile surface into a mounting medium and allow it to soak and soften for two or three minutes before adding the cover slip and adding pressure as directed above. Pieces of dried material may be soaked in a wetting agent, such as 70–95 percent ethyl alcohol, before placing them into a mounting medium. This helps hyphae and other structures to absorb water and regain their original appearance.

Once the cover slip is in place, your slide is ready for use. Begin the examination process by focusing with the 4× or 10× objective lens, then the 40× objective lens. Once focused, place a drop of immersion oil on the cover slip and carefully lower the 100× objective lens into the oil. Fine-focus the image, adjust the

lighting, and examine the spores, cystidia, hyphae, and other structures you wish to observe.

Note that flesh or upper surface tissue may be most beneficial when attempting to determine the presence or absence of clamp connections or hyphal systems. Most of the other important structures, including cystidia and setae, can usually be found by examining samples from the tube layer.

For additional information about microscopic features, refer to *How to Identify Mushrooms to Genus III: Microscopic Features*, by Largent, Johnson, and Watling (1977). This valuable reference describes laboratory techniques, equipment and materials, calibration of the microscope, planes of sectioning, rehydration of dried materials, microscopic structures, and much more.

Chemical Reagents for Polypore Identification

Mycologists have not routinely performed macro-chemical testing of polypores; therefore, little is known about the reactions of reagents applied to most species. Some results of macrochemical tests are known, however, and in these cases the results may be useful to confirm a tentative identification. For example, the application of KOH (potassium hydroxide) to the upper surfaces of *Hapalopilus croceus* and *Hapalopilus rutilans* produces strikingly different results. The upper surface of *Hapalopilus croceus* stains red to carmine, and *Hapalopilus rutilans* stains bright violet to purplish.

Several factors can affect test results, including color variation on a single specimen, the age of the polypore, moisture content, and the presence of parasitized tissue. The most accurate results may be obtained when using recently collected, fresh polypores with dry surfaces.

Historically, procedures for applying reagents to polypore tissues have taken many forms. Collectors use various applicators as well as differing quantities of reagents, ranging from scant to copious amounts. We have experimented with a variety of applicators and differing amounts of applied reagents. Each applicator, reagent quantity, and their combinations produced accurate results at times but did not provide consistent, repeatably accurate results all of the time. The technique we finally settled on that provides consistently accurate results is to apply a cotton-tipped swab with reagent gently to the mushroom tissue using a sweeping motion and minimum pressure. Use a clean swab for every test to prevent contamination of your reagent and of the specimen being tested. Avoid large drops and puddles of reagent. This is especially important when trying to observe a "flash" or fleeting chemical reaction. Too much reagent can obscure this response, sometimes obliterating rapidly changing color sequences.

Reagents should be fresh, not outdated. Although they will keep for several weeks, or sometimes months, we strongly recommend testing them periodically on tissues with known macrochemical reactions. Reagents should be stored at room temperature, preferably in plastic bottles. Some reagents, especially KOH, can react with glass to form silicates and may no longer produce accurate macrochemical test results.

Chemicals are also used for microscopic examination. They are used as rehydrating and mounting media in slide preparations and for identifying some species based on the appearance and specific staining reactions of spores, hyphae, cystidia, setae, and other microscopic structures. The following chemical reagents are routinely used for macrochemical testing or microscopic study:

- Ammonium hydroxide (NH_4OH), in a 3–14 percent aqueous solution or household ammonia without added soap, is used for testing and also as a mounting medium for microscopic work. It is ideal for use with dried material that has been rehydrated in a 70–95 percent ethyl alcohol solution.
- Iron sulfate ($FeSO_4$), in a 10 percent aqueous solution, is used only for macrochemical testing.
- Potassium hydroxide (KOH), in a 2–5 percent aqueous solution, is used for testing and also as a mounting medium for fresh and dried specimens.
- Melzer's reagent is a solution of iodine (0.5 g), potassium iodide (1.5 g), chloral hydrate (20 g), and water (20 ml). Since chloral hydrate is a controlled

substance, it is difficult to obtain. The best options may be connecting with a college or university biology professor or obtaining a prescription from a physician and having Melzer's prepared at a compounding pharmacy. Searching online for prepared Melzer's reagent is another option. This important chemical is used for identifying some mushroom species based on the appearance of their spores, hyphae, cystidia, and other microscopic structures. The structures sometimes stain specific colors when mounted in Melzer's reagent. If they stain bluish gray to bluish black, they are described as amyloid; those that stain dull red to reddish brown are dextrinoid, and those that stain yellow or remain colorless are inamyloid.

- Lactophenol cotton blue is a mixture of lactic acid, phenol, and cotton (or methyl) blue. It is useful as a mounting fluid and stain because it stains cytoplasm pale blue and hyphal wall structures and ornamentation a darker blue.
- Phloxine is a red dye used for microscopic examination, especially of hyphae. It stains cytoplasm red and makes other contrasting structures, such as cystidia, much easier to differentiate.

Because of striking inconsistencies in the literature, variable results in testing, and the subjective nature of color interpretation, and because testing results are simply unknown, macrochemical reactions for many of the species in this book have been omitted. We have provided macrochemical test reactions only when they are reliable, valid, or diagnostic for some species.

APPENDIX C

How to Make a Spore Deposit

A spore deposit is useful when attempting to identify polypores not only because it allows you to determine the composite color of the spores but also because it is the best source of mature spores for microscopic examination. Using tissue from a polypore for slide preparations can skew the spore size range if immature spores are present, resulting in inaccurate measurements.

A spore deposit may be collected on clean white paper, aluminum foil, waxed paper, or glass. To collect spores, begin by selecting a portion of a polypore with well-developed tubes. Carefully cut the polypore sample to fit on the surface you choose, and place it tube side down. If the specimen is small, it may be used intact. Be certain the tubes are oriented as vertically as possible. Tubes that are not precisely vertical will likely not deposit spores. Place the specimen and collecting surface in a draft-free location and cover them with a glass, cup, or bowl. For best results, allow the spores to fall for several hours, or overnight.

Not all attempts at collecting spores will be successful. If the specimen you are using is too young or too old, too dry, or infested with excessive numbers of larvae, it most likely will not produce a spore deposit. Specimens that are too wet will likely become parasitized by molds or other fungi and will usually not produce a spore deposit.

APPENDIX D

The Medicinal Uses of Polypores

A Brief History and Summaries of Current Research

The summarized research presented below was the most current and up-to-date at the time of this book's writing in 2020.

Researchers throughout the world have been working to discover compounds in fungi that may prove useful in expanding our options for preventing, treating, and curing diseases. Much of this research has been conducted in Asian countries where traditional Chinese medicine was originally adopted and adapted to the indigenous medical practices of the ruling classes in the neighboring countries of Japan and Korea. Traditional Chinese medicine incorporated Taoist natural philosophy along with Confucian ideals and was practiced by China's educated elite to care for family members in premodern times. Chinese theories of health incorporated cultural ideals regarding filial piety and respect for, and acceptance of, political and social behavioral norms. Various therapies, including variants of moxibustion, acupuncture, breathing, and meditation practices, as well as recipes featuring assorted organic and inorganic materials, were presumed to have the potential to affect one's health positively. Almost all foods, herbs, weeds, grains, soils, metals, precious stones, animal parts, and excretions, as well as fungi, were assigned qualitative properties that fit within a rather complex system of correlations with seasonal, astronomical, geographical, and ritual events. These were used in complicated combinations to produce tonics and pills that redressed imbalances manifested as pain, exhaustion, physical or mental stress, skin eruptions, menstrual problems, inability to conceive, and so on. The more exotic pharmaceuticals included rhinoceros horn, elephant tusks, deer antlers, sea horses, tiger penis, toad secretions,

shark fins, and pangolin scales, among others. Some of these initially entered official pharmacopeias as tribute gifts from tropical Southeast Asia to demonstrate respect for the Chinese imperial government. Valued as extraordinary medicinals, their use was reserved to satisfy the desires of the monarch and government officials to lengthen their respective life spans and boost their virility and fertility into old age. Herbs, roadside weeds, insects, bark, twigs, and assorted other medicines were used in times of war and famine by commoners in efforts to stave off starvation.

In the twentieth and early decades of the twenty-first centuries, the Chinese government promoted the scientization of these traditional medicinal theories in response to a shortage of physicians trained in biomedicine to care for its rural populations. This entailed the removal of practices such as incantations, which were considered superstitious, and select prescription ingredients of questionable value, such as parts of humans and certain animal excretions. However, physicians trained in traditional Chinese medicine, and their government backers, believed that pharmaceuticals and recipes of Confucian officials in the premodern period were a treasure trove of efficacious medicines based on their alleged long history of use. Researchers were charged with finding conditions described in historical medical documents that matched modern disease syndromes, and to search for formulas employed by premodern healers to treat them. As cheaper and presumably better natural medicines that stood the test of time, these were to be manufactured and sold throughout the world as more affordable alternatives to costly biomedical pharmaceuticals. Those who published positive findings were, and still are, remunerated by the government with financial rewards and higher professional status. Three books published in China on medicinal fungi and their uses in traditional medicine include *Fungi Pharmacopoeia Sinica* (Liu and Bau 1980), *Icons of Medicinal Fungi from China* (Ying 1987), and *Medicinal Fungi of China* (Wu et al. 2013). As of 2015, more than 850 species were considered efficacious. Antitumor functions have been attributed to 331, or 61 percent, of these fungi.

Chinese researchers are making important advances in all the sciences, especially in the fields of medicine, genetics, physics, chemistry, and mycology. Excellent research articles written by China's growing scientific workforce can be found in all of the world's most respected journals. From the 1980s through the beginning of the twenty-first century, however, there has been a competitive and evolving two-tiered system for advancing medical science research. Graduates at the top of their class in the most prestigious universities who are also members of the Communist Party are selected for high-status medical research positions or to be physicians at prestigious city hospitals. Equally capable graduates of less impressive schools who lack political connections are steered toward advancing the aims of westernizing traditional Chinese medicine as researchers or as physicians. Generally, their training has been much less rigorous but perhaps more difficult, since they are required to square their studies with the theoretical foundations of a changing but still premodern medical philosophy. Their research can be found in journals that accept articles on ethnological and alternative world medicine, which tend to be less stringent in their criteria for publication.

Much of the worldwide popular interest in the potential of macrofungi to cure a plethora of disease conditions is based on the promising results of preliminary studies published in these journals. Published research suggesting potential medicinal efficacy is almost always founded on observations of what happens when malignant human cancer cells are exposed to fungal compounds in a test tube or Petri dish (in vitro testing). This is just the first step in determining the potential medicinal utility of any substance. Sometimes Phase I trials on animals and informal Phase II clinical trials on a limited number of hospitalized patients (in vivo testing) are performed. Results on human subjects tend not to be conducted in accordance with accepted biomedical standard procedures for clinical trial testing. Published Phase III and IV trials on medicinal fungi are nonexistent. Many American hospital systems currently offer complementary or integrative medicine to their patients. However, they do not advocate or use herbal, fungal, or other unproven formulations or treatments acceptable to practitioners of alternative medicine as viable natural replacements for standard medical practice. This is because there is an absence of reliable data supporting their efficacy and safety in humans based on rigorously controlled repeatable scientific trials. Along with exercise, massage, dietary advice, and acupuncture, traditional Chinese medicine therapies are used to give needed physical and emotional comfort and to assist patients in the recovery process. Incidentally, China, Japan, South Korea, and several other Asian countries use fungal preparations as adjunct therapies to standard medical treatment for acute diseases requiring surgery and hospitalization. Indeed, the acknowledged strength of traditional Chinese medicine is in its focus on maintaining and improving good health by means of eating a varied, well-balanced diet, incorporating exercise and breathing techniques to relax the body and mind, and the avoidance of bad habits such as overindulgence in food, alcohol, and smoking. Pharmaceuticals incorporate traditional herbs and assorted other substances believed to have therapeutic effects based on their inclusion in traditional medical texts. Modern biomedicine and Chinese medicine continue to coexist. Traditional Chinese medicine is preferred for minor health conditions, general well-being, and prevention of acute diseases. However, rural Chinese and migrant workers and their more highly educated professional counterparts in urban centers prefer to be treated by biomedical physicians for major illnesses—if they can afford the expense. We bring up these issues because many of us are unfamiliar with the processes involved in producing evidence-based science, and being human, we are prone to accept inadequately proven medical claims in hopes of finding a "magic bullet."

The polypores most researched for potential use as pharmaceuticals include *Grifola frondosa, Inonotus obliquus, Polyporus umbellatus, Trametes versicolor*, and *Ganoderma lingzhi*. These, along with *Cordyceps* spp., *Hericium* spp., shiitake, and oyster mushrooms, are hailed in advertising and popular literature as among the most potent natural and comprehensively effective "super-medicines" and immune-stimulating "functional foods" that can prevent and cure maladies ranging from colds, wrinkles, balding, infertility, and impotence to obesity, diabetes, heart diseases, cancers, and Alzheimer's.

What is in fungi that makes them medicinal? There are hundreds of polysaccharides such as beta-glucans and other bioactive compounds of high and low molecular weight that make up the chitin cell walls in various fungi. These compounds are commonly used in the food industry as additives in sour cream, cheese spreads, frozen desserts, and salad dressings. Beta-glucans are sugars that can also be found in the cell walls of plants, bacteria, and algae. Many glucans appear to be capable of triggering immune responses and possibly antioxidant, antiviral, and antibacterial activity responsible for accelerating the healing of wounds. They are considered *potentially* useful for an amazing variety of disorders, including HIV/AIDS, chronic fatigue syndrome, asthma, multiple sclerosis, Lyme disease, lung infections, burns, canker sores, ulcerative colitis, yeast infections, irritable bowel syndrome, rheumatoid arthritis, ear infections, psoriasis, diabetes, physical and emotional stress, and liver problems. Additionally, they are also purported to lower cholesterol and reduce blood pressure. In tests, both in vitro and in vivo, some of these polysaccharides (plant as well as fungal) appear capable of inducing macrophage activity and having positive biological effects on tumors, diabetes, and hepatitis by stimulating the immune system. In Asia, these compounds are used as adjuvants to boost the immune systems of patients with weakened body defenses, who also receive modern biomedical treatments and pharmaceuticals.

Grifola frondosa

Hen of the Woods, or Maitake, is a highly regarded edible fungus. It has been cultivated in the past two decades for food and as a dietary supplement.

Claims have been made for Maitake's beneficial use in preventing and slowing cancer, HIV infections, hepatitis B, diabetes, and hypertension. It is believed that the active compound it contains is the protein-bound polysaccharide beta-1,6-glucan, which may be able to affect macrophages, killer T cells, interleukin-1, and superoxide anions. Early laboratory in vitro studies suggested that Maitake exhibited anticancer properties. In animal studies it appears to slow the growth of some cancerous tumors and lower blood sugar levels. In a small, uncontrolled study conducted by Memorial Sloan Kettering Cancer Center, completed in 2009, *Grifola frondosa* extract appeared to stimulate the immune systems of 34 postmenopausal breast cancer patients who were already free of cancer. However, toxicity to the extract was also observed, and other bioactive compounds it contains were discovered to stimulate the growth of other cancers. High and intermediate doses of the liquid extract were found to increase some immunological parameters and depress others. The study concluded, "Oral administration of a polysaccharide extract from Maitake mushroom is associated with both immunologically stimulatory and inhibitory measurable effects in peripheral blood. Cancer patients should be made aware of the fact that botanical agents produce more complex effects than assumed and may depress as well as enhance immune function" (Deng et al. 2009).

A recent meta-analysis of previous studies concludes that although Maitake extract may elevate the functional capacity of monocytes, T, and NK cells in cancer patients, evidence for direct anticancer effects is lacking. Nevertheless, popular articles continue to cite preliminary studies and testimonials from the 1990s, making false claims about the mushroom. Writing for the Underground Health Reporter's web pages, Dancia Collins cites preliminary Phase I and II studies and anecdotal evidence in a misleading article asserting that Maitake "has been clinically proven to prevent and heal cancer, as well as decrease and even eliminate cancerous tumors." Another important consideration regarding the use of Maitake is that it is not recommended for people taking blood pressure medications, as it can increase their effects. Patients taking warfarin should not consume Maitake. Other possible side effects include an increase in white blood cell count, indicating a possible allergic response.

Inonotus obliquus

Chaga is the sterile, black, cankerlike growth of a white rot fungus found on the trunks of white and yellow birch trees. Popular books, commercial websites such as cancerdefeated.com, and even research articles on this conk inaccurately assert that it was used for thousands of years in China and was called the Mushroom of Immortality. The claims are based on the misinterpretation of first- and second-century text references from the Chinese Classical Treatise on Health (*Shen Nong Ben Cao*) to supermundane substances. The Chinese call Chaga *bai hua rong*, the white birch fungus. According to Beijing's *Daxue Consulting* newsletter of April 27, 2018, Chinese pharmacists started to import the sterile conk in 2016 from other parts of the world, including Finland, Russia, Japan, and Canada, for processing and domestic use as a nutraceutical to meet the demand of Chinese millennials for this popular western supplement. It is also marketed for export to cure every imaginable disease.

The word "chaga" comes from the language of the Komi-Permyak Indigenous people, who live west of the Ural Mountains in the Kama River basin. The term simply means "clinker," referring to the sterile conk's resemblance to coal slag and its probable use in fire-making. Chaga occurs in the circumboreal regions of the northern temperate and subarctic areas at higher latitudes on several species of birch trees, which have long been honored in many cultures of the world. In Scandinavia, Eastern Europe, and Siberia the white birch is known as the "tree of life and fertility." Numerous online Russian magazine articles, novels, poetry, and paintings feature the highly esteemed white birch. All parts of the tree are revered and utilized. The fragrant sap is used for medicines and beverages, the wood for building furniture, and the bark for fashioning shoes and jewelry. The twigs are used by sauna bathers to stimulate circulation, and the leaves color cotton, wool, and silk.

The use of *Inonotus obliquus* was made popular after it was featured as the cause of a miraculous cure in the 1967 novel *Cancer Ward*, by Alexander Solzhenit-

syn. At about the same time, the Soviet government approved Chaga as an anticancer agent, although evidence for its efficacy in humans was nonexistent. Chaga is nevertheless credited with unlimited benefits, including protection against free radicals and against DNA degradation. Chaga is said to detoxify the liver and to fight hepatitis, diabetes, and gastritis, as well as inflammation and inflammatory diseases such as shingles. It continues to be used in Russia to treat inoperable breast cancer, and hip, gastric, pulmonary, stomach, skin, and colon cancers, as well as Hodgkin's lymphoma. While some sources claim Chaga has been used for cancerous tumors of the breast and sex organs, they fail to mention whether it was effective for those purposes. There simply are no published human trials proving the utility of Chaga as an effective anticancer medicine. Endopolysaccharides from Chaga are not toxic, but they are also not cytotoxic to cancer cells.

Eastern Europe and Russia continue to promote outside interest in this nonprescription drug under the name Befungin. An oral solution manufactured in Russia sells on Amazon. Chaga extracts are believed to nourish and protect the skin and hair from sun damage via its melanin compounds. Nowadays, Chaga is also used as a diuretic and as a substitute for coffee or tea.

Chaga's supposed efficacy has variously been attributed to its beta-D-glucans and the triterpenoids betulin and betulinic acid (a secondary metabolite of betulin), which are found primarily in the bark of white birch, as opposed to the conk. The amount of betulinic acid in a Chaga conk, however, is minimal compared with the amount in the bark (approximately 22 to 30 percent in the bark and only 3 percent in the conk). Its usefulness is hard to confirm because of its poor solubility in aqueous solutions. According to a 2012 online article on the bioavailability of betulinic acid, a daily dose of 250–500 mg per kilo of bodyweight, or between 30 and 80 capsules, each containing up to a total of 500 mg of betulinic acid, over a period of many weeks would be required to achieve any of the therapeutic effects observed in studies using mice (Supplement-Facts.org). Another study in the journal *PLoS One* suggests that an oral spray formulation of betulinic acid may increase its bioavailability and its usefulness for treating certain cancers (Godugu et al. 2014).

In commercial advertising and popular literature on medicinal fungi, mention is often made of Chaga being studied by the U.S. National Cancer Institute (NCI). Such statements lend plausibility to the belief that evidence exists that proves Chaga works. To be clear, such a statement only means that it is being studied; however, no published NCI study exists either affirming or denying its potential. According to the Memorial Sloan Kettering Cancer Center, "To date, no clinical trials on humans have been conducted to assess its safety or efficacy for disease prevention or for the treatment of liver cancer, cardiovascular diseases or diabetes. Chaga mushrooms are high in oxalates and excessive intake may have toxic effects."

Chaga is high in oxalates; consumption of large quantities may have toxic effects for susceptible people (Kikuchi et al. 2014). It is counterindicated for those taking blood thinners or diabetic medications because it interacts with anticoagulant and antidiabetic drugs. To date, no repeatable clinical trials have been performed on humans that demonstrate the effectiveness or safety of Chaga.

Since it is slow-growing, decimation due to overharvesting is a real possibility. It will soon be an unreliable source of potential medicines.

Polyporus umbellatus

The Umbrella Polypore is credited with immuneenhancing properties (Wesa 2015). Claims are made that it is antioxidative, anticancer, anti-inflammatory, and protective of liver functions, and that it promotes hair growth. Extracts from the dried sclerotia of *Polyporus umbellatus* are employed by practitioners of modern so-called traditional Chinese medicine for ailments related to edema, scanty urine, urinary dysfunction, vaginal discharge, jaundice, and diarrhea (Zhao 2013). One study suggests fungal metabolites from *Polyporus umbellatus* appear to have been effective in inhibiting bladder cancer in rats (Zhang et al. 2011). The main metabolite believed responsible for its diuretic effects is ergone, a steroid derived from ergosterols found in the sclerotia. In vitro studies may have

demonstrated that ergone may be cytotoxic to human rhabdomyosarcoma cell lines (Fernando et al. 2016; Lee et al. 2007).

Ganoderma lucidum and Relatives

Researchers studying the medicinal properties of *Ganoderma lucidum* claim it has a long history in China, referring uncritically to its alleged use going back to prehistoric times up to 7,000 years ago. More modest, but equally unsupported, are claims that it is one of the substances described in the no longer extant Chinese Classical Treatise on Health, the *Shen Nong Ben Cao*, compiled in the first and second centuries AD. As explained in the 2019 *McIlvainea* article by Dianna G. Smith, "Ling Zhi, *Ganoderma lucidum*: The Chinese Mushroom of Immortality," *Ganoderma lingzhi* is the correct name for the mushroom formerly and incorrectly referred to as *Ganoderma lucidum*. The term "lingzhi" historically referred to a large number of allegedly superior substances believed to be immortality elixirs. It did not refer exclusively to fungi, much less to any species of *Ganoderma*.

Elixirs were not health tonics as we think of them today. In the first millennium and beyond, elixirs consisted of various durable minerals and metals that could be combined, heated over slow-burning fires for weeks or months, liquefied, and fashioned into pills. These were drugs used for the purpose of cultivating transcendent spiritual perfection and immortality. Taoist adepts, court magicians, several emperors, and spiritual disciples of revered Taoists over the past two millennia believed that preparing and ingesting these ingredients could transform humans into winged spirits capable of traveling the cosmos as corporeal or dematerialized beings. Worthy adepts had powers to walk on water, ascend at will to the pole star, or fly off to legendary islands where immortals hung out among bejeweled trees and fantastic creatures while imbibing ritually perfected elixir stones. Those interested in learning more about the use of alchemical elixirs in premodern China are referred to the many scholarly articles and books of Nathan Sivin, Joseph Needham, Ted Kaptchuk, Giovanni Maciocia, Paul Unschuld, Asaf Goldschmidt, and others, as well as translated Taoist texts (Bertschinger 2011, 2015, 2018;

Campany 2002; Dudgeon 1895; Harper 1998; Knoblock and Riegel 2000; Legge 1891; Morgan 1933; Read 1936; Sivin 1969; Unschuld 1985, 1986, 2003; Unschuld and Tessenow 2011; Ware 1966).

Evidence in the form of paintings, poetry, and the late sixteenth-century *Compendium of Materia Medica*, by Li Shizhen, indicates that *Ganoderma lingzhi* (as opposed to the European *Ganoderma lucidum*) acquired by association some of the spiritual and psychophysical benefits previously attributed to the deadly metallic elixirs adopted by adepts and emperors in earlier centuries. The shiny red polypore was associated with the emperor, his palace, cinnabar, the heart, the color red, immortality, happiness, marriage, and assorted other positive qualities. Contrary to popular belief, *Ganoderma lingzhi* was never to be employed as an elixir or a health-promoting supplement. There is no historical documentary evidence that it was actually ever taken by Ming or Qing dynasty monarchs. Two monarchs, however, are known to have perished from poisoning after taking the metallic elixirs, Jiajing (died 1567) and Yongzheng (died 1735). By the second half of the twentieth century, the Chinese political elites and physicians of traditional medicine were eager to take this previously forbidden treasure of mythological spirits and emperors and cultivate it for the mass production of commercial health products for everyone.

The benefits attributed to this polypore in the late twentieth century are based on Chinese medical theories and not on empirical evidence. They include unsubstantiated reports of the prevention of cardiovascular disease by lowering high blood pressure and elevated blood glucose and cholesterol levels. It is also credited with immune system immunomodulating, antibacterial properties, and protection of the liver. Hailed as "the king of herbs" (a twenty-first-century marketing slogan) and a panacea for many ailments, *Ganoderma* is a featured ingredient in numerous common products. These include toothpaste, shampoos, face creams, and dietary supplements. The latter are taken for their perceived anticancer, antiaging, antimicrobial, and antiviral functions, as well as their purported ability to promote hair growth, restore the libido, and extend life. Asian laboratory studies suggest that *Ganoderma lingzhi* may stimulate certain cells of the immune system, but evidence is lacking regarding its ability to fight infections. In vitro experiments have revealed that it does not have a significant effect in terms of killing cancer cells directly. Some studies, however, suggest that cancer patients taking *Ganoderma lingzhi* extract are slightly more likely to respond positively to chemotherapy and radiation than those not using it. In one study, patients taking an extract report that they enjoyed a better quality of life than patients in a control group (Jin et al. 2016). Although it is said to have extended the life span of mice (Wu et al. 2011), no studies record whether patients who take this medicine live longer than those who do not.

Ganoderma lingzhi has also been used to reduce inflammation. Some testimonials affirm that taking a *Ganoderma* tincture may alleviate allergic symptoms, but this feature has not been scientifically tested in humans. The polypore is also employed to increase strength and stamina, although no scientific evidence with humans supports this use. One study done on mice is said to have "improved the anti-fatigue capacity without any effect on weight loss/gain" (Zhao et al. 2013). Extracts have also reportedly led to weight gain of birds infected with a fungal parasite called *Eimeria tenella* (Ogbe et al. 2009). *Ganoderma lingzhi* has also been used to treat lower urinary tract symptoms (LUTS), with one study suggesting that extracts may improve urinary flow in men with slight to moderate LUTS (Noguchi et al. 2008). Larger, long-term studies are needed to see if it can improve LUTS in men who have more severe symptoms. On the plus side, it is said to protect rat brains from trauma-induced oxidative stress (Özevren et al. 2017).

The active compounds in *Ganoderma lingzhi* involve diverse secondary metabolites, including alkaloids and terpenoids. Identification of the compounds that are actually responsible for the reported positive health effects remains elusive.

In a study conducted with 18 healthy adults between the ages of 22 and 52, a commercially available capsule containing 1.44 grams of dried *Ganoderma lingzhi* was taken over a four-week period. It was determined there was no liver, renal, or DNA toxicity except for a few minor reactions (Wachtel-Galor et al. 2004). One reference to toxicity with the medicinal use of *Ganoderma* involved a cancer patient who took an adulterated commercially produced powder formulation over a period of a month, resulting in elevated liver enzymes (Wanmuang et al. 2007).

More concerning, however, is a recent study by Canadian researchers. Toxicity was observed in peripheral blood monocular cells of both healthy adults and healthy children, as well as in pediatric patients undergoing chemotherapy for cancers (Gill and Rieder 2008). The researchers advise that *Ganoderma* extracts be used with caution, as there appears to be potential for toxicity. *Ganoderma* is not recommended for those who are pregnant, take a blood thinner, or use an immunosuppressant. It may also make chemotherapy drugs less effective.

Roughly 200 species of *Ganoderma* occur throughout the world. Many of the shiny laccate species are referenced in both research journals and popular parlance under the name *Ganoderma lucidum*, which is mainly a European species. Many different species that are marketed as *Ganoderma lucidum* actually consist of other genetically and chemically distinct species (Cao et al. 2012, 2018; Hong and Jung 2004). Some mycophiles eager to promote and sell homemade tinctures using *Ganoderma tsugae* appear to believe that fruitbodies of all *Ganoderma* species contain the same beneficial compounds that are in the Immortality Herb. They do not. Although there are numerous species of *Ganoderma* in China (including Taiwan), the official *Pharmacopoeia of the People's Republic of China* (2010) describes only two: *Ganoderma lingzhi* and *Ganoderma sinense*. The Chinese government has stipulated that only products made from *Ganoderma lingzhi* are to be cultivated and processed as medicines, presumably because *Ganoderma lingzhi* is the species believed to have been referenced in classical pharmacopoeias and because *Ganoderma sinense* and native specimens of *Ganoderma lucidum* lack the triterpenes found in *Ganoderma lingzhi*. Prior to DNA sequencing, they were thought to be the same species or at least biologically equivalent. As a result, some products coming out of China were (and probably still are) made from *Ganoderma sinense*.

A recent study, "Evaluation on quality consistency of *Ganoderma lucidum* dietary supplements collected in the United States," revealed that the vast majority sold here do not have the purported medicinal compounds in them (Wu et al. 2017). Just 8 of 19 products sampled contained the triterpenes of *Ganoderma*

lingzhi. Only 6 of the 19 were free of starches from the combined mycelium and its rice or grain substrate. Just 5 of the 19 products included *Ganoderma lingzhi* molecules. The remaining 14 contained no high-molecular-weight beta-glucans. A study of 20 manufactured reishi products sold in the United States, in the form of teas, tablets, and pills, and 17 grow-your-own kits found that 93 percent of the products and about half of the kits contained *Ganoderma lingzhi* native to China; 11 also contained additional material from *Ganoderma sinense* and nonnative *Ganoderma applanatum*, *Ganoderma australe*, *Ganoderma gibbosum*, and *Ganoderma sessile*. One grow-your-own kit was the European *Ganoderma lucidum*. This finding underscores the need for retailers and foragers to be cognizant of the potential consequences to our native forests of cultivating nonnative species and releasing their spores into our environment.

Trametes versicolor

Japanese researchers have discovered two interesting substances derived from Turkey-tail, PSP (polysaccharide peptide) and PSK (polysaccharide krestin). These are believed to function as immunomodulatory stimulants. Results from several small human trials suggest these compounds may have extended the survival rate of victims of gastric cancer over a three-year period by 40 percent (Niimoto et al. 1988), and of colorectal (Ohwada et al. 2004; Torisu et al. 1990) and breast cancer patients by 9 percent over a five-year period (Wong et al. 2005). If these results are consistent, then this is a significant result.

The polysaccharides in *Trametes versicolor* do not kill cancer cells. The PSK in *Trametes versicolor* does not work for esophageal or cervical-uterine cancers. In some cases, it may stimulate mutations. PSP has no cytotoxic effect on mouse lines of hepatoma (Wang et al. 1996), sarcoma, melanoma (Liu et al. 1993), placental choriocarcinoma, or breast cancer (K. W. Luo et al. 2014). Nor can they clear arteries of clogging cholesterol or modulate glucose levels. PSP may, however, protect healthy mice from the effects of whole-body irradiation. One study demonstrated that PSP stimulated the immune system to offer more protection for mice with tumors who didn't undergo radiation compared with those that did. The addition of

PSP with radiation actually led to the growth of larger tumors (Voronov et al. 2013).

Turkey-tail extract may have antiviral effects, as it seems to reduce the frequency of herpes simplex outbreaks (Krupodorova et al. 2014). It appears to ameliorate side effects of cancer radiation and chemotherapy when used as an adjunct therapy by strengthening the immune system following treatment (PDQ 2017).

Conclusions

The September–October 2019 issue of *Cancer Journal* features an article describing an analysis of research data, uses, effects, and drug interactions of 284 herbs and fungi cited in the Integrative Medicine Service website at Memorial Sloan Kettering Cancer Center (Hou et al. 2019). Since November of 2002, the "About Herbs" website had garnered well over 26 million hits. Among the ten most searched herbs and fungi in 2018 were Chaga (1), Reishi (4), and *Trametes versicolor* (10). The authors conclude that over the course of 16 years, evidence for the use of supplements made from these fungi and herbs is primarily based on preclinical results. They also noted that few of the studies were well-designed. Moreover, the number of trials on cancer patients was too limited to determine their efficacy. Before being able to trust that consuming fungal supplements is going to help, do nothing, or cause problems for our health, we need to better understand the complexities of the human body and immune systems. Many studies on the health benefits of fungi in the mid- to late twentieth century, whether performed in Russia, China, or elsewhere, were not conducted in accordance with accepted scientific standards to eliminate biases of researchers or patients. Further studies using improved methods of testing, measuring results, and determining which compounds are truly useful are needed to ascertain whether the hundreds of different species used in commerce can actually prolong the lives of healthy individuals, as well as patients. We need to determine which, if any, of the thousands of different chemicals in macrofungi may have useful medicinal properties, learn proper dosages and duration of care, and learn how they interact with the immune system in mitigating or aggravating particular diseases.

Additionally, there are no universally accepted standards regarding which part of any fungus is being processed for supplement use, testing, and sale. There is no consensus about when, in the life span of a given polypore, its compounds are most beneficial. Furthermore, there is a lack of consistency in commercial products, with some retailers using only spores, others mycelium combined with starches from grain substrates used to grow the fungus, others powdering the hardened fruitbodies, and still others using a combination of different fungal parts or forms, such as the antler form of *Ganoderma lingzhi*. As a result, we are in the dark regarding which, if any, existing formulations are beneficial and what a safe dosage should be. Earlier studies seemed to suggest that all the enzymatic activities of medicinal polypores work synergistically with each other. Recent research appears to be looking at single compounds.

Research design methods have improved somewhat in the twenty-first century, leading to more modest claims regarding the healing potential of different fungal organisms. Some compounds may enhance a patient's immune system, enabling it to recover more quickly following chemotherapy and radiation. Fungal formulas should not be taken while undergoing these treatments, however, because they can counteract the effects of immune suppression therapies. There is also the problematic observation that some compounds appear to co-opt the immune system to promote the growth of cancers. Promising initial research has led to the "suggestion" that fungal products may have the same effect on human subjects that they have on cells in a Petri dish or in genetically engineered mice lacking normal immune responses. Suggestions, however, are not evidence. The conclusion is that further research needs to be done.

These facts have not deterred believers from continuing to espouse the as-yet-unproven utility of "medicinal" macrofungi to prevent or alleviate a plethora of disease conditions. In the future, we hope to be able to report unequivocally that at least some of the many compounds in macrofungi are indeed efficacious beyond their recognized nutritional assets. In the meantime, we urge readers to use caution and refrain from taking unproven supplements for prophylactic or curative reasons until reliable science-based data are produced.

Polypores Organized by Order, Family, Genus, and Species

The following organization of polypores and other fungi described in this field guide is based on studies by Alfredo Justo, Otto Miettinen, Dimitrios Floudas, Leif Ryvarden, David Hibbett, and their colleagues (Justo et al. 2017), as well as data retrieved from the websites of Index Fungorum, Mushroom Observer, MycoBank, and MycoGuide. Groundwork studies on these fungi and their phylogenetic relationships to one another are in a preliminary stage of development. Numerous polypores still require genetic analysis. Even in cases where molecular studies have been published, there is not complete agreement among mycologists regarding the proper taxonomic placement of specimens within various proposed clades and associated family-level classification schemes (Zmitrovich 2018). By furnishing readers with projected revisions to polypore taxonomy, combined with existing placements for fungi that will require further analysis, we have tried to reflect where the mycological community currently stands in this complicated endeavor. Expect further changes as scientific knowledge progresses. *Note:* The term "spp." denotes that the authors of this field guide have described more than one species of a given genus.

Class AGARICOMYCETES
Order AGARICALES
    Family Amylocorticiaceae Jülich (1982)
      Genus and species:
        Plicaturopsis crispa
    Family Cyphellaceae Lotsy (1907)
      Genus and species:
        Chondrostereum purpureum
    Family Fistulinaceae Lotsy (1907)
      Genus and species:
        Fistulina hepatica
        Porodisculus pendulus
        Pseudofistulina radicata
    Family Mycenaceae Overeem (1926)
      Genus and species:
        Panellus pusillus
    Family Radulomycetacea (fam. nov)
      Genus and species:
        Radulomyces copelandii
    Family Schizophyllaceae Quél. (1888)
      Genus and species:
        Schizophyllum spp.
Order BOLETALES
    Family Coniophoraceae Ulbr. (1928)
      Genus and species:
        Gyrodontium sacchari
Order CANTHARELLALES
    Family Hydnaceae Chevall. (1826)
      Genus and species:
        Sistotrema confluens
Order CORTICIALES
    Family Punctulariaceae Pat (1895)
      Genus and species:
        Punctularia strigosozonata
Order GLOEOPHYLLALES
    Family Gloeophyllaceae Jülich (1981)
      Genus and species:
        Gloeophyllum spp.
        Neolentinus lepideus
        Osmoporus mexicanus
Order HYMENOCHAETALES
    Family Hymenochaetaceae Imazeki & Toki (1954)
      Genus and species:
        Coltricia spp.
        Coltriciella spp.
        Fomitiporia spp.

Fulvifomes spp.
Fuscoporia spp.
Hydnoporia spp.
Hymenochaete spp.
Inocutis spp.
Inonotus spp.
Onnia spp.
Phellinopsis conchata
Phellinus spp.
Phylloporia spp.
Porodaedalea spp.
Pseudoinonotus dryadeus
Trichaptum spp.
Xanthoporia spp.
Family Nigrofomitaceae Jülich (1982)
    Genus and species:
        Nigrofomes melanopus
Family Oxyporaceae Zmitr. & Malysheva (2014)
    Genus and species:
        Oxyporus populinus
Family Schizoporaceae Jülich (1981)
    Genus and species:
        Xylodon spp.
Order POLYPORALES
    Family Cerrenaceae O. Miettinen, A. Justo & D. S. Hibbett (2017)
        Genus and species:
            Cerrena spp.
            Spongipellis spp. (excluding *S. spummeus*)
    Family Cystostereaceae Jülich (1981)
        Genus and species:
            Cystostereum murrayi
    Family Dacryobolaceae Jülich (1981)
        Genus and species:
            Amylocystis lapponica
            Fuscopostia fragilis
            Postia spp.
    Family Fomitopsidaceae Jülich (1981)
        Genus and species:
            Antrodia spp.
            Brunneoporus spp.
            Buglossoporus quercinus
            Calcipostia guttulata
            Daedalea quercina
            Fomitopsis spp.

Neoantrodia spp.
Nigrofomes melanoporus
Niveoporofomes spraguei
Osteina obducta
Pycnoporellus spp.
Rhodofomes spp.
Rhodofomitopsis feei
Family Ganodermataceae (Donk) Donk (1948)
    Genus and species:
        Foraminispora rugosa
        Ganoderma spp.
Family Gelatoporiaceae O. Miettinen, A. Justo & D. S. Hibbett (2017)
    Genus and species:
        Gelatoporia dichroa
Family Grifolaceae Jülich (1981)
    Genus and species:
        Grifola frondosa
Family Incrustoporiaceae Jülich (1981)
    Genus and species:
        Skeletocutis lilacina
        Tyromyces spp.
Family Irpicaceae Spirin & Zmitr. (2003)
    Genus and species:
        Byssomerulius incarnatus
        Ceriporia purpurea
        Hydnopolyporus palmatus
        Irpex lacteus
        Leptoporus mollis
        Trametopsis cervina
Family Ischnodermataceae Jülich (1981)
    Genus and species:
        Ischnoderma spp.
Family Laetiporaceae Jülich (1981)
    Genus and species:
        Laetiporus spp.
        Phaeolus schweinitzii
Family Meripilaceae Jülich (1981)
    Genus and species:
        Meripilus sumstinei
        Radulodon americanus
        Rigidoporus spp.
Family Meruliaceae Rea (1922)
    Genus and species:
        Climacodon spp.
        Pappia fissilis

Phlebia spp.

Sarcodontia setosa

Family Panaceae O. Miettinen, A. Justo &
D. S. Hibbett (2017)

    Genus and species:

        Cymatoderma caperatum

        Panus spp.

Family Phanerochaetaceae Jülich (1981)

    Genus and species:

        Bjerkandera spp.

        Hapalopilus spp.

        Phlebiopsis crassa

Family Podoscyphaceae D. A. Reid (1965)

    Genus and species:

        Abortiporus biennis

        Podoscypha aculeata

Family Polyporaceae Corda (1839)

    Genus and species:

        Bresadolia spp.

        Cerioporus spp.

        Coriolopsis spp.

        Cryptoporus volvatus

        Daedaleopsis spp.

        Datroniella scutellata

        Earliella scabrosa

        Favolus tenuiculus

        Fomes spp.

        Fomitella supina

        Funalia floccosa

        Globifomes graveolens

        Hexagonia spp.

        Lentinus spp.

        Lenzites betulinus

        Microporellus spp.

        Neofavolus spp.

        Perennioporia spp.

        Picipes spp.

        Polyporus spp.

        Poronidulus conchifer

        Pycnoporus spp.

        Pyrofomes juniperinus

        Spongipellis spumeus

        Trametella trogii

        Trametes spp.

        Truncospora spp.

        Vanderbylia robiniophila

Family Sparassidaceae Herter (1910)

    Genus and species:

        Sparassis spp.

Family Steccherinaceae Parmasto (1968)

    Genus and species:

        Antrodiella spp.

        Loweomyces spp.

        Metuloidea fragrans

        Mycorrhaphium adustum

        Nigroporus vinosus

        Steccherinum spp.

        Trullella polyporoides

        Xanthoporus peckianus

    Genus and Species incertae sedis:

        Climacocystis borealis

Order RUSSULALES

    Family Albatrellaceae Nuss (1980)

        Genus and species:

            Albatrellus spp.

            Jahnoporus hirtus

            Laeticutis cristata

            Neoalbatrellus caeruleoporus

            Polyporoletus sublividus

            Scutiger pes-caprae

    Family Bondarzewiaceae Kotlába & Pouzar
    (1957)

        Genus and species:

            Amylosporus campbellii

            Bondarzewia berkeleyi

            Heterobasidion irregulare

    Family Stereaceae Pilát (1930)

        Genus and species:

            Stereum spp.

            Xylobolus subpileatus

Order THELEPHORALES

    Family Bankeraceae Donk (1961)

        Genus and species:

            Boletopsis grisea

    Family Thelephoraceae Chevall. (1826)

        Genus and species:

            Thelephora spp.

Class EUROTIOMYCETES

Order MYCOCALICIALES

    Family Mycocaliciaceae A. F. W. Schmidt (1970)

        Genus and species:

            Phaeocalicium polyporaeum

Glossary

acute (margin): Tapered to a thin edge.

agarics: Mushrooms having a cap and stalk, and gills on the undersurface of the cap.

agglutinate, agglutinated (hyphae): Glued together.

allantoid: Sausage-shaped.

amyloid: Staining bluish to grayish or blackish violet in Melzer's reagent.

anastomosing: Connecting and fusing together.

angiosperm: A plant having seeds contained in an ovary inside a fruit.

annual: Completing growth in one season.

apiarists: Persons who keep, care for, and raise bees.

apical, apically: At the uppermost portion or farthest from the attachment point.

apiculus: A short projection at the basal end of a spore by which it attaches to the sterigma.

appressed: Closely flattened down.

appressed-fibrillose: Composed of thin, hairy filaments that are closely flattened down.

appressed-fibrous: Composed of tough, stringy tissue that is flattened down.

appressed-scaly: Composed of scales that are flattened down.

appressed-strigose: Composed of coarse, stiff hairs that are flattened down.

appressed-tomentose: Composed of woolly hairs that are flattened down.

appressed-velvety: Composed of short, fine, soft hairs that are flattened down.

aqueous solution: Any solution in which water is the solvent.

arborescent: Resembling a tree in growth or appearance.

arbuscular mycorrhizae: A mutualistic symbiotic relationship in which hyphae penetrate into plant root cells.

Archaeopteris: A genus of plants, known only as fossils from the late Devonian Period, believed to have woody trunks and fernlike leaves.

arcuate: Curved like a bow.

ascomycetes: A subclass of fungi in which ascospores are formed in a saclike structure called an ascus.

attenuated base (spores): Gradually narrowed, becoming smaller and thinner.

azonate: Having uniform color, without distinct zones.

basal: At the end nearest the point of attachment.

basidia: Club-shaped cells on which basidiospores are formed.

basidiospore, basidiospores: A sexual spore of the phylum Basidiomycota.

binding hyphae: Branched, solid to very thick-walled, aseptate hyphae with tapering side branches that are twisting and thinner than skeletal hyphae.

bioactive compound: Any substance present in the food of humans, other animals, or plants, such as caffeine in coffee, that has an effect on the organism consuming it.

biopulping: Fungal pretreatment of wood chips for the production of wood pulp used to make paper.

bolete: A fleshy cap-and-stalk mushroom with a tube layer and pores on the underside of the cap.

bracket: A type of polypore that forms a shelflike fruitbody on living or dead wood.

broadleaf: Referring to any non-cone-bearing, angiosperm, or flowering deciduous tree or shrub.

brown rot, brown cubical rot: A type of wood decay caused by removal of cellulose and hemicellulose, leaving behind modified lignin.

buff: Pale yellow-brown to pale grayish brown.

bulbous: Enlarged at the base and rounded.

butt (standing trees): The bottom portion of a tree above the roots.

Bya: Billion years ago.

carmine: A shade of dull deep red.

cartilaginous: Tough and breaking with a snap when bent far enough.

cellulose: A polysaccharide composed of chains of glucose molecules that is the main component of plant cell walls.

central (stalk): Located at the center.

cephaloid: Having tubes that are not laterally fused and are easily separated one from another.

chitin: Polysaccharides forming the major constituent in the cell walls of fungi.

chlamydospore: A thick-walled secondary spore developed from hyphae.

chytrid: A simple, microscopic, aquatic fungus that has a single posterior flagellum and typically does not form mycelia.

circumboreal: Distributed throughout the northern portion of the Northern Hemisphere.

clade: A group of organisms believed to have evolved from a common ancestor.

Cladoxylopsids: A group of plants, known only as fossils, that are thought to be ancestors of ferns and horsetails.

clamp connections: Microscopic semicircular bridgelike structures that connect two adjoining cells.

clasping: Surrounding and holding tightly.

clavate: Club-shaped.

close (lamellae): Spacing that is halfway between crowded and subdistant.

coalescing: Coming together to form a whole.

columnar: Having the shape of a column.

concave: Depressed and shaped like a bowl.

concentric, concentrically: Having rings or zones within one another in a series.

concolorous: Having the same color.

confluent: Running into one another.

conical: More or less cone-shaped.

conifer: A cone-bearing tree with needlelike leaves, such as hemlock or pine.

conk: A fruitbody of a wood-rotting polypore, especially those that are perennial.

contracted (stalk): Decreased in size, typically short and stubby.

convex: Curved or rounded.

crenate: Finely scalloped.

crenulate: Very finely scalloped.

crimped: Having small folds or ridges.

cross section: A straight cut at right angles to the long axis.

crowded (lamellae): Almost touching.

crustose: Having a hard, compact surface layer.

cuticle, cuticular: The outermost tissue layer of the cap or stalk.

cyanophilous: Becoming bright blue by absorbing cotton blue.

cycads: Seed plants with a stout and woody trunk and a crown of large, hard, and stiff evergreen leaves.

cylindric, cylindrical: Elongated and of uniform diameter.

cylindrical-ellipsoid: Elongated and resembling an oval with similarly curved ends.

cylindrical-elliptic: Pertaining to a distinctly elongated oval.

cylindrical-oblong: Elongated and longer than wide, with somewhat flattened ends.

cystidia: Sterile cells that project between and usually beyond the basidia.

decorticated: Without the bark.

decurrent: Descending or running down the stalk.

decurved: Bent downward.

dentate: Having teethlike projections.

depressed: Indented or somewhat sunken in.

dextrinoid: Staining orange-brown to reddish brown in Melzer's reagent.

dikaryotic: Having two different haploid nuclei.

dimitic: Consisting of two types of hyphae, usually generative and skeletal, but generative and binding in *Laetiporus* species.

disk: The central area of the cap surface.

dissepiments: The partitions or end walls of the tubes surrounding the pores.

distal: Farthest away from the point of attachment.

distant: Spaced widely apart.

di-trimitic: Consisting of two or three types of hyphae.

dorsal: On the upper or back side.

duplex: Having two distinct zones of different textures.

eccentric (stalk): Away from the center, but not lateral.

echinulate: Having slender, sharp spines.

ecosystem: A complex community of organisms and the environment functioning as a unit.

effused: Spread out over the substrate.

effused-reflexed: Having part of the fruitbody spread out and part forming a shelflike cap.

ellipsoid: Resembling an elongated oval with similarly curved ends.

elliptic, elliptical: Pertaining to an elongated oval with similarly curved ends.

elliptic-cylindrical: Pertaining to a distinctly elongated oval.

elongate-angular: Irregular and elongated in outline.

elongate-ellipsoid: Resembling a distinctly elongated oval with similarly curved ends.

encrusted: Covered with a thin, hard crust.

entire (margin): Even; not broken, serrated, or lacerated.

epithet (species, specific): The second part of a Latin binomial scientific name.

equal (stalk): Having uniform diameter along its length.

ergosterol: A compound found in fungal cell membranes that serves the same purpose as cholesterol in animal cells.

eroded: Partially worn away.

extant: Still in existence, surviving.

exude, exuding: To come out slowly in drops.

farinaceous: An odor variously compared to sliced watermelon rind, cucumber, meal, bread dough, or farina flour.

fascicles: Small bundles.

fertile surface: The spore-bearing surface.

FeSO₄: Iron sulfate, usually a 10 percent solution.

fibrillose: Composed of fibrils.

fibrillose-scaly: Having tiny scales composed of appressed fibrils.

fibrils: Tiny fibers.

fibrous-spongy: Compressible and composed of fibers.

fibrous-tough: Composed of durable fibers.

fimbriate: Composed of radiating fibers and appearing minutely fringed on the edge (margin).

fissured: Having deep cracks.

flagella: Relatively long, whiplike extensions on motile spores.

flesh: The inner tissue of a fruitbody above the tubes or other reproductive structures.

fleshy-fibrous: Composed of soft, flexible fibers.

forked: Divided into two sections.

fringed: Having an edge composed of hairs or fibers.

fruitbody: The entire hard or fleshy reproductive structure (in this work, a polypore).

furrows: Tiny surface grooves.

fusiform: Spindle-shaped.

fusoid: Somewhat spindle-shaped.

gelatinized, gelatinous: Composed of a jellylike substance.

generative hyphae: The basic unit of structure present in all polypore fruitbodies, thick- or thin-walled, with clamp connections or simple septa.

genus, genera: A taxonomic category ranking below a family and above a species.

geotropically: Pertaining to turning toward the ground.

germ pore: A thin circular area in the spore wall.

gills: On some mushrooms, bladelike structures located on the underside of the cap.

glabrous: Lacking hairs.

glancing: Changing from dull to lustrous when the viewing angle shifts in incident light.

globose: Spherical or nearly so.

gloeocystidia: Sterile elements with distinctly oily or refractive contents.

Glomeromycota: A taxonomic phylum of the kingdom Fungi, consisting of species that form arbuscular mycorrhizae with plants.

glucans: Polysaccharides that are polymers of glucose, such as glycogen or cellulose.

guttule: A small oil-like drop visible (via a microscope) inside a fungal spore.

gymnosperm: A plant whose seeds are exposed and not enclosed in an ovary.

habit: The manner in which a fruitbody grows.

habitat: The environment in which a species grows.

heartwood: Innermost nonliving wood in a tree trunk. Compare with sapwood.

hemicellulose: Any one of several complex carbohydrates that surround cellulose molecules in plant cell walls.

hemispherical: Shaped like one-half of a sphere.

hexagonal: Having six angles.

hirsute: Having an outer covering of coarse, elongated hairs.

hispid: With stiff, erect hairs.

homogeneous: Uniform in consistency and color.

horny: Hard, brittle, and difficult to section.

hyaline: Colorless, transparent.

hydrophilic: Having an affinity for water.

hymenial: Pertaining to the hymenium.

hymenial cystidia: Sterile cells located in the hymenium.

hymenial setae: Thick-walled sterile cells found in the hymenium.

hymenium: The layer of basidia and sterile elements that line the inside of the tubes or outside of gills, spines, etc.

hypha (pl. hyphae): Threadlike microscopic filament of a fungus.

hyphal system: The specific type or combination of hyphae that occurs in a fruitbody.

immunomodulatory: Refers to agents having the potential to either stimulate or inhibit immune system responses.

inamyloid: Unchanging or pale yellow in Melzer's reagent.

incised: Appearing cut into.

incurved: Bent inward toward the stalk.

infestation: The presence of an unusually large number of insects in a specific place, typically so as to cause damage or disease.

inrolled: Bent inward toward the stalk and upward.

interwall pillars: Connecting lines between the inner and outer walls of some types of spores (e.g., species of *Ganoderma*).

KOH: Potassium hydroxide, usually a 2–5 percent solution in water.

labyrinthine: Composed of sinuous spaces and resembling a maze.

laccate: Appearing varnished or shellacked.

lacerated: Appearing as if torn.

lacrimoid: Tear-shaped.

lactophenol cotton blue: A mounting medium and staining agent used for microscopic examination of fungi.

lamellae: Horizontally oriented plates of various lengths and thicknesses on the fertile surface of some fungi.

lamellate: Made up of lamellae.

lateral, laterally: Attached to one side.

lichen: An organism consisting of a fungus and certain types of bacteria or algae in a mutually beneficial relationship.

lignin: Complex cross-linked polymers that resist decay and give strength and rigidity to plant cell walls.

lobed: Having rounded divisions.

longitudinally: Oriented along the vertical axis.

lustrous: Bright and shining.

lycopod: Erect or creeping evergreen plant known as a club moss or ground pine.

macromorphology: Gross structure of an organism visible to the unaided eye.

macroscopic, macroscopically: Visible to unaided eyes, without magnification.

margin: The edge of a cap.

Mariana Trench: An ocean trench to the southeast of the Mariana Islands in the western Pacific Ocean.

megafauna: The large mammals of a particular habitat, region, or geological period.

Melzer's reagent: A solution containing iodine, potassium iodide, chloral hydrate, and water used for testing color reactions of fungal spores and various tissues.

membranous (ring): Of or like a membrane.

microscopic, microscopically: Visible only with the aid of a microscope.

minute: Of extremely small size or quantity.

monokaryotic: Containing only one haploid nucleus.

monomitic: Composed only of generative hyphae.

monophyletic: Descended from a common evolutionary ancestor or ancestral group, especially one not shared with any other group.

mottled: Marked with spots or smears of color.

moxibustion: Burning of herbal agents, such as dried mugwort, on the skin as a counterirritant in the treatment of disease.

multicolored: Having more than one color.

multizonate: Having many zones.

Mya: Million years ago.

mycelium: A mass of hyphae visible to unaided eyes.

mycorrhizal: Pertaining to a mutually beneficial relationship between a fungus and the roots of a vascular plant. The fungus greatly increases the plant's root system for uptake of minerals, nutrients, and water. The plant provides the fungus with carbon-based products of photosynthesis.

NH₄OH: Ammonium hydroxide, usually a 3–14 percent aqueous solution, or household ammonia without added soap.

niche: The functional role that an organism plays within an ecosystem.

nondecurrent (gills): Not running down on the stalk.

nonlichenized: A fungus not in a mutually beneficial relationship with a bacterium or algae.

oblique, obliquely: Slanting, neither parallel nor at a right angle to a specified line.

oblong: Longer than wide with somewhat flattened ends.

oblong-ellipsoid: Longer than wide and resembling an elongated oval with similarly curved ends.

oblong-elliptical: Longer than wide and pertaining to an elongated oval with similarly curved ends.

oblong-ovoid: Longer than wide and somewhat egg-shaped.

obovate: Egg-shaped with the narrow end at the base.

obpyriform: Reversely pear-shaped.

obtuse: Rounded or blunt.

ochraceous: Pale brownish orange-yellow.

ochre: Brownish orange-yellow.

olivaceous: Having olive tints.

opportunistic pathogen: An organism that takes advantage of specific conditions to cause harm or injury.

orthographic variant: A spelling, typing, or writing mistake within a scientific publication that resulted in a somewhat different name unintentionally being used for a previously named organism.

ovoid: Somewhat egg-shaped.

pantropical: Distributed across the tropical regions of both hemispheres.

parasite: An organism that lives on or in a host organism, derives nourishment from it, and harms it.

parasitic: Living on or in another organism and deriving nourishment from it.

partial veil: A layer of tissue that covers the lamellae.

pathogen: An organism that is capable of causing disease or injury.

pathogenic: Pertaining to an organism that is capable of causing disease or injury.

pendant: Hanging downward.

perennial: Continuing to grow from year to year.

permineralized: Organic material fossilized through the precipitation of dissolved minerals in the very small spaces of hard tissue.

phloxine: A red dye used for microscopic examination, especially of hyphae.

phylogenetic: Pertaining to the development or evolution of a particular group of organisms.

pileate: Having a shelflike cap with a sterile upper surface.

plane: Having a flat surface.

polyphyletic: Relating to a group of organisms that are classified in the same group but came from different ancestors.

polysaccharide: A carbohydrate, such as cellulose or starch, consisting of a number of sugar molecules bonded together.

pore: A small opening; the mouth of a tube.

poroid: Having pores.

primordium: A structure in the earliest stage of development.

proximal: Located at the closest point.

pubescent: Having short, soft, downy hairs.

pungent: Sharp or irritating.

quillworts: Spore-bearing plants with grassy, spikelike leaves, found mainly in cooler, swampy habitats.

radial, radially, radiating: Having structures arranged around and pointing away from a common central point.

radicating: Continuing as a rootlike underground extension.

resinous: Exuding a sticky and oily substance.

resupinate: Spreading over the substrate with no cap-like portion.

reticulate: Marked out in a pattern like a fishnet.

rhizomatous: Having a rootlike subterranean stem that is commonly horizontal.

Rhynie chert: An early Devonian sedimentary deposit exhibiting extraordinary fossil detail.

ribbed: Having a pattern of raised bands.

ring: Remnants of a partial veil that remains attached to the stalk after the veil ruptures.

rosette: An arrangement resembling the shape of a rose.

rudimentary (stalk): Undeveloped and restricted in size and shape.

ruddy: Having a reddish tint.

saprotroph: An organism that lives off dead or decaying matter.

saprotrophic: Pertaining to living off dead or decaying matter.

sapwood: The living, outermost portion of wood.

scales, scaly: Flattened or recurved projections or torn portions of the cap or stalk surface.

scale trees: Extinct treelike plants related to quillworts and club mosses.

scientization: The process of applying or the attempt to apply scientific principles to something.

sclerids: Thick-walled, hard, unbranched, skeletal hyphae of highly variable shape.

sclerotium: A resting structure composed of a hardened mass of hyphae, usually underground.

scurfy: Roughened by tiny flakes or scales.

sensu stricto: Strictly speaking; in the narrow sense.

septa, septate: Crosswalls within a hypha.

serrate, serrated: Notched or toothed on the edge, like a saw.

sessile: Attached without a stalk.

setae: Sterile, thick-walled elements in the hymenium that are typically dark-colored.

setal hyphae: Thick-walled, pointed hyphae found in the tissue between tubes in some fungi.

sinuous: Wavy and twisting or turning.

skeletal hyphae: Unbranched, thick-walled, aseptate hyphae typically of even width.

sordid: Dull or appearing dirty.

spike mosses: Mossy or fernlike perennial members of the genus *Selaginella*.

sporangia: Structures in which reproductive spores are produced and stored.

spores: Microscopic reproductive cells of a fungus.

sporulation: The process of forming spores.

stalk: The erect structure that supports the cap.

sterigma, sterigmata: A microscopic slender stalk on which a basidiospore is borne.

sterigmate: Borne on a sterigma.

stipitate: Having a stalk as a point of attachment.

stratified (tubes): Arranged in distinct layers.

striae: Small, more or less parallel lines or furrows.

striate: Having small, more or less parallel lines or furrows.

strigose: Covered with long, coarse, stiff hairs.

subangular: Somewhat angular; without sharply defined angles.

subcentral (stalk): Located near the center.

subcylindrical: Somewhat cylinder-shaped.

subdecurrent: Extending slightly down on the stalk.

subdistant (lamellae): Spacing that is halfway between close and distant.

subduction: The sideways and downward movement of the edge of a plate of the earth's crust into the mantle beneath another plate.

subfusiform: Somewhat spindle-shaped.

subglabrous: Nearly bald.

subglobose: Nearly round.

subhymenium: The tissue immediately below the hymenium.

substipitate: Having a very short attachment.

substrate: The food source on which a fungus is growing.

subulate: Shaped like an awl.

sulcate: Having shallow grooves.

tawny: Orange-brown to dull yellowish brown.

terrestrial: Occurring on land.

tomentose: Coated with a thick, matted layer of hairs.

tomentum: A covering of soft hairs.

trama: Sterile supporting tissue.

translucent: Allowing light, but not detailed shapes, to pass through.

translucent-striate: Appearing striate when viewed through translucent tissue.

trimitic: Composed of generative, skeletal, and binding hyphae.

truncate: Appearing cut off at the end.

tubes: Narrow, parallel, spore-producing cylinders on the fertile surface.

tufted, tufts: A cluster closely held together.

type (specimen): The specimen or specimens from which a species was described and named.

umber: Dark yellowish brown.

umbonate: Having a raised area like a knob at the center of the cap.

undulating: Having a wavy or uneven surface.

ungulate(s): A hoofed mammal such as a cow, horse, or deer.

velvety: Covered with short, soft, somewhat erect hairs.

ventricose: Swollen in the middle and tapering to somewhat of a point.

verrucose: Having small, rounded warts.

vinaceous: Pinkish red to pale purplish red.

violaceous: A bluish purple; resembling violets.

viscid: Sticky or tacky.

warted, warty: Having small, rounded bumps.

white rot: A type of wood decay caused by the degradation of all components of wood, cellulose, hemicellulose, and lignin.

woolly-tomentose: Covered with a thick layer of matted hairs.

zonate, zoned: Marked with bands of different color or texture.

zoospore: A motile spore, usually with one or more flagella.

zosterophylls: A group of extinct land plants believed to be ancestors of ferns.

zygomycetes: A subclass of fungi in which sexual reproduction is by zygospores.

Bibliography and Resources

Print

Akbar, R., and W. K. Yam. 2011. Interaction of ganodermic acid on HIV related target: Molecular docking studies. Bioinformation 7(8):413–417.

Armstrong, J. E. 2014. How the Earth Turned Green: A Brief 3.8-Billion-Year History of Plants. University of Chicago Press. 578 pp.

Ayuso-Fernández, I., F. J. Ruiz-Dueñas, and A. T. Martínez. 2018. Evolutionary convergence in lignin-degrading enzymes. PNAS 115(25):6428–6433.

Baek, J., H. S. Roh, K. H. Baek, S. Lee, et al. 2018. Bioactivity-based analysis and chemical characterization of cytotoxic constituents from Chaga mushroom (*Inonotus obliquus*) that induce apoptosis in human lung adenocarcinoma cells. J Ethnopharmacol 224:63–75.

Balla, A. 2015. Fungal fashions: The craft of the polypore couturier. Mushroom: The Journal of Wild Mushrooming 112(31):46–47.

Banik, M. T., D. L. Lindner, B. Ortiz-Santana, and D. J. Lodge. 2012. A new species of *Laetiporus* (Basidiomycota, Polyporales) from the Caribbean basin. Kurtziana 37(1):15–21.

Bauml, J. M., S. Chokshi, M. M. Schapira, E. O. Im, et al. 2015. Do attitudes and beliefs regarding complementary and alternative medicine impact use among patients with cancer?: A cross-cultural survey. Cancer 121(14):2431–2438.

Beinfield, H., and E. Korngold. 1992. Between Heaven and Earth: A Guide to Chinese Medicine. Ballantine Books, New York. 448 pp.

Bell, J. 2019. The Earth Book: From the Beginning to the End of Our Planet. Sterling Milestones. 528 pp.

Ben-Arye, E., N. Samuels, L. H. Goldstein, K. Mutafoglu, et al. 2016. Potential risks associated with traditional herbal medicine use in cancer care: A study of Middle Eastern oncology health care professionals. Cancer 122(4):598–610.

Bengston, S., B. Rasmussen, M. Ivarsson, J. Muhling, et al. 2017. Fungus-like mycelial fossils in 2.4-billion-year-old vesicular basalt. Nat Ecol Evol 1:0141.

Benjamin, D. R. 1995. The nutritional and culinary aspects of edible mushrooms. Chap. 4 in Mushrooms: Poisons and Panaceas. W. H. Freeman & Co., New York. 62–74.

Bensky, D., S. Clavey, and E. Stöger. 2015. Chinese Herbal Medicine, Materia Medica, portable 3d ed. Eastland Press, Seattle. 1325 pp.

Benson, K. F., P. Stamets, R. Davis, R. Nally, et al. 2019. The mycelium of the *Trametes versicolor* (Turkey tail) mushroom and its fermented substrate each show potent and complementary immune activating properties in vitro. Open access. BMC Comp Altern Med 19, 342.

Benson, W. 2012. Kingdom of Plants: A Journey Through Their Evolution. Royal Botanic Gardens Kew. Collins, London. 256 pp.

Benton, M. J. 2015. When Life Nearly Died: The Greatest Mass Extinction of All Time. Thames & Hudson, London. 576 pp.

Berbee, M. L., T. Y. James, and C. Strullu-Darrien. 2017. Early diverging fungi: Diversity and impact at the dawn of terrestrial life. Annu Rev Microbiol 71:41–60.

Bertschinger, R. 2011. The Secret of Everlasting Life: The First Translation of the Ancient Chinese Text on Immortality. Singing Dragon, London. 306 pp.

—————. 2015. Essential Texts in Chinese Medicine: The Single Idea in the Mind of the Yellow Emperor. Singing Dragon, London. 322 pp.

—————. 2018. A Record of the Assembled Immortals and Gathered Perfected of the Western Hills: Shi Jianwu's Daoist Classic on Internal Alchemy and the Cultivation of the Breath. Singing Dragon, London. 192 pp.

Bessette, A. R., and A. E. Bessette. 2001. The Rainbow Beneath My Feet: A Mushroom Dyer's Field Guide. Syracuse University Press. 176 pp.

Beug, M. W., P. Kroeger, and R. Li. 2019. Cautions regarding ingestion of *Inonotus obliquus* (Chaga). Fungi 12(2):32–37.

Bhardwaj, N., P. Katyal, and A. K. Sharma. 2014. Suppression of inflammatory and allergic responses by pharmacologically potent fungus, *Ganoderma lucidum*. Recent Pat Inflamm Allergy Drug Discov 8(2):104–117.

Binder, M., D. S. Hibbett, Z. Wang, and W. F. Farnham. 2006. Evolutionary relationships of *Mycaureola dilseae* (Agaricales), a basidiomycete pathogen of a subtidal rhodophyte. Am J Bot 93(4):547–556.

Binder, M., A. Justo, R. Riley, A. Salamov, et al. 2013. Phylogenetic and phylogenomic overview of the Polyporales. Mycologia 105(6):1350–1373.

Binion, D. E., S. L. Stephenson, W. C. Roody, H. H. Burdsall Jr., O. K. Miller Jr., and L. N. Vasilyeva. 2008. Macrofungi Associated with Oaks of Eastern North America. West Virginia University Press, Morgantown. 467 pp.

Bjornerud, M. 2020. Timefullness: How Thinking Like a Geologist Can Help Save the World. Princeton University Press. 224 pp.

Blanchette, R. A., C. C. Renner, B. W. Held, C. Enoch, and S. Angstman. 2007. The current use of *Phellinus igniarius* by the Eskimos of western Alaska. Mycologist 16(4):142–145.

Bone, E. 2018. Microbia: A Journey into the Unseen World Around You. Rodale Press. 226 pp.

Bonneville, S., F. Delpomdor, A. Préat, C. Chevalier, et al. 2020. Molecular identification of fungi microfossils in a Neoproterozoic shale rock. Science Advances 6(4):1–11.

Bowers, J. Z., J. W. Hess, and N. Sivin (eds.). 1988. Science and Medicine in Twentieth-Century China: Research and Education, Science, Medicine, and Technology in East Asia 3. University of Michigan Center for Chinese Studies, Ann Arbor. 304 pp.

Boyce, C. K., M. Albrecht, D. Zhou, and P.U.P.A. Gilbert. 2010. X-ray photoelectron emission spectromicroscopic analysis of arborescent lycopsid cell wall composition and carboniferous coal ball preservation. Int J Coal Geology 83(2–3):146–153.

Brannen, P. 2018. The Ends of the World: Volcanic Apocalypses, Lethal Oceans, and Our Quest to Understand Earth's Past Mass Extinctions. Harper Collins Publishers, New York. 336 pp.

Burdsall, H. H. Jr., and M. T. Banik. 2001. The genus *Laetiporus* in North America. Harvard Papers in Botany 6(1):43–55.

Burdsall, H. H. Jr., and F. F. Lombard. 1989. *Polyporus lowei*, a new species from the Great Lakes Region. Memoirs of the New York Botanical Garden 49:147–151.

Campany, R. 2002. To Live as Long as Heaven and Earth: A Translation and Study of Ge Hong's Traditions of Divine Transcendents. University of California Press, Berkeley. 607 pp.

Cao, Y., and H. S. Yuan. 2012. *Ganoderma mutabile* sp. nov. from southwestern China based on morphological and molecular data. Mycol Prog 12:121–126.

Cao, Y., S. Wu, and Y. Dai. 2012. Species clarification of the prize medicinal *Ganoderma* mushroom "Lingzhi." Fungal Divers 56(1):49–62.

Cao, Y., X. Xu, S. Liu, L. Huang, and J. Gu. 2018. *Ganoderma*: A cancer immunotherapy review. Front Pharmacol: Ethnopharmacology 9:1217.

Capasso, L. 1998. 5300 years ago, the Ice Man used natural laxatives and antibiotics. Lancet 352(9143):864.

Carlson, A., A. Justo, and D. S. Hibbett. 2014. Species delimitation in *Trametes*: A comparison of ITS, RPB1, RPB2 and TEF1 gene phylogenies. Mycologia 106(4):735–745.

Cohen, M. R. 2015. You are what you eat. Chap. 6 in The New Chinese Medicine Handbook. Far Winds Press, Beverly, MA. 9–111.

Collins, D. 2018. Amazing cancer cure case studies with maitake mushroom. https://underground healthreporter.com/maitake-mushroom-effect-on-cancer/. Accessed June 22, 2018.

Cooke, W. B. 1949. *Oxyporus nobilissimus* and the genus *Oxyporus* in North America. Mycologia 41(4):442–446.

Coy, C., L. J. Standish, G. Bender, and H. Lu. 2015. Significant correlation between TLR2 agonist activity and TNF–α induction in J774.A1 macrophage cells by different medicinal mushroom products. Int J Med Mushrooms 17(8):713–722.

Crozier, R. C. 1977. The ideology of medical revivalism in modern China. Pp. 341–355 in Asian Medical Systems: A Comparative Study, edited by Charles Leslie. University of California Press, Berkeley.

Da, J., W. Y. Wu, J. J. Hou, H. L. Long, et al. 2012. Comparison of two officinal Chinese pharmacopoeia species of *Ganoderma* based on chemical research with multiple technologies and chemometrics analysis. J Chromatogr A 1222:59–70.

Dai, Y. C., and B. K. Cui. 2011. *Fomitiporia ellipsoidea* has the largest fruiting body among the fungi. Fungal Biology 115:813–814.

Dai, Y. C., Z. L. Yang, B. K. Cui, C. J. Yu, and L. W. Zhou. 2009. Species diversity and utilization of medicinal mushrooms and fungi in China (Review). Int J Med Mushrooms 11(3):287–302.

Dai, Y. C., L. W. Zhou, T. Hattori, Y. Cao, et al. 2017. *Ganoderma lingzhi* (Polyporales, Basidiomycota): The scientific binomial for the widely cultivated medicinal fungus Lingzhi. Mycol Prog 16:1051–1055.

Davidson, E. W. 2006. Big Fleas Have Little Fleas: How Discoveries of Invertebrate Diseases Are Advancing Modern Science. University of Arizona Press, Tucson. 208 pp.

Deng G., H. Lin, A. Seidman, M. Fornier, et al. 2009. A phase I/II trial of a polysaccharide extract from *Grifola frondosa* (Maitake mushroom) in breast cancer patients: Immunological effects. J Cancer Res Clin Oncol 135(9):1215–1221.

Dosychev, E. A., and V. N. Bystrova. 1973. Treatment of psoriasis with Chaga fungus preparations. Vestnik Dermatologii Venerologii 47(5):79–83.

Du, Z. Y., K. Zienkiewicz, N. Vande Pol, N. E. Ostrom, C. Benning, and G. M. Bonito. 2019. Algal-fungal symbiosis leads to photosynthetic mycelium. eLife 8:e47815.

Dudgeon, J. 1895. Kung-Fu, or Tauist Medical Gymnastics. Available online at www.sacred-texts.com/tao/kfy/index/htm.

Eastman, J. 1992. The Book of Forest and Thicket: Trees, Shrubs, and Wildflowers of Eastern North America. Stackpole Books, Mechanicsburg, PA. 224 pp.

Engel, M. S. 2018. Innumerable Insects: The Story of the Most Diverse and Myriad Animals on Earth. American Museum of Natural History, Natural Histories. Sterling, New York. 232 pp.

Evans, A. V. 2014. Beetles of Eastern North America. Princeton University Press. 556 pp.

Fernando, D., A. Adhikari, C. Nanayakkara, E. D. de Silva, R. Wijesundera, and P. Soysa. 2016. Cytotoxic effects of ergone, a compound isolated from *Fulvifomes fastuosus*. BMC Complementary Altern Med 16(1):484.

Floudas, D., M. Binder, R. Riley, K. Barry, et al. 2012. The Paleozoic origin of enzymatic lignin decomposition reconstructed from 31 fungal genomes. Science 336(6089):1715–1719.

Floudas D., and D. S. Hibbett. 2015. Revisiting the taxonomy of *Phanerochaete* (Polyporales, Basidiomycota) using a four-gene dataset and extensive ITS sampling. Fungal Biology 119(8):679–719.

Fries, E. M. 1821. Systema Mycologicum. Lund.

Gao, Y., S. Zhou, W. Jiang, M. Huang, and X. Dai. 2003. Effects of ganopoly (a *Ganoderma lucidum* polysaccharide extract) on the immune functions in advanced-stage cancer patients. Immunol Invest 32:201–215.

Gäumann, E. A. 1928. Comparative Morphology of the Fungi. McGraw-Hill Book Co., New York. 701 pp.

Géry, A., C. Dubruelle, A. Véronique, J. P. Riout, et al. 2018. Chaga (*Inonotus obliquus*), a future potential medicinal fungus in oncology? A chemical study and a comparison of the cytotoxicity against human lung adenocarcinoma cells (A549) and human bronchial epithelial cells (BEAS-2B). Integ Cancer Therapies 17(3):832–843.

Gilbertson, R. L., and L. Ryvarden. 1986. North American Polypores. Vol. 1. Fungiflora, Oslo. 433 pp.

———. 1987. North American Polypores. Vol. 2. Fungiflora, Oslo. 451 pp.

Gill, S. K., and M. J. Rieder. 2008. Toxicity of a traditional Chinese medicine, *Ganoderma lucidum*, in children with cancer. Can J Clin Pharmacol 15(2):275–285.

Ginns, J. 2017. Polypores of British Columbia (Fungi: Basidiomycota). Crown Publications, Victoria, BC. 260 pp.

Godugu C., A. R. Patel, R. Doddapaneni, J. Somagoni, and M. Singh. 2014. Approaches to improve the oral bioavailability and effects of novel anticancer drugs berberine and betulinic acid. PLoS One 9(3):e89919.

Goldhor, S. 2008. The good side of rot. Mushroom: The Journal of Wild Mushrooming 100(26:3): 29–36.

———. 2011. Lost in the fungal web: The Chaga saga. Mushroom: The Journal of Wild Mushrooming 108(29:1–2):22–28.

Goldschmidt, A. 2009. The Evolution of Chinese Medicine: Song Dynasty, 960–1200. Routledge, London. 272 pp.

Goldsmith, E. 2017. Nutritional Healing with Chinese Medicine: 175 Recipes for Optimal Health. Robert Rose, Toronto. 480 pp.

Grienke, U., M. Zöll, U. Peintner, and J. M. Rollinger. 2014. European medicinal polypores: A modern view on traditional uses. J Ethnomycology 154(3):564–583.

Haight, J.-E., G. A. Laursen, J. A. Glaeser, and D. L. Taylor. 2017. Phylogeny of *Fomitopsis pinicola*: A species complex. Mycologia 108(5):925–938.

Haight, J.-E., K. K. Nakasone, G. A. Laursen, S. A. Redhead, L. Taylor, and J. A. Glaeser. 2019. *Fomitopsis mounceae* and *F. schrenkii*: Two new species from North America in the *F. pinicola* complex. Mycologia 111(2):339–357.

Halbwachs, H. 2020. Fungi in the rear mirror. Fungi 13(2):14–27.

Hallock, R. M. 2019. A Mushroom Word Guide: Etymology, Pronunciation, and Meanings of Over 1,500 Words. Published by the author. 152 pp.

Halpern, G. M., and A. Miller. 2002. Medicinal Mushrooms: Ancient Remedies for Modern Ailments. M. Evans & Co., Lanham, MD. 186 pp.

Harrington, T. C. 1980. Release of airborne basidiospores from the pouch fungus, *Cryptoporus volvatus*. Mycologia 72(5):926–936.

Hao, Y. F., and J. G. Jiang. 2015. Origin and evolution of China Pharmacopoeia and its implication for traditional medicines. Mini Reviews in Med Chem 15(7):595–603.

Harper, D. J. 1998. Early Chinese Medical Literature: The Mawangdui Medical Manuscripts. Sir Henry Wellcome Asian Series, Royal Asiatic Society, London. 562 pp.

Hazen, R. M. 2013. The Story of Earth: The First 4.5 Billion Years, from Stardust to Living Planet. Viking Penguin, New York. 320 pp.

———. 2019. Symphony in C: Carbon and the Evolution of (Almost) Everything. W. W. Norton & Co., New York. 288 pp.

He, M. Q., R. L. Zhao, K. D. Hyde, D. Begerow, et al. 2019. Notes, outline and divergence times of Basidiomycota. Fungal Divers 99(1):105–367.

Hearn, B. A., C. C. Renner, Y. S. Ding, C. Vaughan-Warson, et al. 2013. Chemical analysis of Alaskan Iqmik smokeless tobacco. Nicotine and Tobacco Res 15(7):1283–1288.

Hibbett, D. S., E. M. Pine, E. Langer, G. Langer, and M. J. Donoghue. 1997. Evolution of gilled mushrooms and puffballs inferred from ribosomal DNA sequences. PNAS USA 94(22):12002–12006.

Hibbett D., K. Abarenkov, U. Kõljalg, M. Öpik, et al. 2016. Sequenced-based classification and identification of fungi. Mycologia 108(6):1049–1068.

Hipp, A. L., D. A. Eaton, J. Cavender-Bares, R. Nipper, and P. S. Manos. 2013. Using phylogenomics to infer the evolutionary history of oaks. Researchgate .net. Pp. 61–71.

Hobbs, C. 2002. Medicinal Mushrooms: An Exploration of Tradition, Healing, and Culture. Herbs and Health Series. Botanica Press, Summertown, TN. 251 pp.

Hofstetter, V., B. Buyck, G. Eyssartier, S. Schnee, and K. Gindro. 2019. The unbearable lightness of sequenced-based identification. Fungal Divers 96:243–284.

Hong, S. G., and H. S. Jung. 2004. Phylogenetic analysis of *Ganoderma* based on nearly complete mitochondrial small subunit ribosomal DNA sequences. Mycologia 96(4):742–755.

Honneger, R., D. Edwards, L. Axe, and C. Strullu-Derrien. 2018. Fertile *Prototaxites taiti*: A basal ascomycete with inoperculate, polysporous asci lacking croziers. Phil Trans R Soc B 373(1739):20170146. Published online Dec. 18, 2017.

Hori, C., J. Gaskell, K. Igarashi, M. Samejima, D. Hibbett, and D. Cullen. 2013. Genome-wide analysis of polysaccharides degrading enzymes in 11 white- and brown-rot Polyporales provides insight into mechanisms of wood decay. Mycologia 105(6):1412–1427.

Hou, Y. N., G. Deng, and J. J. Mao. 2019. Practical application of About Herbs website: Herbs and dietary supplement use in oncology settings. Cancer J 25(5):357–366.

Houlton, S. 2018. Cancer immunotherapy spreads rapidly. Chemistry World. Published online Oct. 17, 2018.

Huang, T. 2015. Healthy Eating: Traditional Chinese Medicine-Inspired Healthy Eating Guides for All Four Seasons. Amazon Digital Services. 514 pp.

Hupy, C. M., and C. H. Yansa. 2009. The last 17,000 years of vegetation history. Pp. 91–105 in Michigan Geography and Geology, edited by R. J. Schaetzl, J. T. Darden, and D. Brandt. Pearson Custom Publishing, Boston.

Huseyin, O., I. Sevgi, D. Engin, A. Firat, P. Gülsüm, and D. Şenay. 2017. *Ganoderma lucidum* protects rat brain tissue against trauma-induced oxidative stress. Korean J Neurotrauma 13(2):76–84.

Isokauppila, T. 2017. Healing Mushrooms: A Practical and Culinary Guide to Using Mushrooms for Whole Body Health. Avery, New York. 244 pp.

Jiang, Y., Y. Chang, Y. Liu, M. Zhang, et al. 2017. Overview of *Ganoderma sinense* polysaccharide, an adjunctive drug used during concurrent chemo/radiation therapy for cancer treatment in China. Biomed Pharmacother 96:865–870.

Jin, X., J. Ruiz Beguerie, D. M. Sze, and G. C. Chan. 2012. *Ganoderma lucidum* (Reishi mushroom) for cancer treatment. Cochrane Database Syst Rev Jun 13(6):CD007731.

———. 2016. *Ganoderma lucidum* (Reishi mushroom) for cancer treatment. Cochrane Database Syst Rev Apr 5 (4):CD007731.

Justo, A., and D. S. Hibbett. 2011. Phylogenetic classification of *Trametes* (Basidiomycota, Polyporales) based on a five-marker dataset. Taxon 60(6):1567–1583.

Justo, A., O. Miettinen, D. Floudas, B. Ortiz-Santana, et al. 2017. A revised family-level classification of the Polyporales (Basidiomycota). Fungal Biology 121(9):798–824.

Kadowaki, K. 2010. Species coexistence patterns in a mycophagous insect community inhabiting the wood-decaying bracket fungus *Cryptoporus volvatus* (Polyporaceae: Basidiomycota). Eur J Entomol 107(1):89–99.

Kameshwar, A. K. S., and W. Qin. 2017. Comparative study of genome-wide plant biomass-degrading CAZymes in white rot, brown rot and soft rot. Mycology 9(2):93–105.

Kang, J. H., J. E. Jang, S. K. Mishra, H. J. Lee, et al. 2015. Ergosterol peroxide from Chaga mushroom (*Inonotus obliquus*) exhibits anti-cancer activity by down-regulation of the β-catenin pathway in colorectal cancer. J Ethnopharmacol 173:303–312.

Kaptchuk, T. 2000. The Web That Has No Weaver. Contemporary Books, Chicago. 528 pp.

Kassinger, R. 2019. Slime: How Algae Created Us, Plague Us, and Just Might Save Us. Houghton Mifflin Harcourt, Boston. 323 pp.

Ketchum, R. M. 1970. The Secret Life of the Forest. American Heritage Publishing, New York. 108 pp.

Kikuchi, Y., K. Seta, Y. Ogawa, T. Takayama, et al. 2014. Chaga mushroom-induced oxalate nephropathy. Clin Nephrol 81(6):440–444.

Kim, Y. O., H. W. Park. J. H. Kim, J. Y. Lee, S. H. Moon, and C. S. Shin. 2006. Anti-cancer effect and structural characterization of endo-polysaccharide from cultivated mycelia of *Inonotus obliquus*. Life Sci 79(1):72–80.

Klump, L. 2018. Climate change and marine mass extinction. Science 362(6419):1113–1114.

Klupp, N. L., D. Chang, F. Hawke, H. Kiat, et al. 2015. *Ganoderma lucidum* mushroom for the treatment of cardiovascular risk factors. Cochrane Database Syst Rev 17(2):CD007259.

Klupp, N. L., H. Kiat, A. Bensoussan, G. Z. Steiner, and D. H. Chang. 2016. A double-blind, randomised, placebo-controlled trial of *Ganoderma lucidum* for the treatment of cardiovascular risk factors of metabolic syndrome. Sci Rep 6:29540.

Knoblock, J., and J. Riegel. 2000. The Annals of Lü Buwei: A Complete Translation and Study. Stanford University Press, Palo Alto, CA. 880 pp.

Knoll, A. H. 2003. Life on a Young Planet: The First Three Billion Years of Life on Earth. Princeton University Press. 296 pp.

Kohler, A., A. Kuo, L. G. Nagy, E. Morin, et al. 2016. Convergent losses of decay mechanisms and rapid turnover of symbiosis genes in mycorrhizal mutualists. Nat Genet 47:410–415.

Kolbert, E. 2014. The Sixth Extinction: An Unnatural History. Henry Holt & Co., New York. 336 pp.

Kouidhi, S., F. B. Ayed, and A. B. Elgaaied. 2018. Targeting tumor metabolism: A new challenge to improve immunotherapy. Front Immunol 9:353.

Kout, J., and J. Vlasák. 2007. *Trametes gibbosa* (Basidiomycetes, Polyporales) in the USA and Canada. Can J Bot 85:342–346.

———. 2009. *Antrodia serialiformis* from the eastern USA, a new and abundant polypore similar to *Antrodia serialis*. Mycotaxon 108:329–335.

Krah, F. S., C. Bässler, C. Heibl, J. Soghigian, H. Schafer, and D. Hibbett. 2018. Evolutionary dynamics of host specialization in wood-decay fungi. BMC Evol Biol 18:119.

Krigs, M., N. Dotzler, J. Galtier, and T. Taylor. 2011. Oldest fossil basidiomycete clamp connections. Mycoscience 52:18–23.

Krupodorova, T., S. Rybalko, and V. Barshteyn. 2014. Antiviral activity of basidiomycete mycelia against influenza type A (serotype H1N1) and herpes simplex virus type 2 in cell culture. Virologica Sinica 29(5):284–290.

Kuo, M. 2007. 100 Edible Mushrooms. University of Michigan Press, Ann Arbor. 344 pp.

Kupferschmidt, K. 2018. A call to arms against the other retrovirus. Science 360(6391):844.

Lane, N. 2005. Power, Sex, Suicide: Mitochondria and the Meaning of Life. Oxford University Press, New York. Kindle edition.

———. 2010. Life Ascending: The Ten Great Inventions of Evolution. W. W. Norton & Co., New York. 352 pp.

———. 2015. The unseen world: Reflections of Leeuenhoek (1677) concerning little animals. Phil Trans R Soc 370:1666. Published online April 19, 2015.

———. 2016. The Vital Question: Energy, Evolution and the Origins of Complex Life. W. W. Norton & Co., New York. 360 pp.

Largent, D. L., D. Johnson, and R. Watling. 1977. How to Identify Mushrooms to Genus III: Microscopic Features. Mad River Press, Eureka, CA. 144 pp.

Lee, M. W., H. Hur, K. C. Chang, T. S. Lee, K. H. Ka, and L. Jankovsky. 2008. Introduction to distribution and ecology of sterile conks of *Inonotus obliquus*. Microbiol 36(4):199–202.

Lee, W. Y., Y. K. Park, and J. K. Ahn. 2007. Improvement of ergone production from mycelial culture of *Polyporus umbellatus*. Mycobiology 35(2):82–86.

Legge, J. (trans.) 1891. Tao Te Ching by Lao-tzu. Available online at Sacred-Texts Taoism, https://sacred-texts.com/tao/taote.htm.

———. 1891. The Writings of Kwang-dze (Chuang-tse) (Books I–XVII). Available online at https://sacred-texts.com/tao/sbe39/index.htm.

Li Hui-Lin. 1977. Hallucinogenic plants in Chinese herbals. Harvard University Botanical Museum Leaflets 25(6):161–181.

Li, S., C. Dong, H. Wen, and X. Liu. 2016. Development of Lingzhi industry in China—emanated from the artificial cultivation in the Institute of Microbiology, Chinese Academy of Sciences (IMCAS). Mycology 7(2):74–80.

Liao, B., X. Chen, J. Han, Y. Dan, et al. 2015. Identification of commercial *Ganoderma* (lingzhi) species by ITS2 sequences. Chin Med 10:22.

Liu Bo and Bau Yun-sun. 1980. Fungi Pharmacopoeia Sinica. Kinoko, Oakland, CA. 297 pp.

Liu, G. 2015. Foundations of Chinese Medicine: A Comprehensive Text. Singing Dragon, London. 976 pp.

Liu, W. K., T. B. Ng, S. F. Sze, and K. W. Tsui. 1993. Activation of peritoneal macrophages by polysaccharopeptide from the mushroom *Coriolus versicolor*. Immunopharmacology 26(2):139–146.

Livermore, R. 2018. The Tectonic Plates Are Moving! Oxford University Press, New York. 492 pp.

Lloyd, G., and N. Sivin. 2003. The Way and the Word:

Science and Medicine in Early China and Greece. Yale University Press, New Haven. 368 pp.

Loron, C. C., C. François, R. H. Rainbird, E. C. Turner, S. Borensztajn, and E. J. Javaux. 2019. Early fungi from the Proterozoic era in arctic Canada. Nature 570:232–235.

Lowenfels, J. 2017. Teaming with Fungi: The Organic Grower's Guide to Mycorrhizae. Timber Press, Science for Gardeners, Portland, OR. 172 pp.

Loyd, A. L., B. S. Richter, M. A. Jusino, C. Truong, et al. 2018. Identifying the Mushroom of Immortality: Assessing the *Ganoderma* species composition in commercial reishi products. Front Microbiol 9:1557.

Loyd, A. L., C. W. Barnes, B. W. Held, M. J. Schink, et al. 2018. Elucidating *lucidum*: Distinguishing the diverse laccate *Ganoderma* species of the United States. PLoS ONE 13(7):e0199738.

Luo, D., S. E. Baker, A. G. Pisabarro, J. D. Walton, et al. 2014. Extensive sampling of basidiomycete genomes demonstrates inadequacy of the white-rot/brown-rot paradigm for wood decay fungi. PNAS 111:9923–9928.

Luo, K. W., G. G. Yue, C. H. Ko, J. K. Lee, et al. 2014. In vivo and in vitro anti-tumor and anti-metastasis effects of *Coriolus versicolor* aqueous extract on mouse mammary 4T1 carcinoma. Phytomed 21(8–9):1078–1087.

Macfarland, R. 2019. Underland: A Deep Time Journey. W. W. Norton & Co., New York. 496 pp.

Maciocia, G. 2015. Foundations of Chinese Medicine: Shang Han Lun and Contemporary Medical Texts. Churchill Livingstone, London. 1289 pp.

Maloof, J. 2016. Nature's Temples: The Complex World of Old-Growth Forests. Timber Press, Portland, OR. 200 pp.

Marchand, P. J. 1987. North Woods: An Inside Look at the Nature of Forests in the Northeast. Appalachian Mountain Club, Boston. 160 pp.

Margulis, L. 1998. Symbiotic Planet: A New Look at Evolution. Science Masters Series, Basic Books, New York. 176 pp.

Margulis, L., and D. Sagan. 2007. Dazzle Gradually: Reflections on the Nature of Nature. Sciencewriters Book, Chelsea Green Publishing, White River Junction, VT. 259 pp.

Marley, G. 2009. Mushrooms for Health: Medical Secrets of Northeastern Fungi. Down East Books, Camden, ME. 112 pp.

Marsone, P., and J. Lagerwey, eds. 2015. Modern Chinese Religion I: Song-Liao-Jin-Yuan (960–1368 AD). 2 vols. Brill Publishing, Leiden. 1653 pp.

Maser, C. 1988. Ancient forests, priceless treasures. Mushroom: The Journal of Wild Mushrooming 21:8–18.

Matheny, P. B., and J. A. Fordyce. 2019. Not all ectomycorrhizal fungal lineages are equal. New Phytologist 222(4):1670–1672.

Mathieu, A., I. Korsakissok, D. Quélo, J. Groëll, et al. 2012. Atmospheric dispersion and deposition of radionuclides from the Fukushima Daiichi nuclear power plant accident. Elements 8(3):195–200.

McCoy, P. 2016. Radical Mycology: A Treatise of Seeing and Working with Fungi. Chthaeus Press, Portland, OR. 672 pp.

McEnvoy, T. J. 2014. Introduction to Forest Ecology and Silviculture. Forestry Press, Mount Juliet, TN. 177 pp.

McIlvaine, C. 1900. One Thousand American Fungi: Toadstools, Mushrooms, Fungi Edible and Poisonous. Bowen-Merrill Co., Indianapolis. 729 pp.

McNamara, A. 2019. Lichen age discovery reshapes understanding of complex ecosystem evolution. BBC Science Focus Magazine. Published online Nov. 15.

McPhee, J. 2020. Annals of the Former World. Farrar, Straus and Giroux, New York. 720 pp.

Medina, E. M., J. J. Turner, R. Gordân, J. M. Skotheim, and N. E. Buchler. 2016. Punctuated evolution and transitional hybrid network in an ancestral cell cycle of fungi. eLife 5:e09492.

Memorial Sloan Kettering Cancer Center Integrative Medicine. 2020. Clinical summary of Chaga mushroom. Published online. https://www.mskcc.org/cancer-care/integrative-medicine/herbs/chaga-mushroom.

Miettinen, O., J. Vlasák, B. Rivoire, and V. Spirin. 2018. *Postia caesia* complex (Polyporales, Basidiomycota) in temperate Northern Hemisphere. Fungal Syst Evol 1(1):101–129.

Miettinen, O., K.-H. Larsson, and V. Spirin. 2019. *Hydnoporia*, an older name for *Pseudochaete* and *Hy-*

menochaetopsis, and typification of the genus *Hymenochaete* (Hymenochaetales, Basidiomycota). Fungal Syst Evol 4(1):77–96.

Millman, L. 2019. Fungipedia: A Brief Compendium of Mushroom Lore. Princeton University Press. 177 pp.

Money, N. P. 2014. The Amoeba in the Room: Lives of the Microbes. Oxford University Press, New York. 240 pp.

———. 2016. Are Mushrooms Medicinal? Fungal Biology 120(4):449–453.

———. 2016. Fungi: A Very Short Introduction. Oxford University Press Very Short Introductions, New York. 144 pp.

———. 2017. Mushrooms: A Natural and Cultural History. Reaktion Books, London. 224 pp.

———. 2018. The Rise of Yeast: How the Sugar Fungus Shaped Civilization. Oxford University Press, New York. 224 pp.

Morgan, E. S. 1933. Tao, The Great Luminant: Essays from the Huai Nan Tzu. Available online at https://sacred-texts.com/tao/tgl/index.htm.

Motato-Vásquez, V., E. Grassi, A. M. Gugliotta, and G. L. Robledo. 2018. Evolutionary relationships of *Bresadolia* (Basidiomycota, Polyporales) based on molecular and morphological evidence. Mycol Prog 17(9):1031–1048.

Nagy, L. G., R. Riley, A. Tritt, C. Adam, et al. 2016. Comparative genomics of early-diverging mushroom-forming fungi provides insights into the origins of lignocellulose decay capabilities. Mol Biol Evol 33(4):959–970.

Nakasone, K. K., and H. H. Burdsall Jr. 1995. *Phlebia* species from eastern and southeastern United States. Mycotaxon 54:33–359.

Naranjo-Ortiz, M. A., and T. Gabaldón. 2019. Fungal evolution: Diversity, taxonomy and phylogeny of the fungi. Biol Rev 94(6):2101–2137.

Needham, J. 1976. Science and Civilisation in China: Chemistry and Chemical Technology, vol. 5, part 3. Cambridge University Press. 742 pp.

Nelsen, M. P., W. A. DiMichele, S. E. Peters, and C. K. Boyce. 2016. Delayed fungal evolution did not cause the Paleozoic peak in coal production. PNAS USA 113(9):2442–2447.

Nelsen, M. P., R. Lücking, C. K. Boyce, H. T. Lumbsch, and R. H. Ree. 2020. No support for the emergence of lichens prior to the evolution of vascular plants. Geobiology 18:3–13.

Nelson, G., C. J. Earle, and R. Spellenberg. 2014. Trees of Eastern North America. Princeton Field Guides. 720 pp.

Niimoto, N., T. Hattori, K. Sugimachi, K. Inokuchi, and N. Ogawa. 1988. Postoperative adjuvant immune-chemotherapy with mitomycin C, futraful and PSK for gastric cancer. Jpn J Surg 18(6):681–686.

Ning, X., Q. Luo, C. Li, Z. Ding, J. Pang, and C. Zhao. 2014. Inhibitory effects of a polysaccharide extract from the Chaga medicinal mushroom, *Inonotus obliquus* (higher Basidiomycetes), on the proliferation of human neurogliocytoma cells. Int J Med Mushrooms 16(1):29–36.

Noguchi, M., T. Kakuma, K. Tomiyasu, A. Yamada, et al. 2008. Randomized clinical trial of an ethanol extract of *Ganoderma lucidum* in men with lower urinary tract symptoms. Asian J Androl 10(5):777–785.

Nowak, H., E. Schneebeli-Hermann, and E. Kustatscher. 2019. No mass extinction for land plants at the Permian-Triassic transition. Nat Comm 10(384):1–8.

Ogbe, A. O., S. E. Atawodi, P. A. Abdu, A. Sannusi, and A. E. Itodo. 2009. Changes in weight, faecal oocyst count and packed cell volume of *Eimeria tenella*–infected broilers treated with a wild mushroom (*Ganoderma lucidum*) aqueous extract. J South Africa Vet Assoc 80(2):97–102.

Ogrydziak, D. 2013. Trees of New England: An Identification Guide. Levellers Press, Amherst, MA. 57 pp.

Ohm, R. A., J. F. de Jong, L. G. Lugones, A. Aerts, et al. 2010. Genome sequence of the model mushroom *Schizophyllum commune*. Nat Biotechnol 28(9):957–963.

Ohwada, S., T. Ikeya, T. Yokomori, T. Kusaba, et al. 2004. Adjuvant immunochemotherapy with oral Tegafur/Uracil plus PSK in patients with stage II or III colorectal cancer: A randomised controlled study. Br J Cancer 90(5):1003–1010.

O'Malley, M. A., M. M. Leger, J. G. Wideman, and I. Ruiz-Trillo. 2019. Concepts of the last eukaryotic common ancestor. Nat Ecol Evol 3(3):338–344.

Otrosina, W. J., and M. Garbelotto. 2010. *Heterobasidion occidentale* sp. nov. and *Heterobasidion irregulare* nom. nov.: A Disposition of North American *Heterobasidion* biological species. Fungal Biology 114:16–25.

Overholts, L. O. 1953. The Polyporaceae of the United States, Alaska, and Canada. University of Michigan Press, Ann Arbor.

Özevren, H., S. İrtegün, E. Deveci, F. Aşır, G. Pektanç, and Ş. Deveci. 2017. *Ganoderma lucidum* protects rat brain tissue against trauma-induced oxidative stress. Korean J Neurotrauma 13(2): 76–84.

Pan, H. H., X. T. Yu, T. Li, H. L. Wu, et al. 2013. Aqueous extract from a Chaga medicinal mushroom *Inonotus obliquus* (higher Basidiomycetes) prevents herpes simplex virus entry through inhibition of viral-induced membrane fusion. Int J Mushrooms 15(1):29–38.

Papaioannou, N., O. V. Beniata, V. Panagiotis, O. Tsitsilonis, and P. Samara. 2016. Harnessing the immune system to improve cancer therapy. Ann Transl Med 4(14):261.

PDQ Integrative, Alternative, and Complementary Therapies Editorial Board. 2017. Medicinal mushrooms. PDQ Cancer Information Summaries. National Cancer Institute, Bethesda, MD. https://www.cancer.gov/about-cancer/treatment/cam/hp/mushrooms-pdq. Accessed September 26, 2020 (PMID:27929633).

Penn, J. L., C. Deutsch, J. L. Payne, and E. A. Sperling. 2018. Temperature-dependent hypoxia explains biogeography and severity of end-Permian marine mass extinction. Science 362:1130.

Pharmacopoeia Commission of the Ministry of Health of the People's Republic of China. 2010. The Pharmacopoeia of the People's Republic of China. 3 vols. Chemical Industry Press, Shanghai. 3,382 pp.

Pleninger, D. B. 2009. Iqmik: Troubled child of *Phellinus* and *Nicotiana*. Fungi 2(2):5–6, 47–48.

Pouzar, Z. 1974. An observation on *Albatrellus subrubescens* (Polyporaceae). Folia Geobotanica and Phytotaxonomica 9(1):87–94.

Powell, M. 2014. Medicinal Mushrooms: A Clinical Guide. Mycology Press, Brighton, UK. 152 pp.

Presley, G. N., E. Panisko, S. O. Purvine, and J. S. Shilling. 2018. Comparing the temporal process of wood metabolism among white rot fungi by coupling secretomics with enzymatic activities. Appl Environ Microbiol 1–29.

Price, P. M., W. E. Mahmoud, A. A. Al-Ghamdi, and L. M. Bronstein. 2018. Magnetic drug delivery: Where the field is going. Front Chem 6:619.

Prothero, D. R. 2018. The Story of the Earth in 25 Rocks: Tales of Important Geological Puzzles and the People Who Solved Them. Columbia University Press, New York. 368 pp.

Quammen, D. 2018. The Tangled Tree: A Radical New History of Life. Simon and Schuster, New York. 480 pp.

Ramakrishnan, V. 2018. Gene Machine: The Race to Decipher the Secrets of the Ribosome. Basic Books, New York. 288 pp.

Read, B. E. 1936. Chinese Medicinal Plants from the Pen Ts'ao Kang Mu, AD 1596. 3d ed. B: Peking Natural History Bulletin. 389 pp.

Read, B. E., and C. Pak. 1928. A compendium of minerals and stones used in Chinese medicine from the Pen Ts'ao Kang Mu by Li Shih Chen, AD 1597. Peking Soc Nat History Bull 3:21.

Reid, D. A. 1955. New or interesting records of Australasian basidiomycetes. Kew Bulletin 10(4): 631–648.

Rencun, Y., and H. Hai. 2018. Cancer Management with Chinese Medicine: Prevention and Complementary Treatments, rev. ed. World Scientific Publishing, Hackensack, NJ. 260 pp.

Retallack, G. J., and E. Landing. 2014. Affinities and architecture of Devonian trunks of *Prototaxites loganii*. Mycologia 106(6):1143–1158.

Retallack, G. J., J. J. Veerers, and R. Morante. 1996. Global coal gap between Permian-Triassic extinction and middle Triassic recovery of peat-forming plants. GSA Bulletin 108(2):195–207.

Riley, R., A. A. Salamov, D. W. Brown, L. G. Nagy, et al. 2014. Extensive sampling of basidiomycete genomes demonstrates inadequacy of the white-rot/brown-rot paradigm for wood decay fungi. PNAS USA 111(27):9923–9928.

Rimington, W. R., S. Pressel, J. G. Duckett, K. J. Field, D. J. Read, and M. I. Bidartondo. 2018. Ancient plants with ancient fungi: Liverworts associate with early-diverging arbuscular mycorrhizal fungi. Proc R Soc B 285(1888):1–9.

Rogers, R. 2011. The Fungal Pharmacy: The Complete Guide to Medicinal Mushrooms and Lichens of North America. North Atlantic Books, Berkeley, CA. 608 pp.

———. 2020. Medicinal Mushrooms: The Human Clinical Trials. Prairie Deva Press (self-published). 156 pp.

Rossi, P., R. Difrancia, V. Quagliariello, E. Savino, et al. 2018. B-glucans from *Grifola frondosa* and *Ganoderma lucidum* in breast cancer: An example of complementary and integrative medicine. Oncotarget 9(37):24837–24856.

Ruiz-Dueñas, F. J., T. Lundell, D. Floudas, L. G. Nagy, et al. 2013. Lignin-degrading peroxidases in Polyporales: An evolutionary survey based on 10 sequenced genomes. Mycologia 105(6):1428–1444.

Runnel, K., V. Spirin, O. Miettinen, J. Vlasák, et al. 2019. Morphological plasticity in brown-rot fungi: *Antrodia* is redefined to encompass both poroid and corticioid species. Mycologia 111(5):871–883.

Sagiv-Barfi, I., D. K. Czerwinski, S. Levy, I. S. Alam, et al. 2018. Eradication of spontaneous malignancy by local immunotherapy. Sci Transl Med 10:426.

Sargent, E. 2017. From venoms to medicine. Royal Society of Chemistry. Published online Dec. 12, 2017.

Sato, H., and H. Toju. 2019. Timing of evolutionary innovation: Scenarios of evolutionary diversification in a species-rich fungal clade, Boletales. New Phytologist 222:1924–1935.

Schmidt, O. 2006. Wood and Tree Fungi: Biology, Damage, Protection, and Use. University of Hamburg, Germany. Springer-Verlag, Berlin. 329 pp.

Shaw, S. R. 2015. Planet of the Bugs: Evolution and the Rise of Insects. University of Chicago Press. 246 pp.

Sheldrake, M. 2020. Entangled Life: How Fungi Make Our World, Change Our Minds and Shape Our Futures. Random House, New York. 380 pp.

Shirouzu, T., S. Matsuoka, H. Doi, N. Nagata, M. Ushio, and K. Hosaka. 2020. Complementary molecular methods reveal comprehensive phylogenetic diversity integrating inconspicuous lineages

of early-diverged wood-decaying mushrooms. Sci Rep 10:3057.

Shizhen, L. 2006. Compendium of Materia Medica (Bencao Gangmu, 1593). 6 vols. Foreign Language Press, Beijing. 4400 pp.

Shubin, N. 2020. Some Assembly Required: Decoding Four Billion Years of Life, from Ancient Fossils to DNA. Pantheon Books, New York. 288 pp.

Shun, J., J. Chen, T. J. Algeo, S. Yuan, et al. 2019. Evidence for a prolonged Permian-Triassic extinction interval from global marine mercury records. Nature Communications 10(1):1563.

Sivin, N. 1969. On the Pao p'u tzu nei p'ien and the life of Ko Hung (283–343). Isis 60:388–391.

———. 1987. Traditional Medicine in Contemporary China, Science, Medicine, and Technology in East Asia 2. University of Michigan Center for Chinese Studies, Ann Arbor. 584 pp.

Smith, D. 2018. Medicinal fungi: Hype and hope. McIlvainea 27. https://namyco.org/medicinal_fungi_introduction.php.

———. 2019. Ling Zhi, *Ganoderma lucidum*: The Chinese mushroom of immortality. McIlvainea 28. https://namyco.org/ling-zhi_ganoderma_lucidum.php.

———. 2020. Glass half-full or half-empty? McIlvainea 29. https://namyco.org/docs/Glass_Half_Full_by_Dianna_Smith.

Smith, H. 2017. Forgotten Disease: Illnesses Transformed in Chinese Medicine. Columbia University Press, New York. 248 pp.

Snell, W. H., and E. A. Dick. 1957. A Glossary of Mycology. Harvard University Press, Cambridge, MA. 181 pp.

Somà, V. 2018. *Fomes fomentarius*: A fungus with a long history and a thousand applications. Fungi 11(1):264–267.

Sotome, K., Y. Akagi, S. S. Lee, N. K. Ishikawa, and T. Hattori. 2012. Taxonomic study of *Favolus* and *Neofavolus* gen. nov. segregated from *Polyporus* (Basidiomycota, Polyporales). Fungal Divers 58:245–266.

Spahr, D. L. 2009. Edible and Medicinal Mushrooms of New England and Eastern Canada. North Atlantic Books, Berkeley, CA. 248 pp.

Spillis, T. 2004. Fire and fungus: An etymological

journey. Mushroom: The Journal of Wild Mushrooming 11(82):6–12.

Spirin, V., J. Vlasák, and J. Kout. 2015. Studies in the *Truncospora ohiensis–T. ochroleuca* group (Polyporales, Basidiomycota). Nova Hedwigia 100(1):159–175.

Spiteller, P. 2015. Chemical ecology of fungi. Natural Products Report Roy Soc Chem 32:971–1003.

Spooner, B., and P. Roberts. 2010. Fungi. Collins New Naturalist Library 96. 596 pp.

Stamets, P. 2005. Mycelium Running: How Mushrooms Can Help Save the World. Ten Speed Press, Berkeley, CA. 356 pp.

———. 2012. *Trametes versicolor* (Turkey Tail mushrooms) and the treatment of breast cancer. Glob Adv Health Med 1(5):20.

Stamets, P., and D. Yao. 2002. Mycomedicinals: An informational treatise on mushrooms. MycoMedia Productions, Olympia, WA. 46 pp.

Stanley-Baker, M. 2013. Daoists and doctors: The role of medicine in the six dynasties Shangqing Daoism. Dissertation, University College London. 324 pp.

Steyaert, R. L. 1972. Species of *Ganoderma* and related genera mainly of the Bogor and Leiden herbaria. Persoonia 7(1):55–118.

———. 1980. Study of some *Ganoderma* species. Bulletin du Jardin botanique National de Belgique / Bulletin van de Nationale Plantentuin van België 50(1/2):135–186.

Stokland, J., and L. Ryvarden. 2008. *Fomitopsis ochracea* nova species. Synopsis Fungorum 25:44–47.

Sun, Y., T. Yin, X.-H. Chen, G. Zhang, et al. 2011. In vitro antitumor activity and structure characterization of ethanol extracts from wild and cultivated Chaga medicinal mushroom, *Inonotus obliquus* (Pers.:Fr.) Pilát (Aphyllophoromycetideae). Int J Med Mushrooms 13(2):121–130.

Suzuki, D., and W. Grady. 2018. Tree: A Life Story, rev. ed. Greystone Books, Vancouver, BC. 208 pp.

Tang, J.-L., S.-Y. Zhan, and E. Ernst. 1999. Review of randomised controlled trials of traditional Chinese medicine. BMJ 319(7203):160–161.

Tedersoo, L., T. Suvi, K. Beaver, and I. Saar. 2007. Ectomycorrhizas of *Coltricia* and *Coltriciella* (Hymenochaetales, Basidiomycota) on Caesal-

piniaceae, Dipterocarpaceae and Myrtaceae in Seychelles. Mycol Prog 6:101–107.

Tedersoo, L., T. W. May, and M. E. Smith. 2010. Ectomycorrhizal lifestyle in fungi: Global diversity, distribution, and evolution of phylogenetic lineages. Mycorrhiza 20:217–263.

Tedersoo, L., S. Sánchez-Ramírez, U. Kõljalg, M. Bahram, et al. 2018. High-level classification of the Fungi and a tool for evolutionary ecological analyses. Fungal Divers 90(1):135–159.

Teschke, R., A. Wolff, C. Frenzel, A. Eickhoff, and J. Schulze. 2015. Herbal traditional Chinese medicine and its evidence base in gastrointestinal disorders. World J Gastroenterol 21(15):4466–4490.

Thompson, J. R., D. N. Carpenter, C. V. Cogbill, and D. R. Foster. 2013. Four centuries of change in northeastern United States forests. PLoS One 8(9):e72540.

Tian, N., Y. D. Wang, S. Zheng, and Z. P. Zhu. 2018. White-rotting fungi with clamp connections in a coniferous wood from the lower Cretaceous of Heilongjiang Province, NE China. Cretaceous Res 105:1–9.

Tomsovsky, M., P. Vampola, P. Sedlák, Z. Byrtusová, and L. Jankovsky. 2010. Delimitation of central and northern European species of the *Phellinus igniarius* group (Basidiomycota, Hymenochaetales) based on analysis of ITS and translation elongation factor 1 alpha DNA sequences. Mycol Prog 9(3):431–445.

Torisu, M., Y. Hayashi, T. Ishimitsu, T. Fujimura, et al. 1990. Significant prolongation of disease-free period gained by oral polysaccharide K (PSK) administration after curative surgical operation of colorectal cancer. Cancer Immunol Immunother 31(5):261–268.

Torkelson, C. J., E. Sweet, M. R. Martzen, M. Sasagawa, et al. 2012. Phase I clinical trial of *Trametes versicolor* in women with breast cancer. Int Schol Res Network: Oncology 251632.

Torres, W., V. Lameda, L. C. Olivar, C. Navarro, et al. 2017. Bacteria in cancer therapy: Beyond immunostimulation. J Cancer Metastasis Treat 3:250–261.

Trudell, S. A., P. T. Rygiewicz, and R. L. Edmonds. 2003. Nitrogen and carbon stable isotope abundances support the myco-heterotrophic nature of host-specificity of certain achlorophyllous plants. New Phytologist 160(2):391–401.

———. 2004. Patterns of nitrogen and carbon stable isotope ratios in macrofungi, plants and soils in two old-growth conifer forests. New Phytologist 164(2):317–335.

Tsai, C. C., Y. S. Li, and P. P. Lin. 2017. *Inonotus obliquus* extract induces apoptosis in the human colorectal carcinoma's HCT-116 cell line. Biomed Pharmacother 96:1119–1126.

Tudge, C. 2000. The Variety of Life. Oxford University Press, New York. 704 pp.

———. 2005. The Tree: A Natural History of What Trees Are, How They Live, and Why They Matter. Three Rivers Press, New York. 480 pp.

Unschuld, P. U. 1985. Medicine in China: A History of Ideas. University of California Press, Berkeley. 464 pp.

———. 1986. Medicine in China: A History of Pharmaceutics. University of California Press, Berkeley. 384 pp.

———. 2003. Huang Di Nei Jing Su Wen: Nature, Knowledge, Imagery in an Ancient Chinese Medical Text. University of California Press, Berkeley. 520 pp.

Unschuld, P. U., and H. Tessenow. 2011. Huang Di Nei Jing Su Wen: An Annotated Translation of Huang Di's Inner Classic, Basic Questions, 2 vols. University of California Press, Berkeley.

Varga, T., K. Krizsán, C. Földi, B. Dima, et al. 2019. Megaphylogeny resolves global patterns of mushroom evolution. Nat Ecol Evol 3:668–678.

Veith, I. (translator). 2015. The Yellow Emperor's Classic of Internal Medicine. University of California Press, Oakland, CA. 296 pp.

Vlasák, J., and J. Kout. 2011. Pileate *Fomitiporia* species in the USA. New combinations *Fomitiporia calkinsii* and *F. bakeri*. Mycol Progress 10:445–452.

———. 2011. Tropical *Trametes lactinea* is widely distributed in the eastern USA. Mycotaxon 115:27–279.

Vlasák, J., J. Vlasák Jr., 2016. Two new polypore species from the southwestern USA: *Fomitiporia fissurata* and *F. deserticola*. Mycotaxon 131:193–203.

Vlasák, J., J. Vlasák Jr., P. G. Harvey, P. R. Leacock, and V. Spirin. 2018. *Pyrofomes juniperinus* comb.

nova, the North American sibling of *P. demidoffii* (Polyporales, Basidiomycota). Annales Botanici Fennici 55(1–3):1–6.

Volk, T. 2005. *Phellinus igniarius*, Iqmik, used by native Americans with tobacco. Tom Volk's Fungi of the Month Nov.

Voronov, E., S. Dotan, Y. Krelin, X. Song, et al. 2013. Unique versus redundant functions of IL-1α and IL-1β in the tumor microenvironment. Front Immunol 4:177.

Wachtel-Galor, S., Y. T. Szeto, B. Tomlinson, and I. F. Benzie. 2004. *Ganoderma lucidum* (Lingzhi): Acute and short-term biomarker response to supplementation. Int J Food Sci Nutr 55(1):75–83.

Wachtel-Galor, S., J. Yuen, J. A. Buswell, and I. F. F. Benzie. 2011. *Ganoderma lucidum* (lingzhi or reishi): A medicinal mushroom. Chap. 9 in Herbal Medicine: Biomolecular and Clinical Aspects, 2d ed. CRC Press, Taylor and Francis, Boca Raton, FL. 488 pp.

Wagner, T., and M. Fischer. 2002. Proceedings towards a natural classification of the worldwide taxa *Phellinus* s.l. and *Inonotus* s.l., and phylogenetic relationships of allied genera. Mycologia 94(6):998–1016.

Waldholz, M. 2018. Why our own immune systems attack our best drugs—and how to stop it. Scientific American 318(1):58–63.

Wang, H. X., T. B. Ng, W. K. Liu, V. E. Ooi, and S. T. Chang. 1996. Polysaccharide-peptide complexes from the cultured mycelia of the mushroom *Coriolus versicolor* and their culture medium activate mouse lymphocytes and macrophages. Int J Biochem Cell Biol 28(5):601–607.

Wang X., X. Zhao, D. Li, Y. Q. Lou, Z. B. Lin, and G. L. Zhang. 2007. Effects of *Ganoderma lucidum* polysaccharide on CYP2E1, CYP1A2 and CYP3A activities in BCG-immune hepatic injury in rats. Biol Pharm Bull 30(9):1702–1706.

Wanmuang, H., J. Leopairut, C. Kositchaiwat, W. Wananukul, and S. Bunyaratvej. 2007. Fatal fulminant hepatitis associated with *Ganoderma lucidum* (Lingzhi) mushroom powder. J Med Assoc Thai 90(1):179–181.

Ware, J. R. 1966. Alchemy, Medicine, and Religion in

the China of AD 320: The Nei P'ien of Ko Hung. MIT Press, Cambridge, MA. p. 388.

Wasser, S. P. 2005. Reishi or lingzhi (*Ganoderma lucidum*). Encyclopedia of Dietary Supplements. Oxfordshire, UK. pp. 680–690.

———. 2010. Medicinal mushroom science: History, current status, future trends, and unsolved problems. Int J Med Mushrooms 12:1–16.

Welti, S., and R. Courtecuisse. 2010. The Ganodermataceae in the French West Indies (Guadeloupe and Martinique). Fungal Divers 43:103–126.

Welti, S., P. A. Moreau, A. Favel, R. Courtecuisse, et al. 2012. Molecular phylogeny of *Trametes* and related genera, and description of a new genus *Leiotrametes*. Fungal Divers 55:47–64.

Wesa, K. M., S. Cunningham-Rundles, V. M. Klimek, E. Vertosick, et al. 2015. Maitake mushroom extract in myelodysplastic syndromes (MDS): A phase II study. Cancer Immunol Immunother 64(2):237–247.

Wessels, T. 2005. Reading the Forested Landscape: A Natural History of New England. Countryman Press, Woodstock, VT. 160 pp.

———. 2010. Forest Forensics. Countryman Press, Woodstock, VT. 200 pp.

Westphalen, M. C., M. Tomšovský, A. M. Gugliotta, and M. Rajchenberg. 2019. An overview of *Antrodiella* and related genera of the Polyporales from the Neotropics. Mycologia 111(5):813–831.

Williams, Gareth. 2019. Unraveling the Double Helix: The Lost Heroes of DNA. Pegasus Books, New York. 504 pp.

Williams, M. D. 2007. Identifying Trees: An All-Season Guide to Eastern North America. Stackpole Books, Mechanicsburg, PA. 416 pp.

Willis, K. J., and J. C. McElwain. 2014. The Evolution of Plants, 2d ed. Oxford University Press, Oxford, UK. 425 pp.

Wilson, E. O. 2010. The Diversity of Life: With a New Preface. Questions of Science Series, Belknap Press, Cambridge, MA. 440 pp.

Wohlleben, P. 2016. The Hidden Life of Trees. Greystone Books, Vancouver, BC. 288 pp.

Wojtech, M. 2011. Bark: A Field Guide to Trees of the Northeast. University Press of New England, Lebanon, NH. 280 pp.

Wolfe, D. 2002. Tales from the Underground: A Natural History of Subterranean Life. Basic Books, New York. 240 pp.

Wong, C. K., Y. X. Bao, E. L. Y. Wong, P. C. Leung, et al. 2005. Immunomodulatory activities of Yunzhi and Danshen in post-treatment breast cancer patients. Am J Chin Med 33(3):381–395.

Wu, D. T., Y. Deng, L. X. Chen, J. Zhao, A. Bzhelyansky, and S. P. Li. 2017. Evaluation on quality consistency of *Ganoderma lucidum* dietary supplements collected in the United States. Sci Rep 7:7792.

Wu Xingliang, Mao Xiaolan, Tolgor Bau, et al. 2013. Medical Fungi of China. Science Press, Beijing. 923 pp.

Wu, Z., Y. Zhang, N. Tan, C. Zhao, J. Yang, and J.-S. Zhu. 2011. ReishiMax extends the lifespan of mice: A preliminary report. FASEB J 25(S1):601.2.

Xu, H.-E., C. M. Berry, W. E. Stein, Y. Wang, P. Tang, and Q. Fu. 2017. Unique growth strategy in the earth's first trees revealed in silicified fossil trunks from China. PNAS USA 114(45):12009–12014.

Yeung, K. S., J. Gubili, and J. J. Mao. 2018. Herb-drug interactions in cancer care. Oncology (Williston Park) 32(10):516–520.

Ying Jianzhe. 1987. Icons of Medicinal Fungi from China. Science Press, Beijing. 575 pp.

Zhang, G., X. Zeng, C. Li, J. Li, et al. 2011. Inhibition of urinary bladder carcinogenesis by aqueous extract of sclerotia of *Polyporus umbellatus* Fries and Polyporus polysaccharide. Am J Chin Med 39(1):135–144.

Zhao, C.-L., F. Xu, and D. H. Pfister. 2016. Morphological and molecular identification of a new species of *Truncospora* (Polyporales, Basidiomycota) in North America. Phytotaxa 257(1):89–97.

Zhao, Y. Y. 2013. Traditional uses, phytochemistry, pharmacology, pharmacokinetics and quality control of *Polyporus umbellatus* (Pers.) Fries: A review. J Ethnopharmacol 149(1):35–48.

Zhao, Z., X. Zheng, and F. Fang. 2014. *Ganoderma lucidum* polysaccharides supplementation attenuates exercise-induced oxidative stress in skeletal muscle of mice. Saudi J Biol Sci 21(2):119–123.

Zhong X., Zhong Y., Yang S., and Zheng Z. 2015. Effect of *Inonotus obliquus* polysaccharides on physical fatigue in mice. J Tradit Chin Med 35(4):468–472.

Zhou L.-W., and L. Tedersoo. 2012. *Coltricia australica* sp. nov. (Hymenochaetales, Basidiomycota) from Australia. Mycotaxon 122(1):123–128.

Zhou, L.-W., Y. Cao, S.-H. Wu, J. Vlasák, et al. 2015. Global diversity of the *Ganoderma lucidum* complex (Ganodermataceae, Polyporales) inferred from morphology and multilocus phylogeny. Phytochem 114:7–15.

Zhou, L.-W., K. K. Nakasone, H. H. Burdsall Jr., J. Ginns, et al. 2016. Polypore diversity in North America with an annotated checklist. Mycol Prog 15:771–790.

Zimmer, C. 2001. Parasite Rex: Inside the Bizarre World of Nature's Most Dangerous Creatures. Simon and Schuster, New York. 320 pp.

———. 2015. A Planet of Viruses, 2d ed. University of Chicago Press. 128 pp.

Zmitrovich, I. V. 2018. Conspectus Systematis Polyporacearum v. 1. St. Petersburg, Russia: Folia Cryptogamica Petropolitana 6:3–45.

Websites

Fungi Growing on Wood: www.messiah.edu.

Index Fungorum: www.indexfungorum.org.

Memorial Sloan Kettering Cancer Center Integrative Medicine: www.mskcc.org/cancer-care/integrative-medicine/herbs.

MushroomExpert.com: www.mushroomexpert.com.

Mushroom Observer: www.mushroomobserver.org.

MycoBank: www.mycobank.org.

MycoGuide: www.mycoguide.com.

Supplement Facts: https://supplement-facts.org/2012-5.php.

About the Authors

Alan E. Bessette, PhD, is a professional mycologist and emeritus professor of biology at Utica College of Syracuse University. He has published numerous papers in the field of mycology and has authored or co-authored more than 20 books, including *Boletes of Eastern North America, Mushrooms of Northeastern North America,* and *Ascomycete Fungi of North America: A Mushroom Reference Guide.* His latest book is *Mushrooms of the Gulf Coast States: A Field Guide to Texas, Louisiana, Mississippi, Alabama, and Florida.* Alan was the scientific adviser to the Mid-York Mycological Society and served as a consultant for the New York State Poison Control Center for more than twenty years. He has been the principal mycologist at national and regional forays and was the recipient of the 1987 Mycological Foray Service Award and of the 1992 North American Mycological Association Award for Contributions to Amateur Mycology. He teaches and lectures regionally and nationally. Alan's interests center on the fungi of eastern North America with a primary focus on subtropical and tropical fungi.

Dianna G. Smith, MA, is an emeritus president of the Connecticut-Westchester Mycological Association, a cofounder of the Pioneer Valley Mycological Association, and a past editor of *The Mycophile,* the newsletter of the North American Mycological Association. She is the current chair of the North American Mycological Association's Medicinal Fungi Committee. Dianna has won national photography awards, and many of her photos have been featured in recently published field guides and mushroom applications for smart devices. She is the recipient of the 2012 NAMA Harry and Elsie Knighton Service Award for her contributions to amateur mycology and the 2012 NAMA President's Award for her work as editor of *The Mycophile.* Dianna is the creator of the educational mycology website http://www.fungikingdom.net and was the webmaster and past president of the Northeast Mycological Federation. She was the producer and editor of the community cable television program *SCAPES,* which aired for 22 years and featured half-hour shows on gardening, botany, and mycology.

Arleen R. Bessette, MA, is a psychologist, mycologist, and botanical photographer who has been collecting and studying wild mushrooms for more than 40 years. She has published several papers in the field of mycology and has authored or coauthored more than 15 books, including *Mushrooms of the Southeastern United States, The Rainbow Beneath My Feet: A Mushroom Dyer's Field Guide,* and *A Field Guide to Mushrooms of the Carolinas.* Her latest book is *Mushrooms of the Gulf Coast States: A Field Guide to Texas, Louisiana, Mississippi, Alabama, and Florida.* Arleen has won several national awards for her photography, including highest honors in both the documentary and the pictorial divisions in the North American Mycological Association's annual photography competition. Arleen teaches courses on mycology, dyeing with mushrooms, and the culinary aspects of mycophagy on both national and regional levels. Her current interests, combining her experiences as a psychotherapist and mycologist, relate to the effects of psychedelic substances on consciousness.

Illustration and Photography Credits

Pat Buchanan produced the map of the North American forest regions (fig. 6) and all the line drawings.

Erin Greb produced the map of the geographic area covered by this book (fig. 1).

Except for the following, all the photographs in this book were taken by the authors.

Jason Bolin: *Laetiporus persicinus* (A)

Oluna and Adolf Ceska: *Calcipostia guttulata, Datroniella scutellata, Jahnoporus hirtus, Stereum sanguinolentum* (A)

Neil Dollinger: *Fomitiporia apiahyna, Foraminispora rugosa, Ganoderma colossus, Ganoderma lobatoideum, Ganoderma tuberculosum*

Gary Emberger: *Globifomes graveolens* (B), *Sarcodontia setosa*

Alan Franck: *Earliella scabrosa, Ganoderma parvulum, Hexagonia papyracea, Trametes villosa, Trullella polyporoides*

Django Grootmyers: *Antrodiella semisupina, Fomitopsis durescens*

Drew Henderson: *Ganoderma megaloma, Pycnoporellus alboluteus* (A), *Scutiger pes-caprae*

Jason Hollinger: *Lentinus berteroi*

Mike Hopping: *Hapalopilus croceus*

Jacob Kalichman: *Antrodia heteromorpha, Cerioporus mollis, Coltriciella dependens* (A), *Gloeophyllum trabeum, Metuloidea fragrans*

Laurel Kaminsky: *Inonotus amplectens* (B)

Andrew Khitsun: *Bjerkandera fumosa, Cerioporus stereoides, Postia tephroleuca* (A), *Stereum hirsutum, Vanderbylia robiniophila*

Joan Knapp: *Irpex lacteus, Xanthoporia andersonii* (B)

David Lewis *Hexagonia cucullata, Hydnopolyporus palmatus, Trametes nivosa*

Martin Livezey: *Buglossoporus quercinus, Inonotus obliquus*

Justin Mathers: *Podoscypha aculeata*

Jared McRae: *Fomitiporia texana, Fulvifomes badius, Ganoderma martinicense, Hymenochaete rubiginosa, Inocutis texana, Lentinus tricholoma, Pyrofomes juniperinus* (B), *Schizophyllum fasciatum, Steccherinum oreophilum, Trichaptum perrottetii, Truncospora mexicana, Xanthoporia radiata*

Daniel Mills: *Brunneoporus juniperinus*

Jonathan Mingori: *Vanderbylia fraxinea*

Daniel Molter: *Inocutis dryophila*

Jamie Newman: *Polyporoletus sublividus*

Maricel Patino: *Gyrodontium sacchari*

John Plischke III: *Leptoporus mollis, Neoantrodia variiformis, Truncospora ohiensis*

David Raney: *Spongipellis unicolor*

Bill Roody: *Abortiporus biennis, Albatrellus ovinus, Bresadolia craterella, Brunneoporus malicola, Cerioporus squamosus, Climacodon pulcherrimus, Coltricia montagnei* (A), *Coriolopsis byrsina, Favolus tenuiculus, Fomitella supina* (A), *Funalia floccosa, Fuscopostia fragilis, Ganoderma sessile, Gloeophyllum sepiarium, Gloeophyllum striatum, Grifola frondosa, Hymenochaete iodina, Ischnoderma resinosum, Laeticutis cristata, Laetiporus cincinnatus, Laetiporus sulphureus, Lentinus arcularius, Lentinus brumalis, Neoalbatrellus caeruleoporus, Neoantrodia serialis, Neofavolus alveolaris, Neofavolus suavissimus, Osteina obducta, Phellinopsis conchata, Phellinus lundellii, Phellinus tremulae, Pseudoinonotus dryadeus, Punctularia strigosozonata, Rhodo-*

fomes roseus, Rigidoporus microporus, Rigidoporus ulmarius, Sparassis spathulata, Steccherinum ochraceum, Stereum gausapatum, Stereum subtomentosum, Trametes ectypa, Trametes hirsuta, Trametes versicolor (B), *Trametopsis cervina, Trichaptum fuscoviolaceum, Trichaptum laricinum, Trichaptum subchartaceum, Tyromyces kmetii*

Stephen Russell: *Tyromyces galactinus*

Christian Schwarz: *Sistotrema confluens, Stereum sanguinolentum* (B)

Bill Sheehan: *Ceriporia purpurea, Phlebiopsis crassa, Skeletocutis lilacina, Steccherinum subrawakense, Xanthoporia andersonii* (A)

Luke Smithson: *Globifomes graveolens* (A), *Perenniporia fraxinophila, Porodaedalea pini*

Walt Sturgeon: *Ischnoderma benzoinum, Laetiporus huroniensis, Plicaturopsis crispa*

Huafang Su: *Inocutis rheades, Inonotus glomeratus, Postia tephroleuca* (B), *Thelephora cuticularis, Trametella trogii*

David Tate: *Pyrofomes juniperinus* (A)

Garrett Taylor: *Trametes suaveolens*

Phillip Thompson: *Phaeocalicium polyporaeum*

Tanith Tyrr: *Picipes lowei*

Debbie Viess: *Pycnoporellus alboluteus* (B)

Index to Common Names

Index to Scientific Names

Pages on which species descriptions and illustrations appear are indicated by **boldface**.

sulphureus, 207, 209, **212, 213,**
212, 272
Laxitextum
crassum, 265
Lecanicillium
fungicola, 270
Leiotrametes
lactinea, 341
Lentinus
arcularius, **214, 215,** 235
berteroi, 216, **217**
brumalis, **215**
crinitus, 216, **217**
lepideus, 237
siparius, 249
strigosus, 248
suavissimus, 236
tephroleucus, 249
tigrinus, **218, 219**
torulosus, 247
tricholoma, **220, 221**
Lenzites
betulina, 222
betulinus, 110, **222,** 236
laricinus, 358
mexicana, 242
quercina, 110
sepiaria, 166
septentrionalis, 112
Leptoporellus
fumidiceps, 369
kmetii, 372
Leptoporus
erubescens, 223
lapponicus, 66
mollis, **223**
Leucoporus
tricholoma, 220
Loweomyces
fractipes, **224**
subgiganteus, 250

Meripilus
giganteus, 225
persicinus, 210
sumstinei, 171, **225**
Merulioporia
purpurea, 91

Merulius
incarnatus, 82
strigosozonatus, 292
tremellosus, 264
Metuloidea
fragrans, **226, 227**
Microporellus
dealbatus, **228,** 229
obovatus, 228, **229**
Mucronoporus
andersonii, 376
everhartii, 137
Mycorrhaphium
adustum, 230

Naematelia
aurantia, 324
Neoalbatrellus
caeruleoporus, 231
Neoantrodia
serialiformis, 232
serialis, 67, 232, **233,** 234
variiformis, **233, 234**
Neofavolus
alveolaris, 214, **235**
suavissimus, **236**
Neolentinus
lepideus, **237**
Nigrofomes
melanoporus, 238
Nigroporus
vinosus, **238**
Niveoporofomes
spraguei, **239,** 286

Ochroporus
lundellii, 259
tremulae, 260
Oligoporus
balsameus, 96
fragilis, 142
fumidiceps, 369
guttulatus, 83
leucomallellus, 142
obductus, 243
stipticus, 84
tephroleucus, 288
undosus, 96

Onnia
circinata, **240,** 241
tomentosa, 240, **241**
Osmoporus
mexicanus, **242**
Osteina
obducta, **243**
Oxyporus
populinus, **244, 245**

Panellus
pusillus, **246**
Panus
conchatus, **247,** 248
crinitus, 216
lecomtei, **248**
neostrigosus, 248
siparius, **249**
suavissimus, 236
tephroleucus, **249**
tigrinus, 218
Pappia
fissilis, **250, 251**
Perenniporia
fraxinea, 374
fraxinophila, **252, 253,** 374
ohiensis, 367
robiniophila, 375
Phaeocalicium
polyporaeum, 349, 353, **355**
Phaeolus
alboluteus, 294
schweinitzii, 241, **254, 255**
Phanerochaete
crassa, 265
Phellinopsis
conchata, **256, 257**
Phellinus
alni, 124, 258
apiahynus, 123
badius, 136
bakeri, 124
chrysoloma, 281
cinereus, 124
conchatus, 256
elegans, 123
everhartii, 137
gilvus, 140

squamosus, 88
suaveolens, 347
subchartaceus, 362
sublividus, 278
subrubescens, 64
sulphureus, 212
supinus, 121
tenuiculus, 116
texanus, 188
tomentosus, 241
tricholoma, 220
tsugae, 160
tulipiferae, 199
ulmarius, 304
umbellatus, 171, **280**, 391
variiformis, 234
varius, 85
versicolor, 348
villosus, 350
vinosus, 238
viticola, 141
volvatus, 107
wahlbergii, 261
Polystictus
fimbriatus, 179
Poria
versiporia, 381
Porodaedalea
chrysoloma, **281**, 282
pini, 281, **282**, 283
Porodisculus
pendulus, **284**
Poronidulus
conchifer, **285**
Porostereum
crassum, 265
Postia
balsamea, 96
caesia, 286
caesiosimulans, 286
fragilis, 142
guttulata, 83
leucomallella, 142
livens, 239, **286**, **287**
populi, 286
simulans, 286
stiptica, 84
tephroleuca, 84, **288**, **289**
undosa, 96

Pseudofavolus
cucullatus, 176
Pseudofistulina
radicata, 117, **290**
Pseudoinonotus
dryadeus, **291**
Punctularia
strigosozonata, **292**, **293**
Pycnoporellus
alboluteus, **294**, **295**
fulgens, **296**, **297**
Pycnoporus
cinnabarinus, 337
sanguineus, 346
Pyrofomes
demidoffii, 299
juniperinus, **298**, **299**
Pyropolyporus
bakeri, 124
calkinsii, 125
fomentarius, 118
juniperinus, 298
robiniae, 138

Radulodon
americanus, 300
copelandii, 300
Radulomyces
copelandii, **300**
Rhodofomes
cajanderi, **301**, 302
roseus, 301, **302**
Rhodofomitopsis
feei, 301
Rigidoporus
lineatus, 303
microporus, **303**
populinus, 244
ulmarius, **304**
Royoporus
badius, 267

Sarcodontia
copelandii, 300
delectans, 317
pachyodon, 316
setosa, 300, **305**
spumea, 317
unicolor, 317

Schizophyllum
commune, **306**, **307**
fasciatum, **308**, **309**
mexicanum, 308
Schizopora
paradoxa, 381
Scutiger
cristatus, 206
ellisii, 62
griseus, 72
hispidellus, 204
ovinus, 63
pes-caprae, 62, 206, **310**
sublividus, 278
subrubescens, 64
Sistotrema
confluens, **311**
Skeletocutis
lilacina, 91, 265, **312**, **313**
Sparassis
americana, **314**
crispa, 314
herbstii, 315
spathulata, **315**
Spongipellis
delectans, 317
pachyodon, 199, 300, **316**
spumeus, 317
unicolor, **317**
Sporophagomyces
chrysostomus, 143
Steccherinum
adustum, 230
ochraceum, 98, **318**, **319**
oreophilum, **320**
pulcherrimum, 98
septentrionale, 99
subrawakense, 227, **321**
Stereum
balsameum, 326
caperatum, 108
complicatum, **322**, 323, 324
frustulatum var. subpileatum, 380
gausapatum, 322, **323**, 324
hirsutum, 322, 323, **324**
murrayi, 109
ostrea, **ii**, **325**, 329
purpureum, 95
quercinum, 323